WILLIAM M. BAKER is a member of the Department of History at the University of Lethbridge, Lethbridge, Alberta.

Born in Ireland in 1822, Timothy Warren Anglin emigrated to New Brunswick in 1849 and quickly became involved in the life and politics of the city of Saint John and the colony. As founder and editor of the newspaper the *Freeman*, he became lay spokesman for the large, mainly lower-class Irish Catholic population in Saint John, supporting its attempts to alleviate the poverty and harshness of life in New Brunswick and voicing its desire to be accepted as a responsible part of the community. Although Anglin shared his countrymen's resentment of the British presence in Ireland, he saw Britain's role in North America as a positive one. Both as a newspaperman and later as a practising politician he pressed for the constitutional and non-violent redress of grievances. His Irish background and sympathies coupled with his moderate political stance and strongly middle-class outlook made him an effective mediator between the Irish Catholics in New Brunswick and the rest of the community.

In the 1860s Anglin was an active participant in the complex political manoeuvrings in New Brunswick, the *Freeman* providing a platform for his strenuous opposition to Confederation. Although the anti-Confederates were unsuccessful, Anglin's career provides insight into both the muddy politics of Confederation and the process of adjustment to the new order. Ultimately the union that Anglin had opposed won his loyalty, a demonstration of the fact that, despite its problems, the strength of the new nation of Canada was considerable. He was a member of the Canadian House of Commons from 1867 to 1882 and Speaker of the House from 1874 to 1878.

This study of the public career of Timothy Warren Anglin – newspaperman, politician, Irish Catholic leader – sheds light on the political and social history of British North America in the second half of the nineteenth century and on the emergence and growth of the Canadian nation.

T.W. Anglin
By permission of A.J.C. Anglin, Toronto

WILLIAM M. BAKER

Timothy Warren Anglin
1822-96
Irish Catholic Canadian

UNIVERSITY OF TORONTO PRESS
Toronto and Buffalo

Library of Congress Cataloging in Publication Data

Baker, William M.   1943–
Timothy Warren Anglin, 1822–96, Irish Catholic Canadian.

Originally presented as the author's thesis, University of Western Ontario.
Bibliography: p.
Includes index.
1. Anglin, Timothy Warren, 1822–1896. 2. Statesmen – Canada – Biography.
1. Title.
F1033.A532B34   1977   328.71'092'4 [B]   76-49480
ISBN 0-8020-5368-8

This book has been published during the
Sesquicentennial year of the University of Toronto

To my family

Contents

Acknowledgments

A legion of teachers, students, colleagues, librarians, archivists, secretaries, and organizations have aided and facilitated the preparation of this study. To all I extend my sincere appreciation. To my parents, both of whom made useful comments on my work, and to my wife Sharon, who also made helpful suggestions on the study as well as making it possible for me to combine hard work with a modicum of sanity, I acknowledge my debt. To the Province of Ontario, the Canada Council, and the University of Lethbridge I wish to express my appreciation for financial assistance which enabled me to complete the research. I am most grateful to the late Dr D.G.G. Kerr, my research director when this study was initially undertaken as a doctoral dissertation at the University of Western Ontario, for his unfailing willingness to assist my endeavour in every possible way and for his judicious comments on my work. I acknowledge with thanks permission to use material which I have already published in the following articles: 'T.W. Anglin: Speaker of the House of Commons, 1874–1878,' *Queen's Quarterly*, LXXX (1973), 256–66; 'Turning the Spit: Timothy Anglin and the Roasting of D'Arcy McGee,' *Canadian Historical Association, Historical Papers, 1974*, pp 135–55; and 'Squelching the Disloyal, Fenian Sympathizing Brood: T.W. Anglin and Confederation in New Brunswick, 1865–6,' CHR, LV (1974), 141–58.

This study has been published with the help of a grant from the Social Science Research Council of Canada, using funds provided by the Canada Council, and a grant to University of Toronto Press from the Andrew W. Mellon Foundation.

W.M.B. / February 1977

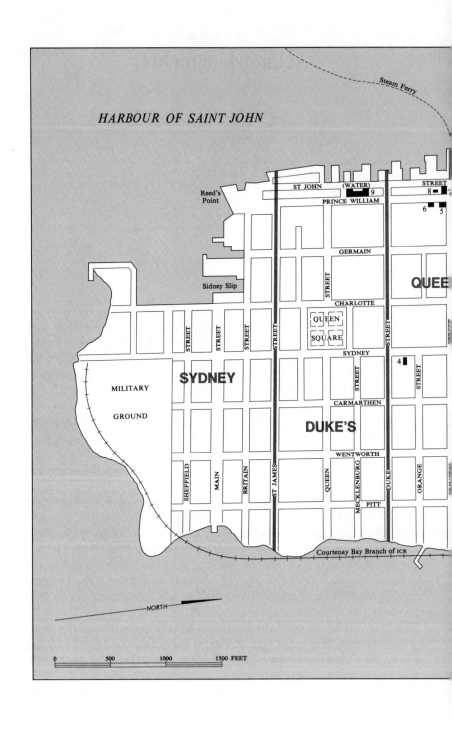

HARBOUR OF SAINT JOHN

Reed's Point

ST JOHN (WATER) STREET

9

8

6 5

PRINCE WILLIAM

GERMAIN

Sidney Slip

STREET

QUEE

CHARLOTTE

QUEEN SQUARE

SYDNEY

MILITARY

SYDNEY

STREET STREET STREET STREET STREET

4

STREET

GROUND

CARMARTHEN

DUKE'S

WENTWORTH

SHEFFIELD MAIN BRITAIN ST JAMES QUEEN MECKLENBURG DUKE ORANGE

PITT

Courtenay Bay Branch of ICR

NORTH

0 500 1000 1500 FEET

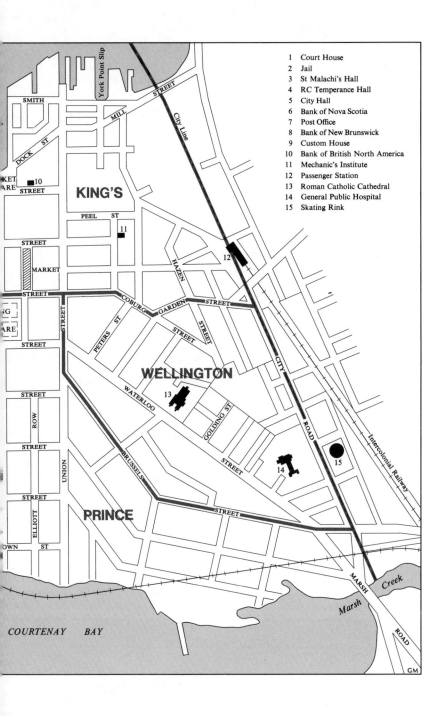

1 Court House
2 Jail
3 St Malachi's Hall
4 RC Temperance Hall
5 City Hall
6 Bank of Nova Scotia
7 Post Office
8 Bank of New Brunswick
9 Custom House
10 Bank of British North America
11 Mechanic's Institute
12 Passenger Station
13 Roman Catholic Cathedral
14 General Public Hospital
15 Skating Rink

Note on Sources

An extensive listing of the materials consulted in preparing this study seems unnecessary. The notes and footnotes indicate the items which have been most useful, Anglin's own newspaper, the *Freeman*, being the most significant single source.

The gaps in the available material are unfortunate. The fact that there are four collections of Tilley Papers (the two held by the Public Archives of Canada are being combined into one) does not make up for the lack of an Anglin collection or the fact that there are no A.J. Smith papers. The A.H. Gillmor Papers, recently acquired by the Public Archives of New Brunswick, demonstrate how valuable collections of the Anglin and Smith papers would have been. It is also unfortunate that the primary materials on D'Arcy McGee are so sparse.

Even the files of Anglin's newspapers have regrettable omissions. Only seven issues of the *Freeman* prior to 1858 are extant, and there is an unfortunate gap between 2 November and 21 November 1865, the period of the York by-election and Anglin's resignation. Moreover, the extant copies of the *Tribune* during the period of Anglin's editorship begin only in July 1885. Thereafter there is an incomplete file as far as March 1887. These omissions, while significant, do not, however, make analysis impossible. Anglin created such a stir in the newspaper world that other papers frequently quoted him. By reading them for the period of the 1850s, for example, one can obtain at least an impressionistic account of Anglin's life during that period. For information on the various newspapers utilized in this study the reader should consult Canadian Library Association, *Cana-*

dian Newspapers on Microfilm Catalogue (Ottawa, 1959–), and J.R. Harper, *Historical Directory of New Brunswick Newspapers and Periodicals* (Fredericton, 1961).

Finally, interviews with the late Colonel E.A. Anglin, R.E. Anglin, and A.J.C. Anglin, grandsons of T.W. Anglin, and the use of the Anglin Family Scrapbook, a copy of which is in the possession of R.E. Anglin, have been helpful in providing information on the family.

All manuscript collections referred to in the notes and footnotes are located in the Public Archives of Canada, Ottawa, unless otherwise specified. The following abbreviations are used in the notes and footnotes:

CHR   *Canadian Historical Review*
NBMA   New Brunswick Museum Archives
PANB   Public Archives of New Brunswick
PAO   Public Archives of Ontario
SJRL   Saint John Regional Library
UNBA   University of New Brunswick Archives

TIMOTHY WARREN ANGLIN, 1822–96

1

Prologue

Timothy Warren Anglin was an Irish Catholic politician in Canada during the second half of the nineteenth century. Born and raised in a small town along the southeastern coast of Ireland, he emigrated to Saint John, New Brunswick, in 1849. Shortly after his arrival he established a newspaper, the Saint John *Freeman*, which was, for a third of a century, the mouthpiece of Anglin and the Irish Catholic community of New Brunswick. In 1861 Anglin was elected by the city and county of Saint John to the New Brunswick Assembly. He became an opponent of the Confederation proposals and took a leading role in the Confederation elections in New Brunswick in 1865 and 1866. With the defeat of the anti-Confederate government, in which he had been a minister for a time, and his own electoral defeat in Saint John in 1866, Anglin resolved both to give Confederation a fair trial and to stand for the North Shore constituency of Gloucester for the Canadian House of Commons. Anglin represented that county in Ottawa from 1867 to 1882, gaining recognition both as a prominent Irish Catholic politician and as a leading Reformer. During the prime ministership of Alexander Mackenzie Anglin was Speaker of the House of Commons. His defeat in the 1882 election and his declining success with the *Freeman* prompted Anglin to move to Toronto. The transition began auspiciously but ultimately proved unsuccessful. It was, therefore, a struggle for Anglin to maintain his normal lifestyle in the decade prior to his death in 1896.

Such a condensation of Anglin's career suggests that Anglin was hardly a figure of the first rank in British North American affairs. To be sure,

Anglin was not as significant as Sir John A. Macdonald or George Brown. But there were occasions on which Anglin was exceptionally prominent. He, probably more than anyone else, led the New Brunswick fight against Confederation. He was, without doubt, the most powerful Catholic layman in the public arena in New Brunswick for a quarter of a century. It is true that he apparently lost many of his battles, but historians rightfully recognize that so-called losers make enormous contributions to the course of events.[1] Thus, even if Anglin was a secondary figure, he had a significant impact on nineteenth-century British North America. Moreover, Anglin's career merits study because he was a leader and spokesman of the Irish Catholic community, one of the potentially most obstreperous groups ever to settle in Canada. Recent work in the field of Canadian political science has suggested that Canada, which has been characterized by decades of reasonably stable government despite the society's 'cultural fragmentation' and 'limited identities,' is a good example of 'consociational democracy.' The functioning of this order has required that 'political leaders of ... separate subcultures ... practise accommodation at the elite level in order to maintain the national political system and make it work.'[2] Obviously it is of very great significance that political leaders of these subcultures tend to accept and support the society of which they are a part rather than attempt to destroy it. Anglin was one such man. The basic thrust of his leadership was towards constitutional and non-violent redress of grievances. Anglin was a moderate, a reformer, not a revolutionary. In accounting for the relatively harmonious evolution of Canadian history this 'no shillelagh' type of leadership is not without significance.

In most ways Anglin's character and personality reflected the age in which he lived. True, his astonishing memory[3] may have been a throwback to an earlier era, but this was an exception to the general pattern. Even the fleshy face and body draped on his hefty frame betrayed the fact that he had adopted the sedentary work habits which became prevalent among the middle class in the nineteenth century. The scarcity of personal letters left behind by Anglin makes difficult a presentation of a character sketch of the man. But the absence of material on Anglin's personal life in itself indicates the private nature of the man. Indeed, while we have evidence that Anglin was a pompous, vain man, he was also reserved, actually modest at times. He was capable of writing a gracious letter, such as the one to Lord Dufferin when he was vacating the office of Governor General.[4] But these gentle characteristics seldom appear. More frequently we see an austere, businesslike, formidable man with a degree of inner strength which bordered on arrogance. But such a public image was far from atypical in the Victorian age.

If one compares Anglin's personality with traits characteristic of the era as depicted in Walter Houghton's *The Victorian Frame of Mind*, one quickly discovers similarities. One of the most noted features of the nineteenth century was the quickened pace of life and the elevation of the concept of work into a virtual idol.[5] Under the influence of puritanism, 'hardly less common among Anglo-Catholics than Evangelicals and Dissenters,' work became a moral and religious virtue.[6] Anglin certainly showed an intense commitment to work, putting in long, arduous hours writing articles at a plain table and chair in a corner of the composing room of the *Freeman* office,[7] or attending sessions of the House of Commons hour after hour in order to send reports back to the *Freeman* and to participate in debate. Anglin was without question industrious and diligent. Indeed one would guess that the unhappiness of his later years was caused as much by enforced idleness as by economic anxiety.

One reason for hard work was to attain the bourgeois Victorian goals of respectability and success. A desire to achieve these twin goals probably contributed to Anglin's rather dour, at least serious, and businesslike manner.* If the Anglin household was far from joyless, with the youngsters sliding down the big banister and Margaret out in the stable acting out plays for her schoolmates,[8] yet Frank Anglin's presentation at the closing exercises of the Christian Brothers Academy in 1875, entitled 'There is no such word as fail,'[9] indicates that life was not all fun and games with Timothy Anglin as father. Indeed, Anglin was not much of a supporter of games at all. '[T]here are too many still who take more interest in a boat race than they do in matters of the greatest possible public importance,' his paper not untypically commented on one occasion.[10]

The desire for respectability may also have contributed to Anglin's tremendous self-control; for example, on one occasion in Richibucto, after he was hit on the forehead with an egg, he simply continued his speech 'as if nothing had happened,' suggesting to the audience that here was the type of men who composed the opposition.[11] An offshoot of such apparent self-assurance was a certain amount of arrogance. An incident which betrays this characteristic occurred in Ireland in 1846 on the occasion of the christening of Mary Jane Irwin, Anglin's first cousin and the future wife of the firebrand Irish nationalist Jeremiah O'Donovan-Rossa.

Mr. Anglin who had agreed earlier to be godfather of the expected arrival, reached the house very late on the day of the christening and was rushed at once to the

---

* This characteristic was probably being mocked by the Halifax *Express*, 15 June 1866, when it stated that as a result of the Confederation elections in New Brunswick Anglin would never again be seen to smile.

church with the baby and its nurse. When the priest impressively announced 'I now christen thee ____' and looked inquiringly at the proud godfather, Mr. Anglin loudly proclaimed, 'Timothy Warren Irwin, Your Reverence.' 'Oh, Your Reverence, No, No!' gasped the astounded nurse, 'It can't be!' 'And why not, pray?' demanded Mr. Anglin sternly, 'what's wrong with that fine name?' 'Nothing at all, Sir, nothing,' stammered the blushing maid, 'but, begging your Honor's pardon, Sir – it's not that kind of a baby!' So the priest, in lieu of anything better, calmly christened mamma 'Mary Jane,' and Mary Jane she stayed.[12]

Anglin's personality also showed strong evidence of dogmatism and rigidity, two more features characteristic of the Victorian mind.[13] One reason for Anglin's rigidity was that neither an editor nor a politician could change his views very frequently.[14] Another factor was that he, along with other middle-class Victorians, was whistling in the dark to keep up his courage. The Victorian age, after all, was one which was wracked by doubts about many matters. The 'eternal laws of morality,' for example, were being 'defied or ignored in the selfish and worldly life of the time ...'[15] Responses to the climate of doubt varied, but grasping one's beliefs tightly around oneself and using them to fend off disruptive uncertainties was highly typical. To a very real extent Anglin employed this technique, particularly where religion was involved. Not only did he believe truth to be unchanging – 'it is time that we all knew and understood that the principle of right is immutable as it is eternal' – but also he maintained that independent thinking and standards were dangerous – 'we can not with safety to the State make each his own standard of right.' Of course, for Anglin the Catholic 'the voice of the Bishops is the voice of authority ...'[16] Even in political life Anglin's isolation betrayed a certain stubbornness and rigidity of opinion. Both in the pages of his paper and in the halls of parliament Anglin could become obstinate. This was, of course, part of the style of the age, a characteristic which does not commend itself to the modern mind. Perhaps that is why Anglin seems today to have been most effective and convincing when he argued his case in a calm and logical manner. But being dogmatic and tough was an operating principle in the nineteenth century and Anglin could be both. He had no qualms, for example, about getting men fired from their government jobs after their alleged opposition to him in the 1877 election, or about dismissing a couple of House of Commons clerks found larking about when he was Speaker.[17] Thus, while Anglin was inevitably forced into shifts of position because of changing circumstances, there was a stubbornness and a tenacity of belief in Anglin's make-up which cannot be ignored.

According to Houghton, 'At the center of Victorian life was the family.'[18] The home was a shelter from outside pressures and a place for the preservation of moral and religious values.[19] Anglin protected his shelter very well from the prying eyes of the outside world: virtually nothing is known about Anglin's relationship with his wife Ellen, except that they had ten children. As for his rapport with his offspring, the christening story suggests the level of his interest in very young children. In letters written in the 1880s and 1890s to Bishop John Sweeny of Saint John Anglin frequently mentioned the success of his oldest boys in school, in establishing their careers, and in marrying well, but aside from a few remarks about all the young ones at home the letters say little about the young children. To judge a family relationship on such flimsy evidence is risky, but it fits the pattern of Anglin's personality – serious, businesslike, concerned with success, and rather distant.

Anglin thus emerges as an earnest, hard-working, morally upright, and somewhat remote individual. He was the sort of man who commanded respect but not affection. Whether there was a necessary connection between his personality and his position in life is difficult to determine. His reserve and remoteness may have been essential to maintain the credibility of his liaison role between the ranks of the lower-class Irish Catholics and the ranks of the ruling, middle-class politicians. In any case his character had an effect on his career. He was not as successful a politician as he might have been had his colleagues considered him to be a good-natured, jolly chap, as well as respecting him for his talents. But too ready acceptance by leading politicians and easy success in receiving a cabinet position could threaten an Irish Catholic leader's support. D'Arcy McGee, who did achieve considerable political success and was accepted by the Canadian establishment, was thought to have 'sold out' by many members of the Irish community before his death. Thus it would appear that Anglin's character was not ill-suited to the nature of the tasks he undertook in life.

It is not to be expected that Anglin's contemporaries fully comprehended, or that his political opponents sympathized with, the delicacy of his situation. Much of the criticism he received at the hands of his opponents can be dismissed as mere politicking in an age and country where political antagonisms were extremely sharp and direct.[20] In any case, such criticism can be balanced by the praise of friendly journals and supporters. But what does emerge from all the characterizations of Anglin made by his contemporaries is the recognition of Anglin as a man of very considerable talent. Perhaps he was a traitorous snake to some, a dog that should be horsewhipped to others, a 'miserable devil' to still others, but the very vituperation of such attacks indicate that Anglin was a man to be reckoned with.[21] As the *New Dominion and True Humorist*, no supporter of Anglin, put it in 1873:

The fact is, if Mr. Anglin could be trusted, his mental endowments, which we acknowledge are of a superior order, would have ensured him a position in the Council of the country long ago, but he is too bigoted in his religious views to have any voice in our government.[22]

Even the Saint John *News*, which had been at loggerheads with Anglin and his *Freeman* for a quarter of a century by the time Anglin departed for Toronto in 1883, recognized Anglin's multi-faceted talents: 'He has a strong intellect, a clear and simple style as a writer, is a fluent and forcible speaker ... He is fitted to make his mark anywhere.'[23] Other contemporary assessments reinforce the image of Anglin as a man of talent. He was 'well-informed, ready and witty,' 'versatile, brainy and fair-minded,' 'an exceedingly powerful debater, possessing a comprehensive knowledge of Canadian affairs,' 'a man with a strong and stubborn intellect, capable of a vast grasp,' and a person whose 'mind was logical, clear and vigorous.'[24] And so the image Anglin projected in his own day is not so different from the one the modern mind sees. His was a personality which was not particularly attractive then and does not appeal today. He was too remote, too dogmatic, and too self-righteous. But in the final analysis his was a character and career which commanded respect and admiration. Thus, at his funeral in St Michael's Cathedral in Toronto not only did a large number of priests participate, but also many luminaries, such as Sir Oliver Mowat, Sir Frank Smith, Justice Falconbridge, and Commander Law representing the Lieutenant-Governor, served as pall-bearers.[25] Respect without affection is, in a nutshell, this writer's attitude towards the subject of this study. One can dislike the superciliousness and arrogant self-righteousness of Anglin, yet admire the idealism, earnestness, and diligence of the man who could write:

Both the member of the House of Commons and the editor of a newspaper should always do what is right and speak the truth ... Truth and right obstruct no policy that is good, endanger no system that is worth preserving.[26]

2

Ireland and New Ireland

Timothy Warren Anglin was born in the little Irish coastal town of Clonakilty, county Cork, on 31 August 1822, into a middle-class Roman Catholic family. On Easter Monday 1849 he left Clonakilty to embark on a ship bound for Saint John, New Brunswick.[1] Of the first twenty-five years of Anglin's life little is known. Because of his father's wealth (the family owned a large home and property possessing eighty-six cottages),[2] Timothy received a good classical education. He was, apparently, preparing for a legal career when the Great Famine hit Ireland in 1845 and forced him to turn to schoolteaching in his home town.[3] While no other important details of Anglin's childhood and early adulthood have been discovered, it is clear that his years in Ireland were very influential.

The Ireland in which Anglin grew up was a society involved in struggle: struggle for political integrity, religious freedom, and economic viability. Protestant English ascendancy in Ireland had meant severe religious and political restrictions for the majority of Irishmen and had contributed to the economic stagnation of the country. The result was Irish hostility towards the Union of 1801 with Great Britain, a hostility Anglin shared.[4] This was an important factor in Anglin's later opposition to Confederation, for, looking at what the Union had meant for Ireland, he feared a similar fate for New Brunswick in a British North American union.[5] Indeed, Anglin virtually equated centralization with despotism and the division of power with freedom and progress.[6] In the case of Ireland, certainly, Anglin always hoped that the British yoke would be removed from the neck of his native land. While there is no evidence to suggest that Anglin was actively involved in the Young Ireland movement which eventually led the abortive uprising of 1848, he was a sympathizer.* In short, early nineteenth-century Irish politics created in Anglin as in other Irishmen an attitude of hostility and suspicion towards those in authority.

Not all the influences of Irish politics were negative. In Daniel O'Connell the Irish had, after all, one of the great nineteenth-century leaders. The victory of Catholic emancipation in 1829 had not only provided Irish Catholics with some hope for the future, but also demonstrated the effectiveness of the political methods of the 'Liberator.'

O'Connell invented constitutional agitation, the voice of the people, the march of opinion. He demonstrated the possibility, in a democratic parliamentary constitution, of carrying through revolutionary changes by evolutionary methods ... His basic theory [was] that there is no political change which cannot be brought about by the force of opinion, by peaceful and democratic organization ...[7]

This was a theory of no little significance. It broke the chains of Irish apathy, undercut the Irish inclination to resort to violence, implied that the state was not necessarily to be hated and distrusted, and urged Irishmen to organize in an effective and legal manner to win for themselves a rightful place in the counsels of government and in society at large. O'Connell's impact on those who assumed the leadership of the Irish Catholic community was profound. D'Arcy McGee, for example, declared in 1861 that he 'never approached a person who seemed more truly deserving of the title of great than Mr. O'Connell.'[8] Anglin agreed. His admiration concentrated on two major concepts which he considered O'Connell had espoused: the principle of moral force, and opposition to state control over the church. O'Connell's position proved, to Anglin's satisfaction at least, that one could be both a liberal and a Catholic, 'that there is nothing incompatible in the most earnest Catholicity with the largest possible measure of popular

---

* *Freeman*, 12 July 1864; and *New Brunswick, House of Assembly, Debates, 1866*, p 105 (7 Apr.). During Anglin's lifetime the charge was often made that Anglin had been a Young Ireland rebel in 1848 and had even been present at the tragicomic battle at Ballingarry (see, for example, New Brunswick, Lieutenant Governor's Letter Book, Vol LXII, Arthur Gordon to Duke of Newcastle, 31 Dec. 1862). This contention cannot be substantiated. In his newspaper Anglin stated that he had never been within fifty miles of Ballingarry in his life and that he had not escaped from Ireland as a rebel as 'there never was any reason why he should seek to escape from any person, thing or power whatever' (see *Freeman*, 19 May 1866). Independent evidence indicates that Anglin was telling the truth.

liberty.'[9] Throughout his political career Anglin was influenced by the model which O'Connell had provided in his youth.

II

While Anglin's political arena was not to be the same as O'Connell's, there were more points of comparison between Ireland and New Brunswick than the mere fact that the colony had once had the name 'New Ireland' suggested for it.[10] New Brunswick, despite its youth in comparison with Ireland, faced similar problems at mid-century.[11] The New Brunswick economy was teetering on the brink of failure. New Brunswick politics were confused and turbulent. Moreover, if Anglin thought that he had left destruction, violence, and death behind him, he was disabused of this idea only a few weeks after landing in Saint John. On 12 July 1849 an Orange parade exploded into a full-scale battle. Some deaths and numerous injuries occurred before order was restored.[12]

Economic difficulties, caused in part by Britain's expressed intention to end the tariff preference which colonial timber enjoyed, had made it impossible for New Brunswickers to welcome the thousands of diseased and destitute Irishmen who had arrived in the late forties. Not only were the immigrant Famine Irishmen weak from hunger and sickness – so much so that 2,115 of the 17,074 persons who embarked for New Brunswick in 1847 died in passage, in quarantine, or in hospital[13] – but also they apparently had to be taught how to perform even the simplest tasks.[14] Few employers were willing to hire such unskilled labourers especially as they might be carriers of disease. From the perspective of the old inhabitants of the province Irish immigration had brought the threat of widespread disease, been a strain on the purse of the colony, and introduced a turbulent element, foreign in religion and customs, to the community.

For their part the Irish, perhaps a third of whom were from Anglin's home county of Cork, had little to be thankful for. Here they were in a strange country, hungry, sick, unemployed, and surrounded by unfriendly inhabitants. It must have seemed that suffering was an Irishman's fate. Irish experience had taught Irishmen that life was a trial and they had developed a profoundly pessimistic attitude towards the world and its affairs. They saw little to counter this attitude in the new world.

Filthy homes, wretched working conditions, and constant hunger mocked the merchants' optimism, and bred, instead, the identical pessimism ... as in Ireland.

On both sides of the Atlantic, Irish experience generated a brooding recognition that human relationships were transient, subject to the ever-threatening intervention of impersonal evils ... Both as peasants whose anxious livelihood derived from the capricious soil, and as cogs in an unpredictable industrial machine, they were victims of incalculable influences beyond their control. For those who met it so frequently in their own experience, untimely disaster, even death, was normal, a part of life accepted without complaint, indeed without even the need for explanation.[15]

Such pessimism made the Irishman profoundly religious. Having lost faith in earthly improvement, he turned for consolation to religion, for the bulk of the Irish immigrants the faith of the Church of Rome. Fervent attachment to the Catholic Church made the Irish conservative, for with the exception of a few months in 1848 the nineteenth-century church fought radicalism everywhere. As well, of course, there was a persistent antagonism between Catholicism and Protestantism. On religious, cultural, economic, political, and social levels, therefore, the Irish immigrants were unlike the New Brunswickers of the Saint John valley. Thus it is not be be wondered at that these differences led to verbal, and at times physical, disagreements, the violence resulting from the Orange parade of 1849 being simply a particularly serious example.

As it turned out, the 12 July riot provided Anglin with an *entrée* into public life in New Brunswick. In the *Morning News* of 18 July a letter was printed over the initials 'J.A.' The writer was Anglin. The lengthy letter deprecated sectarian strife and implored men to cooperate for the good of the country. The author claimed that one benefit of the Great Famine had been that, because it had affected all men alike, all had drawn together to combat the problem at hand:

... the good, the wise, and the charitable of every religion, and of every class in Society, forgetting every thing that had so long divided them, united heart and soul to work for the relief of their suffering countrymen. The Catholic Priests and the Protestant Rectors struggled together, might and main, to succour and relieve their afflicted people, never stopping to ask if this man were a Catholic, or that a Protestant. Those insane and contemptible feuds that had so long divided and weakened the people, and delivered them as it were bound hand and foot, to be dealt with by their Alien Government as it pleased, were now looked back with regret by men who had once engaged in them earnestly. Irishmen began at length to see that if they wished to save their country, the union of all classes and of all religion was necessary ...

If an old, established country such as Ireland found that the common good required cooperation between people, how much more did a new, undeveloped territory like New Brunswick require it? In putting forward the Catholic viewpoint concerning the riot Anglin claimed that city authorities were culpable for allowing things to get out of hand. The easiest remedy would have been to disallow the Orange procession or at least to prevent it from going through York Point, an Irish Catholic section of the town. Failure to do this and failure to make proper use of the troops available had led almost inevitably to violence. The Catholics had not been blameless and should have ignored the insult offered them, as many did, but the Orangemen should not have been allowed to try them so. In any case, the result of the riot on the mind of the Catholic community of Saint John had been serious.

All confidence in the authorities is lost, more especially by the humble men of the Catholic party, who took no part in the late fight, because they wished to show an example of christian charity and forgiveness, and because they believed that the authorities would preserve the peace. Many of these now look on these same authorities as partizans, and literally regret that they did not stand by their friends in the hour of danger.

The difficulty with such a situation was that the Irish Catholic community might become completely alienated from the society in which it lived, and an alienated segment of society has no respect for the laws and institutions of that society. Anglin was therefore warning the authorities that, unless they demonstrated a different spirit towards Catholics, difficulties were bound to ensue. Thus at the outset of Anglin's career in New Brunswick he assumed the role of leadership for the Irish Catholics. He publicized the Catholic viewpoint and at the same time indicated that it was reform not rebellion that he was interested in. He told New Brunswick that, if it wished to have Irish Catholics respect its institutions and obey its laws, it had to meet more of their needs and give them the benefits of its society. Failure to do so would mean that the peace-loving and moderate men of the Irish Catholic community would lose all influence and lawless and more radical elements would gain the ascendancy. The methods of leadership which Anglin used throughout his career can be glimpsed in this letter to the *News*. He was sufficiently censorious of the authorities to merit the support of the Irish Catholics, but at the same time it was clear that what he desired was the pacification of the Irish community; thus the authorities were willing to listen to his criticism and to take some action to rectify the situation. For a group such as the Irish Catholics in a society such as New Brunswick, this was perhaps the only type of leadership likely to produce results desired, in the long run, by all. Anglin was admirably suited for such leadership, for, although he was a staunch Irish Catholic and thus a natural leader of his fellow immigrants, his educational attainments and his socioeconomic background made him almost acceptable to those in authority in New Brunswick.

This letter was Anglin's introduction to journalism. The fairness of its approach and its conciliatory manner won the attention of Saint John and before long the anonymous letter-writer was unmasked. A number of supporters of the so-called Liberal party liked what they had seen and were willing to support the newcomer in establishing a newspaper.[16] Anglin, despite his ignorance of the newspaper business, agreed to accept this support along with that, presumably, of Catholic leaders in the community. Despite Anglin's qualifications, his rapid rise to prominence and the tone of his letter to the *News* lead one to suspect that his leap to leadership was not wholly fortuitous. Perhaps Anglin had been 'imported' to lead the 'Fighting Irish' of Saint John. Whatever the case, there was no denying that Anglin's rise from anonymity was rapid. Only nine days after his letter appeared in the *News*, the same paper carried an advertisement which was the prospectus for a newspaper called the *Freeman*. * This statement claimed that the Irish did not possess the position in the community to which numbers and 'respectability' entitled them.

In the Executive Council, in the House of Assembly, even in the Common Council of the City they are unrepresented. In fact such is the unprotected position of a certain class of Irishmen in this City at present, and so little influence do they possess in its magisterial and police departments, that they seem to have very slight security indeed for either their lives or their properties.[17]

---

* Apparently it was Dr Boyle Travers, an old boyhood chum of Anglin's in Kearney's Classical School in Clonakilty and probably the man who had enticed Anglin to Saint John, who suggested the name of the paper (see *New Freeman* (Saint John), 6 Jan. 1900). It was an interesting and rather conservative choice. Dublin's *Freeman* had been, according to Gavan Duffy, 'the organ of the commercial class – a class who desire what is right and just as far as they understand it, but who are commonly deficient in imagination and political faith, and easily alarmed by novelty or enthusiasm' (see G. Duffy, *Four Years of Irish History 1845–1849: A Sequel to 'Young Ireland'* (London, 1883), p 297). In the new world another *Freeman* already existed, *Freeman's Journal and Catholic Register* of New York City. It was the mouthpiece of Bishop (later Archbishop) John Hughes, the vigorous defender of Catholic rights in the United States (see R.A. Billington, *The Protestant Crusade 1800–1860: A Study in the Origins of American Nativism* (Chicago, 1964), p 146).

What was needed was a means whereby the Irish could unite and make their voice heard and their weight felt. Anglin promised that his newspaper, the *Freeman*, would supply this need. On 4 August the first issue of his new paper made its appearance. The *News*, which had acted as a sort of fosterfather, welcomed it to the newspaper world of New Brunswick:

This [the *Freeman*] is the title of a paper recently started in this City, to advocate Catholic and Irish interests. Its Editor is Mr. J. Warren Anglin. The articles are exceedingly well written, and in a good tone of spirit. The descendants of Ireland in this City will now have what they never had before to represent them – viz: a talented and respectably conducted journal; and they ought to give it their best support.[18]

Even if the *News* did not know the first initial in Anglin's name, it was a flattering reception for his newspaper to receive.

With the founding of the *Freeman* Anglin entered an occupation which he was to follow for the next forty years. Of course, in 1849 he realized only that becoming a newspaper editor provided an opportunity to present the Irish Catholic viewpoint to the New Brunswick populace, and also gave him the chance to earn the leadership of the Irish Catholic community in New Brunswick.

III

In order to fill such a position Anglin could not stray far from the needs and thoughts of the Irish community of New Brunswick. Throughout his career, therefore, Anglin was required to champion the Irish cause, both in the homeland and in British North America, in both printed and spoken words. He had to defend the Irish name from apparent slurs cast by police reports, banquet speakers, historians, and the like.[19] He participated in Irish fund-raising activities, promoted the interests of Irish societies and organizations, and gave lectures and speeches about Irish affairs to sundry groups.[20] He had to cover Irish subjects in the newspapers he edited, a task he gladly accepted. Finally, and most importantly, as leader he had to be an interpreter for and defender of the Irish Catholic community within the larger society. That duty would probably require him to seek political office so that he could scrutinize the acts of government and speak directly to legislators and indirectly to the public at large with some hope of being heard and of influencing legislation. Unfortunately, for Irish leaders political involvement could be a double-edged sword; because of the Irish tradition of the 'Castle Catholic' – men who 'sold out' to the English – the more successful one became in politics, the more suspect one became in the Irish mind. Indeed, this may help to account for the fact that Anglin was generally to be found in the ranks of the opposition during his political career.

Second, being a Catholic spokesman, as well as an Irish leader, also made demands on Anglin. It required participation in specifically Catholic functions as well as regular attendance at devotional services: graduation ceremonies at Catholic schools, cornerstone laying for Catholic buildings, banquets honouring high-ranking clergy.[21] Being a Catholic lay leader also meant supporting Catholic enterprises such as reform schools and orphanages.[22] It demanded speaking and writing in order to present the Catholic perspective on such questions as marriage and divorce.[23] It even required Anglin's attendance at certain ultra-Protestant gatherings in order to ascertain if erroneous or slanderous statements were being made about Catholics.[24] As a Catholic spokesman it was necessary for Anglin to maintain close contact with leading local churchmen such as the New Brunswick bishops, John Sweeny of Saint John and James Rogers of Chatham.[25] Similarly Anglin had to accommodate himself to the conservative perspective of the nineteenth-century Catholic Church which in the famous Syllabus of Errors of 1864 had denounced everything from atheism and rationalism to liberalism and the doctrine of progress.[26] Fortunately for Anglin, responding to these pressures raised few problems, for he was already attuned to the church's message, probably because he had grown up in an Ireland where the bond between layman and priest had been exceptionally close.[27] But whatever the case he had a profoundly religious outlook on life. He believed that religion ought to be

the great vital principle that should ever guide, govern, actuate, and controul man in his family, in the workshop, the market place, the court of justice, the public meeting, and the place of amusement ... causing him to refer every thought, word and deed of his whole life to God ...[28]

As a Catholic he agreed 'unreservedly with the Pope in all matters of doctrine – the one condition on which he could be a Catholic.'[29] Anglin's Catholicity was indeed far more than mere show for his own temporal benefit; it was a faith to live by.

3

The Founding Decade
The 1850s

The greatest challenges facing Anglin upon coming to New Brunswick were to acclimatize himself to his new environment and to earn himself a position of prominence in these surroundings. His status was obviously related to the condition of the Irish community as a whole, and it is clear that the Irish in Saint John remained an isolated portion of the population throughout the 1850s. The decade witnessed the emergence of Anglin as the recognized spokesman for Irish Catholics, with the *Freeman* as his mouthpiece. Finally, the 1850s was the time of Anglin's apprenticeship for public life as he familiarized himself with and became partially involved in the major issues of New Brunswick politics.

I

The fact that Irish Catholics formed at least one-third of the 38,475 persons in the county of Saint John did not assure them a comfortable position.[1] The acculturation[2] of any immigrant group is a difficult process; Irish Catholics were no exception. As it has turned out, of course, Irish Catholic Canadians have retained only their religious distinctiveness, not any significant cultural particularity. The Irish had one significant advantage – that of speaking the same language as the majority group. While this was of undoubted benefit, it also had disadvantages. In most cases an immigrant picks up the thought processes and cultural values of the majority in learning the language. In a sense, therefore, not being forced to undergo this learning process made the acculturation of the Irish even more difficult than that of a foreign-language group. Speaking the same language but holding a vastly different philosophy of life than native-born British North Americans, the Irish were fated to go through a lengthy adjustment to the new society.[3]

In the initial stages the Irish made a quite successful effort to retain their peasant sociocultural values. One recent study has demonstrated that in three pre-Famine Irish rural settlements in eastern British North America many aspects of the material culture of Old Ireland were retained or were changed slowly.[4] Even in the urban communities of North America the Irish attempted to re-create a familiar social environment. It may be that the urban setting was more appealing to the Irish emigrant who was unable in the 'isolation imposed by the structure of Canadian agriculture' to find the 'constant companionship in large social groups' to which he was accustomed.[5] Working in construction crews, railway gangs, lumber camps, timber yards, and saw mills was probably not all that different from labouring in the mobile harvesting crews which had become prevalent in Ireland.[6] The faults of Irish emigrants – lawlessness, drunkenness, and poverty – were also traceable to unfortunate tendencies in the homeland. In short, the Irish clung tenaciously to their former way of life in the new world.

If the Irish chose this direction, there were also external forces which pushed them towards remaining a sub-society within the larger community. In Saint John, for example, Irish Catholics were ostracized from many of the associations of the city. The YMCA was, of course, a Protestant organization, but Catholics do not appear to have been involved in more ostensibly neutral groups such as the Early Closing Association, one meeting of which had thirteen Protestant clergymen in attendance.[7] Even the St Patrick's Society of Saint John, with its Anglican chaplain and Scotch-Irish executive, was isolated from the Catholic natives of Ireland.[8] The organization of charity in the cities of the Atlantic colonies became divided along Catholic-Protestant lines, mainly because Protestants were disturbed that the bulk of their donations was being used for the maintenance of impoverished Catholics.[9] Colonial hostility towards Irish Catholics was not unanimous, but unquestionably many residents of Saint John agreed with a Fredericton newspaper's thinly veiled condemnation of the Irish:

If ever there was a Town suffering under the infliction imposed by the dregs of a criminal-pauper population, that town is Fredericton ... Drunkeness [sic], that great source of general evil, but especially of seduction and debauchery, has entailed upon us a large number of persons of all ages and sexes, who maintain themselves by the commission of crimes too indecent to be named, or in the event of being committed, lie upon our hands for support in the jail or Alms House ...[10]

It is clear that Irish Catholics were not welcomed with open arms, and thus it is hardly surprising that they were segregated.

The isolation of Irish Catholics in Saint John stemmed from their socioeconomic circumstances. Irish immigrants had landed in Saint John impoverished; many remained in destitution. Initially, of course, there was the mid-century depression in the timber and related industries.[11] Employment opportunities improved by the mid-1850s when the wood-related enterprises, such as shipbuilding and saw milling, were in a healthy state and construction on the Saint John suspension bridge and on the European and North American railway was in progress.[12] But the cholera epidemic of 1854 and the sharp economic decline of 1857 disrupted the economic stability and progress of the city. These events, plus the endemic seasonal unemployment which plagued British North America in this era,[13] made it extremely difficult for Irish workmen to achieve economic well-being. Clearly Irish Catholics in Saint John 'tended to dominate occupations on the lower end of the status scale ...'[14] and to be the most impoverished group in the community.[15] They became, in fact, proletarians with little hope of anything but unskilled or semi-skilled jobs in the timber ponds, lumber yards, flour mills, iron foundries, construction gangs, and the waterfront dockyards. However unpleasant that situation may have been for the workers themselves, the labour they provided was an essential ingredient in enabling New Brunswick to build its rail line, to process its wood products, and to develop its industries.[16] In other words, the value of the services provided by Irish Catholic labourers was hardly matched by an equivalent economic reward for the workers.

Families at a subsistence level or on charity could hardly afford opulent surroundings, even had living accommodations been plentiful in Saint John.[17] Many Irish had to take whatever lodgings they could get, no matter how dismal. The Irish became extensively distributed throughout Saint John, a city in which poor and rich frequently lived side by side.[18] Thus Irish Catholics constituted at least one-quarter of the residents in all wards of the metropolitan area.[19] But they also formed two-thirds of the population of King's ward, situated at the northwest corner of the main part of the city, next to the harbour and north of the business district. Included in this ward was York Point, the Irish section which the Orangemen had marched through in 1849. 'These streets were notoriously dirty and crowded, with packed tenements set between slaughterhouses and tanneries.'[20] The fact that two-thirds of the houses at York Point were without privies undoubtedly contributed to the high death rate in that area during the cholera epidemic of 1854.[21] Other parts of the ward were little better. Flaglor's alley, 'where two hundred people lived in stinking apartments perched over "an enormous Cesspool and several privies flowing upon the surface ...,"' was eventually closed by the Saint John Board of Health as unfit for human habitation.[22] Irish living conditions elsewhere in the city may have been more acceptable but were probably still inadequate.

Given these conditions and the Irish tradition of violence, it is hardly surprising that the colonial Irish were unruly at times. Much of this was somewhat purposeless violence, such as vandalism and wife-beating, along with robbery and murder. But some of it was clearly an attempt to improve the economic circumstances of the group. There is little doubt, for example, that the labour strife which occurred on occasion was fomented on the workers' side by Irishmen. In 1855, for instance, Mr Cushing, the owner of saw mills near the city, insisted that his men work a ten-and-a-half-hour day despite the workers' desire to work only ten hours. In true capitalistic style he told them that if they did not like the terms they could quit. Some workers succumbed to the logic of his argument and went back to work. Others left.

Those who left went round to the other Mills, and to the wharves, and succeeded in mustering a gang of some 60 or 70 rowdies. They then went to Mr. Cushing's Mills and demanded him to shut down his saws. On his refusing, they knocked down him and his son, beat several of the men, and endeavoured to drive out all who were working there. In this, however, they failed. On Saturday night last a volley of seven shots was fired into the sleeping apartment of Mr. Cushing's men, evidently aimed for their beds, as several of the shots passed close to the heads of those who were sleeping there. There can be no doubt but the murderous attack was made by the same party who attacked the Mills.

It was a classic example of pre-union labour strife, for the malcontents were forced to seek work elsewhere.[23]

The Saint John Irish Catholics were, therefore, an unsettling element in the community, Separated by socioeconomic status, philosophical outlook, and even to some extent geographical location, the Irish posed a threat to the stability of the colonial society. For Anglin this situation created both a problem and an opportunity. The difficulty, of course, was that as an Irish Catholic he bore a stigma, however praiseworthy his education, diligence, and attainments. He could not be accepted readily by the dominant groups in Saint John in spite of the fact that he shared many of their middle-class values. As they were apprehensive about the Irish Catholics as a group, they naturally were suspicious of the leader of that group. On the other hand, the opportunity was the fact that both the Irish Catholics and the established colonial society required someone to provide liaison between the two groups, as the 1849 riot had demonstrated, particularly to the native-born. For their part the Irish had almost daily evidence of the need for a spokesman who had sufficient standing to be listened to by the established authorities. This fact, plus the deferential character of nineteenth-century society, accounts for Irish Catholic support of their middle-class leader.

As an Irish leader Anglin was well aware that any group requires self-respect as an initial step towards improvement. For this reason Anglin almost always defended the Irish as a group against charges that they were a depraved and useless burden on society. He chose, naturally enough, to view such criticisms as the result of ignorance and bigotry. To promote Irish self-respect and a feeling of worth within the society Anglin perpetually urged the commercial and industrial expansion of the city, though always with a sharp eye for fiscal irresponsibility of legislators. Economic development would provide employment for Irish Catholics; in turn this would improve their economic circumstances, which would enable them to raise their living standard and ultimately integrate them into the community. To give the Irish a sense of belonging Anglin's paper carried news of Ireland, the implication being that the new world was not completely detached from the old and that improvements in Ireland would assist the North American Irish to overcome sneering criticisms of the national character of Irishmen. As well, the organization of Irishmen in Saint John for various purposes was also supported by the *Freeman*. As the St Patrick's Society had no place in it for Catholics, another body would have to be formed. And so the Irish Friendly Society, some five hundred strong by 1859,[24] was formed. If Protestants were reticent to provide social welfare for Catholics, then Catholic societies would have to undertake this task.[25] Volunteer fire companies composed of Irish Catholics provided a useful public service as well as a focus for companionship and an opportunity to participate in parades.[26] Probably most significant in making Irish Catholics feel at home in Saint John was the growth of the Catholic Church. Under the energetic leadership of Thomas L. Connolly, who became bishop of New Brunswick in 1852, the church responded to the needs of

Irish Catholics, witnessed, for example, by the building of the cathedral, one of the city's most distinguished edifices. Anglin certainly supported the efforts of the church for he was one of those selected to serve on a committee to raise funds to build the cathedral, just as he was on the committee named to frame a welcoming address to Bishop Connolly.[27]

Anglin's efforts to accommodate the Irish to their new surroundings did not cease at this point. Attempting to develop employment opportunities, promoting social organizations, and defending the name of the Irish were not sufficient. If the Irish were to be accepted in the community, they had to avoid activities which threatened the social fabric or made the dominant groups fearful. This, at least, was the basis of Anglin's policy. One might envisage an Irish spokesman promoting violence, an Irish tradition, as a technique for attempting to gain control of a community,[28] but Anglin was not such a leader. For one thing his middle-class status meant that he sympathized with most of the goals sought by the ruling groups – social stability and economic development using capitalist techniques if at all possible. Anglin did not promote the organization of labour unions to improve the working conditions and wages of the Irish workingman. Nor did he mount a campaign for state involvement in the field of social welfare. These topics would have been of major interest to the mass of Irish Catholics for they clearly spoke to essential problems. To blame Anglin for his failure to come to grips with these issues, however, would be to expect an individual to transcend both his class and his era.

Anglin's perspective on matters relating to social problems, which had been moulded by his Irish background, was clearly expressed in the *Freeman*.

The belief underlying the Irish Catholic view of the cause of social evils is that man, due to original sin, is fallen; as a result, he has many frailties and suffers grave hardships not susceptible of great transformation by mere mortal efforts ...

From the Irish point of view, the most effective prescription for ameliorating the difficulties and dilemmas inherent in the human condition was acknowledgment and repentance of sin, of error, and the hope that Divine intervention would be forthcoming ...[29]

Anglin also shared 'the prevalent attitude to the poor at the beginning of the nineteenth century' in which 'severity (bordering on contempt) was incongruously blended with compassion.'[30] The trick was to differentiate between the deserving and undeserving poor: the infirm, aged, and widowed were deemed worthy of support; the able-bodied poor were not.[31] For the former Anglin was always ready to support fund-raising activities.[32] The *Freeman* was even willing to appeal for contributions for the creation of a House of Refuge for fallen women.[33] Beggary, on the other hand, Anglin considered to be an 'evil' which demanded attention. He recognized that some of the urchins who sought handouts were in genuine need but he was also convinced that a large number of them were 'trained to begging as a profession, by parents who are too idle to work, or too dissipated and worthless to support their family on their earnings.'[34] Needless to say, Anglin had little sympathy for the able-bodied poor.

Anglin's sympathy disappeared completely when it came to adult 'rowdyism.' Activities such as breaking windows, fighting, drinking in taverns without paying, and a host of other rather minor offences should be, the *Freeman* believed, 'most vigorously punished' by the police.[35] Since by the mid 1860s there were '9 Billiard Saloons, 2 Bowling Saloons, 20 Gambling Houses, 65 Beer Shops, 280 Licensed Taverns and 37 Houses of ill fame'[36] in the city, there were plenty of opportunities for trouble to erupt, and the *Freeman* found the situation most disturbing:

There is the terrible fact staring the moral and respectable in the face, that in this city are a number of 'haunts of infamy and abodes of crime,' to which resort swarms of young men and old, who drink and gamble and brawl night after night ... to whom religion is an entire stranger; whose knowledge of the Divinity is only such as enables them to blaspheme his name; whose respect for society and the laws is merely a dread of the policemen and the watch-house; who are so reckless, so hardened, so depraved, or so ignorant, that even when the violent death of one of their companions has been the result of their 'scrimmage' or their 'row,' they see in it nothing to be ashamed of, nothing to be sorry for; and even when giving evidence on a murder trial, they display an indifference in regard to crime that is quite as shocking as crime itself.[37]

Anglin believed that prevention of such deplorable conditions was the only long-range answer to the problem, but aside from implying that the church should be able to play a role, indicating that a general supervision of 'haunts of infamy' was needed, and suggesting that 'the innocent and well disposed' would do well to shun bad companions and avoid crowds, tumults, and disturbances, even as spectators, he had few suggestions.[38] Anglin's concern for morality and lawfulness was indicated by the concerted effort of the *Freeman* to cover the police court cases in Saint John, partly no doubt to ensure that justice was done, but mainly in order to preach to the Irish the folly and sinfulness of activities which would bring them in front of the courts. To Anglin this seemed to be part of his role. He had to 'improve' Irish Catholics in order to make more legitimate his case for increased recognition and rights for them. The *Freeman* was, therefore, a supporter, though not an uncritical supporter, of the forces of law and order.

Anglin's approach was very much middle-class, promoted by the church establishment and tempered by some realization of the conditions in which large numbers of Irish Catholics lived. It was a feasible and not inappropriate position for Anglin to adopt as an Irish Catholic leader bent on accommodating the Irish to their new surroundings. The efficacy of his endeavour depended, of course, on the success of his mouthpiece, the *Freeman*.

II

Like the Irish community, the *Freeman* had a struggle to establish itself. In the first place there was much competition among the Saint John newspapers for readers. When the *Freeman* was founded in 1849, there were nine other newspapers in Saint John including the *New Brunswicker*, the *Courier*, and the *News*.[39] This competition, coupled with the failure of a number of *Freeman* subscribers to pay their debts, forced Anglin to suspend publication for several months in the winter of 1850–1.[40] But adversity apparently brought increased strength, for when the paper was reestablished it was no longer published once but three times a week. This reorganization was obviously successful, for the *Freeman* made a regular triweekly appearance in New Brunswick for the next quarter-century.* In 1858 Anglin adopted a strict cash-in-advance policy for subscriptions and offered inducements for forming clubs.[41] The circulation of the *Freeman* is not known, although on a couple of occasions during the period it boasted of having sold more than 4000 copies.[42] This number would have been unusual, however, for the *Freeman* faced the competition of two other Saint John papers on the mornings it was published.[43] Nevertheless, it seems likely that before long the *Freeman* had as wide a distribution throughout the province as any other paper. It became the life-blood of the Catholic community in every nook and cranny of New Brunswick.†

---

*   Fewer than a dozen issues of the *Freeman* prior to 1858 remain extant. Fortunately the *Freeman* was often quoted by other provincial newspapers.

†   At one time there was a project afoot for Anglin to edit a purely religious paper as well as the *Freeman* (see Bishop James Rogers Papers, Bishop John Sweeny to Rogers, 16 Dec. 1860, in UNBA). Nothing materialized from these plans.

By means of the *Freeman* Anglin made himself known in Saint John and throughout the province. It did not take him very long to become embroiled in controversy with various newspapers and personages.[44] It was standard practice at the time for one editor to berate another, and Anglin quickly developed a skill and bite unsurpassed in New Brunswick. While his argument was usually thorough and convincing, it was not always stated moderately. On one occasion, for example, he claimed that 'it would not be more absurd to discuss Temperance in a grog shop, Honesty with a receiver of stolen goods, or Chastity in a brothel, than to enter on a religious controversy with the *Chronicle*.'[45] Vigorous writing of this type made Anglin's name well known – if not always liked – in New Brunswick.

There was no question that the *Freeman* was Anglin's voice, for not only was he its proprietor, but he also stated on several occasions that all editorials were written by himself save only very brief notices when he was away from the city. Even here the evidence seems to suggest that he usually left a few editorials ready for his printer.[46] One of Anglin's most notable talents was his reporting ability. He had an amazing memory, apparently being able to listen to a meeting, take nary a note, and yet present in the *Freeman* a full and accurate report 'not only of the nouns used by the speakers but the adjectives qualifying them.'[47] Before long other newspapers, particularly the *Courier*, began to rely upon the accounts furnished by the *Freeman*. Anglin's talent resulted in his travelling to Fredericton in 1852 and reporting the debates of the Assembly to the Saint John press.[48] The fact that in subsequent years Anglin was present listening to and reporting the speeches made in the Assembly gave him almost as much knowledge of political affairs in the province as if he had been an elected member.[49]

Producing a triweekly kept Anglin extremely busy. After 1850 Anglin's name did not appear on executive or membership lists of the various organizations in the city, except for work for the church.* In part this was because a morning newspaper required much evening work if it was to be on the streets for sale on time.[50] If the production of the *Freeman* was an arduous task, however, it was interesting work which gave Anglin a sense of importance and involvement in the community. The *Freeman* office itself was unpretentious, situated, for the most part, above stores on or near Prince William Street,[51] in the business district of the city where lawyers, bankers, dry-goods merchants, printers, and a dozen other types of

---

* Anglin had been a vice-president of the St John Total Abstinence Relief Society in 1849 and 1850 (see *Courier*, 20 Oct. 1849; and 5 Oct. 1850).

businessmen and professionals had their offices.[52] When things were dull, Anglin could always have sauntered a block south of the *Freeman* office to Chubb's Corner where, according to an 1877 account, 'more gossip has been talked during the last forty years than would furnish the stock-in-trade of forty well-organized sewing circles ...'[53] To the north of the *Freeman* office was Market Square and to the west the harbour, both within a few minutes walk. The harbour, when it was not enveloped by fog as was so frequently the case, would have provided Anglin, a man raised by the sea, with many sights of interest. Around the harbour were boatsmen, raftsmen, and millmen busy plying their trades. Boats of all sizes and descriptions abounded, from the ferry boats which carried passengers to the west side of Saint John for four cents,[54] to the steamers which made four trips a week to Eastport, Portland, and Boston,[55] and to the timber and sailing ships bound for Liverpool.[56] The environs of the *Freeman* office provided much to stimulate Anglin.

There were other interesting subjects in Saint John which diverted Anglin's attention, as the *News* of 2 December 1853 showed:

'*Nabbed at Last!*' – One of our contemporaries, to whom we proposed a short time since, a series of topics to write upon, has, since Saturday last, been turning one subject – that of *Batchelors* – to a very practical, and we hope it will turn out useful account. After all, we have not hinted to him in vain, and we shall expect a large slice of wedding cake for having been the means of stirring his courage up to the sticking point. Our friend will now have a place to spend his evenings besides in the Printing Office. We shall have some capital editorials after this.

Anglin, at the age of thirty-one, married Margaret O'Regan. The newly-weds, along with the bride's sister, resided on Peters Street.[57] The fact that Anglin believed it appropriate to get married suggests that he had achieved some measure of economic stability and prestige in the community. His position, however, was hardly one of great affluence. The house on Peters Street, probably a rented building, was located only six blocks away from the *Freeman* office, but the area left something to be desired. A complaint was registered in 1848, for example, that 'the flat near the foot of Peters Street is a perfect bog ...' because of a lack of drainage.[58] Anglin's first marriage was tragically short, for Margaret died on 2 June 1855.[59] To her memory, and that of her sister who also died before 1859, Anglin presented Bishop Connolly with a stained-glass window which was set in the south transept of the cathedral.[60] It was probably fortunate that no children had been born to the couple for Anglin would probably not have been a successful single parent. Whatever might have been, the fact was that by 1855 Anglin was a youthful widower making his way in the world. On 30 July 1857 he purchased property on Waterloo Street just north of Golding from Thomas and Elizabeth Gass for £1,200.[61] This lot was only a few blocks north of Anglin's former residence, but it was on more elevated ground and closer to the cathedral. It was, in fact, a valuable piece of property: 'The HOUSE is very large, commodious[,] thoroughly built, and well finished. The Pipe Water is carried through the house; there is an excellent Spring in the yard, and the property is well drained.'[62] Clearly Anglin had established himself during the 1850s as a reasonably prosperous resident of Saint John.

III

Anglin's middle-class orientation probably explains his economic philosophy. In retrospect Anglin's economic views seem intensely conservative but in his day they were typical liberal conceptions. Even the Irish Famine had not shaken his basic faith in nineteenth-century laissez-faire individualism. Stripped of any qualifications, Anglin's opinion was best expressed in a speech made to the New Brunswick Assembly in 1865:

Ever since I have been a member of this House I have opposed every Bill which interfered with the exchange of goods between buyer and seller. I have never seen any good result from a measure placing restrictions upon Trade ... If I go to ... market and cannot choose between good and bad, then I must be my own loser; no rules can protect me.[63]

This attitude led Anglin to oppose such things as protective tariffs during the Confederation debates and in the debate over Macdonald's national policy during the late 1870s and 1880s. He even believed that it was not right for New Brunswick to demand that Great Britain maintain a differential duty on timber for the benefit of the colony.[64] Anglin was opposed to other forms of legislation which restricted free enterprise, such as the usury law in New Brunswick which, he claimed, made it disadvantageous for bankers to lend money to local manufacturers when compared to the lumber and ship exporters.[65]

Indeed, while Anglin demonstrated some interest in developing markets for New Brunswick's wood-based enterprises,[66] he was particularly concerned with the growth of local industries which would, as he put it, 'give employment to hundreds,'[67] undoubtedly including many Irishmen.[68] The building of railways centred on Saint John was part of the process of developing manufacturing and commerce, and thus the *Freeman* was in the forefront of railway promotion. Anglin was proud of the economic strides Saint John was making during the fifties and participated freely in the traditional running battle with the Halifax newspapers over the relative merits of the two cities:

... all real rivalry between a manufacturing, commercial ship-building, ship-owning city, and one which depends solely on its garrison and its fisheries, is simply impossible. We should be amused, rather than annoyed, at the malevolence of our neighbours ...[69]

While in many ways Anglin had a 'chamber of commerce' growth mentality, he also paid homage to another commonplace idol of nineteenth-century North Americans – the agrarian myth. As Anglin put it in 1861, 'ownership of the soil is that which must ultimately confer the greatest advantages.'[70] He urged the industrious, sober, and frugal members of the labouring class to leave the cities and seek independence by building farms in the wilderness.[71] The *Freeman* found it difficult to understand why workingmen would want to remain in the cities:

With an infatuation that can scarcely be accounted for, thousands of men cling to the wretched life of towns and cities, their casual employment, their fluctuating wages, their miserable lodgings, scanty food, insufficient fuel and ragged clothes, their filth and abominations and vices with as much tenacity as if these alone rendered life desirable; as if the free air of the country were poison, and labour in the woods and fields were the greatest slavery.[72]

To promote agricultural settlement the *Freeman* gave full support to a colonization scheme developed by Dr John Sweeny, who became Bishop of Saint John in 1860.[73] All of this, of course, was more a matter of 'do as I say' than 'do as I do.' Whether Anglin was simply mouthing platitudes in his support of the agrarian life is difficult to assess. Clearly, however, the only way in which Anglin's views on agrarian settlement can be accommodated with his desire to promote the industrial development of Saint John is that both were geared to alleviating the destitution of Irish Catholics.

Perhaps because he represented a poverty-stricken minority group, Anglin strongly believed that the privileges of those directing the provincial economy had to be matched by a stern sense of public responsibility. In prosperous times, for example, 'prudence, caution and economy' were necessary in order that the public debt be abolished.[74] If the state treasury was low, then expenditures should not be increased by extravagant schemes. And of course the government's management of finances had to be carefully scrutinized. Mismanagement, corruption, and extravagance were, in Anglin's eyes, grossly irresponsible in men who had been entrusted to guide the colony's economic development. Among other things, fiscal incompetence would result in a need for greater taxation, whether via tariffs or in some other form.[75] In turn, this would restrict freedom of trade, an eventuality which was repugnant to Anglin's economic thought.

While Anglin always kept a close eye on government expenditures, he had no major objection to the general direction taken by the New Brunswick economy during the 1850s. Improved economic conditions by 1852 and the achievement of reciprocity with the United States in 1854 removed most of the economic grievances which had spawned political agitation at mid-century. The timber, lumber, and shipbuilding industries, characterized by great instability from year to year, still dominated the economic life of the colony, but manufacturing was developing and railway-building did proceed. Railway-building was, of course, the major politico-economic issue of the 1850s throughout British North America. Discussions of railways in New Brunswick newspapers were extremely voluminous, complex, and confusingly intermingled with the politics of the province.

In brief, there were two main possibilities.[76] An intercolonial railway could be built which would connect New Brunswick with Canada on the one hand and Nova Scotia on the other. An alternate line was one which would link the province with the United States. These two projects were not necessarily mutually exclusive, as it was possible that parts of both lines could run on the same tracks.[77] However, competition developed because the New Brunswick North Shore counties were not willing to see the Saint John valley reap all the benefits of the iron horse. Nor were British authorities anxious to help build an intercolonial railway, supposedly of military value, that was not as far away from the American border as possible. On the other hand, any intercolonial railway scheme which did not provide connections for the Saint John valley would meet with tremendous opposition from the southern and western counties.[78] Anglin favoured the integration of both schemes. Build the European and North American Railway, the grandiose name given to the line which was to connect Portland, Maine, and Shediac, New Brunswick, he said, but let the province also develop her railway network on the foundation of the Euro-

pean and North American so that New Brunswick would become connected to the railroad systems of Canada and Nova Scotia as well as the
United States.[79] Anglin, as a proponent of Saint John interests, supported
the European and North American line above all others, if a choice had to
be made.[80] In 1850 Anglin had been secretary of a meeting in Saint John
which had drafted plans for that railway and he had then been on a
committee established to solicit funds.[81] The construction of this railway
would also provide work for many Irish labourers looking for jobs around
Saint John. Anglin was so concerned about the 'E. & N.A. Railway' (as the
Freeman frequently called it), that he was most unsympathetic to anything
that seemed to put barriers in its way – anything, that is, except genuine
financial difficulties. Given that qualification, he continually prodded the
government to make ever greater efforts.[82]

IV

Railways were potent sources of political division in New Brunswick but
there was another issue which divided men in public life. By mid-century
New Brunswick had not yet adopted the apparatus which is conventionally
assumed to be part and parcel of the system of responsible government.
The fact was that the Assembly itself had won control of the purse in 1837
and did not want a 'responsible' executive to infringe upon its prerogative.
As a result the province was not developed by any comprehensive plan.
Also party politics were very slow to develop, each assemblyman being out
to get the most he could for his constituency. This involved a good deal of
back-scratching – known in the province as 'log-rolling.' Thus, personal
connections, local interests, and patronage considerations took precedence over grand developmental schemes. Nevertheless, for purposes of
simplicity one could stretch a generalization to its utmost limit and say that
there were reformers in the province; reformers who wished to see the
introduction of complete responsible government, including the diminution of the power of the Colonial Office as represented by the Lieutenant
Governor. Ironically, perhaps the most important agents promoting constitutional change in the colony were the British themselves, for they
wanted to regularize the system in New Brunswick and reduce their involvement in provincial affairs. The Lieutenant Governor appointed in
1848, Sir Edmund Head, was directed to introduce responsible government
into the province.[83] But the old system was difficult to change and the
coalition administration which revamped itself after the 1850 election carried on in power until 1854.[84]

When Anglin arrived on the Scene in 1849 the most outspoken exponent of reform principles was the *News*. It is significant, therefore, that it was to the *News* that Anglin sent his letter of July 1849. By natural inclination the *Freeman* sided with the reformers, and it did not take long for the newspaper wars of New Brunswick to confirm its position. Anglin's unequivocal attitude towards the administration was clearly evident, for example, in August 1851, when he heard the astounding news that two of the supposed opponents of the government had taken office in it. He accused the two men, John H. Gray and Robert D. Wilmot, of 'political corruption, treachery, and baseness' and of betraying the interests of their constituents for personal gain.[85] Throughout the reign of the coalition the *Freeman* acted as a critic of the government and was something of a financial watchdog.[86] In short, the *Freeman* was a good and true opposition organ.

The election of 1854 brought about a change of government. Charles Fisher, a reformer, was called upon to form the administration and succeeded in procuring the services of Samuel Leonard Tilley, John M. Johnson, W.H. Steeves, Albert J. Smith, James Brown, and William J. Ritchie.[87] Fisher was no great favourite of the *Freeman*: the paper feared that he could be bought off if the price were right.[88] Moreover, no Catholic was named to the Executive Council as had been expected.[89] Thus the establishment of the new government did not meet with the wholehearted approval of the *Freeman* despite Anglin's staunch opposition to its predecessor. Anglin began to find himself in a peculiar position in regard to the politics of the province.

For a time the *Freeman* seemed to waver in its support. It became more unhappy with the so-called Liberals but it was still leagues away from the Tories. Anglin became aware, however, that the former would do little more for Catholics than had the latter. By May 1855 he was complaining that among the new appointments no Roman Catholic was to be found.[90] Anglin was also becoming discontented with government railway policy.[91] Yet throughout 1855, or at least until the autumn, the *Freeman* could not be classified as being in the opposition camp. Even in January 1856 the Fredericton newspapers assumed that the *Freeman* was basically on the side of the government.[92] The issue which, in all of its ramifications, turned Anglin decisively against the new government was prohibition.

New Brunswickers liked their liquor.[93] Inevitably abuses existed, and during the fifties efforts were made to curb its consumption. The result was the rise of the temperance movement in New Brunswick.[94] There was a strong moral and religious spirit associated with the temperance agitation, but unfortunately a denominational division tended to develop on this issue. There were undoubtedly many Catholics who followed the precepts of the great Cork temperance advocate, Father Mathew, and abhorred the results of excessive drinking. But the large mass of the poverty-stricken, at whom the North American temperance crusade was aimed, were Irish Catholics. As a result, a prejudice against the Irish grew out of the movement as evangelical and puritanical Protestantism became associated with it.[95] Largely because of the religious overtones of the temperance movement, but no doubt partly because they enjoyed their liquor, Irish Catholics became opposed to the movement. The agitation in favour of prohibition seemed discriminatory, another Protestant ploy to discredit the Catholics. Undoubtedly this situation went far to define Anglin's attitude on prohibition.

Under the leadership of Leonard Tilley, the Sons of Temperance movement in New Brunswick grew by leaps and bounds. With the support of this organization a private bill prohibiting the importation or production of liquor except for medicinal purposes was passed in 1855 by the Assembly and the Legislative Council (New Brunswick's equivalent to the Senate or House of Lords). Tilley, the Provincial Secretary, thus put forward a bill which would curtail provincial income without making any provision for making up for this loss. Three members of the executive opposed the bill throughout its progress through the legislature, and yet accepted that it was a private bill – despite the fact that it had to affect the government, since it involved finances and required enforcement – and so declined to advise Lieutenant Governor J.H.T. Manners-Sutton not to assent to the bill.[96] Many members of the legislature had apparently shown great hypocrisy when they had voted for the bill. The *Head Quarters* claimed that, of the twenty-two supporters of the bill, fourteen were in the habit of imbibing, some to excess. Apparently one had even 'built up his courage' before making his speech.[97] Finally the law was allowed to go into effect without having the firm backing of the populace. In such a situation prohibition was likely to cause far more difficulties than it could possibly solve.

The reaction of the provincial press to this legislation was general disapproval. There was fear that the bill would not only be as unenforceable as its predecessor, which was passed in 1852, operative in 1853, and repealed in 1854, but would also stir up bitterness and strife.[98] Of all the newspapers the *Freeman* was the most outspoken in its criticism. After presenting to its readers the terms of the bill, it proceeded to assess it:

These are the principal features of a Bill, the most arbitrary and tyrannical conceived in modern times, destroying the sanctity of the domicile, rendering the *habeas corpus* a nullity and investing Justices (ignorant, fanatical, or unprincipled as they may be) and their myrmidons with a degree of power and authority never before entrusted to any Magistrates or officers in any part of the British empire, not under martial law.[99]

Undoubtedly Anglin felt that it was impossible to exhort his compatriots to be law-abiding citizens when the legislature passed absurd laws and the government irresponsibly allowed them to be put into force.

In assesssing Anglin's motives for so vigorous a condemnation of the legislation and the government, one must include personal factors as well as the fact that Irish Catholics generally did not approve of prohibition. Anglin may have opposed the liquor law for fear of losing lucrative advertising contracts from liquor interests, although he claimed that because of his stance the *Freeman* lost not only government advertising but also that of Saint John businessmen whose party feeling prevailed over 'their good sense.'[100] Such financial calculations probably did not greatly concern Anglin.

It is not the first nor the twentieth time that I have deliberately risked the loss of money and friends and lost them for the sake of maintaining what my reason tells me is the course of justice and truth. The man who would hesitate to do so is unworthy of being a journalist.[101]

To Anglin prohibition was simply a most serious question of principle in politics.

It is an utter fallacy to say that the Prohibitory Law is not politics. It is political in the highest sense of the word: for everything that effects [sic] the State is political and the success or defeat of any particular parties is not politics of a minor and less important sort. The Prohibitory Bill I must regard as the introduction of a most unwarrantable kind of Legislation that would prescribe to the public at the will of the minority [sic] what they should eat and drink and wear and how they should worship. The end is unquestionably good but the end does not justify the means: for if it did then whenever the majority of the people or of the Legislature thought Mormonism or Spiritualism to be the only true religion they might with as good reason compel us all to take a plurality of wives or profess a belief in Spirit Rappings … Once admit Legislation of this kind to be indulged in and there can be no limit to it but the will of the majority or the forbearance of the minority.[102]

The Liquor Law did not work. Its regulations were sporadically applied in most of the province and the *Gleaner*, the Miramichi newspaper, claimed that the only difference before and after the law went into effect was that before liquor dealers had paid money into the county treasury and after they paid nothing.[103] In Saint John the situation was different. There court cases involving even petty offences were numerous. Much ill-feeling arose and agitation for the repeal of the law gained strength daily. By March 1856 the *Freeman* favoured repeal of the bill even if the offices of the Colonial Secretary had to be used, a stance which brought ridicule from the *News*:

We knew that he [Anglin] was a Liberal, and in favor of 'local Parliaments' and self government, and like ourselves opposed to the flippancy and dictation of a Colonial Secretary. Yet, we find him supporting the principle ... of going down upon our knees to ask the Colonial Secretary to interpose his authority and prevent the Liquor Law going into effect. We were opposed to the Law, but far more opposed to the miserable spirit of crying to 'Mammy' to save us.[104]

The 1856 session of the New Brunswick legislature met in a mood of tenseness and disorderliness.[105] In such an atmosphere rational considera-tion of the defects of the Liquor Law could not take place and no motions for repeal or amendment were carried. The colony seemed on the verge of chaos, and shortly after the House rose from its labours Lieutenant Gover-nor Manners-Sutton gave the Executive Council a choice: either enforce the law or remove it from the statute books. He recommended an im-mediate election as the only solution to the existing state of affairs. Council members did not accept the view that the act was wholly inoperative and advised the Governor that, if it proved unsatisfactory after what they considered to be a fair trial, then the existing legislature would repeal it. They would not advise a dissolution. This was not acceptable to the Governor, and when he dissolved the parliament the members of the executive felt obliged to hand in their resignations. A new administration was quickly sworn in and the election was on.

Manners-Sutton's action aroused a good deal of debate as to its constitu-tionality and propriety. Most New Brunswick newspapers disapproved, many sympathizing with the desire to rid the province of the problems created by the Liquor Law, but feeling that the problem did not warrant the Governor's exercise of the prerogative.[106] The *Freeman* did not agree with this reasoning and in supporting the Governor broke all ties with the former government and rose to the defence of the new, despite the fact that it contained some of the very men to whom it had been most opposed a short time before. While Anglin would undoubtedly have felt more comfortable arguing the other side of the case, the *Freeman* maintained that the Governor had acted constitutionally and the the conditions created by the Liquor Law required his action. Anglin boiled down the problem to a straightforward proposition:

Those who regard the Law as wrong in principle, injurious in its effects, and in every way an enormous and intolerable evil, are now called upon to say whether they shall willingly consent to the continuation and aggravation of this evil; or whether the Governor, in affording them an opportunity of getting rid of it, has done wrong because the existing state of things does not warrant this exercise of the prerogative.[107]

The 1856 election results legitimized the action of the Governor as far as this could be done. An overwhelming majority of the members returned were pledged to vote for repeal of the Liquor Law. It seems probable that the *Freeman*'s influence had been strongly felt since the government candidates swept the Saint John electoral districts, even Tilley being defeated.[108] But a government elected merely to repeal the Liquor Law found its existence most precarious, for after repeal there was little to prevent the assemblymen from going in various directions.[109]

In the meantime Anglin's relations with his former allies had rapidly deteriorated. A robust game of charge and counter-charge developed between the *Freeman* and the *Courier*, the *News* and the *Reporter* also getting into the game.[110] 'One of Them,' in a letter to the *Courier* published on 20 December 1856, compared Anglin to a snake:

The *Freeman* will remember quite well that some members of the Liberal party saw this adder when he was frozen, and, taking pity, assisted him into life; but, when natural strength returned, his original nature was fully developed in stinging his benefactors. They were then obliged, in self-defence, to put him away from them; his subscription and advertising lists bear evidence of this. Some saw the creature's propensities, and heard him hiss long ago: while others hoped on, almost against hope, until recent events fully satisfied them that no forbearance would even alter the creature's nature.

Such criticisms were standard fare in that era, but it is clear that Anglin was not the most popular man in the colony. It was at this time that the stories of his supposed involvement in the Irish Rebellion of 1848 began to circulate and also complaints about the critical attitude he had taken towards the Crimean War were bandied about.[111] But Anglin was not one who needed much sympathy, for he could hand out abuse with the best of them. Also, although this factor was part of the process that maintained the isolation of the Irish community of New Brunswick, the charges laid against him probably enhanced his prestige with that group. One thing that Anglin was sensitive about, however, was being labelled a Tory.[112] He reacted strongly to this accusation, as he felt that not he had changed but rather his opponents. But since they still retained the label of Libeal, he was forced to assert both that there were really no true parties in the province, and that the Liberals were not really true liberals and did not merit the name.[113]

Thus by the time the 1857 session of parliament began the *Freeman* was firmly committed to the government and thoroughly alienated from the 'Smashers,' as the *Freeman* and other government papers called the Liberals. But by the end of March the government was in such a moribund state that it was forced to dissolve the Assembly and call an election. The Smashers swept back into power, returning twenty-six of their supporters compared to fifteen government supporters.[114] The election had, however, indicated that Anglin's opposition to the Smashers coincided with the views of other Irish Catholics of Saint John, for the Irish Friendly Society of Saint John passed a resolution in support of the government candidates.[115]

V

In a sense political developments at mid-decade did not involve a great shift for Anglin. True, there had been a break with the Liberals, but more important was the fact that Anglin, as the leader of the minority group of Irish Catholics, found himself in opposition to the government. This was what was typical of his political stance of the 1850s, and indeed throughout his career. The prohibition issue, therefore, simply provided the mechanism whereby Anglin resumed his familiar role as an opposition journalist. Aside from the fact that his newspaper no longer received lucrative government advertisements,[116] he did not object to this position, for he thought it 'much easier and more pleasant' to attack than to defend.[117] The *Freeman* found plenty to attack.

One reason for Anglin's opposition to the new government of Fisher and Tilley was its tendency to adopt anti-Catholic attitudes. It is not surprising that it did, for the Smashers lived in the general atmosphere of religious discord which existed at the time in New Brunswick and throughout much of the English-speaking world.[118] The religious antagonism which polluted the social atmosphere of the colony spilled over into its political life. From

Anglin's point of view at least, the Smashers showed distinct WASP characteristics. Perhaps their attitude was a transfer of the discrimination which they, as Dissenters, had received from the Anglican establishment at the beginning of their political careers. Perhaps political exigencies led them to anti-Catholicism. Whatever the case, it was a fact with which Anglin and other New Brunswick Catholics had to deal. Fortunately anti-Catholicism was not as noticeable among the political leaders as among some of their backroom supporters, such as John Boyd, whose letters to Tilley often included outbursts such as the following:

You heard something of a Protestant boy having been stolen out of the Protestant Orphan Asylum by the Papists; well he has escaped from the Papists, and that is all I can tell you at present; but when the affair is finished it will be a history of Popery in N.B. and how it has been *done*, that will astonish you.[119]

Poor Boyd was always seeing Catholic plots at work in the province, and Anglin as one of the chief agents.[120] Tilley's own views are not clear. He does not seem to have been a bigot himself and yet he never seems to have taken a stand against the anti-Catholicism of others.[121] Perhaps he was living Mark Twain's silent lie.

The *Freeman* was indefatigable in its efforts to expose the basic anti-Catholic principles upon which the government operated. Often, the *Freeman* propounded, these were not particularly obvious; but they were effective nonetheless.

It is a pity the Know-Nothings of the United States do not learn a lesson from their brethren in New Brunswick, and instead of stupidly seeking an odious law to exclude all foreigners from the right to vote until after a 21 year residence, seek and obtain a registration law such as ours, which would enable them as the great secret organisation of the country effectually to exclude the vast majority of the foreigners obnoxious to them, and all the 'penniless' who are not of their party.[122]

Of course the clearest test of the government's attitude towards Catholics was the amount of patronage which Catholics received. The *Freeman* pointed out that it was so small that even the most bigoted and intolerant could not be dissatisfied. Catholics, Anglin demonstrated, were almost completely excluded from positions of importance.[123] The *Freeman* even claimed that Catholics did not fear the rise of a Protestant Alliance because they had so little to lose in a political sense that threats to take away what they had were simply laughable.[124]

Although the darkness of religious antagonism hung over New Brunswick like a cloud, the light of tolerance could not be extinguished. One might claim that by continually referring to the anti-Catholicism prevalent in New Brunswick, Anglin did little to foster toleration. Yet perhaps by pointing out the problem to the community at large, he did help to mitigate it; in fact, the *Freeman* claimed that a change was already occurring.

The Province no longer suffers as it once did, from religious feuds, and although trial by jury is not yet what it should be, and although the Reporter and its associates do all in their power occasionally to revive religious frenzy, we have full confidence that the good sense of the people will prevail, and that whatever may be the temporary effects of unprincipled scoundrels, who from time to time seek to prostitute religion in the service of party, the feelings which true religion always excites will prevail more and more each day, and as people know each other better, kindness and good-will will more and more take the place of senseless hatred and animosities, so injurious to the best interests of all the people.[125]

The policy of the government towards Catholics was only one of the reasons why Anglin opposed the Smashers. The government was an anti-Catholic Know-Nothing administration, said the *Freeman*, but, as well, it was a Do-Nothing one. Over and over again Anglin insisted that the government was not accomplishing anything of significance and that its whole policy consisted of keeping itself in office and enjoying its position.[126] There was much validity to his accusations. Once the issue of responsible government had been settled,[127] the government devoted itself to the game of patronage politics. Politicians, newspaper editors, and other personages scrambled over each other for the richest prizes. It is not surprising, therefore, that Anglin continually denounced the government for corruption, extravagance, mismanagement, and all other forms of financial sin.[128] In 1861 the *Freeman* proved that Fisher had been guilty of gross misconduct in regard to Crown lands, and that several other members of the government, including Tilley, had been implicated. Although the *Freeman* mined the issue for all it was worth, the government escaped fairly easily by making Fisher the scapegoat for everyone concerned. He was forced to resign, leaving Tilley as the undisputed king of the hill.[129]

But if the *Freeman* found little about the government to commend, it considered the opposition members in the Assembly little better. True, Anglin did reject the charge that opposition to the government was equivalent to supporting the Family Compact and even claimed that the government was establishing its own Compact.[130] But he thought that the men in

TOP Former Anglin home in Clonakilty
Photograph taken by A.J.C. Anglin and used by permission

BOTTOM Cottages formerly owned by Anglins in Clonakilty
Photograph taken by A.J.C. Anglin and used by permission

ABOVE View of Saint John, c. mid-nineteenth century (Geo. N. Smith)
Public Archives of Canada C 30960

OPPOSITE, TOP Mrs Anglin (née McTavish), 1874
Public Archives of Canada PA 26436

OPPOSITE, BOTTOM Charles Fisher, 1868
Public Archives of Canada PA 25342

TOP Samuel Leonard Tilley, 1869
Public Archives of Canada PA 12632

BOTTOM Albert James Smith, 1868
Public Archives of Canada PA 25257

the Assembly who opposed the government were generally a weak lot, no more concerned with the welfare of the country than the Smashers.[131] Obviously the *Freeman* considered the political system to be inadequate and in need of reorganization:

The change must be complete. It will be well if not only the party now dominant, but the whole system which curses the Province, be got rid of at once and for ever, and that at length men be selected to govern the country, who are really honest, really intelligent, and really independent; men who will not be the slaves of any faction that may style itself a political party, for no other reason than that it is desirous of putting out or keeping out another clique which also styles itself a party.[132]

Not only were such statements in the tenacious tradition of non-party politics of the province, but they also indicated that Anglin could find a comfortable home in neither of the two so-called parties.

Still, the prime target of Anglin was the Smasher government. Many government supporters considered Anglin to be the main source of opposition and they castigated him for this. T.B. Barker, Tilley's business associate, for example, thought Anglin was 'a miserable lying scoundrel'[133] who 'ought to be horsewhipped like a dog.'[134] The very bitterness of such comments, which found parallels in the newspapers, betrayed the seriousness and importance with which government supporters regarded Anglin. Anglin was, in fact, becoming recognized as a major figure in the province. The real test of his prominence and power, however, would come when he himself stood for election.

4

Political Principles
and Policies
1860-4

I

Anglin's first venture into active politics came in 1860 when he ran for an aldermanic seat on the Saint John Common Council in King's ward. The way the *Freeman* told it, its editor had been approached by a number of the residents and pressed to run. He had tried to dissuade them, and only after they had appealed to his sense of duty did he give his reluctant assent. He warned them that the Smashers and their hangers-on would do all in their power to defeat him and that a religious cry would be raised. This was exactly what occurred, said the *Freeman*, when Anglin was defeated by a three to two margin.[1] It was not an auspicious beginning for a political career.

   Anglin's opportunity to revenge this defeat came a year later when the life of the New Brunswick Assembly came to an end, much to the satisfaction of the *Freeman*.

It is gone! and the whole Province experiences an ineffable sense of relief. It is gone!! may no country ever look upon its like again. It is gone!!! sunk in infamy unfathomable, and its memory will ever be loathed and abhored [sic] by good men. It is gone!!!! but it has left behind it a mess of corruption and pollution which it will require all the energy of the good and wise to get rid of; which if not got rid of at once will taint the political atmosphere for many years to come.[2]

On 9 May the *Freeman* published Anglin's card to the electors of the county of Saint John announcing his candidacy. It proclaimed that his political opinions and principles were well known and that, if he was elected, his aim would be to put these principles into practice, and to 'secure for the country an honest, energetic, prudent and economical administration of public affairs.' He would run – but under what label? The answer to this question was not decided for some time. A clique of the Conservative party in Saint John got together at an unpublicized meeting – a 'hole-and-corner' meeting Anglin later called it – and drafted a Conservative slate of candidates for the city and county constituencies. Anglin had expected to be nominated as one of the ticket on account of the services he had provided for the Conservatives during the five previous years. But this did not occur,[3] and he would have to run as an independent. This was not unfitting, as all along the *Freeman* had exhorted the New Brunswick electors to 'choose without regard to party men of honour and character who hold the political opinions of which they approve.'[4] As it turned out eleven candidates were nominated for the four seats available in the county of Saint John – four Liberals, four Conservatives, and three independents.

Anglin had learned enough of Saint John politics to take at least one important precaution. In the King's ward election the year before a number of placards and handbills had been circulated purporting to come from Anglin and urging Catholics to vote for one of their own. Anglin had not, in fact, issued them and he considered the whole thing to be a plot by his opponents to initiate a Protestant reaction.[5] The plot had succeeded then; he took steps to ensure that the same thing did not happen again:

Mr. Anglin also wishes to state that, in order to prevent the possibility of misrepresentation, he will not issue any handbills or placards, and to warn the public that if any be issued in his name they will be spurious and fraudulent.[6]

Detailed evidence on the campaign in Saint John is not available. The *Freeman* placed itself under a self-imposed censorship while its editor was a candidate.[7] But when the political dust cleared, Anglin had polled the second highest number of votes of the eleven candidates.[8] Taking the other three seats for the county were Smashers, a fact which meant that two very important Conservative leaders, John Gray and Robert Wilmot, were left at home. What accounted for Anglin's victory? Undoubtedly the publicity which the *Freeman* had brought him was an important factor. Probably many Conservatives felt they owed him a vote for his past services. Unquestionably the Catholic vote helped him.[9] But there was another factor involved: the electors recognized that he was a capable, hard-working, and intelligent individual.

Throughout his public career Anglin's political thought was pragmatic.

Nevertheless, one can discern certain concepts which lay at the basis of his political activity and remained relatively consistent. In essence Anglin was both a liberal, in the British sense, and a luke-warm democrat. Given Anglin's social standing, his Irish background, and the tendency of minority groups to attach themselves to liberal movements,[10] Anglin found it natural to adopt liberalism, that British middle-class doctrine of laissez-faire individualism. To the editor of the *Freeman* liberalism was more closely tied to the concepts of justice and freedom than to specific political systems or particular legislative programs:

... liberty depends no less on the nature and spirit of the laws than on the *mode* in which they become laws. *A man may enjoy the fullest liberty if governed according to law, and the laws are in themselves good, even though he had no voice in their adoption* ... True freedom, real liberty, cannot exist even in a republic, where all men are legally equal, if false principles in legislation prevail with, or are submitted to by the majority, and are acted upon in legislation. Where the rights of the individual are trampled upon there is despotism.[11]

Majority rule, then, was not to be equated with liberalism or necessarily with good government. There is no question that Anglin's fear of the power of the majority stemmed from particular conditions in New Brunswick. Anglin was, after all, part of a distinct minority group in that colony, and it is important to note that his statement on the essence of 'real liberty' was made during the struggle over prohibition.

It may seem curious, therefore, that while Anglin placed little faith in any majority, he favoured extension of the franchise.

For our own part, we have never yet been able to find any reason why the possession, real or nominal, of a few pounds more, should make one citizen better than another, or give him more legal and political rights. Every man in the community is compelled to submit to the laws made by the Legislature and to pay in full his share of the taxes or duties they impose, and there is no good reason, and there can be none why the people should be classified into a law-making class, and a class who must have no voice in making the laws they have to obey, or determining the burdens they have to bear. Still less can there be any reason why the distinction should be based on money ...[12]

Anglin's support for what amounted to universal manhood suffrage is explained partly by the fact that many Irish Catholics met neither the property nor income qualifications for voters and partly by his conviction that much corruption and discrimination existed in drafting lists of electors, for the Irish found it extremely difficult to have their names placed on voters' lists.[13] And so, as the *Freeman* told the *News*, 'we will not consent that you should have Universal Suffrage on your side and almost universal disfranchisement on ours.'[14] Consequently Anglin waged a strenuous annual campaign to overcome what he considered to be the tampering with electoral lists for the benefit of the Smashers.[15] The same concern about corruption also led Anglin to urge the adoption of the secret ballot and simultaneous elections throughout New Brunswick.[16]

In a very important sense, therefore, Anglin was a democrat.[17]

Democracy, it is true, has many errors and faults and crimes to account for; but in this country what form of government not democratic is at all tolerable? Is it to be endured that we are to have a governing class here, and a class that must submit to such laws as the governing class choose to impose? That men like the editor of the Reporter, the Messrs. Fisher, or our own Assessors, are to determine who are to constitute the governing class, to say to this man, you have not 'soul enough,' and to that, you have not 'a common interest in the community;' and although you are intelligent, sober, industrious, and a good citizen; though your whole life has been devoted to a trade or pursuit beneficial to the country, and although, moreover, you have as large an income and as much property as that other man whom we permit to vote, we will exclude you, and merely because we think proper to do so? Yet such are the principles these Liberals now openly advocate, and even the Ballot they would, if possible, do away with, because it protects the working man from the undue influence of his employer; the poor man from the vindictiveness of his creditor.[18]

Yes, said Anglin, the vote was a right which all men of the province ought to possess. But it was a precious right and carried with it serious responsibilities.

The right to vote, and by voting to take part in the government of the country, in the making of its laws, and raising and expending the revenue, is the greatest political right any man can possess, and he who disregards it is not fit to be a citizen of a free country.[19]

Anglin's commitment to democracy was far from total. His comment on the responsibility of voters gives some indication of this. As well Anglin's support for democratic principles seems to have been restricted to political and legal matters, for in social and economic affairs there is little evidence to suggest that he considered equality to be either possible or desirable. One might even suggest that his espousal of political democracy in the late 1850s and early 1860s was a result of his desire to win the franchise for a larger number of Irish Catholics, persons who might be expected to support his political ambitions. Clearly the circumstances of the time, in particular the growing desire of some Smashers further to restrict the franchise, played a role in determining Anglin's views, for in the 1880s, when writing to Lord Lorne about what the franchise ought to be in Ireland, Anglin suggested a small property or income qualification geared to giving the vote 'to all who take an intelligent interest in the affairs of the country.'[20] This may have been a compromise proposal, for Anglin also wrote in the same letter that 'It is difficult to find a permanent standing place on this question short of universal suffrage in any country,' but it does suggest that Anglin was uneasy about the concept of universal suffrage. Finally he was far too middle-class and far too atuned to the Christian belief in the depravity of mankind to place much faith in the goodness and rationality of man, particularly the ordinary man.

To many nineteenth-century democrats the solution to the problem of ignorant and degraded masses would be found in the use of state power, particularly in providing free education for all members of society. For Anglin, the liberal and the Catholic, the answer was not in the use of state power, but in the influence of religion. Anglin believed that religion ought to be 'the great vital principle that should ever guide, govern, actuate and controul man ...' and that clerics ought to play an important role in shaping attitudes and standards in the political arena and throughout society.[21] Anglin undoubtedly agreed with the Catholic theorist de Bonald who believed that 'the safeguard against the misuse of power does not lie in institutions to curb power ... but in the ethical limitations of power set by the religious conscience.'[22] Many nineteenth-century Catholics used this conception to justify opposition to political reform; Anglin did not. He believed that the application of Christian principles was essential for the adequate operation of *any* governmental system. As the *Freeman* stated on 9 June 1863, 'no agencies or means merely human can controul or subdue, much less quite extinguish the evil tendencies, the corrupt inclinations of human nature ... To controul human nature is a supernatural work which can only be accomplished by supernatural means.' Since this was true whatever the form of government, why not support democratic reforms which would give men political rights to which they were entitled?

Finally Anglin believed that liberalism was not antagonistic to the role of religion in a society. One of the key beliefs of nineteenth-century liberalism, after all, was that government legislation should be avoided if at all possible. To most liberals this precept had particular application to economic affairs. Anglin took it beyond this, for from his point of view liberalism was an appropriate ideology to combat the encroachment of the state in matters of religion, particularly the attempt to restrict the power of the church. This was the lesson that Daniel O'Connell's career had taught, Anglin believed, and Anglin was an admirer of 'The Liberator.'[23]

To bring together liberalism, democracy, and Catholicism in the nineteenth century was no easy task. One must admit that Anglin's response to the challenge was impressive. There was a coherence to his beliefs which, while not always apparent in the disconnected comments he made throughout his career, enabled Anglin to relate his political activities to something close to a reasoned ideology. He was, in short, a liberal with leanings towards democracy and with a firm belief in the efficacy of Christianity to bring harmony and justice to the political and social order.

In the hurly-burly of New Brunswick politics intellectual debate on the merits of various philosophical approaches was infrequent. Anglin himself seldom raised his criticism of the Smashers above the mundane level. He was, to be sure, a thorn in the flesh of the government from the beginning of his parliamentary career. In the Assembly and through reports to the *Freeman* over the signature 'Al'[24] Anglin scrutinized the activities of the administration especially in financial matters. His efforts were acknowledged by political antagonists such as John Boyd, who believed that Anglin assumed the leadership of the opposition forces once in the Assembly. Boyd was quick to proffer advice to Tilley.

But if Anglin returns to St. John without having upset the Govt. or fastened upon you the charges he has so long, and so shamefully made, then he will indeed be weak, and the laughing stock, and scorn of all here. Give him rope as you say but then hang him high up, that the whole Province may see the great big vulgar lantern jawed Paddy in his true native deformity.[25]

In spite of political infighting the 1862 session, Anglin's first in the Assembly, passed rather smoothly. Anglin himself had seldom been in a more auspicious position. His happiness was made more complete on 25 September 1862, when he married nineteen-year-old Ellen McTavish. Anglin, was, to be sure, a desirable widower, a 'good catch,' but he was forty years old at the time of his second marriage. Ellen was the daughter of the substantial dry goods merchant and justice of the peace, Alexander McTavish. The Lord Bishop officiated at the wedding, assisted by two other ministers, and the large cathedral in the city 'was crowded to excess' in spite of the time of the service – 6 AM. Nuptials completed, the newly-weds left for Boston on board the *New England*.[26] What could be more middle-class?

II

At this stage of Anglin's life, with his parliamentary career launched and with the *Freeman* well established, the political and economic life of New Brunswick was becoming increasingly involved in wider relationships. The dominant formative influence was the American Civil War. But that war also had repercussions on connections with the mother country and with the rest of British North America. In the changing circumstances Anglin found it essential to adopt positions on the public questions of the day and to make his views known.

One defining characteristic of British North Americans was their anti-Americanism of a variety of kinds. To most Irish Catholic emigrants, on the other hand, the United States was an earthly utopia and the hope of the world. As one might expect, Anglin's attitude was a mixture of the two views, as befitted an Irish Catholic British North American. Anglin never forgot that the United States had provided a home for thousands of his destitute countrymen and that it represented a great ideal for mankind. On the other hand, he became sufficiently condemnatory of the United States to approach the Canadian norm.[27] He pointed out the gap between American theory and practice, arguing, for example, that Irishmen and Catholic-ity were worse off in the United States than in British North America. He was not loath to denounce American society as irreligious, amoral, and its government as corrupt, extravagant, and inefficient.[28] Nevertheless, Anglin had no desire to see civil war split the union apart; throughout January and February 1861 the *Freeman* voiced the hope that full-scale warfare would not break out.[29]

When war actually began, Anglin placed greatest emphasis on two causal factors: the failure of politicians such as Lincoln to deal with a soluble problem and the fanaticism which existed in both the North and the South.[30] The *Freeman* foresaw a long drawn out war and the end of the union *de facto* if not necessarily *de jure*:

In all probability no human efforts can ever repair the Union, which has been so wantonly shattered. Conquest could not restore the old Union. For even if the

North could conquer the South, then there would be, instead of a union of equal Sovereign States, a conquering and dominant section dictating terms, and a conquered and subject section compelled to yield to such dictation.[31]

As the war proceeded, Anglin could see that rapid and unpleasant changes were taking place across the border:

In 1870 the United States will be a very different country from what it was in 1860. Its people, their institutions, manners, customs, ideas; their memories and aspirations, their ambition, and their means of satisfying it, will all have undergone a mighty change.[32]

Voices of moderation were being drowned by the press, politicians, preachers, and 'the Sovereign mob.'[33] As well, the country was becoming militarized, and under the guidance of corrupt politicians and with the support of the mob such a development threatened to end liberty and replace it with 'the worst of despotisms.'[34]

Yet, while the *Freeman* found much to criticize, it found no cause for rejoicing in the difficulties of the United States. Anglin believed that the destruction of that country would be a tragedy for the entire world.[35] Moreover, in contrast to so many British North Americans, he could see no great constitutional lesson to be learned from the Civil War. The complexity of Anglin's attitude on this and other questions relating to the Civil War was clearly demonstrated in the summer of 1863, on the occasion of a speech made in Saint John by another colonial Irish Catholic leader, Thomas D'Arcy McGee.*

In the course of his lecture McGee termed the great republican experiment in the United States a virtual failure. He asserted that liberty and authority had to be properly weighted in a constitution and that the weakness of the principle of authority in the republican institutions of the United States, was responsible for the defects of American society.[36] Anglin rejected this analysis. Republicanism had not caused the Civil War, said the *Freeman*. No form of government could have prevented the economic struggle nor have overcome the two great evils that monarchical Britain had left behind in 1783: a 'fierce bitter intolerant fanaticism which in England had brought a King to the block' in the North, and in the South 'the slavery of colour as the basis of the social fabric ...'[37] The *Freeman* could

---

* It would appear that until 1863, at least, relations between McGee and Anglin, while not especially intimate, had been harmonious.

not see that the Civil War was worse than the wars that the monarchies of
Europe had been engaged in for centuries:

Is it, in the opinion of any sensible man, worse that a people should be convulsed by
such a question as slavery, or that a majority of the States and people of a Great
Republic should be determined at any cost to maintain the unity of a country which
nature has made one than that a country should be desolated by wars of succession?[38]

McGee had missed the point, Anglin asserted:

Social evils and vicious habits are not the effects of any form of Government, but
are caused by a want of religious training or religious feeling, or by the malign
influence of what seems to be religion while it is but a pander to human pride and
selfrighteousness ...[39]

Anglin was not propagandizing for republicanism in particular, although
in his open-minded approach he was unlike most of his fellow-residents of
British North America.[40] He did not think the American system perfect and
indeed preferred the British cabinet system, although there too he saw
abuses that needed correction.[41] He was simply trying to demonstrate that
the attitude of the people was far more important than constitutional forms.

It is not merely by the existing laws or by any written form of constitution, much
less is it by exceptional circumstances alone that we are to judge the value and
worth of what we – perhaps erroneously – call the institutions of a country. Judged
by such a standard, what a monstrous machine of oppression and injustice would
not the Constitutional Monarch of Great Britain sometimes have seemed. We must
rather seek the spirit that pervades the people and finds expression in their laws and
customs ... In its very pliancy and elasticity, in its capacity to be moulded to any
shape some find the greatest merit of this [British] Constitution; but in fact, and
indeed, it would be as worthless as any other form of Govenment, definite or
indefinite, if the spirit of freedom and order and good government did not pervade
the people as a whole, if they did not know how to reconcile the largest measure of
individual liberty and of personal rights with a profound respect for 'authority' and
'laws.'[42]

In analysing the merits and deficiencies of republicanism Anglin remained faithful to his political philosophy. The form of government, Anglin
argued, was not the basic factor shaping the life of a nation. Even laws

blessed by custom or devised precisely to provide protection for people's liberties could be employed as a means 'of oppression and injustice,' Anglin believed.[43] The keys to the well-being of society as a whole were right ideas, proper attitudes, and true religion. This was hardly a startling discovery in the realm of political thought, but it was a convincing rebuttal to McGee's facile attack on republicanism.

III

The American Civil War tested, even strained, the connections of the British North American colonies with Britain. Even before the Civil War Anglin's attitude towards the mother country had undergone transformation. Colonial Irish Catholics could never muster any affection for England; at most they could only re-examine the meaning of a connection with Britain. They were convinced, of course, that in the case of Ireland the results were uniformly bad. In British North America, however, they discovered not only that the imperial connection was appreciated, if only for the strength it provided in dealing with the United States, but also that it was seldom bothersome or deleterious to colonial interests. As a result colonial Irish Catholics began to adopt a dualistic attitude towards Great Britain. On the one hand, the British connections had some real benefits for British North America and there was little objection to seeing that relationship continued. As one observer watching Halifax Catholics remove their caps while the band played 'God Save the Queen' put it: 'Irishmen can be loyal in Nova Scotia, but not at home.'[44] Anglin was one of those who developed a compartmentalized attitude to Britain; although he never accepted British dominance of Ireland, he did learn that it was neither necessary nor just to criticize the imperial connection from the British North American point of view. In fact, in criticizing the New Brunswick Assembly for quibbling over the amount of money to be spent during the visit of the Prince of Wales in 1860, Anglin confessed that his views towards Britain had changed since his Irish days.

We have never been accused of any excess of what in New Brunswick is called loyalty; we have never professed an intensity of attachment to her Majesty's person, or to her crown and dignity. When the power exercised in her name is oppressive and tyrannical, we never hesitate to denounce it, and there was a time when, in another country, we heartily desired its utter overthrow; but in this Province, where the people now enjoy so full a share of civil and religious liberty, where the Crown is the symbol of liberty and order and justice, founded on law, and there is no longer any wrong, save of the people's own doing, or any tyranny but such as we ourselves create for one another, the head of the Government is surely entitled to more than empty professions, even from those who have been warmest in asserting the people's rights, and when, for the first time in the history of the Continent, the heir apparent visits the trans-atlantic empire of which he is one day to be sovereign, the Province so boastful of its loyalty, the Province which owes so much to the empire, should not show itself to the world a petty huckster, calculating the profits on the little venture; a Barnum considering the propriety of investing a few hundreds in the rarest kind of peep show.[45]

Yes, said Anglin, there was value in the imperial connection. The British North American provinces were not ready for independence; it would be too great a burden for them to carry; 'and such a degree of the responsibilities of independence as is thus forced upon them, will scarely excite the spirit necessary to retain it, and may degenerate into mere licentiousness, for we are not a people ready to make great sacrifices in any cause.'[46]

There was no question of Anglin's sympathies, therefore, when the famous *Trent* incident of 1861 made war between Britain and the northern United States a good bet. If it came to blows, he would not be found supporting the Yankees.

In this case England can not fail to do what the circumstances imperatively demand without incurring not only a loss of dignity and honour, but what is of far more consequence in these degenerate days a loss of prestige and influence which must inevitably lead to other and greater losses, and to an immediate decline in her rank and position as a naval power.[47]

But the *Freeman* was far from desiring war. A lead editorial in tumultuous mid-December, entitled 'Common Sense,' hoped for a way out of the impasse. Anglin could see both the justness of the British case and the difficulties faced by the American government. But he queried whether colonists were anxious to shoulder the responsibilities and horrors of war and gave a caution to his readers:

Let us, by our acts and words, prove that if there must be a war, it will, as far as we are concerned, at all events, be a war for the maintenance of the right and not for the indulgence of senseless hatreds and rabid animosities. While there is a chance of accommodation let us show that we wish an accommodation to be made on such terms, that while it vindicates the honour of England, it shall wound the self respect of our neighbours as little as possible. Under all circumstances let us remember that taunts, and threats, and insults tarnish most deeply the character of those who use them, and that in the most important crisis the most valuable article is 'Common Sense.'[48]

Fortunately war was averted. Anglin was convinced, however, that Americans still laboured under several dangerous delusions. He claimed that they did not seem to grasp the fact that British North Americans had no desire to be incorporated into the American republic:

The people of the United States hold obstinately to the idea that these Provinces enjoy no freedom, and pine for the liberty which annexation to the United States would give. They seem incapable of learning that an immense change has taken place in our condition during a few years; that we now enjoy, to an almost unlimited extent, the right of self government; that our connection with England, except in an hour of danger ... is merely nominal; that we pay not one penny of tribute to the Imperial Government, directly or indirectly; that we are not bound to furnish a single man for her army or navy; that we make our own laws, levy our own taxes and expend the proceeds as we choose, and that although the want of larger markets prevents the development of our manufacturing skill and energy, and we are in consequence often blamed for want of enterprise, when the real want is want of a market, we have no fault to find with England on that score, as she claims no preferences or privileges for her productions, and imposes no restrictions on our trade. To suppose then that the Provinces are as dissatisfied as when a few persons strove to rule them arbitrarily in the name of the Imperial Government, is indeed an erroneous idea, and this the Yankees will discover to their cost should they ever attempt to build up any scheme of conquest upon it.

Another false conception held by many Americans – and some colonists as well – was that the Irish Catholic community in British North America formed an anti-British pocket within the imperial fortress. Anglin's response was eloquent testimony to the falsity of this assumption:

It is also an erroneous idea, that the 'Irish population,' because they detest a bad and odious Government in Ireland, must necessarily be disloyal to a good and beneficent Government in these Provinces because it is called by the same name. The majority of them have friends and relatives in the Union, and they owe to America for all it has done for the Irish exiles a debt of gratitude, which even Know Nothing absurdities and violence could not make them wholly forget. No part of the population is bound by so many ties to the people of the United States, and none would be more reluctant to engage in a quarrel with them; none more determined to take no part in any aggression; but they too know their duty, and they have never yet been found unfaithful to the Government that protected or to the flag that sheltered them. *Semper et ubique fideles*, they will not be found in these Provinces to forfeit their glorious motto nobly earned, and even those who would willingly at an hour's notice peril life and limb in the cause of Irish freedom, will show that the same sense of justice and love of right which in Ireland would make them rebels makes them conservatives in these Provinces. They value the blessings of liberty, sustained and regulated by law, and tho' bearing no ill-will towards the Americans, entertaining no wish to see the great Republic weakened or humbled, they know their duty to the country in which they live and of whose people they are truly an integral part, and knowing it will perform it.[49]

The danger of American attack did not disappear in 1862 along with New Year's resolutions. The question of defence continued to be an important issue in the *Freeman*.[50] Before the Civil War Anglin had accepted the legitimacy of British military withdrawal from North America.[51] Indeed, he continued to believe that for Britain the imperial connection was unprofitable, and that the colonies would have no cause for bitterness, just regret, if the mother country broke the tie. But on the other hand Anglin believed that the colonies were jeopardized by their relationship with Britain. Any war with the United States would not be for the sake of British North America but for the sake of the mother country.[52] Were the colonies independent, they could determine their own policies towards the United States and 'by prudence, moderation, and fair play ... possibly avoid a quarrel for many years to come.'[53] The point was, that since Britain was causing the problem with the United States, she ought to bear the responsibility.

If England chooses to sever the connection it is for us to submit with all patience and do the best we can to protect and take care of ourselves; but while we form part of the Empire England must and will do all she can to protect our soil – not indeed for our sake but for her own.[54]

Still, it was clear that Anglin favoured the retention of the British tie. Equally obvious was the fact that for Anglin the connection was deemed good not for itself but because it was serviceable to New Brunswick.

In his 1863 speech in Saint John McGee had suggested that British North American union would provide increased military security against the United States.[55] Anglin again disagreed. In the first place he correctly assumed that union must be a step towards independence.[56] Total independence would mean that the provinces might escape invasion in the event of an Anglo-American war, but it would also mean that Britain would lend no aid if the provincials quarreled with the United States. In the latter case the fate of the provinces was considered hardly open to debate. But total independence was unlikely, and in this situation the Empire could organize colonial defence far better than could any central colonial government. Thus, for Anglin, there were only two realistic choices: either British North America had to retain strong imperial ties or none at all.

All any of the Provinces could do, they could do far more effectively co-operating with the military and naval power of England, and subordinate to it, than by any attempt at united, independent action ...

If we were independent, perhaps the United States would never assail our independence; but a union of the Provinces would not increase our strength to repel the attacks, did they assail us, and it would not enable us to co-operate more effectually with Great Britain, if we were still to form part of the empire.[57]

IV

A topic which was often discussed in the same breath as defence was that long-considered venture, the Intercolonial Railway. Under the impact of the Civil War imperial authorities became more willing to provide financial backing for a potentially useful military work. In 1862 an agreement acceptable to all parties concerned seemed to have been reached. New Brunswick was to pay three and one-half twelfths of the total cost, and the selection of route was to be left to the imperial authorities.[58] Not only was the railway issue the most important political question in 1863, but also, as it turned out, it proved to be an important precursor of and prelude to the Confederation debates which were to follow.

Anglin's position was that of a sceptical member of the opposition and a representative of Saint John interests. He was unhappy that the choice of route had been left to imperial authorities. It was clear that for military reasons their selection would be the North Shore route for it was farthest away from the Maine border.[59] As far as the *Freeman* was concerned, the Saint John valley route was best for New Brunswick. This route, connecting the European and North American from Shediac to Saint John with the partially developed St Andrews and Quebec Railway, would unify the railway system of New Brunswick and would be the best possible commercial line. With a small extension beyond St Andrews the province would have railway connections with the United States as well as with Canada. True, it would be of little military value in time of actual warfare and even this route might not be a profitable proposition. But, Anglin felt, it would come much closer to paying its way than either the North Shore or the central route. Indeed, because it would use track already in existence, it would be cheaper to build even though it was the longest route. Finally, the interests of Saint John, the commercial centre of the province, would be served. If Saint John were seriously hurt, New Brunswick as a whole would suffer and find its revenues insufficient.[60]

Of the three routes the *Freeman* had made a choice. Yet could New Brunswick afford to build a railroad anywhere? Anglin had doubts which were shared by Lieutenant Governor Arthur Gordon and by A.J. Smith, who resigned from his position as Attorney General on the issue.[61] In the first place, Anglin was sure that New Brunswick could get a better deal. Not only should the route be specified, but also Canada, which Anglin believed stood in much greater need of the Intercolonial, should assume a greater portion of the expense. However desirable railway connections might be, the province had to be able to pay for them. To Anglin's mind the Saint John valley route for the Intercolonial, in combination with the Western Extension of the European and North American Railway, was the least expensive railway policy possible. The initial and most important phase of this policy was Western Extension from Saint John to Saint Stephen. This was to be the commercial road, the one that would be a great trade artery between European and American markets, provided that New Brunswick and Maine filled in the missing links between Shediac and Portland, Maine. If the Saint John valley route for the Intercolonial was not selected, then the Western Extension must come first. Anglin probably expected that this would force the building of the Intercolonial via the Saint John valley route. But, in whatever form, the building of a line from Saint John to the Maine boundary ought to be New Brunswick's top priority in railway development, Anglin argued.[62]

In a six-hour speech 'showing a very remarkable research into forbidding details, and the power and capacity of his memory'[63] Anglin gave the 1863 House of Assembly the benefit of his views on the railway question. In spite of his speech and, more importantly, in spite of the fact that Canadian authorities had not gone along with the railway scheme, New Brunswick passed an Intercolonial Railway Bill in the hope that its initiative would push Canada into action.[64] But the Intercolonial did not proceed and Canada belatedly repudiated the 1862 arrangements.[65]

As the Intercolonial Railway fell on evil days, interest in the Western Extension of the E. & N.A. showed a marked revival by the autumn of 1863. Even government papers began to come out in favour of the enterprise, and early in January 1864 a Western Extension committee was formed.[66] The membership of the committee seemed heavily weighted with supporters of the government. Indeed, many of them apparently had taken up the Western Extension as a second choice and were more interested in promoting the Intercolonial as soon as the opportunity presented itself.[67] The fact that the Western Extension committee was dominated by Smasher sympathizers turned out to be extremely important over the next few years.

As the 1864 session approached, the Tilley government found itself in a dilemma. There was apparently little chance of getting the Intercolonial, yet the Intercolonial Railway Act of the year before was still in force. Pressure from both inside and outside the province was strong. On the other hand, the demand for the Western Extension was irresistible.[68] In the circumstances the legislation put forward by the government was little short of brilliant, at least from a political perspective. It provided that the Intercolonial Railway Act would be binding for another year. If that period expired, the province would pay £20,000 a year for an indefinite number of years to anyone undertaking to build a line to Canada, as long as the government approved of the project. As well, for various lines within the province, the act provided a subsidy of $10,000 a mile. So many were projected that the province would have had almost as many rail lines as a lobster has legs – hence the act was labelled the 'Lobster Bill.'

Anglin was impressed, but not favourably:

This was a great day's work surely. Seriously and solemnly at first, with much earnestness too; afterwards with jeers and laughter and fun and jokes, the House played one farce after another, passing Bills which ... will for years to come be monuments to the folly and recklessness of the majority of the Assembly. One saving clause they did put to all the Bills. It was that unless operations were commenced within two years, and unless the roads were built within five years, the Bill expire.

Anglin was understandably angry. This was not sure and stable progress but reckless extravagance. He charged the government with purchasing support by allowing all bills introduced by those who supported the government measure to pass, 'no matter how they conflicted with public policy or with the general interests.' The only motion he could support was one making provision for a survey for the Western Extension.[69] Anglin wanted the Western Extension, but he suspected that the government had added insult to injury by incorporating a company which was incapable, and perhaps not even in earnest, of building the line.[70] As June came and went, the Western Extension Company floundered. The Common Council of Saint John failed to make a financial contribution and the businessmen of the city did not buy shares.[71]

There was another political matter which by then had sunk from view: the issue of Maritime union. During 1863 and early 1864 the project of a union of the Atlantic colonies had gained some prominence. Anglin had shown disinterest in the topic, as had most Maritimers.* It was a movement lacking in enthusiasm, Lieutenant Governor Gordon being the main force behind it. While the three Maritime legislatures agreed to send delegates to a conference to discuss union, no conference was arranged and none but Gordon seemed to care.[72] It was at this point – when railways and Maritime union were at a standstill – that the Canadians again entered the picture.

* The one time the *Freeman* discussed the topic Anglin merely said that Maritime union seemed to be a good idea and that he supported the general concept (see *Freeman*, 10 May 1862).

5

Anti-Confederation:
From Theory to Practice
1863-5

The Canadian initiative stemmed from the colony's constitutional difficulties. As early as 4 June 1864 the *Freeman* informed its readers of some interesting news:

The Canadian Premier has stated that his Government have applied to the Governments of the Lower Provinces to confer with the Canadian Government on the subject of a Union of the Provinces, the object of the Canadian Government being to put an end to the present state of affairs in Canada, which is almost a deadlock, neither party having strength to govern the country, and anarchy and confusion, financial difficulties and troubles of all kinds being apprehended.

By the end of the month the 'Great Coalition' had been formed, basing its program on British North American union.[1] On the very day the new administration took office, a despatch was transmitted to the Maritime colonies asking if Canada could send delegates to the approaching conference on Maritime union.[2] The Canadian interest forced the unprepared Maritime provinces to make plans for a conference which only Canadians believed was going to take place. Hurriedly it was set for 1 September at Charlottetown. Canada was to be allowed to send delegates but only in an unofficial capacity.[3] As this series of vital events unfolded during the summer and early autumn of 1864, Anglin was thoroughly involved. He was an active participant in some of these events, but on all of them he expressed his views publicly week by week. He emerged as a leading opponent of Confederation. Throughout the winter of 1864–5 he publicized the anti-Confederate cause and contributed in no small way to the anti-Confederate victory in the 1865 elections in New Brunswick.

I

By 1864 Anglin had already clarified many of his views on the subject of British North American union. Since 1858 he had voiced his scepticism about the practicability, necessity, and advantages of such a union, particularly if the imperial tie were to be maintained.[4] He did acknowledge that, if either mother country or colonies were determined to break the connection, 'then this union would become a necessity ...'[5] In the 1863 session of the Assembly he had even agreed 'that the British North American Colonies should be joined in one great nation' and that such a union 'was likely to occur some time ...'[6] But it was not until the summer of 1863, in response to D'Arcy McGee's glorious vision of union presented in his Saint John lecture, that Anglin gave the issue much consideration.

Anglin was a practical man. He dealt with facts not dreams. He had little patience with those for whom 'no flight of fancy is too wild, no exaggeration of facts too gross, no hyperbole too absurd,' when speaking about a union of the provinces. 'If you could believe these men,' Anglin mockingly stated, 'the mere act of union would give us military and naval strength, would bring us a population, would develop our resources, bring mines and minerals to light, secure to us the trade of the Great West, and direct through the magnificent valleys of the St. John, the St. Lawrence, etc., etc., the tide of travel from Europe to Asia.' This was too great a strain on credibility as far as Anglin was concerned. Union would not bring military strength. He simply could not understand 'how the Union of the Provinces and the transfer of our representatives to Ottawa, would confer such wonderful advantages on our farmers, and fishermen, and miners, and shipbuilders, and lumberers.' Anglin believed that a British North American nation was desirable as a future goal but it was obvious to him that the time for union had not arrived. The greatest impediment was the lack of contiguous settlement in British North America. The fact that it held as many people as had the Thirteen Colonies nearly a century earlier was not a fair comparison, for they had not faced an overpowering neighbour in 1783 as did British North America in 1863. Anglin was most sceptical that union would encourage an influx of immigrants and capital, for union would not remove the European impression that the United States was the best place in the new world both to invest and to settle. Having a 'big' name would not help economically.[7] Union would confer no benefits on New Brunswick's farmers or fishermen because free trade with Canada existed in farm and fish products. The lumbermen and shipbuilders of the province would find only that Canada remained their great rival. Would not New Brunswick's already neglected roads, bridges, and harbours fall into an even worse state 'when we had to petition that great Assembly for our own money'? Finally, Anglin had no sympathy with those who desired to create a bigger country in order to enlarge the scope for public men. It was distinction enough 'to be known merely as inhabitants of British America as subjects of the British Empire ...' He demanded no 'new nationality.'[8] Not only were there many challenging tasks for public men to perform but also neither circumstances nor the people demanded British North American union.

These Provinces are now as free as any country can be, as independent as our circumstances and position will permit. Our people are happy and contented, industrious and enterprising, their trade unrestricted and untrammeled, except where their own tariffs create restrictions which they can remove when they please. Let us not, to gratify the cravings of any selfish or wild ambition, sacrifice or emperil [sic] any of those advantages by any act of our own, and retard our progress by assuming the burdens of Court extravagance and standing armies. The time will come, perhaps soon, when a union will be practicable and advisable; when the vast wilderness which now separates us will have disappeared, to make way for farms and villages and towns, stretching in an unbroken line from the Atlantic to the great Lakes, and far beyond them, and from the United States frontier far into the Hudson's Bay country, and we shall all be one people in reality. We do not remain in *status quo* ... We are progressing steadily and constantly. Every new road that is opened, every new clearance that is made, every new house that is built is another step in the steady progress to this great end, and the humblest backwoodsman is doing more to build up this great country than the orator who would substitute fancy for fact, or the politician who believes that statesmanship consists in aiming at the impossible, or in essaying to do by legislation what can only be done by strong hands, directed by wise heads. The true work of the real statesman in these Provinces to-day is not to indulge in wild visions or to weigh down the energies of the people by imposing on them burdens far beyond their power that he may carry out some extravagant scheme, but to labour patiently, prudently, removing, when possible, all difficulties in the way of the merchant and manufacturer, increasing all the facilities for opening up new districts for settlement, and new fields for enterprise, building new bye [sic] roads and great roads and Railroads wherever they are required, as fast as the means of the people will permit, indulging in no chimeras and fancies at the public expense, and not making the gratification of his own vanity, and avarice the chief object of his ambition. He must know much ought to be done at each period, and so much and no more should he attempt.[9]

It was to be expected, therefore, that Anglin's reaction to the Canadian initiative of 1864 was one of annoyance. As far as he was concerned, the Canadians were responsible for their own problems and should not expect the Lower Provinces to solve them. He did not want to be a party to any attempt to crush the French Canadians 'between the upper and the nether mill stone' of Upper Canada and the Lower Provinces. He gave Canadians a sanctimonious word of advice:

Moderation, prudence, a regard in word and deed for the rights and feelings of one another, economy – in a word common sense is all they require to get rid of all their difficulties. But if they will plunge deeper they must not hope to drag us down with them.[10]

Anglin did recognize, however, that another force in favour of union was at work. He saw that the imperial government had seized upon the opportunity provided by the agitation for union to prepare 'the way virtually to get rid of the care of this part of the Empire ...'[11]

Anglin's attitude was plain to see during the visit of a group of Canadians to New Brunswick at the beginning of August. In conjunction with the interest in union a Canadian delegation, led by McGee and made up of politicians, members of the press, and an array of businessmen, had decided to accept the invitation of the Saint John Chamber of Commerce to visit New Brunswick. This invitation had previously been declined, 'but the sudden *replatrage* which unites Cartier and George Brown, and the wish to find favour for the new policy of a Federation make a visit to the Lower Provinces now desirable.'[12] During the visit a dinner was presented in honour of the Canadians. On this occasion, which Anglin attended as a member of the New Brunswick Assembly, the editor of the *Freeman* not only demonstrated his stubborn opposition to Confederation but also made a statement which was later to be misquoted and cause him much grief. The speakers at the banquet had made frequent allusions to union but had been careful not to convert the dinner into a political demonstration. Then John Gray, the former Conservative who had joined the Tilley forces in 1863 on the question of the Intercolonial Railway, stood up to propose a toast and made a strong speech in favour of union. Anglin feared that Gray would actually propose a toast to the union of the provinces. At this point the editor of the *Freeman* turned to the gentleman beside him and stated that if such a toast were put he would protest, and if his protest did not avail he would leave the room. The toast, fortunately for the tranquillity of the dinner, was made to the 'sister provinces' or something equally noncommittal. However, when Anglin was persistently called upon to make a speech, he began by making it clear that not all had come to the dinner to make a demonstration in favour of union. He stated that he and many others had come simply to welcome the Canadians and show them kindness and hospitality. What Anglin then stated was best reported by the *Freeman*:

But as Mr. Gray had chosen to introduce and discuss the question of a Union, he must say that in his opinion the time for a Union had not yet arrived, and he then proceeded to argue briefly that the people of the Provinces are too widely separated; that the physical obstacles still to be overcome are too many; that a Union in our present circumstances would not be strength but weakness, and that even if all these objections were removed, we should proceed with the greatest care and caution lest we make a mistake that may be irremediable. He argued also that the demand for a Union for [the] purpose of defence was absurd, inasmuch as we now are united with and through the Imperial government, which in case of trouble would take controul of all the military power of the Provinces, and would direct it as wisely and efficiently as any Provincial General Government. He went so far and spoke so strongly, that it [was] necessary to add, as nearly as we can recollect, the following words, 'But he did not wish them to suppose from what he had said that he was absolutely opposed to a Union of the Provinces at any time or on any terms. He believed that ultimately the destiny of these Provinces must be either to drift into annexation with the United states –'Here he was interrupted by a storm of yells and hisses from a part of the company. When he succeeded in making himself heard above the uproar, he completed the alternative by adding: –'– or to form one great Union or Confederation of some sort.'
  He then went on further to say that he wondered that men who talked so much of loyalty did not believe that it was honour and glory enough to belong to the British Empire, and that they thought it would be more glorious to belong to a North American nation, etc.[13]

During the stormy campaigns which followed his words were twisted by his opponents to the assertion that he had stated that union or annexation must take place within a few years. The addition of the words 'within a few years' made a great deal of difference. Anglin's prognostication had not been for the immediate future. By adding this short phrase his opponents attempted to make Anglin look like a fool, a liar, or an annexationist when he opposed Confederation. He was none of these, but it was by no means an unsuccessful effort to make Anglin appear inconsistent.

Anglin viewed the approach of the Charlottetown Conference with suspicion. While he had little confidence in the New Brunswick representatives, Anglin agreed with the closed-door policy of the meetings for he recognized that the vastness of the subject which the delegates were to consider was a great enough problem without the speech-making that public deliberations would have encouraged.[14] He also asserted that the conference had no real power and that anything agreed upon would have to be submitted to the people for judgment and to the legislature for assent.[15] Nevertheless, Anglin recognized that a great effort would have to be made to combat the idea of an immediate British North American union and shortly after the Charlottetown Conference adjourned he began a series of articles on the subject of union.

Breaking in a brand new set of type for the occasion,* Anglin discussed some of the topics the conference delegates had spoken of when they were in Saint John. They had frequently talked about loyalty but Anglin was sure that they did not understand either themselves or their subject. On the one hand they talked about loyalty to the British Empire and on the other about forming a great North American nation. The manner in which the delegates talked of forming a great nation led him to suspect that they thought separation from the British Empire was at hand and that they believed this desirable. Should union and quasi-independence come about, Anglin stated, 'we may by a perversion of terms still call ourselves British subjects, but we would be only allies, bound ... by terms most disadvantageous to us.' Union would be playing right into the hands of those politicians in Britain who desired to get rid of military commitments in North America, for they could then claim, erroneously, that the colonies were capable of defending themselves.[16] This, of course, had long been Anglin's argument on the question of defence and the imperial connection, but he thought it wise to clarify for his readers the misleading nature of the Confederates' loyalty argument. Anglin simply could not equate the disintegration of the Empire with loyalty to it even if a faction in Britain wished to see the imperial connection weakened.

Anglin also dealt with the economic side of union. Existing trade between Canada and New Brunswick was negligible. This fact would remain

---

* Anglin stated that nearly four million copies of the *Freeman* had been printed with the old metal (see *Freeman*, 17 Sept. 1864). This would mean that on the average approximately 1800 copies of each issue had been printed.

true after union even with an Intercolonial Railway, Anglin asserted, unless 'the exploded Protectionist Principles' were instituted to force unnatural trade. But a protective tariff would simply increase the cost to the consumer. Moreover, with or without protection, Maritime manufacturers would receive no great benefits from union, despite what other politicians claimed.* Canada had water power even more abundantly than the Maritimes and labour just as inexpensive. Nearly all manufacturers in New Brunswick had to import raw materials in whole or in part. Obviously the law of comparitive advantage would determine which manufacturing concerns would survive and grow.

Some manufacturers better adapted to our position and circumstances may grow to immense proportions, such as they can never reach while their only market is our own Province; but many others would be immediately extinguished in the competition with the manufactures of Canada, which have the advantages of being long established, of having larger capital, and a larger home market – for a market within a radius of three or four hundred miles, is after all a home market, as compared with a market seven hundred or a thousand miles away.[17]

The unsettling and probably deleterious effects of union upon the manufacturers of Saint John would be compounded by the neglect of the Western Extension and the building of the Intercolonial by the North Shore route whereby Halifax would profit and Saint John would stagnate.[18] The railway issue was merely one extremely important example of what would happen were union to take place. Then the general good of British North America would have to take precedence over the interests of Saint John.[19] For a political representative of Saint John this was no minor matter. Anglin was proud of his adopted city and constituency and did not want to see its light dimmed by union.

In opposing union Anglin was compelled to defend himself from the charge of the government press that his criticism resulted from his being almost congenitally 'unwilling to be found rowing in the same boat with the Government.'[20] There was probably some validity to the accusation, but on the other hand Anglin was more consistent in his attitude to union than many government organs. Anglin, for instance, had always been suspicious of Canada, especially of the Clear Grits of Upper Canada, whereas

* Tilley once stated that Maritimers were 'a manufacturing people to a large extent, and ... would, to the whole of British America, occupy the same position that Massachusetts does to the United States' (see E. Whalen, *The Union of the British Provinces* [Charlottetown, 1865], p 40).

the government papers had waxed hot or cold depending upon the state of the Intercolonial Railway.[21] The *Freeman* was convinced that Upper Canada supported the idea of union because it wished to control British North America.[22] Moreover, Anglin considered Canadians extravagant, not only in their plans for economic development but also in their parliamentary organization. Salaries paid elected members were far higher than those paid in New Brunswick and the ministers had a number of unnecessary assistants. As far as the Irish editor was concerned:

The assimilation of our system of this [the Canadian system] may answer office-seekers, but we doubt much if it would be for the interest of the people, who would have to pay all these salaries, contingent expenses, etc., etc.[23]

On 29 October 1864, while the delegates to the Quebec Conference visited Montreal after the completion of their labours, Anglin stated what his immediate objectives would be. It had been announced that the Quebec scheme would not be submitted to the people for judgment; it would simply be passed or rejected by the provincial legislatures.[24] Anglin strongly disagreed with this. When he learned that the scheme itself would not even be made public until it was introduced in the legislatures, his anger exploded.

This is clearly a conspiracy to defraud and cheat the people out of the right to determine for themselves whether this Union shall now take place.[25]

Anglin demanded that the Quebec Resolutions should be made known immediately in order to give time for consideration and reflection. After this the legislature should be dissolved and an election held on the question of union.*
    Thus, before the exact terms of the proposed union were made known, Anglin had set the lines of his attack and defence. His was a basically anti-union position. The details of the Quebec Resolutions were important but they would have had to be impossibly favourable to New Brunswick to make any difference to Anglin. Union, as far as he was concerned, was a

---

* *Freeman*, 29 Oct. 1864. It is quite true that not everyone in 1864 thought it necessary to submit the scheme to public vote. To many this would have seemed to be following a democratic and republican course of action incompatible with contemporary British practice. One should not assume, however, that this attitude was the only legitimate one, to the exclusion of the concepts presented by Anglin and many others. Both views were valid in the British North America of 1864.

dream of the future not the plan of the present. His views, especially those on the Empire and defence, might be termed narrow-minded and selfish. But then, whose thoughts and actions at the time of Confederation could not be so defined? Anglin's position at least had the merit of familiarity. The existing organization had worked satisfactorily for Saint John and New Brunswick; the new one might not.

II

As the details of the Quebec Resolutions leaked to the press by way of the public speeches of the delegates to the conference and sundry other methods, Anglin and his allies, particularly A.J. Smith, prepared to give Tilley and the other delegates a warm reception. It was known, for instance, that New Brunswick was to elect only fifteen members to an Assembly of 207.[26] Anglin did not doubt that fifteen men 'of whom some would always be mere office-seekers, could do little to ensure the welfare of this Province – to get – for instance – St. John made a terminus of the Intercolonial Railway, or to secure the construction of the Railroad to the United States ...'[27] Nor was Anglin enamoured with the unofficial but relatively accurate reports of the projected constitutional arrangements:

It is absurd to speak of such a Union as is thus described as a Confederation. It is in truth a Legislative Union, and the local Legislatures will be useless, cumbrous, expensive machinery, which no one will desire to see retained ... If this Union must be, it would be better to abolish the local Legislatures at once in appearance as well as in reality than to set up such expensive shams.[28]

Thus when the New Brunswick delegates landed in Saint John they found opposition to union rearing its head in many places. Within two weeks Tilley was forced to conclude that 'the feeling in New Brunswick is at present decidedly adverse ...'[29]

On 15 November the *Freeman* was able to achieve the first of its three-point program when it published the Quebec Resolutions. Anglin's accompanying comments were not gentle. He stated that by the acceptance of such a scheme 'we will by our own act surrender up to the Imperial Parliament all the rights and privileges we now enjoy, hereafter to hold and enjoy all rights of self-government, not as inherent in ourselves, but as gifts from the Imperial Parliament, and by virtue of Imperial Statute.' This was, Anglin maintained, 'unadulterated Toryism such as was known in Canada before the rebellion.' He did not object to the principle of representation by population in theory, but in practice, when he saw how it would ensure the dominance of Upper Canada, he thought it malicious. Representation by population, he asserted, was not equitable when distinct communities with distinct interests existed. Anglin believed that such communities made up British North America.

We are not one people with Canada, and no laws of Imperial or local Legislatures can in an instant make us one. Between our principal centres of population and the nearest of the large towns of Canada, hundreds of miles of wilderness, scarcely dotted with a few settlements, intervene. The channels of their trade do not pass through our territory, not ours through theirs. We are, and for many years we must remain, distinct communities, with many interests either conflicting or not common. With Nova Scotia, great part of which is within sight of this City, with which we now do a large trade, a real union may be possible. A union with Canada can not in our day be such an amalgamation that we will cease to consider ourselves or to be different communities; that we will take the same view of all the measures of the General Parliament as the people of Canada West will take; that we will have no special interests to protect or care for.

Anglin obviously subscribed to the view that you cannot manufacture nationalism; it must grow of its own accord. Anglin's advice to his readers was not only to consider carefully the Quebec Resolutions, but also to ask first of all if union of any kind would bring them any great positive good, otherwise unobtainable. It was apparent to Anglin that under union increased taxation would be inevitable. Unless this was compensated by some great good, it was not worth the risk of finding that union was harmful to New Brunswick's interests when it was unable to do anything about it.[30] Obviously Anglin's Irish past, in particular a fear of union with a larger entity which might exercise something akin to imperial dominance, still haunted him. He exhorted the people, through the use of the power of public opinion, 'to compel the Government to submit the question of Union directly and immediately to the people themselves.'[31]

Confederate efforts to promote union on the basis of the Quebec Resolutions were weak. Tilley made unconvincing assertions of the benefits Confederation would bring, and John Gray, another delegate from Saint John, resorted to name-calling as he accused Anglin of inconsistency on the basis of his statement at the dinner for the Canadian visitors in August 1864. Anglin stood up and answered Gray's charges at the meeting at which they were made.[32] As for Tilley's financial statements, the *Freeman* found them unsatisfactory and bluntly said so. To this Tilley reacted strongly. He wrote a letter to the editor of the *Daily Evening Globe* challenging Anglin to speak for half an hour at the Tilley-Gray meeting to be held on 22 November.[33] He did not, however, have the courtesy to transmit a copy of this letter to Anglin, let alone send him a personal invitation.[34] Anglin, in a long open letter to the people of Saint John, stated why such a challenge was to be refused. In brief, he did not think the terms fair and was afraid of trickery. Furthermore he did not want to make the discussion a personal quarrel between Tilley and himself, for this would influence Tilley's friends, who now doubted the wisdom of the union policy, to 'return to the fold.' Anglin did, however, make a counter-offer. He stated that Tilley could, if he wished, write articles to the *Freeman*, and they could be as long as he desired. All would be published. In making this offer Anglin managed to escape from the trap that Tilley had set. Tilley, however, was not a writer. Nor was he about to assist Anglin in the sale of his newspaper. At the second Tilley-Gray meeting in Saint John he stated that anything he chose to publish would be given to the papers that advocated Confederation. The *Colonial Presbyterian* best summed up this squabble:

The challenge to discuss on the platform with a member of the Government, a great constitutional question, which had never been submitted to the Legislature of New Brunswick, was one of doubtful propriety. It might result in a spectacle that would minister to vulgar curiosity or partizan gratification, but it could hardly advance the public interest. Then Mr. Anglin is not popular; this is no doubt, partly his own fault, but it arises also from the intolerance of the devotees who worship at the shrine of the greater political deities. The former are not content to hear and refute Mr. Anglin or the *Freeman* ... but they use denunciation and physical force. This spirit was manifested in a striking manner at the dinner given to the Canadian delegates, when Mr. Anglin, who spoke at a point near where we sat, was interrupted by hisses in the utterance of an unobjectionable sentiment ... Mr. Anglin, therefore, would have had no chance of a fair hearing on the proposed debate. But then again even if he had, he could not, in readiness and aptness of financial illustration and argument, cope for a single moment with Mr. Tilley. The editor of the *Freeman* can write a strong editorial, but Mr. Tilley shines in the area of debate.[35]

Perhaps Anglin could not have stood up to the financial arguments of Tilley in a public debate but he gave blow for blow in the columns of the

Freeman. In very long, amazingly detailed, and cogent articles Anglin poured scorn on the arguments and figures of Tilley. He cautioned his readers:

We want this to be thoroughly impressed on the minds of our readers. We want them to think of what we have said and to be satisfied that we are right; that in retaining or withdrawing our territorial revenues and export duty, we are little favoured, the other Provinces on their part doing the same; that in getting 80 cents a head, even if it were out of the $3 we now pay, we do not get a fair share; that the $63,000 a year is mere delusion, and that if this scheme be accomplished 'Western Extension' will be postponed for at least another generation.[36]

It was not long before these articles had won the attention of the editor of the *Colonial Presbyterian*, the very man who had assumed that Tilley was the master of financial questions, and he urged the *News*, the chief government organ in Saint John, to deal with the 'weighty facts and figures advanced by the *Freeman* ...'[37] The main reason for the differences in the interpretation on financial matters between Anglin and the Confederates was that they disagreed as to whether 1863 and 1864 were good, bad, or typical years. The Confederates felt that the economy of New Brunswick and its revenues would continue to rise whereas Anglin was much more cautious. He thought that these years were ones of extreme prosperity that might not continue. He based his calculations on more typical years in the New Brunswick economy, such as those before the Civil War or 1862, when the initial depression of the Civil War had passed in New Brunswick but before the American wartime demand had created an artificial boom in New Brunswick. This difference in starting point had a great influence on how Anglin and the Confederates felt the Quebec scheme would work. Anglin believed that New Brunswick was foolish to enter into financial agreements which assumed that the elevated status of the provincial economy would continue. Then too Anglin felt that the Confederates had estimated too low the cost of such things as the Intercolonial Railway and defence expenditure.[38] He took delight in showing the discrepancies between the estimates of Tilley and other Confederates such as A.T. Galt and A.G. Archibald.[39] In short, the *Freeman* was far from out of its depth on financial matters. Even an arch-enemy of Anglin, Judge Lemuel A. Wilmot, tacitly recognized the *Freeman*'s effectiveness. He advised Tilley not to put too much emphasis on 'the financial adjustment' and to concentrate more on the '*great future*' aspects of Confederation.[40] By 31 December

1864 the *Freeman* could claim, with some show of reason, that 'Mr. Tilley has most signally failed.'

III

Anglin could not have known, as the new year dawned, that it was to be the most eventful year of his entire life. But he must have realized that it would be a busy one, for an election was in the offing. Tilley had found that it was unlikely that Confederation could be carried in the existing Assembly.[41] Public pressure had forced him first to promise 'that if there were any question as to the opinion of the people on the subject [of union], then they would refer it to the people themselves to settle at the polls,'[42] and then grudgingly to agree that the issue 'would not be pressed upon the attention of the House, until after the General Election next year ...'[43] Still it was not certain whether the 1865 session would precede or follow dissolution of the House. Not until 19 January did the Executive Council decide that a prompt dissolution should take place.[44] Anglin made it clear what the issue of the election should be:

Confederation or no Confederation, that should be the one and only question now raised, as it is the one question which will be settled at this election. Personal feelings, private regards, even party considerations should at this great crisis be set aside or postponed.[45]

The prospects for the anti-Confederates appeared good. In A.J. Smith, G.L. Hatheway, J.C. Allen, R.D. Wilmot, Anglin, and others, the 'Antis' found leadership and strength despite the fact that some opposed the Quebec Resolutions for opposite reasons than others. In fact this division meant that Tilley was trapped in a pincer. If he said that under the Quebec Resolutions the central government would have virtually all the power, he alienated those, like Smith and Anglin, who wished New Brunswick to remain largely independent of Canada. If he proclaimed that the province would retain almost all its powers, Allen and Wilmot would see in this a reason for opposing Confederation.[46] Still, Tilley had one hope to cling to, as John Boyd noted:

May you succeed, and I am convinced you will in the end, were it for no other reason, than this. Anglin is opposed to you – he never succeeds in opposing you.[47]

The election campaign of 1865 ranged far and wide and Anglin and his allies attacked the Confederates on a number of grounds. In the very important sphere of economics Anglin waged a hard fight. The general economic climate in New Brunswick was not good. The first four months of 1865 showed a drop of nearly 25 per cent on the revenue collected at Saint John.[48] Returns from the European and North American Railway had slumped.[49] By 13 April 1865 it was announced that only half as many ships were being built in Saint John as had been under construction at the same time in 1864.[50] With both the Civil War, which had given a large carrying trade to New Brunswick, and the Reciprocity Treaty rapidly coming to an end there were dark clouds on the economic horizon. The Confederates claimed that they could blow them away. The Antis claimed that they could do better, even though Anglin felt that the expectations of the people were unreasonably high.

On particular economic issues Anglin and Smith asked questions. Why had intercolonial free trade not been obtained before if the benefits were to be so great? They pointed out that Tilley had used the infant industry argument two years before and that he had prevented New Brunswick from achieving free trade with Canada in 1862.[51] Their implication was that intercolonial free trade could be attained without union. In this belief, of course, Anglin was overly sanguine. What about reciprocity – did its impending abrogation mean that New Brunswick was forced to look to British North American union as the Confederates were arguing? Gray had even gone so far as to state that 'the abrogation of the Reciprocity Treaty would be the greatest boon to this Province; the greatest blessing that could be conferred on us; the greatest source of wealth we could have were we Confederated.' Anglin could not credit such a statement: 'Can any one imagine a man in his sound senses making such a declaration at this time of day?'[52] Anglin went so far in the opposite direction as to imply that the union proposals might be the cause of the abrogation of reciprocity. He thought that the United States now looked upon the Quebec Resolutions as an attempt on the part of British North America to take advantage of the Reciprocity Treaty and that consequently the United States had resolved to remove this threat.[53]

As one might expect, railways constituted the most important economic issue. For the Confederates the Western Extension had emerged as a real problem in November and December 1864. Tilley saw that 'a majority of the People of St. John are very anxious to have that line constructed ...' As well, a large number, especially in the eastern part of New Brunswick, desired immediate connection by rail with Nova Scotia. Tilley recognized his difficulty. He knew that demands would be made in the Assembly, should one meet before the election, that additional government aid be provided for these lines, or even that they be undertaken as government works. Unfortunately for Tilley, 'neither of these steps can be taken under our arrangement at Quebec as our debt would be immense beyond what we are permitted to incur ...'[54] John A. Macdonald had urged Tilley not do do anything in relation to railways and, while this may have been advisable from the Canadian viewpoint, it was a heavy burden for the Confederates of New Brunswick to carry.[55] Tilley attempted to put some life into the Western Extension Company, but Anglin was highly sceptical of the effort.[56] Perhaps he was justified in being doubtful, for Tilley knew not only that no more governmental aid could be given the Western Extension, but also that he had to combat a development he thought harmful to the prospects of the Confederates.

I see a combination forming between the friends of Western extension, and the Anti-federation men. The former with the [expectation?] of forcing terms, the latter with the hope of defeating the Union Measure. This is a powerful combination that must be broken up in some manner.[57]

The difficulties presented by Western Extension were one reason Tilley later gave for calling an election prior to meeting the legislature:

The friends of Western Extension (who are mostly the enemies of Confederation) asserted that with the facilities thus provided no roads would be built, and were demanding that they should be undertaken as Government Works – seeing that this could not be done under Federation they would not only oppose that measure but would have embarrassed the Govt. by submitting a proposition, calling upon them to assume these Railways as Govt. Works, knowing that the members of the Government must oppose it, and in doing so, Watters & myself would lose the Confidence of our Constituents.*

Tilley knew that Anglin and other Antis would make use of the issue by

* Macdonald Papers, LI, Tilley to Galt, undated. Tilley was oversimplifying matters when he equated the 'friends of Western Extension' with 'the enemies of Confederation.' The incorporated company for Western Extension included such Tilley supporters as William Wright, John Boyd, William and Thomas Parks, and many others (see *New Brunswick Government Gazette*, XXII, 11 May 1864). There is also an interesting inference to be drawn from Tilley's statement – i.e., that Tilley, as a Confederate, was not a friend of Western Extension. This, of course, is what Anglin had asserted.

showing that the line could not be built under the 'Lobster Bill,' given the terms of the Quebec scheme. It was desirable, therefore, for the government to call an election before it was made clear in the legislature that the Confederates would do no more for Western Extension.

Anglin pursued the issue vigorously in any case. Confident that the railway would not be built under the terms of the 'Lobster Bill,' he was convinced by January 1865 that it should be undertaken as a government project.[58] Of course, it would have to be ascertained that the province could bear the additional expenditure without bankrupting itself, but Anglin felt that there was probably no worry on this score as revenues had greatly increased in 1864 and he thought the provincial coffers would be full.[59] In this assumption Anglin was not taking sufficient cognizance of the downswing in the New Brunswick economy in the early months of 1865 which resulted in a diminution of government revenues. In any case Anglin was so sure of his stand that on nomination day in Saint John he apparently stated 'that Western Extension could never be built under the present scheme, and that it must be built as a government work; and that ... he would go for Western Extension forthwith, and oppose any Government that was not willing to adopt it as a government work, and if the Government to be formed did not do it, or attempted to trifle with it, he would endeavour to turn them out.'[60] Thus Anglin became the most prominent advocate of building Western Extension as a government work. Compared to such a policy the Smashers offered little. The government-inspired agitation for Western Extension in late 1864 was a failure. There is little doubt that those who wished to see Western Extention built, and who were wedded neither to the Smashers nor to private enterprise, would have leaned towards Anglin and his allies in 1865.[61]

Nor did the Intercolonial Railway greatly benefit the Confederates. Tilley could not state which route the Intercolonial would follow and naturally this made residents of the Saint John valley apprehensive, as evidenced by G.L. Hatheway's weak couplet:

> Mr. Tilley will you stop your puffing and blowing
> And tell us which way the railway is going.[62]

The New Brunswick Confederates' problems were compounded when it was reported that Macdonald had asserted that the guarantee of the Intercolonial would not be part of the constitution.[63] It had also been rumoured that there would be no imperial legislation on the Intercolonial. Tilley fired off a note to Macdonald bluntly proclaiming that no delegate from New Brunswick would consent to union unless the railway was guaranteed by imperial legislation. He demanded that Macdonald send a telegram to rectify the problem he had inadvertently created.[64] Macdonald did so, but the damage had been done.

The economic confrontation was a highly important aspect of the 1865 election campaign, but significant skirmishes flared up elsewhere on the battlefield and Anglin ran hither and yon, bolstering and giving leadership to the Anti forces. When Tilley stated that amendments would be made to the Quebec Resolutions if they were not satisfactory, Anglin quoted Macdonald as stating that the resolutions must be accepted in their entirety as they were in the nature of a treaty.[65] Furthermore, the Civil War served as an example to Anglin. He did not agree with the right of southern secession but many New Brunswickers did. As a consequence, the Irish Anti asked the rhetorical question: 'Is there any clause in the Confederation Scheme now before the people giving the right to any of the Lower Provinces to do likewise at any future period?'[66] Macdonald would have shuddered at the thought. Tilley's assertion that he wanted the greatest possible time for the discussion of the union question met with Anglin's ridicule. After all, Anglin stated, it was Tilley who had withheld the Quebec scheme from the people and who had agreed to the plan to introduce the resolutions to the legislature without going to the people. It was Tilley who had chosen the time of the elections. These and many more specific attacks on the Confederates and their scheme added up to a striking condemnation of Confederation that was not without effect. In fact, by the middle of January Tilley received a note from a correspondent who remarked 'that all great measures of improvement, are carried out more by means of side issues, or an undertow, or prejudice, than upon the intrinsic merits of such ...'[67]

Above all, perhaps, the question of defence and the imperial connection was most significant. Anglin had nothing new to say on this topic; he simply restated his position. He still did not believe that the imperial connection was a mere alliance or that England would 'do nothing unless we consented to do what these Delegates have chosen to agree we ought to do.'[68] He again showed the ridiculous situation the new nation would be in should a state of quasi-independence be achieved. It would have no say in the making of war or peace and yet could not be neutral in a war between the United States and Great Britain. He re-affirmed his view that Confederation was a step towards entire separation from the Empire.[69] Anglin wanted to maintain the imperial connection. He had no interest in the plan of the *Carleton Sentinel* for union with the New England States – this was an indulgence in 'fancies.'[70]

Issues were not, of course, the only factors involved in the election. Anglin was the leader of the Irish Catholics and obviously relied upon their political support. But throughout the campaign he suggested that neither Catholics nor Protestants should vote for or against Confederation on religious grounds. Politics should be determined not by religious denomination but by intelligence and conscience.* Undoubtedly, however, many Irish Catholics shared Anglin's Irish-bred fear of a union with a large power. Probably they agreed with his distrust of George Brown and the Clear Grits. The most important factor, however, was that the *Freeman* was the only well-known Catholic newspaper in New Brunswick with wide circulation among the Catholic population. But anyone, Catholic or not, who had read the *Freeman* since the summer of 1863 would have been impressed with its arguments against union.

Anglin's influence among New Brunswick Catholics was challenged by the Confederates. One counter-influence was provided by Charles Watters, a Catholic, a member of the Smasher government, and Tilley's running-mate in Saint John. But Watters was not the source of government strength he might have been. He was slow to support Confederation and provided weak competition for Anglin in the Catholic community.[71] Tilley himself had tried to undermine Anglin by attempting to win Bishop Sweeny over to Confederation. He came away from his meeting with the bishop thinking that he had been successful and that at least Sweeny would not actively oppose Confederation.[72] From Canada came another challenge to Anglin in the form of three packages of pamphlets from D'Arcy McGee in aid of the Confederate cause.[73] But the greatest threat to Anglin's dominance came from the highest Catholic ecclesiastical authority in the Maritime provinces, Dr Thomas L. Connolly, who had left Saint John in 1859 to become the Archbishop of Halifax.[74] At the beginning of January 1865 Connolly had written to the editor of the Halifax *Morning Chronicle* in favour of British North American union.[75] As far as the archbishop was concerned, the choice before the people of British North America was annexation to the United States or the maintenance of the British tie. Because, as he claimed, Catholics were much worse off in the United States, he urged support of Confederation. The Confederates rejoiced in the archbishop's letter:

---

* Anglin once told a reader who urged Catholics to unite to get better treatment from the government that place-hunting was demoralizing and that Catholics 'should feel a pride in being able to say that, however others have bartered and sold their influence at elections, they at all events have been actuated rather by a regard for the general interests than by any desire to exalt themselves individually or collectively, or to degrade any others' (see *Freeman*, 9 Jan. 1864). Anglin also recognized that any union among Catholics would bring about counter-combinations (ibid).

I have not seen anything for a long time pleases me so much as Dr. Connolly's letter, it is so opportune, and falls with such crushing weight on Anglin, who tries even to be witty at the Arch Bishop's expense.[76]

Anglin thought Connolly's propositions ridiculous. To him the choice was either to accept Confederation and the inevitable breaking of imperial ties or to remain as they were. He had no respect for the archbishop's views and termed them 'empty and feeble.'[77] He claimed that what the archbishop thought was of no consequence, because 'in politics Bishops and Priests and Protestant Clergymen are as other men' – adding that New Brunswick priests and Bishop Sweeny opposed Confederation.[78] While Connolly, McGee, Watters, and Tilley may have had some impact on New Brunswick Catholics, it is clear that even their combined weight could not knock Anglin off his pedestal. The *Freeman* was what Irish Catholics and many others were listening to.

The consequence of Anglin's work – which included adding scores of illegal voters to the electoral lists back in September 1864, if the *News* could be believed[79] – along with the efforts of other anti-Confederates was seen in the election results. The Confederate defeat was overwhelming. Of the forty-one members of the Assembly, no more than twelve representatives returned were deemed to be in favour of Confederation.[80] Every man in the Assembly who had represented New Brunswick at the Quebec Conference had been unseated. To be sure, the margin of the Anti victory in many constituencies was small, as was the case in most nineteenth-century elections because of the small number of eligible voters. Tilley, for example, lost by 113 votes in the city of Saint John and Babbitt lost by only 36 votes in Queen's. It is true, therefore, that only a small number of votes would have changed results in a number of cases. But to consider the election close would be to accept contemporary Confederate propaganda, for the Antis received something close to 60 per cent of the total vote cast. The election was, in fact, a smashing Confederate defeat.[81] The Lieutenant Governor was shocked: 'I was aware that the public sentiment of the Province was opposed to Confederation; but I was by no means prepared for such a result ...'[82]

IV

What had caused such a startling result? In a general sense the *Freeman* was quite correct in thinking that the election had simply been a great rejection of Confederation. To be sure the Confederates complained of the views and actions of Lieutenant Governor Gordon and of back-country ignorance about the Confederation scheme, but these complaints were of minor significance and were, in fact, effectively countered.[83] As well, even John Gray poured cold water on the rumour that Yankee gold had bought the electoral verdict.[84] There was one thing, however, on which the Confederates agreed and which they believed had played a large role in determining the final results of the election. They were convinced that New Brunswick Catholics had voted as a bloc against Confederation. Tilley attributed defeat in Saint John to the Catholic vote along with the Western Extension issue. In other counties, he felt, the united vote of the Catholics was the main reason for anti-Confederate victories. Had the Catholic vote been divided, he argued, the Confederates would have carried nearly every seat.[85] John Gray was also of the opinion that the Catholic electors of Saint John, led by their bishop and clergy, had gone against the scheme 'almost to a man.'[86] The emotion-charged issue of clerical influence and the Catholic vote was not only of great significance to Anglin, but also played an important role in directing the Confederates' future tactics in their continuing quest for union.

John Gray was particularly outspoken on the subject. He confided to George Brown his belief that the Catholic vote was all part of a plan:

They voted like a flock of sheep. Out of a thousand votes in this City & County upwards of 950 ... [were] Against Confed[n]. It would be absurd to suppose – that this was because they understood the question – There are no 950 men in creation whose minds would necessarily arrive at one conclusion on a secular question – because they were of the same creed – but for years past the Bishops and Priests of the R.C. Church in this Province have been struggling to make their denomination an *Element* in the Governing Power – not fragmentary as every individual in a state constitutes a part of the Governing power – but distinct – combined – a power. An element which can dictate – Thus in this Case throughout the whole Province In each County – the Catholic body as a body have voted in one way – and have thus effected their great object – that of establishing not only their power – but the *belief* of its Existence – This I consider to have been *their great object* – and having attained that object – they are just as likely on another occasion to be in favor of Confederation as against it.

Hitherto in this Province their Bishops and leading men have considered that they did not hold either socially or politically the influence and position they ought to hold – That attained – first – the interest of the Province will be next – No one can or ought to object – to any man holding place position or power on account of his

Religion. And a Roman Catholic possessing intelligence and a stake in the Country is entitled to as much Consideration as a man of any other creed – but it becomes a terrific power for evil or good – if masses without education and intelligence can be moved one way or the other as they might be directed by an [assertion?] of spiritual authority –[87]

Shortly after the election results began to trickle in, the Confederates began to complain of clerical influence, telling tales of various atrocities, such as a Catholic clergyman refusing to give the sacraments to those who desired Confederation. They accused the Bishop of Saint John of supporting, even from the pulpit, the editor of the *Freeman*. There was also the suggestion that the gentleman ' ... ,' who had written to the *Freeman* frequently during the election campaign, was a clergyman, perhaps even Dr Sweeny himself. Anglin did not have a great deal to say about ' ... ,' but even if he had been a clergyman, his letters seem to have been quite anonymous. Anglin pointed out, on the other hands, that thousands of Dr Connolly's letters had been printed and distributed as well as the regular issues of those religious papers, the *Presbyterian* and the *Religious Intelligencer*. This clerical influence was all right as far as the Confederates were concerned, Anglin complained, but even a small amount used on the other side was, to them, intolerable.[88] He flatly denied that any priest threatened to refuse 'religious ordinances':

No priest dare make such a threat, and if any were mad enough to make it, no Catholic would regard it, as every Catholic knows that the priest is as much bound by the laws of his Church as is the layman, and that punishment would surely follow so great an abuse of his position.

In answer to the charge that he had been supported from the pulpit, Anglin had a marvellous reply:

We do know that we attended Mass at the Cathedral every Sunday for months past, and the only allusion we ever heard to the elections was a short sermon on the subject of bribery, in which the Congregation were told that the man who sold his vote at an election committed a grievous offence against Society and against God; but in which not one word was said to show what were the preacher's views on the question at issue. It the Editor of the *Presbyterian* thinks that such a sermon was calculated to sustain Mr. Anglin, then we must admit that we are proud of being so sustained.[89]

The position of the Catholic hierarchy in New Brunswick on the Confederation question is of considerable interest. Archbishop Connolly, of course, was an outspoken proponent of Confederation. Bishop Rogers of Chatham also favoured the scheme but did not consider it 'judicious' to give public support.[90] Bishop Sweeny's sympathies, it would appear, were with the Antis. Nevertheless, there is no evidence to support the rumour, which Tilley had reported, that the bishop had sent letters to the priests calling on them to oppose Confederation.[91] While the possibility exists, just as it is possible that Bishop Rogers wrote to the priests in the lower part of Gloucester on behalf of Confederation as Peter Mitchell had requested,[92] it seems safe to claim that any clerical influence on the Catholic vote in 1865 resulted from the convictions of individual priests rather than the concerted efforts of the hierarchy. Neither of the two New Brunswick bishops gave public support either for or against Confederation. That they should have been accused of clerical interference when they did a remarkably good job of keeping their opinions to themselves seems very odd. What was certainly not involved was a conspiracy among the Catholic hierarchy to build a solid Catholic bloc vote, as Gray had suggested. This would have been impossible given the hierarchy's divergent views.[93]

Indeed, an analysis of the election results in Saint John county, where there was an especially large Irish Catholic population, suggests that Catholics were more divided in their vote than the Confederates believed. If the assertions of Tilley and Gray had been correct, it would be logical to expect that the percentage of anti-Confederate votes should be correlated to the percentage of Catholics in a particular electoral subdivision: in other words, the larger the number of Catholics, the larger the number of anti-Confederate votes, on a percentage basis. This does not, in fact, prove to have been to case. Compare, for example, the electoral subdivisions of Duke's and King's. In Duke's the Catholic population made up 28.1 per cent of the total, and in King's Catholics formed 65.9 per cent of the total population. Yet in both electoral subdivisions the Anti vote was 51.4 per cent of the total. Thus the statistics would seem to prove that the Catholics did not vote as a bloc in the 1865 election, although it may be possible to explain away the statistics. Given the fact that voting was by ballot, and that the statistics did not prove their case, the assertions of Tilley and Gray were irresponsible. In defence of Tilley and Gray, on the other hand, it is certainly true that the Catholic vote did not hurt the Antis. In every electoral subdivision in Saint John county in which Catholics formed more than one-third of the population a majority of votes were cast for the Antis. But this is about as far as one can go.[94]

Throughout the province at large a survey of the statistics indicates that, while Catholic voters may have had a tendency to vote for the Antis, it was not a bloc vote, with the exception of Acadian Catholics who do appear to have voted overwhelmingly in favour of the Antis in several localities.[95] The conclusions one must draw on the issue of the Catholic vote are, therefore, twofold. First, there was no attempt on the part of the hierarchy to mould a bloc Catholic vote. Second, the whole idea of a monolithic response by New Brunswick Roman Catholics to Confederation is highly questionable.

Anglin and the Antis had won the battle of the 1865 elections. But the Confederation wars did not end there, for almost immediately the Confederates prepared for a renewed campaign. Tilley was optimistic and thought the situation would change in the not far distant future.[96] Accordingly he set about constructing a province-wide association, probably that organization known as the British American Association, and urging the judicious use of imperial pressure to influence the population of New Brunswick.[97] He had always claimed that he needed more time to 'educate' the inhabitants of New Brunswick; now he had it.[98] John Gray was not as content. He felt that the imperial government should pass an act on the basis of the Quebec Resolutions which would allow the provinces to join when they were able. Gray was actually willing to skirt the whole problem of getting the electors or legislature of New Brunswick to approve the scheme:

It seems absurd that the petty jealousies of small Communities should be allowed to stand in the way of a great measure of Imperial Policy – and operate to defeat the future welfare of the Whole of British N. America.[99]

Anglin did not fear great repercussions from across the Atlantic. He approvingly copied a short passage from the *Acadian Recorder* which, when asked what the imperial authorities would say about the rejection of Confederation, had replied:

Why they may disapprove of the course pursued by the Lower Provinces; they may call it short-sighted and narrow; but they will respect their unanimity and defer to the tenacity of their affection for their time-honored constitutions and peculiar interests.[100]

As events proved, this was a naive hope.

6

Executive Councillor, 1865

At the beginning of April 1865 Anglin's attention was diverted from politics by the birth of his first child, Francis Alexander.* Anglin, at forty-two, was taking on the responsibilities of parenthood at an age when many men had had their last child and some men were becoming grandfathers. His young family was to cause Anglin no little anxiety in later years, but in April 1865 pride must have been Anglin's major emotion. Clearly, his stake in his adopted home was growing ever greater.

I

The birth of Frank prevented Anglin from going to Fredericton to be sworn in as an Executive Councillor.[1] The ostensible leaders of the new government were A.J. Smith and R.D. Wilmot, one representative from each wing of the anti-Confederate movement, Smith speaking for those who thought that no union at all should take place, and Wilmot representing those who favoured a more centralized union that the Quebec Resolutions envisaged.[2] Forming a government had been no simple task for, as Anglin later pointed out, 'it is not every day you find parties who have been opposed to one another for years, brought together to labor for the protection of the country.'[3] Still, Lieutenant Governor Gordon, at least, found the results quite impressive:

* Frank Anglin was to become Chief Justice of the Supreme Court of Canada (see appendix).

On the whole, the *personnel* of the new Govt. is an improvement on that of the previous Council. A decided majority of its members are men of undoubted honesty; and 2 or 3 of their number are educated gentlemen. There is man among them of the natural abilities of Mr. Tilley, but on the other hand there is no man so utterly incapable & inefficient as were some members of my late Ex. Council.*

In spite of the government's apparent strength, however, Gordon recognized that appearances were deceiving. There was the difference in attitudes towards the Quebec Resolutions. Moreover, Gordon doubted that 'an Irish rebel [Anglin] and one of the least estimable members of the late Govt. [Hatheway]' would be sufficient to enable the government 'to retain the favour of the democracy ...'[4] Gordon also reported that neither Allen nor Wilmot would long remain in office as Allen was to be appointed to the Bench as soon as the Chief Justice resigned and Wilmot was expected 'to appropriate the vacant Sinecure Office of Auditor General.'[5]

The selection of Anglin as a member of the Executive Council was particularly interesting. To be sure he had been one of the most important, perhaps the most important, anti-Confederate. But his position in New Brunswick had long been a controversial one and his presence in the cabinet was certain to draw severe criticism. Indeed, the *Religious Intelligencer* complained that his appointment was 'an imposition on, and an insult to every loyal protestant subject of Her Majesty in this Province.'[6] Nevertheless it would have been almost impossible to form an Executive Council without including Anglin. Not only had he been a bulwark of strength on the anti-Confederation issue, but also his talents and conscientious attention to duties were expected to serve the government well. 'Mr. Anglin is above mediocrity as a writer,' wrote one retired politician, 'and will be found useful, not only as an adviser of prudent measures, but as a literary critic, in preparing such documents as require to be carefully and correctly written.'[7] In fact, the real question was not whether he merited a position in the cabinet but what kind of post it should be. Eventually it was decided that he would become an Executive Councillor but not hold a departmental office – a minister without portfolio, to use contemporary phraseology. To some observers it seemed curious that neither Anglin nor

* Lieutenant Governor's Letter Books, LXIII, Gordon to Cardwell, 10 Apr. 1865, The composition of the cabinet was as follows: A.J. Smith, President of the Council; J.C. Allen, Attorney General; A.H. Gillmor, Provincial Secretary; Bliss Botsford, Surveyor General; W.H. Odell, Postmaster General; G.L. Hatheway, Chief Commissioner of the Board of Works; R.D. Wilmot, T.W. Anglin, and Richard Hutchinson, all without departmental office (see J. Hannay, *History of New Brunswick* [Saint John, 1909], II, 237).

Wilmot received a departmental office. Tilley thought that they feared defeat in the by-elections which would be required if they were to accept a departmental office.[8] This hypothesis had some merit, especially in Wilmot's case,[9] but it is not the whole story. Certainly the other members of the government were not afraid of bringing on a by-election in Saint John as both Wilmot and Anglin had been offered the prestigious office of Provincial Secretary.[10] Anglin himself never said why he refused to take this or the other offices offered him.[11] Perhaps he did not want another election contest – after all that would have cost money.[12] Perhaps he did not wish to become bogged down with departmental business in Fredericton and leave the *Freeman* lanquishing in Saint John. Perhaps he recalled the Irish 'Castle Catholic' tradition and feared losing the support of his Irish followers. Whatever the case, Anglin received neither the responsibilities nor the salary and prestige of departmental office.

In the absence of extensive documentary evidence it is difficult to generalize about Anglin's performance as an Executive Councillor. As all political leaders must, he concerned himself with matters of patronage and was especially disturbed by the feeling that sprang up that the government was neglecting its friends. He thought that 'no further cause for such a cry should be given if possible' and that outspoken opponents should be relieved of their public offices.[13] He also played a significant part in looking after the details of government business, particularly in Saint John.* With his cabinet colleagues Anglin was distant. Provincial Secretary Gillmor, for example, mentioned that he had wished to have a confidential chat with Anglin but that he had 'hesitated to break the ice' since Anglin was usually so reserved.[14] In fact, Anglin remained a loner throughout his career and never seems to have made political acquaintances into intimate confidants or personal friends. He seldom wrote the lengthy letters that so many politicians of the day considered essential to maintain political contacts. Nor did he have numerous confidential conversations with A.J. Smith, as Gillmor had assumed.[15] Yet lack of close contacts with his colleagues did not mean he had no influence. Gillmor had been especially impressed by Anglin, thinking that he was moderate in his demands and quite unassuming, 'much more so than many would be with your talent and influence ...' As far as Gillmor was concerned, Anglin and Smith, because of their

* Gillmor Papers, Anglin to Gillmour (Anglin used this spelling consistently), 13 June, 9 and 12 Oct., and 6 Nov. 1865. It was a good thing he did take an interest in such things as there were some shocking examples of poor administration. On one occasion Anglin found that the secretaries in the office of Public Institutions had had to borrow money on their own account from friends to pay overdue bills (ibid, Anglin to Gillmour, 9 Oct. 1865).

experience 'and other qualifications which must always give men influence, 'had more weight at cabinet meetings than any two others.[16] As a working member of the government Anglin seems to have been a valuable addition. But as a prime target for attacks on the government Anglin was a detriment.

II

The abuse Anglin's presence drew upon the anti-Confederate government was only one of its problems. In a remarkably short period of time it went from strength to weakness. There were many problems with which the Antis were confronted, some large, some small, but all aided in the destruction of the government.

In the field of economics the pressure of circumstances weighed heavily on the Antis. Notice of the abrogation of the Reciprocity Treaty had been given by the American government in the spring of 1865 and Canada refused to consider intercolonial free trade without political union. In addition, the anti-Confederate government took office at a time when an economic depression was becoming clearly noticeable in New Brunswick. Money was scarce and capital investments and new business enterprises were nowhere to be found. Railway and import revenues remained on a low ebb until the summer. Another great blow to the government was the fact that the provincial treasury was virtually empty.[17] The Tilley government had boasted of a large surplus for 1864 but this had been wiped out by the beginning of April. The new government now had to reorganize its expenditures to bring them more in line with revenues and the chances of the government taking on Western Extension were extremely poor. Obviously Anglin's commitment to build Western Extension as a public work meant trouble for either Anglin or the government. Lowered revenues meant drastic cuts in the budget even though the demands for greater expenditures on Western Extension and defence were now incessant. Controlling provincial expenditures did not win much applause in New Brunswick. The inhabitants were used to grandiose schemes and were not prepared for the conservatism necessitated by financial difficulties.

The Antis found another enemy in the non-elective branch of the legislature, the Legislative Council. One of Anglin's projects in the 1865 session was a Reformatory Bill which would have allowed Catholics to establish Reform Schools, though almost entirely at their own expense.[18] This bill, which was a partial answer, at least, to a crying need in Saint John, was

passed by the Assembly after an amendment.[19] But the Legislative Council, dominated by Confederates, voted seven to five in favour of postponing
the bill.[20] Shortly thereafter it threw out two more pieces of legislation.[21]
Anglin's anger was uncontrollable.

The opponents of the Government; the advocates of Confederation, the men who
long to see the free people of this Province driven or dragged or tricked into
Confederation, have begun to 'thank God that we have a House of Lords;' that a
body of men, many of whom have purchased their seats by the vilest and most
hateful services venal politicians could render to a Government, and who are still
desirous to see the party to whom they owe their seats restored to power, act in
utter disregard of public opinion and of the public interest, impede the course of
legislation and obstruct the public business.[22]

The greatest disintegrating force which faced the government, however,
was the 'loyalty' debate. This was an issue which not only involved Anglin
most acutely, but also went far to determine the fate of the Anti government. The attitude adopted by the British administration and its representative in New Brunswick, Arthur Gordon, towards the government was of
fundamental importance, for if British authorities opposed the anti-
Confederate government and pushed Confederation, the Antis could be
made to appear disloyal to the British Empire. On such an issue Anglin
would be a particularly vulnerable target because of his Irish background
and rumoured rebellion in 1848.

On the other side of the Atlantic influences were at work to help the
Confederates. Earl Russell, for instance, was willing to consider coercion,
and Edward Cardwell and the Colonial Office were resolved to undercut
the new government whenever possible.[23] Gordon was instructed to get
those who were pro-unionist but anti-Quebec resolutions to cooperate with
Tilley and his allies.[24] Cardwell also applied pressure over the question of
defence, implying that, without New Brunswick's cooperation on the
union question, Britain would hesitate to provide military assistance.

It is easy for provincial orators to say that Gt. Britain wants the Confederation in
order that her own burdens may be lightened. They would show more patriotism &
more philosophy if they reasoned thus, 'the country which takes so much interest in
this scheme, which will render our defence easier & more effectual, shows that she
is in earnest about our defences. We should have less reliance on her steadfastness
& sincerity, if she seemed less anxious about us.'[25]

With shallow arguments like this it is small wonder that Anglin felt that Britain was simply trying to escape her defence burden. Still, the pressure created by the defence question resulted in the government supporting an improved militia law and tripling the money spent for training militiamen.[26] Of course, military officials considered the amount trifling and opposition newspapers felt the sum was excessive.[27] Anglin himself thought it was a very large amount and would rather have spent the money on public works.[28] Yet the desire to satisfy imperial authorities on the question led Anglin to vote for the appropriation.[29] Obviously the impact of British official opinion was powerful.

From the outset vice-regal efforts were geared to the defeat of the New Brunswick Antis. Gordon attempted to widen the split between the two wings of the government and informed his Executive Council that he would dissolve parliament as soon as it became apparent that Confederation could be carried.[30] On the very day the new government was formed Gordon requested that Tilley be allowed to retain the rank and precedence of an Executive Councillor.[31] In fact, even during the time of the negotiations for office among the Antis, Gordon was keeping Tilley informed of developments.[32] One must consider it unusual, to say the least, for a Lieutenant Governor to divulge confidential information about one political party to the leader of another. Keeping Tilley as an Executive Councillor enabled Gordon and Tilley to plan strategy. They decided that they should remain quiescent until November. Then Tilley would create an agitation, and when the time was right the legislature would be flooded with petitions. If the government did not act, Gordon would dissolve parliament.[33]

Clearly, then, the British authorities did not accept the voice of the New Brunswick electors as a final decision on the question of union. On 24 June Cardwell sent a very strongly worded despatch to Gordon and the other Maritime governors which made this quite clear. It amounted to an appeal to loyalty and became a milestone in the campaign for Confederation. In part, it stated:

You will ... express the strong and deliberate opinion of Her Majesty's Government that it is an object much to be desired that all the British North American Colonies should agree to unite in one Government ... Such an union seems to Her Majesty's Government to recommend itself to the Provinces on many grounds of moral and material advantage ... But there is one consideration which Her Majesty's Government feel it more especially their duty to press upon the Legislature of [New Brunswick]. Looking to the determination which this Country has ever exhibited to regard the defence of the Colonies as a matter of Imperial concern, – the Colonies must recognize a right and even acknowledge an obligation incumbent on the Home Government to urge with earnestness and just authority the measures which they consider to be most expedient on the part of the Colonies with a view to their own defence. Nor can it be doubtful that the Provinces of British North America are incapable, when separate and divided from each other, of making those just and sufficient preparations for national defence, which would be easily undertaken by a Province uniting in itself all the population and all the provinces of the whole.[34]

Naturally enough, the government attempted to counteract this pressure. In the middle of May the Executive Council sent a gentle reminder to Cardwell via Gordon, 'to inform the Secretary of State for the Colonies how entirely the scheme has been rejected by the people of this Province ...'[35] When this failed to produce any change of attitude, the government suspected that misinformation about the election must have been spread throughout England by the Canadian delegates who were, the *Freeman* wrote, 'working to enslave the people of the Maritime Provinces.'[36] But when two delegates, Smith and Allen, were sent to England to provide correct information and thus change Cardwell's stance, they ran into a stone wall.[37] In the meantime the Executive Council and Gordon prepared a reply to Cardwell's despatch of 24 June.

On 12 July the Executive Minute was sent to Gordon. While acknowledging the 'due weight' which Cardwell's opinions ought to carry, the Minute rejected his views.[38] It suggested that the Quebec scheme had not been a plan of fusion but the means whereby the Canadas could be divided to overcome sectional difficulties. It stated the belief that union along the lines of the Quebec Resolutions would bring no 'moral or material advantage' to either New Brunswick or the Empire. In fact, the Minute claimed, union would tend towards the loosening of imperial ties. It concluded with the opinion that New Brunswickers had the right to determine their fate, or else self-government meant nothing. The *Intelligencer* stated that this memorandum was tantamount to disloyalty and accused Anglin of writing it. Anglin did not answer this charge immediately except to point out that all the members of the Executive Council present had signed it and were therefore responsible for it.[39] Eight months later, however, in the House of Assembly, Anglin was able to tell the whole story.

Anglin took opportunity ... to explain that all the passages in the famous Memorandum of Council which Fisher and the newspapers had so violently assailed – which it was said were written by no gentleman, but a mean, low fellow – which were said to be an insult to the Queen and an outrage to the people – were written, not by him (Anglin), but by the Governor himself; while the loyal paragraphs and others were written by Anglin, and some others by Odell, and he believes Wilmoţ.

He explained the whole process by which it was prepared. Wilmot was the one who finally compiled all the Council agreed to adopt and he was authorized by the others to put their names to it.

He explained also that the changes demanded by their friends were postponed by the urgent request of the Governor, who persuaded them, through Mr. Smith, that it would seriously affect the chances of the success of the delegation if he must write to the Colonial Office that such changes were made. For the good of the great cause they consented to the delay, and not because they truckled to the Governor.[40]

Anglin's role in this is quite clear. He wished to assert that in opposing Confederation there was no disloyalty to the Empire.[41] He hoped to urge the imperial authorities into acceptance of New Brunswick's position by appealing to their sense of fair play and their sympathy for the constitutional rights of British subjects under responsible government. He was attempting to win over Cardwell, for Anglin realized that, if the British government persisted in its course of urging Confederation with all the means at its disposal, the anti-Confederates would be in a bad position in the province of the Loyalists *par excellence.*'[42] But Britain was not prepared to allow opposition to Confederation, as Cardwell's reply to the memorandum of the Executive Council indicated.[43] The anti-Confederates began to look for some means of escape from the predicament in which they found themselves.

One attempt was made near the end of August. Anglin and Hatheway quietly slipped away to Quebec. Charles Fisher, in his virtually illegible handwriting, warned Galt that they were coming to see if better union terms could be obtained, especially on the issues of representation and finances, and advised the Canadians to put Anglin and the Antis in a false position if at all possible.[44] There is no doubt that the two New Brunswick Antis went to Quebec to see how the ground lay. Exactly what they did is unknown, but they did have discussions with some Canadian leaders, including Cartier and Lord Monck.[45] As well, Hatheway and Anglin were given a lunch at Quebec which was attended by oppositionist elements in Canada. Anglin used the occasion to correct the prevalent impressions in Canada concerning the New Brunswick elections. It was an excellent speech which clearly outlined Anglin's position but it was a wasted effort.[46] Confederation was the determined policy of Canada and it would not be changed because of Anglin or New Brunswick.

Another trip by a New Brunswick Executive Councillor late in the summer of 1865 showed that all was not well within the anti-Confederate ranks. R.D. Wilmot's visit to Quebec City to discuss forthcoming reciprocity negotiations with the United States resulted in his taking positions independent of the Anti government.[47] At London in Canada West he told Canadians to bide their time; that vast numbers in New Brunswick desired union but not the Quebec Resolutions.[48] Shortly thereafter he repudiated the 12 July Minute of Council.[49] The *Freeman* denied that New Brunswick wanted union and ridiculed Wilmot's reversal on the Executive Minute.[50] Privately Anglin thought that Wilmot ought to be asked to leave the cabinet.[51]

That continued pressure from imperial authorities was gouging large holes in the ranks of the anti-Confederates was plain to see. The British government's desire for Confederation was also most obvious. New Brunswickers were not unimpressed by this display of support for union and the time rapidly approached when another appeal to the electorate would yield a far different result. But the British attitude towards Confederation was only one part of the loyalty issue. The other phase began to emerge seriously in the autumn of 1865, by which time events in the United States had made Fenianism a difficulty for British North Americans. In New Brunswick this problem became a part of the loyalty issue in conjunction with and even more important than imperial opinions on Confederation. On such a question Anglin quickly became the centre of attention.

III

The Fenian Society was a strange and complex organization.[52] Its main object was the liberation of Ireland from Britain; its chosen means, physical force.

This Fenian Brotherhood, organized in April, 1859, could be defined as an organized body of men devoted to a system of political, financial, and military action on the part of the Irishmen of America, aiding and co-operating with an allied body of revolutionists in the British Isles, for the purpose of gaining the independence of Ireland.[53]

Most of the Fenians had been born in Ireland, but their strength was centred not in the homeland but in the United States where operations could be carried out with a minimum of secrecy. The internal history of the

Fenian Brotherhood is extremely complex. Suffice it to say that the movement assumed a significance after the Civil War that it had not had before.
Realizing this, the British government took effective action to curb
Fenianism in Ireland.[54] With the home movement checked, the American
Fenians grew restive and exhibited the refractory characteristics which
have plagued so many Irish movements. A split developed within the
brotherhood and blossomed forth at the Fenian convention held in October
1865. The question was whether the society should attempt to capture
Canada in the hope of using it as a base for freeing Ireland or whether it
should work to foment revolution in Ireland. By December two rival
Fenian organizations had been established; the Roberts-Sweeny Fenians,
led by W.R. Roberts and T.W. Sweeny, who supported the 'attack on
Canada' concept, and the more orthodox O'Mahony Fenians, led by John
O'Mahony. To British North Americans such internal squabbling made
little difference; they looked upon all Fenians as presenting a genuine
threat, largely because the attitude of the American government towards
the Fenians was hazy.

Initially, at least, Anglin's view of the brotherhood was ambivalent. As a
substantial North American Irishman he could find little affinity with an
organization composed mainly of the lower classes.[55] Nor was it likely that
the devout Anglin would give much support to a movement condemned by
the hierarchy and most of the priests of the Catholic Church for being
anti-clerical, atheistic, and a 'secret, oath-bound and revolutionary society.'[56] Moreover Anglin, like other British North American Irishmen,
tended to compartmentalize his attitude to Britain. In relation to Ireland the
British connection was bad and ought to be ended; for the North American
colonies it was useful enough and might be maintained. While Anglin knew
that Irish conditions needed amelioration, his own political inclinations and
his experience with responsible government in the new world made him
favour constitutional agitation to remedy the wrongs of Ireland. As for the
plan to attack British North America, Anglin, along with most colonial
Irishmen, had no sympathy.[57] After all, New Brunswick was now home. It
is virtually unthinkable that Anglin would have risked his position in New
Brunswick to become involved with hare-brained Fenian schemers. He
had far too much to lose.

Yet the *Freeman* underplayed Fenianism for a long time. In part, this
may be explained by the fact that Anglin, along with everyone else, was
bewildered by the conduct of the society. Also he was always convinced
that the Fenian menace, both from without and within British North
America, was grossly exaggerated.[58] But the *Freeman*'s posture was also a

result of its editor's indecision. He agreed with the goal of the Fenian Society – greater freedom for Ireland; but he was less sure about the intended means. Certainly he considered the government of Ireland 'one of the worst in Europe,' the people having to support a church establishment, absentee landlords, and increasingly heavy taxation in spite of poor harvests and diminishing population.

> Revolution is always a fearful, often a wicked thing, and the views of these Fenians may be visionary, their hopes may be baseless; some may think their intentions wicked and their schemes rash and wild; but those who approved of revolution in Tuscany and Parma must at least admit that the grievances which the Fenians would redress are unparalleled in their enormity, even if the means by which they would redress them should not meet with approval.[59]

This statement, however, had been made in 1863, before it became apparent that the Fenians might attack British North America, and must be seen in a different light from comments made after the autumn of 1865. Anglin's general policy was to keep the subject as dormant as possible. Whatever position he took, discussion of Fenianism could only hurt him politically, and he undoubtedly felt that on this issue silence was the better part of political valour. But it was too much to expect the Confederates to adopt the same line. By the autumn of 1865 it was apparent that the pro-Confederate papers were keeping a sharp eye on Fenian developments and were going to keep the subject in the public mind.[60] The issue was just too good to overlook. Here was an illegal organization, composed largely of Catholic Irishmen, which wanted to throw off the British connection by violent means. It was a simple mental step to forge a link between Fenianism and New Brunswick Irish Catholics and thereby brand them with disloyalty. What would be the political utility of this for the Confederates? It would polarize the views of the Protestant majority of New Brunswick in favour of Confederation since it was assumed that the Irish Catholics had opposed it in the 1865 elections. It would be a marvellous means of undermining Anglin's political power and, through him, the power of the government. Thus four distinct entities – Roman Catholics, anti-Confederates, Fenians, and Anglin – became inextricably interconnected in the pro-Confederation campaign. It was to be a tremendously successful campaign for loyalty and Confederation against the Fenian-sympathizing, anti-Confederate Catholics, led by Anglin. The first occasion on which this tactic played a major role was during the York by-election of November 1865.

IV

In September 1865 the Chief Justice of New Brunswick, Sir James Carter, resigned. The most senior of the three Supreme Court judges, Robert Parker, was elevated to the Chief Justiceship and J.C. Allen resigned his post as Attorney General in order to become a Puisne Judge. A.J. Smith took over Allen's position as Attorney General.[61] Two elections were thus necessitated. In York a by-election had to be held to fill the vacancy left by the resignation of Allen, and in Westmorland Smith had to go to the electorate to confirm his assumption of the office of Attorney General. No opposition was offered to Smith in Westmorland and he was duly returned.[62] But in York Charles Fisher, who had once been described by the Duke of Newcastle as 'the worst public man in British America,'[63] but who was an accomplished politician, took the field as the opposition candidate and John Pickard was nominated on the government side. Pickard came out flatly against the Quebec Resolutions.[64] He was an Orangeman, but he hoped to pick up Catholic votes from the support given him by Anglin and the *Freeman*. For his part, Fisher decided to ignore the six hundred Catholic voters and concentrate on arousing the Protestant and British feeling of the remaining 3100 voters.[65] Using Anglin as a symbol, Fisher accused the government of disloyalty, of favouring annexation, and of apologizing for Fenianism.[66] Papers supporting Fisher echoed him. The editor of the *Reporter*, for example, reduced the issue of the election to simple terms:

The reckoning day is at hand. Monday next will decide whether Mr. Anglin is to rule this Province, or this Province to rule Mr. Anglin; whether loyalty or Fenianism is the chief power in the land.[67]

The *Religious Intelligencer* proclaimed Roman Catholicism to be the source of the Fenian troubles.

Fenianism is a Roman Catholic movement. There may be a few other mad spirits identified with it, but it is emphatically a conception of Rome, its origin is the intense hatred which Romanism inspires against British Protestantism and British freedom.[68]

Strangely enough, Fisher almost completely ignored the issue of Confederation. He even promised to oppose any scheme of union which might be introduced into the existing parliament by the Antis, an indication that he felt there was some possibility of the government reversing its stand.[69] Local issues played some role in the York by-election,[70] but the most important factor was the loyalty cry raised by Fisher and directed against Anglin. 'Anglin, Fisher announced with patriotic conviction, was the avowed enemy of worthy Orangemen, of pious Protestants, of faithful British subjects, of devoted United Empire Loyalists, of the sons and grandsons of the York volunteers, Queen's Rangers, and other heroes of the American Revolution.'[71] The Halifax *Recorder* thought the anti-Anglin campaign reminiscent of a Nova Scotia movement of a few years back:

The people of York were warned against this Roman Catholic Fenian monster in language as loud, and canting and frothy, and effectual as that which Mr. McCully coined for the Protestant Alliance a few years ago to frighten the fools in Nova Scotia, and induce them to believe that they would be murdered in their beds by the 'Papists.'[72]

Fisher's campaign was thoroughly disreputable but eminently successful. Fisher polled 1927 votes; Pickard only 1217.[73]

The Confederates had discovered the way to win an election. With the Colonial Office refusing to cooperate with the anti-Confederate government of New Brunswick and undermining it whenever possible, the Confederates in New Brunswick found that they could win by playing down the issue of Confederation and by using the loyalty cry and the Fenian bogey which resulted in an anti-Catholic campaign. With improved organization and Canadian money, the Confederates now had little fear of a new general election.[74]

On the same day that Gordon reported to Cardwell the results of the York by-election, he also notified the Colonial Secretary of the resignation of T.W. Anglin from the Executive Council. Were these two events connected? The *Reporter* certainly thought so:

It is possible that the Government, finding it difficult to continue in power while he was included in their ranks, determined to get rid of him, and so by innuendoes and otherwise, induced the hon. gentleman, seeing his presence was disagreeable, to withdraw. Or on the other hand it is just as likely that, admitting he was a weakness to the party, he has slipped behind the scenes, where he continues to pull the political wires for the Government.[75]

The by-election was indeed an issue in Anglin's resignation, not as the cause of it, but rather in its timing. The real reason for his resignation was the great bugbear of New Brunswick politics, the railway question.

V

The difficulties facing Western Extension were legion. In the first place the government could not afford to undertake it as a government work in spite of Anglin's election pledge. Second, the Western Extension Company, still dominated by Tilley's friends, such as William Parks and Charles Skinner, respectively president and secretary of the company, was in a position to make life difficult for the government. It held a charter and would neither relinquish this to the government nor make energetic and realistic efforts to get the line built. Parks had gone to Britain in order to raise funds for the Western Extension, but had not pressed his case until after the 1865 election results were known. He then visited Edward Watkin, the British railway magnate and one time president of the Grand Trunk, who was of the opinion 'that it was utterly impossible to lend a shilling for any public work in New Brunswick in the face of her refusal of Confederation ...'[76] And with these weak efforts Parks gave up his quest for British financial support, leaving 'Mr. Anglin and his Colegues [sic] to Build Western Extension.'[77]

The issue of Western Extension did not immediately render false Anglin's position in the government. He was still sure that only as a public work would the line be built.[78] Anglin asserted that he stood by his election pledges, but that only he, not the government, was to be bound by them.[79] Nor did he feel compelled to resign his position in the Executive Council, for it was not yet clear what the government's position would be. The Western Extension Company had not yet given up its charter and nothing could be done until this occurred.[80] By the middle of June the opposition papers were stating that the Western Extension Company had found new life.[81] Anglin was sceptical and suggested that the majority of the committee members of the company were more anxious to embarrass the government than to complete the line. The brief upsurge of the company fell flat when the Saint John Common Council refused to invest $400,000 in stock, and it was then reported that the company had agreed to surrender its charter.[82] But John A. Poor, a railway magnate from Portland, Maine had accepted the terms offered by the company and, as far as can be ascertained, the charter was never surrendered.[83] Throughout the summer Western Extension remained in a state of suspended animation, most members of the government hoping that the company could arrange to commence construction.[84]

Early in September the *Evening Globe* announced that the government had given its acceptance to the European and North American Railway Company and the Maine Company for the building of Western Extension.[85] The *Freeman* doubted this fact, even after Skinner, the secretary of the company, in a letter to the 'Citizens of Saint John', re-asserted that the company's offer had been accepted under the terms of the 'Lobster Act.'[86] Anglin obviously was not aware that A.J. Smith, without the knowledge of the Executive Council as a whole, had negotiated with Skinner and signed an agreement with him. Though not authorized to take such a step, Smith had virtually determined the government's policy on Western Extension. There is little doubt that Anglin would have accepted this action had he had confidence in the company, but he did not. He was convinced that no company could be formed that would actually build the road and that the existing organization in particular was quite incapable. It became obvious that Anglin would have to resign if the Executive Council acquiesced in Smith's agreement with the company, an agreement which members of the Executive Council became aware of only when it became public knowledge.[87] Anglin knew he would have to resign. In fact by October he pursued a policy of passive silence at council meetings, giving his opinions only when asked, but doing nothing to commit himself to the policy the government was adopting towards Western Extension. Still, the council had not formally accepted Smith's contract with the company and there was some doubt that the company could raise even the small amount required to fulfil the contract. Until these things occurred, Anglin decided to remain in the cabinet. His reasons for delaying his resignation were two. First, it would be foolish to resign if it turned out that the company could not fulfil the bargain or if by some miracle the Executive Council turned it down. Second, there were two by-elections impending and he did not want to give encouragement to the Confederate opposition. Also, it may be that the urgings of Provincial Secretary Gillmor not to resign had some effect. But he had to make his attitude on the government's Western Extension policy clear to his friends and the readers of the *Freeman*.[88]

The line he chose to follow was therefore a very difficult one, and, as it turned out, his tightrope act served little purpose. True, Smith met no opposition in Westmorland, but Fisher's use of Anglin as a target in York showed that his presence in the cabinet was a mixed blessing for the Antis. Indeed, Anglin later claimed that, seeing what was going on in York, he had said to Smith: 'you know best whether the proceedings of the Western Extension Company are such as to satisfy you; if they are, I must leave you, and you might as well have the benefit of my absence;' but Smith, apparently, had refused to knuckle under to the pressure of the anti-

Catholic cry being raised in York.[89] But a couple of days after the York by-election the Western Extension Company turned the first sod for the line, and the following day Anglin wrote a lengthy letter of resignation to Gordon, giving a history of the government's handling of the problem of Western Extension and his reasons for resigning.[90]

Anglin disagreed with his colleagues over the competency of the company to build Western Extension, but he still remained a strong supporter of the government's stand against Confederation.[91] If he thought that the government was trifling with Western Extension, at least he did not feel compelled to fulfil his apparent election pledge to work for the government's destruction. On the contrary, he felt that he would be at least as useful to the government outside the cabinet as within it.[92] From the *Freeman*'s point of view it was a much better arrangement.[93] Anglin now had greater freedom as an editor and could more easily defend himself against the multiple attacks that were being made on him. He probably hoped that his resignation would remove the foundation of the Confederates' anti-Catholic campaign which had been so successful in York. In any case, it must have been a relief for Anglin to resign, if the *Globe*'s description of the treatment he had received, is correct.

... Mr. Anglin was in the Government for only a few months, and during that time subjected to a course of persecution from an unscrupulous press and by Mr. Tilley himself, in season and out of season, by daylight and by dark, in the House of Assembly and out of it, in the lobbies, in the galleries, in the hotels, at the street corners, behind porches, in Canada, in England, by sleeping and by waking, – a course that was humiliating to his own manhood ...[94]

With his resignation Anglin terminated the only cabinet post he ever held during his career. As a working member of the cabinet he seems to have been very competent and conscientious, and his knowledge and efficiency would seem to have merited similar positions in the future. But he was a controversial figure, a fact which his months as Executive Councillor amply demonstrated. His roles as newspaper editor and as leader of the Irish Catholics meant that he brought weaknesses as well as strengths to the government in which he was included. His short term as Executive Councillor may also have been the apogee of his political power. Certainly the next few months saw its rapid decline and, although he managed to recover, he was always known thereafter as one of the old defeated anti-Confederates. One thing is clear. If Anglin thought that the attacks on him would diminish after he resigned, he was sadly mistaken. He was just too useful a target.

7

Anti-Confederation: Defeat
1865-7

I

Anglin had long been viewed by opposition newspapers as a powerful force in the anti-Confederate government. His resignation did not greatly change their opinion; Anglin's influence was now merely more insidious, for he continued 'to pull the political wires for the Government.'[1] To Anglin opposition journalists gave the nickname 'the Dictator.' As an example of his power they pointed to the appointment of William J. Ritchie as Chief Justice after the death of Robert Parker in November 1865. Filling the position had not been an easy task. Apparently A.J. Smith was for a time prepared to take the office himself, but as Parker lingered on his death bed, Smith found that his political friends would not agree to his 'desertion.'[2] His refusal left the choice between Lemuel Allen Wilmot and Ritchie, the two senior judges of the Supreme Court. Wilmot, though a cousin of R.D. Wilmot, had been aggressively pro-Confederate, even in court.[3] He was also *persona non grata* to Anglin because of an attack he had made on Catholicism a few years back.[4] On the other hand, Ritchie was known to be an Anti and his legal reputation was far above that of Wilmot, if the assessments of Gordon and the *Freeman* were correct.[5] The difficulty was that Wilmot was the more senior of the two. Despite this, Ritchie was named Chief Justice. At this turn of events the opposition felt or feigned outrage. The *Telegraph*, for one, was extremely bitter:

We have no hesitation in asserting that the intrigues which will lead to any other than Justice Wilmot receiving the Chief Justiceship ... will be regarded by the country as demonstrating, beyond the shadow of a doubt, that the Government of the Province is again in the hands of Mr. Anglin – that the Government has bowed its neck to the yoke of 'the Dictator.'[6]

Anglin quite rightly pointed out that the Western Extension issue had proven that the government did not dread him.[7] But he did feel most strongly about Judge Wilmot:

We are almost sorry that we cannot accept the high compliment the *Telegraph* pays Mr. Anglin. We could almost wish it were true that the very proper treatment he has received was due to Mr. Anglin's influence.[8]

It is clear that, if Anglin's nickname was an exaggeration, the Confederates were correct in thinking that Anglin's influence was felt by the government. In fact, it was almost as though Anglin had not resigned but become an Executive Councillor who never attended council meetings. As he told the Provincial Secretary shortly after his resignation, his services were still at the disposal of the Government.

I am sorry that I have had to part with you and sorry that you attach undue importance to my resigning. I do not think that the step I have taken will weaken you much and I am satisfied that it must disconcert the plans and schemes of our opponents and that out of the government I can give you as much support as I could in it. My opinion on any subject that may demand consideration will always be at your service.[9]

In numerous minor political matters he fulfilled this pledge; but especially in his knowledge of and advice on the most important government affairs one can see not only his attitude towards a deteriorating situation but also his true significance in government circles after his resignation.

At the time of his resignation Anglin suspected that certain 'plotting' was going on. George Brown had come to New Brunswick in mid-November, ostensibly on a trade mission, but mainly, as Anglin suspected to see how plans for Confederation were shaping up.[10] The Irish Catholic leader called on the leader of the Clear Grits in an attempt to find out 'what was brewing.' 'We tried strength for an hour or so,' Anglin reported, 'and he was almost victor.' About all he could surmise from his talk with Brown was that some secret planning was taking place and that Lieutenant Governor Gordon was involved. With this unknown threat facing the Antis,

Anglin warned Gillmor, the Provincial Secretary, to prepare for the onslaught.

They have been trying Smith and he seems disposed to temporise. I had a talk with him last night. I wished he should understand exactly where Wilmot – who seems to be the agent of this new scheme – would be found, that he may be on his guard. We are beset on all sides and much depends on Smith and you. I can only serve as an auxiliary but you may depend on my doing all I can. Smith promises to let me know on his return how matters stand. I hope he will be prudent and do nothing to weaken his position.[11]

Anglin's supposition that plans were being drafted for the achievement of Confederation was correct. By the beginning of December Gordon had completed arrangements. His view was that the anti-Confederate government had become so weakened, demoralized, and unpopular that it could be persuaded to go for some revised plan of union since 'the most determined isolationist Mr. Anglin is no longer a member of the Government.'[12] Even Smith, Gordon stated, was talking about union. Gordon therefore intended to get the existing government to sponsor union resolutions in the Assembly, and if there defeated to call an election. The Lieutenant Governor was aware of the dangers of this course of action and tried to make plans for meeting those that should arise:

It may be asked whether there is no danger lest the apparent acquiescence of the Government in an Union policy should only be affected for the purpose of producing delay, and under cover of objections in detail to defeat the scheme by continual procrastination. Against this danger I propose to guard by compelling the adoption of a decided policy when the time for the assembly of the Legislature draws near. I then propose to submit to my Council the draft of a paragraph, in my speech from the throne, in which I intend to invite both branches of the Legislature again seriously to consider the question of an union of the B.N.A. Provinces, and shall express a hope that such an Union will speedily be accomplished. If my Government are content to adopt such language all difficulty is at an end, and the resolutions will be adopted by both houses with trifling opposition. If on the contrary my Council as a body decline to make themselves responsible for the enunciation of such sentiments the time will I think have arrived at which a change of Government may be effected, and a dissolution tried.[13]

Gordon expected some of the Executive Council to accept these terms and others to refuse and resign. A coalition of sorts would then be formed and Confederation would triumph. This plan won the approval of George Brown and Lord Monck and they told the New Brunswick supporters of Confederation to trust Gordon and to make preparations for a possible election.[14]

At this crucial time the anti-Confederates began to show further signs of internal dissension. For example, in December A.R. Wetmore, the member for the city of Saint John, decided to change sides, claiming that the opinion of his constituency had changed, although being refused positions both as Attorney General and as a judge might have influenced his analysis of that opinion.[15] Another lingering problem was Wilmot's role in the cabinet. Would he resign or would the government change its policy? The answer to this question was foreshadowed by the announcement on the first day of 1866 that Smith would go to Washington for reciprocity negotiations. Wilmot had represented the province on the reciprocity question at Quebec during the summer and he had expected to make this second trip. Along with the recent slight to his cousin the judge, this decision made him angry. It was rumoured that he had handed in his resignation.[16] As far as Anglin was concerned, Wilmot's resignation was past due. 'His only strength,' Anglin had written prophetically back in November, 'would be in a renewal of the No Popery cry.'[17] However, for the moment Gordon chose not to accept Wilmot's resignation.

Smith's trip to Washington was fruitless, as Anglin had expected.[18] The United States was simply not interested in reciprocity.[19] While Smith was away, however, interesting developments were taking place in New Brunswick. Gordon was trying to carry out his plan concerning the throne speech and coupling this with Wilmot's letter of resignation. Anglin advised great caution about the speech from the throne. A few injudicious words, he thought, could seriously weaken the Antis' position.

If you can not again speak out plainly and unequivocally in condemnation of the Scheme and the whole idea of Confederation the best plan in my opinion would be to make the Speech absolutely non committal merely informing the Legislature that all despatches &c. will be laid before them.[20]

The tactics to be followed were highly important. Anglin could not approve of Smith's idea of temporizing, as the former called it.[21] Still, while he did not like, he was willing to consider, Gillmor's suggestion to detach the government from policies introduced into the Assembly, perhaps by making Confederation an open question.

Your idea would not be a bad one perhaps if nothing better could be done. It would be rather an unconstitutional mode of proceeding and under ordinary circumstances totally inadmissible in my opinion: but if the Imperial Govt. by their agent threaten the very constitution itself and will not be satisfied with the expression of the public will given in the constitutional way and we can not resist the pressure why it would be their fault not ours if this new method were adopted. It was a favourite scheme of some of the advocates of a Prohibitory Law at one time. Perhaps the Governor who is now so completely in the hands of the Schemers would not be satisfied even with that. I hate chicanery and trickery but at present I do almost think that a little finesse would be pardonable when we have so many and such unscrupulous enemies to deal with.[22]

The government's real problem, Anglin was convinced, was the Lieutenant Governor. The Irish editor thought Gordon's conduct disgraceful and wanted to ensure that, if the anti-Confederates were dismissed, they would be able to publicize his conduct.

Should a break up take place we must at all events be able to tell the whole story so that the public may understand all about it and how we were hampered and thwarted by His Excellency under the guise of friendship and how he got us into all this difficulty acting the whole time in concert with the very Mr. Tilley whom in conversation with some of us he so much affected to despise. Of course it will not do to ask permission to tell this in so many words: but permission to explain the cause of the trouble can not be refused and that involves everything.[23]

Anglin vowed that if Gordon played 'traitor,' 'I will skin him as I never yet skinned recreant and deceiver.'[24] Articles in the *Freeman* contained such thinly disguised warnings to Gordon that the Lieutenant Governor wrote a private note to Anglin protesting that there would be no dissolution of the House before it met.[25] Anglin's reply stated that in Saint John there was no change of opinion on Confederation; in effect he warned Gordon to watch his step.

The people think that it would be an outrage to force them into a new election so soon after they have so solemnly deliberately and emphatically pronounced judgement on the great question submitted to them by your Excellency's late advisers; but if an election must come, they are quite determined to fight to the last. I hope most sincerely that when an election does occur no party will have any cause or even plausible pretext for dragging your name before the public, and discussing your conduct or your motives.[26]

While attempting to forestall Gordon's moves, Anglin was also trying to stiffen the anti-Confederate backbone. What was necessary, he thought, was to 'look the enemy in the face, confront him boldly and never show any symptom of want of hope or want of courage.'[27] Unfortunately for the Antis this was a great deal to ask.

When Smith returned from Washington, Gordon confronted him with a stiff proposition – either accept a policy of union or he would turn to Wilmot, whose resignation had not been accepted, in combination with Peter Mitchell as the core of a new administration.[28] Surprisingly, Smith met Gordon's demands, although later developments indicated that the two men had differing opinions about the nature and scope of the agreement. The Executive Council agreed with Smith's decision and Smith was allowed one week to consult with his friends before giving Gordon his final answer.[29] In the meantime Wilmot's resignation was accepted and the government won a little breathing space.[30] Nevertheless Gordon did not completely trust his Attorney General.

I am confident that Mr. Smith *wishes* to adopt the course above described, in acceding to which at all he certainly makes great sacrifices, and lays himself open to reproach from those who have been his warmest supporters, but I see also that if he is unable to induce his followers to accept the change, he will not scruple to avow that his own opinions have undergone no change and that he is still prepared to continue his opposition to the Quebec Scheme of Federation.[31]

One of those supporters with whom Smith consulted was unquestionably Anglin. Even more certain was Anglin's opposition to Confederation. He was willing to accept the submission to the Assembly of Cardwell's despatches and other documents or propositions emanating from the imperial government or the 'sister colonies,' 'common courtesy requiring that the most careful consideration should be given to any propositions from such quarters.'[32] But to go further and make more positive commitments was not acceptable to Anglin. Nevertheless, when Smith returned to Gordon, he told the Lieutenant Governor that the party was generally willing to accept the course he had consented to pursue. Gordon was highly pleased.

This decision of my Government enables me confidently to assert that, whatever be their own fate, & I consider their retention of office under the circumstances very doubtful, the Confederation Scheme will, in a few weeks be acceded to by this province, and I beg to congratulate H.M. Govt. on the success of an object the attainment of which they have so decidedly desired.[33]

The Lieutenant Governor was premature. What he did not realize was that the Antis were capable of playing politics as skilfully as everyone else involved in the Confederation struggle. It would appear that Gordon had spoken to Smith in general terms and that Smith was perfectly happy to allow the Lieutenant Governor to deceive himself. As far as can be ascertained, Smith never agreed to support Confederation.[34] His position seems to have been to allow the subject of union, whether the Quebec scheme or some modified plan, to be introduced into the Assembly for discussion but not to promote it. At least this is what 'the Dictator' thought.[35]

On 8 March the parliament met and listened to the speech from the throne. It contained a paragraph stating 'the deliberate opinion' of the British government that a union was desirable.[36] On 12 March the debate on the reply to the throne speech commenced. Charles Fisher introduced a want of confidence motion.[37] He declared that the government had taken insufficient precautions against the Fenian danger.[38] For almost a month the debate dragged on, the government proceeding with a number of other bills by starting the daily sessions at 11 AM rather than 2 PM.[39] But part of almost every day was spent in discussing Fisher's want of confidence motion. Whether Smith wanted the debate prolonged is a moot point, but it is probable that he and his government, seeing that otherwise the session was progressing favourably, were not particularly concerned about Fisher's motion. They still held a good majority in the Assembly and they may not have been very anxious to rush into a discussion of union, for then the direction in which the government was heading would become obvious.* The likely direction was shown in the proposed reply to the throne speech. It agreed on union in the abstract and then stated:

But in any scheme for a Union of the British North American Colonies which may be proposed, it is, in the opinion of this House, absolutely essential that full protection should be afforded to the rights and interests of the people of this Province; and no measure which fails to obtain these objects should be tolerated.[40]

Anglin agreed with this proposed reply, especially with its assertion that in

---

* The government could not, it seems, have ended the discussion at all without the acquiescence of the opposition. On this point the late W.S. MacNutt has stated that 'at any time' Smith 'could have brought closure to the debate ...' (see MacNutt, *New Brunswick*, p 455). This writer contacted Professor MacNutt about this passage and in a letter dated 23 August 1967 he replied that the word *closure* 'was used in the more figurative and general sense.' It appears to this writer that, as there was no closure rule to be invoked, the opposition could have filibustered as long as it wished.

any union the rights and interests of New Brunswickers would have to be safeguarded, and on 5 April and for the next two days Anglin got his opportunity to speak in reply to Fisher's amendment.[41] During this speech he touched on several topics of recent history. He gave a great deal of information on the formation and inner workings of the Executive Council. He spoke at length on the appointment of Ritchie and about Judge Wilmot. He complained of the pressure put on the government by Cardwell who, Anglin was sure, was the mouthpiece of Canadian politicians. He explained and defended the famous council memorandum of 12 July. He complained that the Smasher government had left only $9,000 to the credit of the province, the Post Office account overdue, and the Crown lands in great disorder. He talked of union as being an old idea but the Quebec scheme as being a new one: 'it was an attempt to graft a new branch on the old stock; but it wouldn't grow; and if they ever did succeed in setting it, it would produce nothing but fungi and rottenness.'[42] He spoke of the York election, of his visit to Quebec, and of the anti-Catholic campaign being run by the Confederates. He defended himself against the charge of disloyalty, claiming that the advocates of Confederation 'found they could not appeal to the common sense of the people with any chance of success; they, therefore, appealed to the passions and prejudices of the people to do their work.'[43] He announced that he would oppose the government should it try to pass a Confederation scheme through the Assembly. He spoke of a multitude of other things but ended on a most fitting note when, in answer to the question whether he was opposed to any kind of political union with Canada, he stated:

I do not believe at the present time a political union of any kind can be formed with Canada which would be a benefit to the people of this Province. I do not know of any one opposed to union in the abstract, but my impression is that the time has not arrived for any kind of union, and I will oppose it to the last. At present the Provinces are distinct communities with conflicting interests, and the Quebec Scheme does not reconcile them, and the difficulties can only be overcome by sacrificing the Lower Provinces altogether.[44]

From 7 April, when Anglin concluded his speech, to 16 April events moved swiftly. While a band of Fenians made threatening gestures on the New Brunswick border, Gordon forced the resignation of the anti-Confederate government and brought in Mitchell, Tilley, Fisher, Wilmot, and the rest.[45] Thus Anglin was given his opportunity to 'skin' the Governor. His first effort, made in the House of Assembly just before the House was prorogued on 16 April, was to give detailed information about the Minute of 12 July, showing that the sections of it which were being attacked as disloyal were those written by the Governor. Prior to April cabinet secrecy and a respect for Gordon's integrity had kept Anglin silent, in spite of the barbs thrown at him. But now, Anglin claimed, Gordon had become the head of a provincial faction by his 'unconstitutional' conduct.[46] Anglin's main attack, however, was made in his usual manner, in the pages of the *Freeman*.

We always believed that the Governor meant well; but his ideas of right and wrong are to some extent peculiarly his own. He acts as if he were raised to an immense height above all mere Provincialists, and as if our leading politicians were as mere pawns in a game of chess, to be moved and worked at his will and pleasure. We do not think that he would wilfully do wrong, knowing it to be wrong; but he is one of those men who never can be made to believe that anything they wish to do can possibly be wrong. No doubt he was sincere in wishing to support Mr. Smith; but the moment he decided on getting rid of him he regarded neither the principles of the constitution nor the rights of the people.[47]

Of course, Anglin felt, this subversion of responsible government was closely linked with the scheme for union, and now he used the terms 'anti-Constitutionalists,' 'Canadian imperialists,' and 'foes of Responsible Government' to designate the Confederate party led by Tilley. But little was to be gained from the constitutional issue, as Anglin and the other Antis were to find in the election campaign which followed prorogation. The electors saw that the Antis had been treated unjustly but, more important, they saw just how great was the support for Confederation which British officials were willing to give. Anglin tried to raise the cry of 'responsible government' but New Brunswickers were not listening very closely. Their ears had become attuned to the tribal war-cry of 'loyalty.'

II

Since his resignation from the cabinet Anglin had continued to fight a rearguard action on the two flanks of the loyalty issue. He argued once again that Confederation meant the loosening of the imperial connection.[48] He attempted to demonstrate that opposing Confederation was no more disloyal than opposing the Reform Bill which was then getting attention in England.[49] New Brunswickers surely had a right to their own decisions:

This is freedom and self-government with a vengeance, when the people of these Provinces must consent to change their constitution merely because a colonial minister who knows nothing about them desires it, and to be governed, not according to their own well understood wishes but according to the wishes of a Mr. Cardwell as interpreted by Messrs. Brown, Cartier, McCully and Company.[50]

Yet Anglin could not get around the fact that the imperial government, whether for good reasons or bad, supported Confederation. The Antis were branded, though most unjustly, with disloyalty. There was nothing, short of unconditional surrender, they could do about it.

Still, it was the second phase of the loyalty question, the Fenian issue, which most closely involved Anglin. The York election showed that connecting Fenianism with Anglin, Catholicism, and the Antis was a most efficacious technique for the Confederates, and they were not about to let the issue slip from public attention. The Confederates believed that Catholics had voted unanimously against Confederation in 1865 and they resolved that, should another election ensue, the Catholic vote would be offset by a greatly increased Protestant vote. One way of accomplishing this goal was to organize an anti-Catholic campaign which would appeal to religious and 'loyal' sympathies among Protestants. The key figure in this campaign was Anglin, and the made-to-measure issue was Fenianism.

Circumstances aided the Confederates. Early in December the Fenian menace began to assume large proportions. Lieutenant Governor Gordon prepared to 'ensure the security of the frontier,'[51] while in Saint John panic spread throughout the city.[52] The excitement, based merely on rumours, died down quickly enough, but Protestant forces were being marshalled, as George Ryan, a King's county politician saw:

I do not look for an election so soon as you predict yet everything appears to be working admirably[.] [T]his Fenian raid that is causing so much excitement now is no harm to our cause though the resignation of Anglin robs it of half its beauty.

I believe the time is not far distant where the contest at the polls will be Protestant and Catholic instead of formerly liberal and Tory ...*

---

* Uncatalogued Tilley Papers, Ryan to Tilley, 7 Dec. 1865. Gordon was aware of the anti-Catholic campaign building within New Brunswick and in several speeches made 'a strong protest against prejudices so pernicious to the harmony and well being of the province, and which I fear some parties for political objects and from selfish motives are not disinclined to foster' (see Lieutenant Governor's Letter Books, vol LXIII, Gordon to Cardwell, 18 Dec. 1865). For an example of the lack of impact these speeches had on the pro-Confederates, see *Religious Intelligencer*, quoted in *Freeman*, 20 Jan. 1866.

Anti-Anglin attacks became very widespread and were deftly connected with anti-Catholic and anti-government sentiments. The *Reporter* accused the Executive Council of holding meetings in Saint John because Anglin was nearby, thereby giving him 'a better opportunity of pulling the Government wires.'[53] The pattern had been formed. The Confederates charged Anglin with being a Fenian sympathizer and thus blackened all Catholics.[54] At the same time they accused Anglin of being the real power behind the anti-confederates and thus branded the government with disloyalty.[55]

It cannot be disguised that a large portion of the people have lost confidence in 'a class' of their fellow subjects, and this, mainly owing to the *disloyal* character of that portion of the press which has represented them; and the people have lost confidence in the Government to which they look for protection and defence, because they have no confidence in the party or press that mainly supports and defends the Government.*

Against the Confederates Anglin was forced to defend himself and his fellow Catholics. He did this not merely for personal and religious reasons, but also on political grounds, for he detected the purpose of the Confederates' tactics.

The Confederate party despair of winning by any means that could be deemed honourable. They have almost abandoned argument, and for some time past their papers have laboured with all their might to create in the Protestant portion of the population a suspicion and dislike of the Catholic portion ... If those persons could establish a Protestant party as they try to do, and get all Protestants to join it, and to follow the Confederate leaders blindly, the whole fight would be fought, and a Confederation victory would be inevitable.[56]

Anglin's defence was multifaceted. He asserted Catholic loyalty:

The Catholics who have chosen this Province as their home regard it as truly their country, in whose welfare they are as deeply interested as any other class of its inhabitants. They have done as much as any others to develop its resources, promote its prosperity and increase its wealth. In attachment to its free institutions, in ready and cheerful obedience to its wise, equitable and beneficient laws, and in

* Quoted in *Freeman*, 24 March 1866. Not all Protestants accepted the equation that the Catholics and their lay leader were disloyal. On New Year's Day 1866 a number of Anglin's Protestant supporters presented him with a gold watch and chain as a token of their esteem (ibid, 4 Jan. 1866).

honest and faithful allegiance to its Government, they yield to no class of Her Majesty's subjects. A better form of government they could not desire, and even if no higher or better motives influenced them, they assuredly would be as ready as others to protect the property which many of them have acquired by many years of incessant toil and strict frugality. Irish Catholics, *semper et ubique fideles*, are loyal in this Province, for the best of all reasons – because loyalty here is reason and justice and common sense; is love of liberty and of independence, and the French Catholics are quite as loyal as the Irish.*

Anglin denied that a Catholic party existed in New Brunswick, as the *Intelligencer* had charged, for, he stated, 'there is no reason why there should be either a Catholic party or a Protestant party in this happy country, where all churches and denominations are equal in the eye of the law.'[57] He maintained that he never had attempted to dictate to the government and he rejected the idea that Catholics controlled it. He scorned the suggestion that the votes of Catholics were monopolized by the clergy from the altar.[58] The reason for the strong Catholic vote for the Antis at the last election, Anglin asserted, had not been religion but the fact that 'the majority of them, like the majority of the whole people, believed the Quebec Scheme would ruin the Province ...'[59] He denied that the Fenians posed a serious threat, asserting that it was insulting to New Brunswick to suggest that it could not defend itself against 'unorganized rabble.'[60] In any case, Anglin protested, the Irish of New Brunswick should not be held responsible for actions of Irishmen outside the province.[61]

But even under extremely difficult circumstances Anglin did not reject his Irish background and sympathies. During his speech on Fisher's non-confidence amendment Anglin branded the Fenians as 'a mad and reckless

* *Freeman*, 12 Dec. 1865. Other Catholics felt as did Anglin. 'One Who Knows' wrote to the *Freeman* stating that 'if the Fenians do pay us a visit, it will be seen that Catholics will be amongst the foremost to repel them, or any foe ...' (ibid, 30 Dec. 1865). The Archbishop of Halifax also proclaimed Catholic loyalty, asserting that Catholics had nothing to gain from annexation to the United States and even less reason to support the Fenians, 'that pitiable knot of knaves and fools ...' 'From their success we have nothing to expect but bloodshed, rapine, and anarchy, and the overthrow of God's religion – for all this is inscribed in their banner' (see Lieutenant Governor's Letter Books, vol LXIII, Connolly to Gordon, enclosed in Gordon to Cardwell, 15 Jan. 1866). This letter was reprinted, after being toned down according to the Archbishop's request (see Correspondence of the Military Secretary of the Commander of the Forces: Fenian Correspondence, vol CLXXXVIA, Connolly to Gordon, telegram, 4 Jan. 1866), in many newspapers and as appendix II of T.D. McGee's *The Irish Position in British and Republican North America: A Letter to the Editors of the Irish Press Irrespective of Party* (Montreal, 1866).

body of men, who did not know what they were about, and with them he had no sympathy ...' But he also talked about the Irish homeland of his youth, and his sentiments indicate one reason for Anglin's prominence among the Irish community of New Brunswick. With much feeling he recalled the horrible scenes the Great Famine had brought to his native village:

... now a child expired in its mother's arms, then a woman; and again, a strong man, worn away to a skeleton, departed. When he looked back and saw these groups, sitting on a lock of straw, with nothing but tattered rags to protect them from the winds of heaven, he would be less than a man and an Irishman, to speak harshly of the men who took steps which they believed would remedy this state of things ... The Fenian party knew little or nothing of these things, and could not remedy them, if they now existed.

More than once during this part of the speech Anglin's emotions overcame him and 'he had to suspend his language, while the falling of a pin might have been heard in the remotest corner of the building.'[62] The occasions when complete silence descended upon the New Brunswick Assembly were rare and precious. Anglin had had his moment. But it might have been more politic to avoid the topic of Ireland, for such an open statement of his beliefs and feelings could be manipulated by his opponents.* Indeed, they continued to pound away at his alleged Fenian sympathies and connections during the election campaign that followed the fall of the government.

III

The Antis started the election campaign at a great disadvantage. While the anti-Confederates had been wrestling Gordon for control of the helm of the New Brunswick ship of state, the Confederates had taken over the engine

* There is some confusion whether Anglin was talking about Fenians or Young Irelanders when he said he could not speak harshly about them. The official *Debates* suggest that he was referring to Fenians (see *Assembly Debates, 1866*, p 105 [7 Apr.]), and the *Telegraph* was of the same opinion (see *Telegraph*, 22 May 1866). The *Globe*'s account, which the *Freeman* copied, indicates that he was talking about the Young Irelanders (see *Freeman*, 12 Apr. 1866). It would seem highly unlikely that Anglin would have committed political suicide by voicing sympathy for the Fenians. In later years he denied ever saying 'that he could not find it in his heart to say anything against the Fenians' (see *Freeman*, 19 Aug. 1882). In the report of Anglin's speech the official reporter, J. Marche, apologized for failing to do justice to Anglin's speech (see *Assembly Debates, 1866*, p 101).

room. In September and October 1865, for example, the Confederates had re-adjusted the balance of the electorate in Saint John. The *Freeman* stated that 118 had been disfranchised and another 178 had gained the vote for the first time.[63] Thus by the time the House dissolved in 1866, the Confederates had little to fear. Because they had formed the Executive Council at the time of dissolution, they were able to time the elections to suit themselves.[64] Tilley expected a hard fight but, he confided to Macdonald, 'the Election in this Province can be made certain if the *means* are used.'[65] Macdonald made sure that 'the monies' were available for Tilley and his associates.[66] For their part the Antis received only a small amount of outside financial aid from their allies in Nova Scotia.[67] The Confederates also managed to overcome a problem they had faced in the 1865 elections. Then the Quebec scheme had hindered rather than aided them. In 1866 they began to talk about terms better than the Quebec plan, in spite of Macdonald's stricture on this point.[68] They also avoided another difficulty in which they had found themselves when the plan was first announced – that is, the right of the people to vote on such an important change in the constitution. Mitchell promised that the new union plan would be submitted to the people.[69] Anglin was scornful of these promises. They were 'chaff by which wise birds will not be caught.'[70] Of course, he was right, and the Confederates never did discharge their commitments. But the fact that the Confederates were not proclaiming the Quebec Resolutions as their scheme was an adroit political move on their part. All the Antis' criticisms of the Quebec plan were thus bypassed. Anglin and his allies had little to attack except the very vagueness of the program of the New Brunswick Confederates.[71]

The Confederates were not wholly responsible for their excellent electoral position. They received considerable aid from economic circumstances. New Brunswick as a whole had recovered from its depression in trade and this recovery brought the revenues of the province to almost exactly the same level in 1865 as in 1863. In other words, 1865 had been one of New Brunswick's better years. Unfortunately for the Antis, however, 1864 had been a phenomenally successful year, and thus it appeared that the economy was slipping.* The people of New Brunswick were therefore unhappy. The lucrative shipping trade caused by the Civil War had ended and capital was difficult to find. Many who felt that something had to be done to improve the economic base of New Brunswick turned to Confeder-

---

* The New Brunswick revenues in 1863 had been $844,894.55; in 1864 $1,060,815.85; and in 1865 $840,390.21 (see *Assembly Journal, 1864*, p 150; *Assembly Journal, 1865*, p 150; and *Assembly Journal, 1866*, p 158).

ation in desperation. Aiding this change was the fact that Tilley was now favouring a low-tariff policy and claiming that a low tariff would be put into effect after union.[72] On more specific economic matters the anti-Confederates had been failures. As Anglin had prophesied, the Western Extension project begun in November crawled along like a decrepit snail.[73] For a change railway policy became a secondary issue in New Brunswick politics as neither party was able to take advantage of the desire for the Western Extension. The Antis would garner no votes on this issue in 1866. Similarly the anti-Confederate government had obtained neither a renewal of the Reciprocity Treaty nor British North American free trade. In fact, about the only issue which Anglin and the other Antis could successfully exploit was the conduct of the Lieutenant Governor.[74] Time and again the *Freeman* complained of the unconstitutional actions of Gordon and tried to promote itself as the defender of responsible government. Indeed, Anglin attempted to turn this issue into the Antis' form of the loyalty issue. The Antis, he proclaimed, were the true loyalists, the defenders of the rights of New Brunswickers against subversion from outside. But in New Brunswick the pressure to conform had become too great. A subtle psychological change took place in New Brunswickers. Steadily, but non-rationally, a pattern formed in the minds of these colonials: Confederation began to mean loyalty to the Empire, prevention of annexation, and a new lease for the economic life of the province. They were not necessarily happy about Confederation but their resistance to such a change had run out. In 1866 they were willing to gamble, and the Confederates provided them with the opportunity.

Though other factors were important, loyalty was by far the most significant issue in the election of 1866. The loyalty cry in conjunction with the anti-Catholic campaign had begun long before the spring of 1866, but it was then that they became most intense and most effective, aided by an extremely fortuitous incident. At the very time that Gordon had forced the resignation of the anti-Confederate government, a number of Fenians gathered at the Maine border town of Eastport.[75] Nothing had materialized from the various Fenian scares during the winter,[76] yet in the first week of April a small band of O'Mahony Fenians, in spite of their earlier opposition to attacks on British North America, arrived on the New Brunswick border.* Under the leadership of B. Doran Killian, the Fenians wandered

---

* What had happened was that in February 1866 *habeas corpus* had been suspended in Ireland. It was 1848 all over again. All suspected persons were incarcerated. For the time being, at least, it seemed unlikely that there would be any effective Fenian movements in Ireland. This chain of events caused the prestige of the Sweeny faction to rise in the United

along the frontier, came to Calais, and made a comic-opera attack on Indian Island before they gave up and dispersed.[77] While they had done virtually no military damage, they nearly wiped out the anti-Confederates' chances of electoral success. The Fenians had spoken against Confederation, releasing the following statement to the citizens of New Brunswick:

Republican institutions have become a necessity to the peace and prosperity of your Province. English policy, represented in the obnoxious project of Confederation, is making its last efforts to bind you in effete forms of Monarchism.[78]

Anglin did not appreciate this 'help' from the Fenians. He urged New Brunswickers to be prepared to give the raiders 'so warm a reception, if they dare to desecrate our soil, that those who escape shall never want to come to New Brunswick again,'[79] but he doubted that they were serious about attacking the province. The Fenians, he noted, talked loud and often, in contradiction to the rapidity and secrecy of action which would have characterized a real movement. Indeed, what sense did the Fenian activity make, Anglin asked, unless the agitators were serving some political object.

The movements of the Fenians on our frontier are quite inexplicable. The O'Mahony Fenians repudiated the idea of invading the Provinces, and ridiculed the proposition made by General Sweeny; yet we find that the small bands now collected at Eastport and the neighborhood belong to that faction and that they are under the immediate control of the redoubtable B.D. Killian himself, once an

---

States; this, in turn, caused the O'Mahony branch, urged on by B.D. Killian, to take up the idea of an attack on New Brunswick. It was, however, to be a raid, a diversion, which they hoped would lead to an Anglo-American war. O'Mahony may have felt it was worth trying on those grounds (see L. Winkler, 'The Fenian Movement and Anglo-American Diplomacy in the Reconstruction Period,' unpublished Master's dissertation, New York University, 1936, p 36; and D. Ryan, *The Fenian Chief: A Biography of James Stephens* [Dublin, 1967], pp 236–7). It is possible, however, that O'Mahony did not approve of the raid, which may have been merely a Killian caper. After the raid O'Mahony dismissed Killian from his post of financial secretary of the brotherhood 'for disobedience of orders, and for inaugurating movements calculated to injure and defeat the Brotherhood' (see *The Irish American* [New York], 19 May 1866). See also Macdonald Papers, vol. LVII, Lord Monck to Macdonald, 16 Apr. 1866; and Drafts of Secret and Confidential Despatches ... , vol I, Archibald to the Earl of Clarendon, 17 Apr. 1866. Gordon estimated the number of Fenian raiders at between 2,000 and 3,000 (see Lieutenant Governor's Letter Books, vol LXIII, Gordon to General Doyle, 22 Dec. 1865); H.A. Davis thinks this estimate about five times too high (see H.A. Davis, 'The Fenian Raid on New Brunswick,' CHR, XXXVI [1955], 322).

intimate friend of the Hon. T.D. McGee and his associate in the management of the *American Celt*, a rabid anti-British journal, now the right-hand man of O'Mahony and some time ago accused of furnishing information to the Canadian Government for a consideration.[80]

Killian, the *Freeman* stated, 'could not have said anything better suited to the purposes of the Canadian party' and for his pains had probably received due recompense from the Confederates.[81]

If those Fenians are on the frontier to do the work of any party in this Province, is it not natural that they would say and do what the party whom they sought to assist wished and directed, or at least what would be best calculated to help that party?[82]

The conclusion Anglin drew was clear. Killian was doing the work of the Confederates, who 'in all probability' had 'a full knowledge of what he is doing.'[83] The raiders and the Confederates were mutually dependent, the *Freeman* charged, for without the assistance of the Fenians the Confederates in New Brunswick 'know they can do nothing.'[84] In Anglin's mind this Fenian agitation was possibly connected with Thomas D'Arcy McGee; after all, Killian had once worked for McGee.[85] McGee's knowledge of and contact with the Fenian Society were considerable. Then, too, he was a strong advocate of Confederation and a proponent of the 'new nationality.' Surely, Anglin thought, both the motive and the opportunity resided with McGee.*

* Anglin found support for this view in the Boston *Herald* (see *Freeman*, 3 May 1866). From the evidence available there is nothing to substantiate Anglin's charges that the Confederates, either in Canada or in New Brunswick, were connected with the Fenian agitation. Yet it is not entirely impossible. Brotherhood leaders were always being accused by members of the society of selling secrets and services, and the organization itself was always low in funds because of the extravagance of its leaders. This writer thinks it most unlikely that Anglin's accusations are correct. If the Fenians were sincere in opposing Confederation, their action was completely foolish. It is likely, however, that these Fenians really did not care one way or the other about Confederation. Their raid on New Brunswick was probably an effort to win support for the O'Mahony faction. As for McGee, every student of Canadian history has heard of his courageous stand against Fenianism – a stand that probably cost him his life. O'Mahony, in his anger at Killian, suspected that his lieutenant was in league with McGee, but this is inadequate and highly suspect evidence (see Drafts of Secret and Confidential Despatches ..., vol I, Archibald to Clarendon, 17 Apr. 1866). It is beyond the realm of imagination that McGee could have had enough duplicity to have carried out such a program while writing and speaking so vehemently against the brotherhood. Two excellent examples of his private convictions,

Anglin's accusations were disreputable for they were based on suspicion, not fact. Nevertheless one can understand why he would have had such suspicions. His experience had led him to think that there was nothing to which the Confederates would not resort. Also, like the Confederates, Anglin was fighting a political war. Consciously or subconsciously he was striving to find something to improve the bad situation the Antis faced. What he came up with, in effect, was his own disloyalty cry against the Confederates. In addition, it was not easy for Anglin to accept the abuse he was receiving without striking back. Along with the usual sort of name-calling, the most persistent charge of the Confederate newspapers was that Anglin was in league with the Fenians, at least by association.[86] He repudiated such accusations and insinuations.[87] As far as Anglin was concerned, the Confederates were out simply to discredit his name, to set Protestant against Catholic, and to brand Catholics with disloyalty – all for the political goal of carrying Confederation. But he was unable to change many minds. The Confederate campaign was working. 'I have noticed lately,' wrote one of Tilley's correspondents, 'a most determined and bitter hostility by every Roman Catholic voter.'

This I ascribe, whether justly or not, to the Fenian Sympathy. This hostility you know is capable of becoming very formidable, and I believe now, that the Confederates, may make up their minds to encounter an almost unanimous Catholic Vote against them. In fact, the obstinacy and prejudice of some, and the interested motives of others, will constitute an opposition, which the friends and supporters of the measures, would scarcely believe to exist.[88]

A side issue of the Confederates' electioneering was an attempt both to have their cake and to eat it. At the very time they were running a campaign characterized by a strong anti-Catholic flavour, they were quietly appealing to the Catholic hierarchy for support – and getting it! Bishop Edward Horan of Kingston and Archbishop Connolly took pains to modify Bishop Sweeny's position.[89] Under such pressure it was likely that Sweeny would keep his opinions, if they remained unchanged, to himself. Also attempts were apparently made to use the priests to promote Confederation amongst the Acadians, but to little avail.[90] Finally Bishop Rogers of Chatham came out in favour of Confederation in public letters.[91] Anglin ridiculed Rogers's

---

which departed in no way from his public views, are found in James Moylan Papers, McGee to Moylan, 27 Oct. 1865; and Charles Murphy Papers, McGee to A.M. Sullivan (editor of the Dublin *Nation*), 25 June 1866.

arguments, and thus started a lengthy paper war between Anglin and the bishop which lasted until the elections were over.[92] Their debate did little credit to either man but did show most clearly that Catholic political views in New Brunswick were not monolithic.[93] It also demonstrated that, while in most of New Brunswick the Confederates were arousing anti-Catholic sentiment, in the eastern counties, where the Catholics were the largest religious group, the Confederates were trying to win them over.[94]

Very little went well for Anglin in the 1866 election campaign. He was criticized and vilified, and made the butt of sarcasm and scorn. Despite all this he fought vigorously, if little less vituperatively than his opponents, for what he thought right. In speeches in Northumberland, Kent, and Saint John and in the pages of the *Freeman* Anglin waged the battle. Time and again he pointed out what the Confederates were doing.

The policy of the Confederate party of late seems to be to insult the Catholics of the Province in every imaginable way. They pretend to regard them all or nearly all as Fenians ready to join in any treasonable attempts to overthrow British supremacy in the Provinces ... [T]hey resort to insinuations well calculated to poison the minds of those who do not know what manner of men they are.[95]

He accused the Confederates of being 'a set of unscrupulous partizans, who themselves have neither religion, honour, nor honesty, who strive to trade in the strong religious feelings and prejudices of others, and to destroy the confidence and good will which, fortunately for the Province, exists between Catholics and Protestants ...'[96] Anglin's apprehensions, though exaggerated, no doubt partly for political purposes, were not imaginary. Various newspapers were running an anti-Catholic campaign in the service of the Confederates. The *Religious Intelligencer*, for instance, stated that 'the vehement opposition to this measure [Confederation] by the Catholic party in New Brunswick the ''Sons of Liberty'' in Canada and the Fenian Brotherhood in the United States, is beginning to be pretty well understood, and is having the effect of waking up the loyal feeling of the people of the Provinces.'[97] By the eve of the elections the *Intelligencer* had come so far in this line of thought that it had a simple solution to the Fenian difficulties.

Whether we shall be overrun and ultimately swallowed up by Fenianism, is more to be decided by the loyal electors of the Province with their ballots at the polls, than by the volunteers who are doing duty in arms on the border, to defend our homes and our lives.[98]

All Anglin's efforts to combat this line of attack failed. In the year since the last election self-satisfaction had given way to fear and anxiety among the inhabitants of the province. New Brunswickers honestly, if irrationally, felt that in voting for Tilley and the Confederates, and against Anglin and the Antis, they were showing their loyalty and saving the country from those who wished to destroy British rule. They scarcely stopped to concern themselves with the policy of Confederation. By 1866 the pressure applied by the Colonial Office had combined with the Fenian scare to make New Brunswickers willing to accept Confederation. They were loyal subjects and wanted to prove it. The Confederates were willing to take advantage of this feeling of loyalty, despite the fact that such a campaign would revive religious and ethnic antagonisms in New Brunswick.

The Confederate campaign was extremely successful. The Fenian raid on Canada at the beginning of June considerably aided the Confederates in New Brunswick and combined with a plethora of other issues to swamp the anti-Confederates. The forces led by Tilley swept into power, winning thirty-three of the forty-one seats in the House of Assembly.[99] In only three counties, all with a large Acadian population, were Antis victorious.[100] Anglin himself lost his seat. His old antagonist, the *Religious Intelligencer*, hailed the Confederate victory as that of 'loyal Protestants and British sentiment which had been so nobly declared at the polls ...'[101] For the *Telegraph* the election meant that 'Fenianism and Annexation, or, in one word, Warren-Anglinism was "taken in and done for," and the disloyal Fenian sympathizing brood fairly squelched.'[102] Anglin thought otherwise. From his point of view 'the conspirators' had won.

IV

Anglin and everyone else knew that the struggle for Confederation was very significant. In retrospect we can see that it had an importance which contemporary observers could not have realized. Without New Brunswick the Atlantic provinces would never have accepted Confederation. Had this union been postponed in the mid-1860s, it might have been postponed indefinitely. What this would have led to remains a matter of speculation, but it is clear that the acceptance of Confederation in New Brunswick is one of the important landmarks in the history of the Canadian nation. It also tells us something about the bases on which Confederation was founded – something of the historical identity of the Canadian nation.

One can wax moralistic about the struggle for Confederation in New

Brunswick, as Anglin certainly did. It was true that the anti-Confederate government had been ill-treated. From the Colonial Office had emanated the desire to defeat the Antis in order that the issue of Confederation might be carried. The means used to promote this end can hardly be deemed acceptable in a system of responsible government. Lieutenant Governor Gordon, too, violated its spirit, not just in April 1866, but right from the beginning, when he informed the government that, as soon as the opportunity presented itself, he would dismiss the administration, even if it held a majority in the Assembly. It was also true that the victorious Confederates used dishonourable means, arousing men's prejudices and passions against their fellow-citizens. Honest men were labelled traitors and an entire ethnic group was singled out as enemies of the majority within New Brunswick. Nor was the anti-Confederate campaign totally fair or honourable. The tactics used in New Brunswick in the political struggle on behalf of Confederation make one wonder whether Anglin was correct in contending that union at this time was premature.

Indeed, in his original criticism of Confederation Anglin had been correct on many counts. By no stretch of the imagination was Canada a unified country until at least thirty years after Confederation. It was not railways that made Canada a cohesive entity, but population, and it took many years for the new country to fill in the vast stretches of unpopulated land between the settled sections. Canada very nearly did not maintain an independent existence, and at times Anglin's fear that a premature union might preclude a solid British North American union in the future seemed to be well based. Especially during the 1880s it appeared that Canada might disintegrate and be annexed by the United States. Fortunately this did not happen. But would not such a possibility have been even more remote had the imperial connection been maintained as it had existed before Confederation? Anglin was correct in his belief that the imperial organization was the best protection that British North America could obtain. Of course, had the provinces not accepted Confederation, Britain might have refused to defend British North America, but such action on the part of Britain would have been most unlikely. In his belief that the acceptance of Confederation was simply playing into the hands of the Manchester School Anglin was again largely correct. No less a person thatn A.T. Galt was forced to agree with Anglin's assertion that Confederation would do little to preserve the British connection.

I am more than ever disappointed at the tone of feeling here as to the Colonies. I cannot shut my eyes to the fact that they want to get rid of us. They have a servile fear of the United States and would rather give us up than defend us, or incur the risk of war with that country. Day by Day I am more oppressed with the sense of responsibility of maintaining a connection undesired here and which exposes us to such peril at home ... But I doubt much whether Confederation will save us from Annexation.[103]

Even in his assertion that the people had the right to pronounce upon any contemplated change in the constitution of the country Anglin could hardly be called wrong. His was the voice of the future, whereas the belief that only parliament need be consulted on such an important issue was the voice of the past.

Yet Anglin was not completely right. His Irish background had given him a fear of union which made him set preconditions which it would have been virtually impossible to meet. He did not recognize the advantages that union would bring. He did not see, for instance, that within Confederation New Brunswick would have a partial insurance policy against the economic disasters that struck periodically. Perhaps the greatest weakness of Anglin's argument was his suggestion that the time for union had not arrived. If he supported the concept of union, as he claimed he did, he ought to have seen that at no point in time would conditions for union be perfect.

In the end Anglin accepted the defeat of 1866.[104] He saw that further struggle would be in vain, and in the period between the New Brunswick election and 1 July 1867 the *Freeman*'s campaign against Confederation was half-hearted.* Anglin realized that it was futile to hope that Confederation could be prevented. He suspected that the London Conference would merely 'harmonize the [Quebec] Scheme with the views of the representatives of the Maritime Provinces, and yet not alter or modify anything ...'[105] While this was not exactly what happened, it is a reasonable generalization of what did.[106] Resignedly and unhappily Anglin resolved to accept Confederation. New Brunswick had, in Anglin's view, expired. The *Freeman* gave it a decent burial:

Died, – at her late residence in the City of Fredericton, on the 20th day of May last, from the effects of an accident which she received in April, 1866, and which she bore with a patient resignation to the will of Providence, the Province of New Brunswick, in the 83rd year of her age.[107]

* Anglin did suggest to Smith that he write to Lord Carnarvon 'setting forth the means and agencies employed at the last Election ...' (see Joseph Howe Papers, vol IV, Smith to Howe, 6 Nov. 1866).

Anglin's acceptance of Confederation was tempered by bitter memories, and he acknowledged the proclamation of the British North America Act with these in mind.

Yesterday at 12 o'clock, noon, we became Canadians, by Act of Parliament.
Let us be *duly* thankful.
For the people, the good they were promised or the evil with which they were threatened, are all yet in the immediate future.
For the politicians, the elysium for which they longed was opened weeks ago.*

* *Freeman*, 2 July 1867. Anglin himself attended a ball in Fredericton on 1 July, although curiously he denied that it was a Confederation ball (see *Reporter*, 5 July 1867; *Freeman*, 11 July 1867).

8

Adjusting to the New Era
1867-72

For Anglin, as for the new Dominion of Canada, the years from 1867 to 1872 were a tremendously important formative period. As D'Arcy McGee told the Montreal Literary Club in November 1867: 'It is usual to say of ourselves, Gentlemen, that we are entering on a new era. It may be so, or it may be only the mirage of an era painted on an exhalation of self-opinion.'[1] The early years of Confederation required a good deal of readjustment by many people, none more so than Anglin. Not only did the new régime demand from all Maritimers comparatively more of this adaptation than from the residents of the old province of Canada, but Anglin had been an anti-Confederate as well. He had resolved to accept the situation, but it remained to be seen exactly what he meant by this. Certainly he was suspect to the Confederates of New Brunswick. In addition, Irish Catholics were in great public disfavour in British North America – even greater than usual – as a result of the Fenian disturbances. Readjustment there would have to be.

Anglin had many questions which demanded an answer. What position was Canada to occupy in the North Atlantic world? Would she in fact be able to expand from sea to sea? What role would New Brunswick and Saint John play in the Dominion? What was to be the basis of political organization and how would parties develop? What was to be the part played by the Irish Catholic community in British North America? What role was Anglin himself to play in the events which alone could give the real answer to these questions? In short, the first years of Confederation were another period of acclimatization for Anglin. He had adjusted from his Irish homeland to

New Brunswick during the 1850s. Now he had to adapt again, for from his perspective New Brunswick had died in 1867.

By 1872 it was clear that Anglin had gone a long way in accommodating himself to the new nation. His Canadianization was important for he thereby assisted two subcultures – the Irish Catholic community and New Brunswick – to operate within the Canadian political system. The story of Anglin's adjustment to the new régime also demonstrates something that is too infrequently acknowledged in this age of considering Canada's first century as a tragic flight from centralization – that is, that the new nation did indeed have the power to co-opt individuals, including one of the most important opponents of Confederation.

I

The first indication that Anglin was willing to modify his viewpoint in response to the new Canadian scene was his decision to become a candidate in the 1867 general election. Since his defeat in 1866 Anglin had asserted that he had no intention of being forced into public life again.[2] In making such statements Anglin was no more disingenuous than the thousands of other politicians who have made similar pronouncements from time immemorial. Undoubtedly Anglin desired to remain in political life. The problem was to find a constituency which would elect him, for the 1866 débâcle showed that he could not count on Saint John. Fortuitously, at some time between his defeat and May of the following year the North Shore constituency of Gloucester had presented him with a requisition with many signatures, to stand for election. In June of 1867 it was announced that he had accepted the call.[3]

Anglin's political interest in Gloucester was long-standing. In 1860 an effort had been made by both Catholic bishops in New Brunswick to secure the Gloucester riding for Anglin. At that time, however, Bishop Rogers of Chatham had discovered that the local priests had their own favourites and he decided that 'it might be considered indelicate in me, a comparative stranger in the Province, to become too urgent in political matters so soon after my appointment.' He decided to work quietly on the matter.[4] Friends of Anglin in Gloucester apparently urged the editor of the *Freeman* to become a candidate, and there was a hint in the *Freeman* that Anglin would not be unwilling to be put forward.[5] Ultimately, of course, Anglin stood for election in Saint John in 1861. But the connection which had been established in Gloucester made Anglin's candidacy in 1867 not wholly unexpected.

The county of Gloucester was numerically dominated by Acadians. At first glance it may seem surprising that a constituency in which French-speaking Acadians made up two-thirds of the population would consider electing an English-speaking Irishman, even if he were a Catholic.[6] There were several factors involved. The Acadians had attempted to survive after the Expulsion of 1755 by avoiding 'civilization.' They had isolated themselves in fishing villages along the North Shore and in back-country communities in the interior. They had passively refused to play major roles in provincial politics or major commercial schemes. Such inactivity left a political vacuum in Gloucester which others filled – the Irishman, William End, being the most prominent in the pre-Confederation period. In the commercial world as well English-speaking entrepreneurs such as John Ferguson, Robert Young, and Kennedy F. Burns were very powerful. Even the Catholic priests were more likely to be Irish or French or québécois than Acadian. At the time of Confederation, therefore, the Acadians of Gloucester were a people dominated by non-Acadians. An incident which was reported in the *Freeman* of 8 September 1874 provides an insight into the totality of this domination. Apparently a man and woman had been brought before the courts on a murder charge and sentenced to death. Curiously enough they showed no perceptible emotion on hearing the verdict. Why? Neither understood English, and not a word had been translated for them even when the death sentence was passed.[7] Furthermore, in terms of actual voting power the Acadians in Gloucester may even have been outnumbered. They were, after all, poor and largely uneducated. In a constituency in which less than 15 per cent of the population were eligible to vote it seems likely that at least as many people who were English-speaking as French-speaking had the franchise.[8] Given these factors, it becomes less surprising that Anglin could find a political base in Gloucester.

This is not to say, however, that Anglin did not have some appeal to Acadian voters. He was, after all, a co-religionist, a prominent public figure, and a man whose views on Confederation had coincided with Acadian opinions. Moreover, Anglin and the *Freeman* had an acceptable record vis-à-vis Acadians. Anglin's attitude towards the Acadians was a combination of admiration, sympathy, and concern. What Anglin admired in the Acadians was their tenacity and peasant-like devoutness. 'The great and steady growth of the French population in this Province,' the *Freeman* stated, 'their piety, their simple, innocent lives, and their attachment to the place of their birth, and to their early associations, appear to mark them out as Providentially preserved and protected for some great purpose.'[9] But Anglin recognized that their struggle for survival was extremely difficult and that they suffered many injustices. He believed, for example, that 'to apply rigidly to them a set of rules framed for the other people of the country, is to deprive them of all rights in the name of right, and in the name of law to make them outlaws.'[10] But then, the *Freeman* claimed, for generations they had been regarded 'as absolutely having no right whatever,' and had been 'neglected, despised and almost forgotten by all but the priests who came to minister to their spiritual wants.'[11] This perception led Anglin to sympathize with and support Acadian efforts to improve their circumstances. Indeed, Anglin did more than give sympathy and support; he strongly urged Acadians to assert themselves. In spite of his view that the Acadians had a providential purpose to fulfil, Anglin feared that, unless they made a successful adjustment to modern society, they would be destroyed.

... for all who desire their welfare the great question now is how best to prepare them for a change that is inevitable; how to transform the whole condition of society, and yet preserve in full vigour all those virtues that form so large a part of their character. The change, to be in all respects beneficial, must proceed from within, as changes in a people effected by pressure from without, are always fraught with evil, even if they are good in the main. To save themselves from evil influences, the French in these Provinces must as soon as possible have their own merchants, professional men, and literati; they must extend their possession of the soil, acquire a proper knowledge of agriculture, and in a word take a position equal in all respects to the best. They can not remain a simple, primitive peasantry, – their retirement and seclusion are coming to an end; they must be ready to meet the world on equal terms, or they must eventually lose their distinct existence as a people.[12]

The irony is that in developing a more assertive, professionally led society better able to meet the challenges of a rapidly changing world, as Anglin urged, the Acadians eventually found that they no longer needed to rely upon outsiders, like Anglin himself, to represent their interests. Nevertheless in 1867 Anglin could be put forward as a friend of the Acadian people, a man who understood and sympathized with their problems and had some sense of the direction in which they should seek to move. Anglin's greatest problem was that, although he had been in favour of publishing a French version of the *Debates* of the New Brunswick Assembly,[13] he could not speak French.[14] This was no small obstacle, but it was not insurmountable as the election was to prove.

Becoming a candidate for Gloucester did not mean that Anglin had to change his political stance on most issues. For example, whether in

Gloucester or Saint John, he could say 'I told you so' to the Confederates as the economy of New Brunswick showed no substantial improvement during the year after the 1866 election had ensured Confederation.[15] He could also sustain a non-committal attitude towards the Canadian party system by proclaiming that the question of union had been fully settled and that former Antis were 'bound to do all we can to make it as beneficial or as little hurtful as possible.'[16] What the electors ought to demand, Anglin stated, were 'men who, while willing to work with any party (no matter what its appellation) that was disposed to do what was just and fair, would above all feel bound to guard the interests of this Province ...'[17] Thus, while Anglin did not trust the New Brunswick component of the Macdonald coalition government, he also immodestly replied, in response to a report circulated by the *News* and *Intelligencer*,[18] that he was 'by no means in unison with Mr. Brown or Mr. Howe and he may find it quite impossible to unite with either of them as leader of a political party.'[19]

There was one issue, however, that caused Anglin no little embarrassment. To become a Gloucester candidate it was imperative for him to change his position on the Intercolonial Railway route. Back in 1863 Anglin had favoured the Saint John valley route for the Intercolonial, should a line be built. But by 4 June 1867 the *Freeman* was suggesting that the North Shore representative who did not support the northeastern route would be 'a traitor to those who have trusted in him ...' Obviously, Anglin was willing to support the North Shore route if Gloucester elected him. In spite of charges of inconsistency, to which he failed to make wholly convincing replies, Anglin kept this commitment.[20] It was a necessary political manoeuvre because it was simply a *sine qua non* that every candidate for election support the rail route which would bring the most benefits to his particular constituency.

The campaign in Gloucester was not an easy one for Anglin. While he apparently had the support of local priests and some important men in the community, he had powerful opponents both within the riding (John Meahan and Robert Young, both victorious Anti candidates in the 1866 elections, and Senator Ferguson, the influential Bathurst lumber baron) and from outside (Archbishop Connolly and Peter Mitchell, the Smasher leader on the North Shore).[21] In spite of all the influence brought to bear against him, Anglin won a resounding victory, polling 1,061 votes to Meahan's 671.[22] The *Freeman* was jubilant:

The chief contest in this Province took place in the County of Gloucester, where the Privy Council and their partizans made the greatest conceivable efforts to defeat

Mr. Anglin. Nothing that could possibly be done was left undone; nothing that the most practised skill could divine was left untried. All that ledger influence could do: all that intimidation and bribery could do was done, and all served but to render the triumph of the people the more signal and glorious.[23]

It was indeed a glorious triumph. Basking in his success, and with his ears ringing from the applause of the crowds who had greeted him at Newcastle and Chatham, in Kent and Westmorland, and finally at the Saint John Railway station as he returned to his family, Anglin must have felt that the new Dominion would find a place for him – and perhaps he for it.[24]

II

As well as being the representative for Gloucester in the Canadian House of Commons, Anglin was still a prominent spokesman for the Irish Catholic community. In 1867 there were several Irish Catholic leaders in British North America. The most famous was Thomas D'Arcy McGee; the New Brunswick champion was Timothy Anglin. By this time the divergence of opinion between the two was firmly entrenched.[25] Among other things there was a significant difference in style between the two men. You could almost see this in their faces: McGee's bold eyes and rather surly thin mouth compared to Anglin's fleshy cheeks and lips and small eyes tucked away behind a pair of glasses. Anglin was more placid and confident, while McGee had an unsettled, almost haunted look. McGee was always the flamboyant actor in politics who could be carried to extremes by the virtuosity of his own performance. Anglin was more reserved, almost stolid, and it took a great deal to ruffle his feathers.* It was McGee who moved from place to place and from job to job throughout his life; Anglin who resided in Saint John editing the *Freeman* for a third of a century. It was McGee who had participated in the rebellion of 1848 and whose life was prematurely ended by an assassin's bullet in the streets of Ottawa; Anglin who never took part in any rebellion and died in his bed at the age of seventy-three. The difference in temperament accounts, in part at least, for the fact that there was little accommodation between them after McGee's speech in Saint John in the summer of 1863 – the speech which the *Freeman*

---

* Anglin's calm response to name-calling from Attorney General John M. Johnson in the 1864 session of the New Brunswick Assembly moved one assemblyman to comment, 'Who would have thought that an Irishman would stand so much and not show fight?' (*Freeman*, 8 March 1864; and *Daily Evening Globe* [Saint John], 4 March 1864).

had thoroughly dissected and destroyed. Then, and also after McGee's famous Wexford speech of 15 May 1865, Anglin had objected to what he considered McGee's slurs on the character of the American Irish.[26] What really angered McGee, however, were the insinuations and accusations in regard to the Fenian raid on New Brunswick which appeared in the *Freeman*. He wrote an angry letter demanding that Anglin prove or retract the charges:

Stand forth then, Mr. Anglin, and make good your words or eat them, or else stand convicted of slandering an absent man, for the sake of promoting your anti-union ends and purposes.[27]

Anglin could prove some things but could not, of course, demonstrate that McGee had been involved in the Eastport raid. His proof here was notable by its absence:

Mr. Killian's mission to Eastport rendered great services to the cause of Confederation, of which Mr. McGee is a prominent advocate. So far, whether by previous agreement or not, they worked together.[28]

In the days that followed the controversy continued heatedly, with the *Freeman* becoming almost slanderous.

He [McGee] became a politician without principle, willing to sell his talents to any party that chose to purchase, and trading in the influence which his eloquence and his previous history gave him amongst the Irishmen of Canada.[29]

It was obvious that there was no love lost between the two men.[30]

One of the most important issues over which Anglin and McGee differed, at least in approach, was the Fenian Society. McGee's way of dealing with the Fenians was to denounce them, publicly, vociferously and totally.[31] If he offended tender Irish Catholic sensibilities, that was unfortunate but could not be avoided. Anglin's approach was quite different. He felt that McGee was berating those he was attempting to influence and defaming his own countrymen,

sometimes by admitting with mock reluctance that they were almost as bad as their worst enemies described them; sometimes by impertinently advising them with an air of the greatest imaginable kindness and solicitude not unmixed with a large share of condescension not to do something or other which only their most bitter enemies ever imagined them capable of doing.[32]

Anglin gave McGee no credit for the prevention of the spread of Fenianism.

We believe that Mr. McGee did absolutely nothing to prevent the spread of Fenianism in Canada, because his language on that subject, uttered to please his patrons, was always calculated to irritate and provoke rather than to persuade. If Fenianism made little way amongst Irishmen in Canada it was we believe because their own good sense and their own knowledge of the duty they owed to the country of their adoption stood in the way ...[33]

Anglin, in contrast, took a rather more quiet approach. Appeal to a man's better nature and he was likely to respond favourably. Anglin certainly had no wish to promote Fenianism in British North America. Fenian attacks upon the British colonies were completely unjustified and 'ought to be resisted with all the force and energy of which we are capable ...'[34] But Anglin, as has been seen, had some sympathy with the ultimate goal of the Fenians, if not with the methods used. He attempted to assess the movement honestly, despite the fact that anyone who did not condemn the Fenians totally was immediately suspect.

The Fenians, however wrong and foolish their purposes may be, do not aim at wholesale robbery and plunder. They believe that English rule is ruinous to Ireland, and that a complete revolution is the only means by which Ireland can be made what she ought to be. To effect such a revolution the mass of the Fenians have proved that they are willing to make great pecuniary sacrifices, to grapple openly with one of the strongest powers of the world, and to expose themselves to almost certain destruction.[35]

Perhaps the arrest of his Fenian cousin, John Warren, in Ireland in the late spring of 1867 was one of the factors which made Anglin unwilling to denounce Fenianism in all places and at all times, although the *Freeman* expressed its regret that Warren's 'patriotism and devotion to a noble sentiment' should be 'so misdirected.'[36] The entire issue was one for which Anglin had to compartmentalize his attitudes: the Fenians were bad in and for British North America; outside that sphere they might not be the worst thing that had even happened to Ireland. It was unlikely that they would succeed in their foolish schemes in Ireland, but perhaps their efforts were better than doing nothing. Anglin's approach was different from that adopted by McGee; it also met with greater approval from the Irish Catholic population of the new Dominion.[37]

Both men undoubtedly realized that the other posed a threat to his position in the Irish community. Certainly it was to be expected that there would be a good deal of competition between them after 1 July 1867 for the leadership of the Irish Catholics throughout the Dominion. The contest promised to arouse some interest:

For it will be pleasant by and by to watch the meeting of Mr. McGee and Mr. Anglin on the floors of the Parliament Chamber. It will be an agreeable pastime, now and then, to see the Hon. little McGee intellectually spin round the Hon. large Anglin on his head, with his feet pointing toward the zenith.[38]

The 1867 session began in Ottawa early in November. No one who wanted to arrange for decent accommodations would think of arriving late, but then no one wanted to miss the opening of the first parliament of the new Dominion. On his way to the remote lumbering city of Ottawa Anglin paused in Montreal long enough to take in a concert sponsored by the St Patrick's Society of that city. This was no accident. The society had rejected McGee's leadership and had elected as president Bernard Devlin, McGee's opponent in the violent 1867 election.[39] Undoubtedly to snub McGee, invitations were sent to Anglin, Joseph Howe, and Patrick Power to attend the organization's annual concert. The usual time for the concert had even been changed in order to suit the convenience of the invited guests.[40] Not unnaturally the society expected more from its guests than their mere presence, although Anglin claimed to be unprepared to speak and seemed very halting and apologetic at the beginning of his address.[41] But as he went along what may have been mere nervousness disappeared and he warmed to the gathering. He told his audience about his political stance – no fixed party position but a willingness to give Confederation his best efforts. Then he told them something about the Irish Catholic community of New Brunswick – its trials and tribulations, the prejudices which it faced, and the way in which he believed these ought to be overcome.

The only way to meet this opposition is to live it down – to do what is right and leave it to time to satisfy the honest portion of our fellow-citizens that we are not what they believe and represent us to be, but that we are sincerely desirous to prove ourselves, in every private and public act, to be good citizens and subjects.

Anglin then presented what might be termed a political manifesto for the Irish Catholics of the new Dominion. It was not by hiding the fact that they were Irish that they would advance. They ought not to be ashamed of the old country nor its history. It would be by living as Irishmen ought to live that they would win the confidence of the rest of the people. Anglin pointed out that it was the Irish who did much of the work – a great deal of the hard work – which was promoting the economic growth of the country. He exhorted his fellows not to look to others for help, but to build themselves up. If they failed to rise to a position equal to others, it would be their own fault. The Irish must prove they were worthy. Anglin knew that this would not be easy under existing circumstances, but do it they must.

There never was a time in the history of the Irish people when their position was one of such exceeding difficulty as it is at the present moment. We are charged with being disloyal – with being traitors to our country. It is said we cannot be trusted, and though we enjoy the protection of this country and eat of its bread we are traitors at heart. You know that is a vile calumny – a lie. We know what we owe to the country … It is our duty to do what is right, and let us make up our mind to do it, and then we will receive the applause of the wise and good. We know the Government of this country is the most benign and just that ever existed, and we know that we owe to this Government unbounded and unqualified allegiance. We should therefore do our duty to our country, our fellow-citizens, and our families, and then take what comes as a matter of course.

It was an impressive speech. In appealing to the better instincts of his Irish listeners, it was fully in line with Anglin's practice of attempting to improve the Irish while fighting for their rights. It also indicated that Anglin would not hesitate to contest, even on McGee's own ground, the leadership of the Irish Catholic community.

In the Commons itself Anglin was not anxious to take a prominent role before he became thoroughly acquainted with procedures in the House.[42] McGee did not allow him this luxury. The debate on the throne speech, dominated by Nova Scotians, had nearly come to an end by 14 November. Early that evening, however, McGee rose in the House, and in a speech which even Anglin admitted contained 'some beautiful passages,' reviewed the situation in Nova Scotia at length, proceeded thence to New Brunswick in the course of which he attacked Anglin, though not by name, and concluded by making charges of Fenianism against a portion of the Montreal Irish.[43] He claimed, among other things, that at the concert which Howe and Anglin had attended in Montreal ten days before, the St Patrick's Society had honoured the names of several Fenian leaders.[44] The speech forced Anglin to his feet where he remained for an hour and a half answering McGee.[45] He dealt at length with the 'vile and infamous means' by which the Confederates had succeeded in New Brunswick. He spoke of many other issues as well, but perhaps most important was his defence of the Irish of New Brunswick and Montreal 'from the calumnies first insinuated and afterwards openly hurled at them by the member for Montreal West.' The speech, at least according to one source friendly to Anglin, created a considerable sensation and made the government unhappy with McGee, for Anglin's counter-attack produced a 'stronger anti-Confederate sentiment than anything yet said.'[46] In this first clash of the two Irish Catholics on the floor of the Commons Anglin had given as good as he had received. He might even claim a victory:

It might not be amiss to state that Mr. McGee, although the assailant, left the House some time after Mr. Anglin began his reply to him, and some were malicious enough to say he ran away.[47]

The St Patrick's Society of Montreal approved of Anglin's defence of the Irishmen of that city and passed a motion expressing its appreciation.[48] It then expelled McGee from membership in the organization, an action which Anglin felt compelled to explain to the press of New Brunswick.

It is because he has ... become the slanderer of his own race and people, and because he has so persistently calumniated the members of the St. Patrick's Society, that he has at length been expelled.[49]

Anglin's association with the Montreal Irish continued on St Patrick's Day 1868. Once again the St Patrick's Society invited Anglin to be its guest, and once again Anglin made a speech which met with the enthusiastic approval of his audience. As befitted the occasion, he emphasized the history and traditions of the homeland and boasted that, in spite of their trials, Irishmen had proved throughout the world that they 'cannot be subdued or exterminated.' Nor could he agree that Ireland's problems had been solved or were likely to be alleviated quickly:

... he would ask the vast audience of over three thousand assembled, if they were content with the condition of their countrymen? (Loud cries of 'No,' 'No,' from every part of the hall answered the question). Mr. Anglin said he trusted that emphatic reply would go across the Atlantic ... he considered the Irish would have to struggle a long time before changes could be made, so that the country will become what it ought to be.

Anglin went on to suggest that British politicians apply the Canadian model of responsible government to Ireland and concluded by urging 'all Irishmen to elevate themselves in the moral, social and intellectual scale ...'[50]

At this juncture it was apparent that Anglin had turned the tables on McGee and was taking issue with McGee on his home ground just as McGee had interfered politically with Anglin in New Brunswick in 1863–4. Not all Irishmen approved of Anglin's activity, of course; the *Canadian Freeman*, for example, denounced his involvement in and aggravation of the split within the Montreal Irish community.[51] But other English-language Catholic newspapers, from the very conservative Montreal *True Witness* to the rabid Irish nationalist paper the Toronto *Irish Canadian*, spoke favourably of the newcomer to Canadian politics.[52]

By 1868 Anglin and McGee did not agree on very many issues. But curiously enough it was on one of their rare notes of harmony that their volatile relationship ended. On 3 April Macdonald had proposed in the House that a section of the oath of allegiance for members of parliament which was obnoxious to Catholics be struck out. First, McGee expressed his gratification, and Anglin followed with similar sentiments.[53] Four days later McGee was dead.

The assassination of McGee placed Anglin in an incredibly difficult position. He had been making very harsh criticisms of the man who now lay dead. The criticisms had been made seriously: Anglin believed that McGee had been wrong in his whole approach and in his accusations. Anglin could not retract these honest beliefs. But there seemed to be little doubt that one or more Fenians had been responsible for the foul deed. Understandably, then, Anglin was reticent to talk or write about McGee personally. He tended to concentrate on other details of the tragedy, but there was no doubt about his horror, as his report to the *Freeman* showed.

The dreadful, the appalling crime of this morning is already known all over this Continent, and, perhaps, all over Europe and everywhere the blood of honest men runs cold as they hear of this most deliberate and most atrocious murder. It would be impossible to believe human nature so degraded, so debased to the level, not of the brute beasts, but of the fiends, did we not know that such crimes are too often perpetrated by fiends wearing the human form ... Mr. McGee frequently denounced Fenianism and the Fenians, in language certainly not too severe or too bitter, if applied to such ruffians as this cold-blooded assassin, who, it may be, found such denunciations a pretext for satisfying his thirst for human blood.

...

A few hours before, and the Commons of the Dominion listened to a Speech, which, although for the greater part a thrice told tale, commanded their attention, and now the brain then teeming with thought, richly stored with learning, and quickened by a genius rarely surpassed, is at rest, and the tongue, so eloquent, is silenced for ever.[54]

In the Commons that day Anglin was brief as he spoke on behalf of the Irish of New Brunswick and the Dominion. He acknowledged his embarrassment at the fact that the deed was undoubtedly the work of an organization of Irishmen – not, he trusted, of Irishmen belonging to the Dominion.

It is an outrage that will probably have a great effect on the future of this country. None of us can realize its effects yet. The shock is too recent, and some of us can on this occasion give vent to the feelings which overmaster us. Perhaps, after all, this is the highest tribute which we can pay to the man who has gone from amongst us.[55]

Anglin must have prayed that it had not been his words of denunciation of McGee that had triggered the deranged mind of the assassin. At the same time the words he had written three months before in the *Freeman* must have come back to him: 'Fenianism continues to be one of the most puzzling, tantalising, troublesome, and unintelligible of combinations.'[56] Perhaps he even began to question whether he ought to have been so sanguine about the contentedness and stability of the Canadian Irish. With McGee's death the entire Irish Catholic community came into disrepute, and Anglin himself was again accused of treating Fenianism too lightly.[57] But even in these days Anglin betrayed neither his principles nor the Irish community he led. He was one of the courageous few who questioned the treatment which Whelan, the accused murderer, received in the name of justice.[58]

The death of McGee was an important watershed in Anglin's career. While McGee was alive, Anglin had an undoubtedly able opponent. Had he lived, it seems probable that McGee would have been a means by which Anglin might have risen to greater prominence than he did. There were already good indications that Irish Catholics throughout the Dominion were beginning to look upon Anglin with favour, while McGee was in growing disrepute. The spectacle of two talented Irish Catholics continuing to battle from opposite sides of the House of Commons would certainly have given Anglin greater publicity than he received after McGee's death.

Irish Catholics, finding themselves in disgrace, reacted to McGee's death by withdrawing from politics. From 1868 to 1872 there were few occasions when the Irish Catholic community of Canada was involved in politics as a distinct group. This change was acceptable to Anglin for, as he had stated in Montreal and elsewhere, he believed that Irish Catholic politics ought not to be isolated from the mainstream of political activity. But he always maintained that, while the Irish were 'living down' their reputation, the rest of the community had to stop discriminating against them. Anglin continued to appeal for ethnic and religious tolerance in the new Dominion.

If this Dominion is ever to be as great, and strong, and powerful as its founders anticipate ... all these old-world feuds must be forgotten, and all its people must work together harmoniously to promote its prosperity and consolidate its strength, no sect, or denomination, or association seeking to degrade, to pull down or keep down any other, but each working earnestly and zealously for the elevation and aggrandisement of all.[59]

The *Freeman* was convinced that Irish Catholics did not receive this kind of justice in Canada. The aftermath of the Fenian raids,* the suspension of *habeas corpus* in 1867, the imprisonment of Irishmen after McGee's murder for months on end without their being charged or brought to trial, the systematic exclusion of Irish Catholics from office, and the ill-treatment meted out to those Irishmen who tried to work their way into positions of influence – all showed to the *Freeman* that discrimination existed.[60] On such issues Anglin was willing to speak out. Still, he saw no need to undertake an aggressive campaign for Irish Catholic rights. Indeed, the half-decade after the assassination of McGee produced little evidence to dispute Anglin's belief that, through effort and right living the Irish would eventually achieve a reasonable position in Canadian life. Thus, while Anglin thought the condition of Irish Catholics in Canada far from perfect, he believed it was improving and at least was better than the situation in the United States.[61] In his role as an Irish Catholic spokesman Anglin found little cause to be unhappy with Confederation. But then he had never opposed Confederation because he thought it would be bad for the Irish Catholic community in particular.

---

* The case of Father McMahon, a Catholic priest who had been imprisoned after the Fenian raid of 1866 although the evidence against him had not been conclusive, brought Anglin to his feet in the House of Commons in 1869 to put forward the Irish Catholic point of view. In spite of the fact that he feared his remarks would be misrepresented and bring abuse upon his head, he considered it to be his duty as an Irish Catholic spokesman to speak out (see 'T.W.A.,' 7 May 1869, in *Freeman*, 13 May 1869).

III

The main reason for Anglin's opposition to Confederation had been his fears about what would happen to New Brunswick. Developments between 1867 and 1872 showed that he had been a true prophet on many counts. Even the first session of parliament showed the New Brunswick representatives what it meant to be a small minority in the Commons. With the exception of Tilley, who sided with the government, and three absent members, all of the New Brunswick representatives voted against placing a duty on imported flour.[62] Their action was to no avail; the duty was accepted. In the sessions which followed New Brunswick found the 1867–8 example of the flour tariff repeated time and again. The position of the spokesmen of the Lower Provinces became painfully obvious.

Sometimes for days together a stranger would hear nothing to induce him to suspect that the Lower Provinces have lately been united to the Upper ... It is easy to observe that when the case of the Lower Provinces is brought up, those who speak of it are endured as if it were a great effort of courtesy – not to listen to them, for few do listen – but to allow them to speak. The true business of Parliament, the great majority seem to think is whatever relates more especially to the Upper and greater Provinces, in the present, the future or the past.[63]

Anglin fought a rearguard action throughout the session, acting as a financial watchdog. He was a most conscientious parliamentarian and earned the $1157.40 he received for his work and travelling expenses during the lengthy first session.[64] There was another reason for Anglin's faithful attendance in the Commons. It would have been rather difficult for 'T.W.A.' to send to the *Freeman* his daily reports of proceedings in the House had its author not been present. Still, other legislators did not always take their duties as seriously as Anglin, as the following account of the Committee of the Whole indicates:

Some half a dozen or a dozen members gather around the clerk's table, and the clauses of the bill are passed one by one in rapid succession; while the rest of the members, who have not escaped to the saloon, amuse themselves in various ways, somewhat after the manner of irrepressible school boys in the absence of the teacher. Some few, more staid and sober than the rest, settle down in their seats in the hope that they may be allowed to pen a letter or perchance read an article in their local paper. Unfortunate man! vain hope! A huge paper ball, thrown from some skilful hand in the rear, scatters pen, ink and paper in rude confusion over the desk, while a seat cushion or a formidable blue book from another quarter comes thundering down upon the worthy member's head, sending his ideas in a hurly burly race after his writing material, and arousing within him the spirit of retaliation. And thus the sport commences. Paper balls, blue books, bills, private and public, cushions, hats and caps of all styles, are brought into requisition, and are sent whirling through the room in every direction.[65]

There is no question that New Brunswick, especially the Saint John valley, had a difficult time in these years, in part because the province never fully recovered from the depression caused by the end of the Civil War,* and in part because changing technology was rendering the wooden shipbuilding industry obsolete. Some of Saint John's problems were caused by the selection of the North Shore route for the Intercolonial Railway, although the virtual completion of the Western Extension in 1869 offset this to some extent.[66] Confederation itself contributed to New Brunswick's economic problems. The tariff on food stuffs, for example, was particularly hard on the province.[67] Not surprisingly, disillusionment with Confederation set in rapidly.[68] New Brunswickers had been led to believe that union would solve their economic problems; obviously it did not. Unhappiness with Confederation reached a peak in New Brunswick in 1870 and 1871, even many of the Confederate journals voicing discontent.[69] Anglin's reaction was rather interesting. He did not agree with those who blamed the Upper Canadians directly. He claimed that it was not that they wished to harm the Lower Provinces or to do them an injustice, but simply that the Maritimes did not have the political power to protect their interests against the influence of Ontario.[70] He also rejected the theory, which some New Brunswick papers proposed, that the province's difficulties were the result of bad administration. Anglin was sure that they were inherent in Confederation itself: a change of the men in power would make little difference.[71] What could be done about this situation? Was repeal of the union the solution? What about annexation to the United States? These were two possibilities that were being talked about. Anglin supported neither.[72] Having committed himself to give Confederation and the new administration a fair trial, he was not going to be accused of obstruction:

---

* Emigration from New Brunswick was the most notable indication of these conditions (see *Freeman*, 12 Oct. 1867). The population of Saint John in 1871 was only 1,500 higher than it had been in 1861 (see *Canada: Census, 1870–71*, 1, 428).

If Confederation fail, it will not be through any fault of Mr. Anglin's. If those who took this Province into Confederation are to be relieved in any degree from the responsibility that they owe the people, it shall not be by any act of his.[73]

On the other hand he felt there was no virtue in ignoring conditions:

It is much wiser and more manly to take the facts and circumstances as they are, weigh and understand them thoroughly, discover if possible what is best to be done, and then set to work earnestly and resolutely to do it.[74]

The *Freeman* offered no solutions to the existing problems. Perhaps irresponsibly, but understandably, Anglin considered that such solutions should come from those who had brought New Brunswick to such a pass – the Confederates. He preached a doctrine of quietism, at least for the moment, partly to give union an honest and reasonable trial. But, after all, he was down on record as saying that New Brunswick would not prosper under Confederation; events were proving him correct and he was enjoying saying 'I told you so.'[75] The people had chosen badly but they had chosen, and they would have to pay the penalty. There was no going back now.

It is no use to wriggle under the yoke which they must carry, or to believe that any change in its adjustment can make it very much less burdensome or less galling.[76]

Anglin found another reason for accepting the new federal government at Ottawa: he could place no faith or hope in the men who formed the New Brunswick administration. The *Freeman* considered them 'weak in character' and lacking in ability, whether legislative, administrative, or parliamentary.[77] After Anglin's old opponent Judge L.A. Wilmot was appointed Lieutenant Governor,[78] Anglin's interest in provincial politics became perfunctory. The only hope for improvement seemed to be the parliament in Ottawa.

Anglin's views on various aspects of New Brunswick's position under the new régime provide clues to his attitude towards the new Dominion. Anglin had vowed to give Confederation a try, and there is no question that he tried to carry out his promise. But perhaps he also found it convenient to do so. He had been, after all, a staunch and sincere anti-Confederate. He could not now just turn around and support the new state of affairs. His 'fair trial' proclamations performed a face-saving role. Not that he was happy with the state of affairs in New Brunswick, no provincial resident could have been. But by 1872 Anglin recognized that things might have been worse, and were not quite as bad as he had expected them to be. Over and over again he showed his *de facto* acceptance of the new system by his involvement in it. In the Commons he was one of the two or three most active members from New Brunswick. His activity, his complaints and criticisms, all implied that he believed that something could be done to alleviate New Brunswick's situation through political means. He had little hope that improvement would result from action on the part of the provincial government and therefore he placed great emphasis on the federal parliament. This was where the people of New Brunswick might be able to save themselves. Although in the various areas which related to New Brunswick's position in the Dominion, Anglin never failed to point out the difficulties that Confederation had brought about, there was a basic acceptance on his part that changes would take place within the system. His very opposition to much of what was transpiring was part of his acceptance of the new régime.

IV

Anglin looked at developments from various viewpoints: as an Irish leader and as a New Brunswick politician, but also as a significant political and newspaper figure, concerned with the consolidation of the new Dominion and its position in the North Atlantic community. This third perspective was at least as important as the other two in determining Anglin's reactions to the Canadian nation.

Anglin's attitude towards the pacification of Nova Scotia was quite predictable. He completely sympathized with Nova Scotian 'efforts to be free,'[79] for there was no question in his mind that Nova Scotians were ill used. There was almost as little question however, that they would not be able to do anything about it, for the imperial authorities would not countenance any great disturbance of the scheme they had so whole-heartedly supported.[80] Furthermore, Nova Scotians could expect little help from New Brunswick Antis in a fight for repeal. Certainly, Anglin declared, they would get none from him.[81] Yet he was not enamoured with Confederation, as the *Freeman* indicated after the failure of Nova Scotia's appeal to Britain.

Begotten of deceit and selfishness, cradled in falsehood, nursed in treachery, fed on lies, Confederation it seems can not exist without a plentiful supply of untruth. It would have been enough to refuse what Nova Scotia asked for some reason of Imperial policy, real or pretended; but this would not have been consistent with the whole course of Confederation. Falsehood is essential to its very being, and so the petitioners were mocked and insulted ...

What will Nova Scotia, thus robbed, insulted, outraged now do? We can not tell. The *News* advises that she should now submit, and calls submission loyalty, patriotism, wisdom. This is to counsel the traveller who, betrayed by his guide, has been knocked down by highwaymen, beaten, robbed of his purse and watch, spat upon, reviled and insulted, to lie quiet and bear it all meekly, lest he be beaten more, and his clothes also be taken from him. This may be good advice, but it is such advice as few men care to follow even when resistance is utterly hopeless.[82]

But Nova Scotia, under Joseph Howe's leadership, did choose to submit, especially after Macdonald offered the province better financial terms. To this Anglin agreed, but at the same time he stated that New Brunswick 'should be ready to claim what she is entitled to – taking into account revenue as well as population.'[83]

Canadian acquisition of the Northwest was another matter. Despite the assurances of the New Brunswick Confederates in 1865 and 1866 that acquisition of the Northwest would not take place for some time, it became clear even in the first session of parliament that it would take place in the very near future.[84] Anglin objected, but, he stated, there was little that could be done about it. Confederation had been for the benefit of the Upper Canadians and they could not be prevented from 'carrying such measures as they deemed essential to their welfare.'[85] By the 1869 session Anglin had come to a partial acceptance of the acquisition on the ground that one might as well get on with the experiment in nation-building.[86] There was, however, one aspect of the arrangements that disturbed Anglin.

At this time of day, and in this part of the world, no community, large or small, will very long endure an arbitrary government of any kind or form. The proposed Government for the North West is merely provisional, and it is to [be] presumed will not be maintained for any great length of time.[87]

The residents of the Red River colony were not, of course, willing to live under this form of government for any length of time whatever. Anglin and the *Freeman* followed the events of 1869 and 1870 with great interest, generally siding with Métis demands and above all urging the avoidance of bloodshed.[88] Fortunately, order was eventually restored and Manitoba became a tiny province.* For the *Freeman* the lesson of the first three years of Confederation was clear: 'So far, disaffection and resistance, constitutional or armed, has been successful in this Dominion.'[89] Not that New Brunswick could adopt these tactics very effectively – she had already made her bargain.

If Anglin objected to the acquisition of the Northwest as premature and likely to be of no benefit to the Maritimes,[90] it is not surprising that he was against the annexation of British Columbia for the same reasons. In his view there was no immediate necessity for this step unless the Pacific colony was willing to come into Confederation on fair terms. As far as Anglin was concerned, the actual terms, both politically and economically, were ridiculous. The cost of the railway alone would probably ruin the country. All in all, Anglin felt, it was a very poor bargain, especially for the Lower Provinces. They would pay a goodly share but reap few benefits.[91]

With the consolidation and expansion of the new Dominion up to 1872 Anglin was not entirely satisfied. He considered that mistakes were being made and that the country was being far too heavily burdened. Yet this view was not a rejection of Confederation but rather an acceptance of it. He was concerned that overburdening the country would result in its destruction. One might say that he was becoming Canadian in his outlook. Certainly this was true of his attitude towards the development of Canada's position in the North Atlantic community between 1867 and 1872.

In the late 1860s Britain was withdrawing from the North American continent as honourably as possible. Anglin had been correct in his view that Confederation was simply one stage of this withdrawal, a retirement which Anglin believed posed very serious dangers for British North Americans vis-à-vis the United States.[92] At times his strictures against the British position amounted to a charge of cowardice or, at least, a shirking of responsibilities.[93] While able to criticize, however, Anglin was not able to make positive suggestions. He claimed that the real responsibility for providing and preparing for the future rested with those who had brought about Confederation.[94] The real reason for Anglin's neutrality on this issue

* Anglin doubted the advisability of establishing the 'little'province of Manitoba. He felt that, because its size was so limited, the area would, for a long time, be controlled politically by the Métis. This would lead new settlers to take up other lands 'and thus the state of things to which many now object would become perpetual and this Province would continue to differ in population, manners, customs and probably in laws from all the Provinces surrounding it' (see *Freeman*, 7 May 1870).

was probably not an ideological principle but simply the fact that he did not know what course ought to be followed. He did not want annexation[95] but he had always believed that independence must lead to it – and independence seemed to be approaching quickly. The alternative that some were suggesting – imperial federation – Anglin considered to be hopelessly utopian.[96]

By the beginning of 1870 the situation seemed to have changed somewhat. The American armies had been disbanded, and British panic to leave the North American continent subsided, although the withdrawal continued.[97] Anglin's views at this time were consistent with the position he had formulated during the Confederation debates. He argued that a quasi-independent Canada would reap the drawbacks of the imperial connection but few compensating benefits. He then proceeded to the logical conclusion that, if the removal of British military support would somehow make Canada safer from American attack, then 'a separation in name as well as in fact would still more effectually remove any such temptation.'[98] Obviously there were two solutions to this state of affairs. The first – continued British military presence in Canada – seemed impossible, given the prevailing British policy and attitudes. The second – independence – was a definite possibility, but the danger that annexation by the United States might be the result seemed equally feasible. There was, however, a third possibility: if the United States and Great Britain were able to come to an agreement on the issues that divided the two countries and establish an *entente cordiale*, would this not make Canada safe?

Anglin first heard that a high commission was to meet in Washington to resolve Anglo-American differences while he was on his way to Ottawa for the 1871 session. His initial reaction was fear that Canadian interests would be sacrificed. Unquestionably Anglin felt that the negotiations would be a very significant factor in deciding the future of the imperial tie.

If Great Britain negotiates respecting our rights but to surrender them, about our interests but to sacrifice them, and appoints our leading politician one of the High Commissioners but to make us seem to assent to our own loss and humiliation, the connection will no longer serve to protect our rights, promote our rights, or gratify our feelings. If, however, these gloomy anticipations should prove unfounded, and Great Britain should once more prove herself a true protector of her colonies, the advocates of Independence may be forced to regard their theory as Utopian.[99]

Immediately after the terms of the Treaty of Washington were made public,

Anglin took a stand from which, unlike many other public men, he never wavered. He acknowledged that Anglo-American amity was greatly to be desired and worthy of considerable sacrifice. But why should Canadians be the victims of imperial policy? Why should they give up everything and receive nothing in return? It was not even that a lasting peace had been secured, Anglin claimed, but merely a 'hollow truce.' For this meagre return 'the honour of the British Empire and the dearest rights and most valuable privileges of the Dominion of Canada' had been sacrificed. The treaty had given 'everything the Americans could possibly have demanded, except the absolute transfer of all British Sovereignty on this Continent ...'[100]

From this powerful indictment of the treaty Anglin refused to budge. He recognized that war would be a frightful alternative, but he thought that this was neither the inevitable nor the probable consequence of the rejection of the treaty in its present form.[101] He accepted the validity of the argument that Canada ought not to stand in the way of a great international agreement between the two countries which had the most influence on Canada, but he could not bring himself to accept the treaty.[102] Acceptance of it would be a greater betrayal of Canadian interests than rejection. Moreover, Britain was carrying out the final phase of its withdrawal from North America during the fall of 1871. Canada would soon have to face the American colossus alone in any case.

Soldiers gone, fortresses dismantled, armories, arsenals and magazines emptied of their contents, what remains to bind us to the Empire but that the Imperial Government appoints a Governor whom the Dominion pays, claims the right of annulling the most solemn decisions of the Canadian Parliament, disposes of our territorial rights to conciliate the United States and exercises some of the rights of sovereignty without giving the protection which the Sovereign is always bound to afford. If the connection means to us constant sacrifices on our part without any corresponding benefit, if it means to Great Britain an increase of responsibility and danger without any compensating advantages how long will the connection last?[103]

Why then sacrifice Canadian rights in the hope of maintaining a connection which could not last? Not surprisingly, Anglin voted against the Treaty of Washington when it came before the Commons in 1872.[104] Parliament accepted the treaty, of course, but Anglin did not think that this action would win much gratitude from Great Britain.[105]

By 1872, therefore, Anglin was pessimistic about the longevity and value of the imperial connection. However, it was clear that Anglin had become a nationalist of some variety. He did not wish annexation to the United States and saw little hope of returning to pre-Confederation status. What remained to him was patriotism towards his land of birth and his land of adoption. Since Confederation, the latter was no longer New Brunswick but the larger entity, Canada. In time, and actually fairly readily, Anglin transferred his loyalty to Canada. By 1872 he was making decisions on external affairs, at least, from a Canadian viewpoint. It was not the first nor the last time that a man found his Canadian patriotism in dealing with the people of other nations. Anglin might not have approved of the development of the North Atlantic community in these years and found many occasions to ridicule the arguments of those who had supported Confederation in order to preserve the British connection, but, when all was said and done, Canada was what he was left with. The debate on the Treaty of Washington showed that he had come to realize this fact. Commitment to Canada was the least repugnant alternative.

V

On the premise that happy men do not foment revolution, the final means of judging Anglin's attitude towards the new Dominion is an examination of his personal situation. Anglin had gone to Ottawa in 1867 thinking 'how unpleasant and even worse it will be to leave family and home and business for months and live so far away ...'[106] On his arrival he found Ottawa busy and crowded; suitable lodgings were hard to find 'at any price,'[107] and accommodations in the House of Commons just as difficult. Anglin would have preferred to sit upon the cross benches or in a place 'below the gangway,' such as existed in the English parliament, but in Ottawa there was no comparable place.[108] He was assigned a seat on the opposition benches, immediately behind A.A. Dorion, the Rouge leader, and beside Albert Smith.[109] Subsequent developments showed that this was not an inappropriate position for Anglin.

After Confederation the government had a much easier time in forming party ties than its opponents.[110] This was partly because the government had to govern the country. This was a positive task which required at least a minimum of unity and also provided patronage. In contrast, the opposition had no real purpose to serve by becoming a unified group. Opposition to the government could be as vigorously prosecuted without unity. Nevertheless, the divergent elements of the opposition, led by the largest group, the Ontario Reformers who looked to George Brown and his *Globe* for leadership, gradually built up common links and began to realize that to over-throw the Macdonald régime greater cooperation would be required.[111]

The attitude Anglin had displayed towards parties in the 1867 election did not change overnight. Although recognizing that Anglin was certainly no ally of the government, even the New Brunswick press did not think it too extreme to assume in the summer of 1868 that, if Tilley resigned from the cabinet, Anglin would take his place.[112] As 1868 wore on into 1869, the *Freeman*'s position changed little. It continued to criticize various writings of the organ of the Ontario Grits, the Toronto *Globe*.[113] But if Anglin did not always agree with the Grits, he was clearly not a government supporter. In the sessions from 1867 to 1870 he voted against the government over half the time and with increasing regularity.[114]

1870 brought important developments. For one thing Anglin's wife and possibly their young family joined him in Ottawa for at least part of the session.[115] Undoubtedly this made Anglin feel more at home in the capital. Moreover, during the 1870 session attempts were made to unify the opposition elements in the Commons.[116] Anglin was not overlooked in the search for talent, and by November the *Globe* was intimating that he was worthy of a position in a Reform cabinet should one be formed.[117] Still, Anglin was not an easy fish to land. In December 1870 Anglin wrote to Sir John A. Macdonald about patronage for a political friend. It may be that Anglin was attempting to see if Macdonald would make him a good offer before he joined the Reform bandwagon, although the language of the letter does not support this interpretation.[118] In any case the Prime Minister was convinced that Anglin's position had already been defined by the *Globe* and that Anglin was disloyal and an annexationist.[119] His belated answer to Anglin was blunt if not downright insulting. 'My principle is,' he stated, 'reward your friends and do not buy your enemies.'[120]

From this point on, Anglin gravitated slowly but surely towards the Reformers.* The 1872 session of parliament, with its two major issues of the Treaty of Washington and the New Brunswick schools question, moved Anglin even further into the Reform camp, and a letter he wrote to Alexander Mackenzie after the 1872 election showed very clearly which side he was on.[121] Thus by 1872 Anglin had gone far to acclimatize himself

---

* At the same time the Grits began to make a more direct appeal to Catholics (see Mackenzie Papers, Brown to John O'Donohue, et al., 9 March 1871). A pamphlet printed in 1872, undoubtedly for election purposes, was devoted to the proposition that Irish Catholics were not receiving a fair deal (especially in terms of patronage) from the Tories and urged that the Reformers be given an opportunity (see J.L.P. O'Hanly, *The Political Standing of Irish Catholics in Canada* ... [Ottawa, 1872]).

to the Canadian party system. He had also adjusted to Ottawa and the House of Commons. And, much as he would have hated to admit it, the fact that he was a prominent member of the House of Commons helped him to think kindly of the new régime.

On other levels his life was satisfactory as well. His family was expanding nicely. He had become a stockholder in the Commercial Bank of Saint John.[122] From the number of dinners he attended and the number of toasts to which he was asked to reply during the period it would seem that either he was becoming acceptable to Saint John society or he was one of the few who could hold his drinks.[123] One unusual aspect of Anglin's career is that he apparently took no role in any club or organization in Saint John, except committees of the cathedral. There may be several explanations for this. In the first place, Anglin would never have been sought after to join clubs on the basis of his affability. Moreover, the Anglins were members of the social élite among Saint John Catholics.[124] As well, there were practical reasons why Anglin could not seek membership in community organizations. As the editor of a morning newspaper many of his evenings had to be devoted to the *Freeman* rather than club gatherings. Also, one must think that politics, religion, and family took up any time the *Freeman* did not consume. Finally Anglin did not need personal membership in many of the Saint John organizations because he could exercise influence and keep abreast of developments through his friends and employees. John O'Brien, for example, a young employee in the *Freeman* office, held numerous executive positions in various organizations, especially temperance movements, until his untimely death.[125]

During this period Anglin was also having considerable success with the *Freeman*. Ownership of such an establishment, including printing press, type, paper, and all the other essential paraphernalia of a newspaper, was no mean investment.[126] In fact, the 1872 tax assessments show that only two hundred individuals on the east side of Saint John, with a population of over 24,000, were wealthier than Anglin, whose real and personal property was valued at approximately $13,000.[127] The quality of the *Freeman* suffered while Anglin was in Ottawa, for he did not give free rein to his assistants while he was away. Consequently there were few editorials worthy of note for a couple of months each year. On the other hand, the readers of the *Freeman* had first-hand reports from the House of Commons. There were the usual problems with the Post Office not delivering papers to places at a distance from Saint John,[128] but the circulation of the *Freeman* seemed to show a considerable increase during this period. In February 1871 the *Freeman* was available for sale at eleven places in Saint

John and vicinity and five other places in New Brunswick and Nova Scotia.[129] Twelve months later it was selling at sixteen spots in and around the city and three places outside.[130] While no exact circulation figures are available, the *Freeman* was prosperous enough for Anglin to buy new type in 1872. At the same time the *Freeman* expanded from seven to eight columns on each of its four pages.[131] Things were going well for Anglin. He was even found not guilty in a libel suit which had been brought against him.[132] It would seem that in personal as well as political matters Anglin must have thought that the Confederation experiment was worth continuing.

Thus during the first five years of the new Dominion the former anti-Confederate came to terms with the new régime. He did not like all aspects of Confederation, but he gave it a fair trial and did not find it entirely wanting.

9

'Godless' Schools and Party Politics

1872-4

The issue which disturbed the serenity of Anglin's life in the early 1870s was the New Brunswick schools question.[1] In this period the education problem was the one major arena in which the Catholic Church in the western world fought the forces of secularism, Protestantism, and all the other 'isms' which it felt were arrayed against it. The famous *Syllabus of Errors* of 1864 had condemned education which ignored the Catholic faith and the authority of the church, and which regarded as its sole, or at least its primary aim, a knowledge of nature and the ends of secular society.[2] To Catholics, therefore, the system of education was of immense importance.

Education has always been an important means of passing on traditions and faith to children. Recognizing this fact, the Catholic Church has always utilized education as a means of conveying morality and instructing communicants in the intricate tenets of Catholicism. Control of the education of Catholic children has meant for the Church an opportunity to place its doctrines into social context for young Catholics, and allows them to give sufficient scope and outlook to their religion when applying its principles to everyday life. This control of education is particularly essential when the society at large is in a state of flux, when society is undergoing a period of transformation of goals, or subject to a new form of mobility. If the variability of religious antagonism is added, the Church's demand for educational control becomes more urgent.[3]

Western society was indeed in a state of flux. The transformation which was taking place in the second half of the nineteenth century led to the primarily secular society of the twentieth century. There was, however, a good deal of religious antagonism which accompanied, and in fact accounted for, much of this development. The Protestant attitude towards education in North America was very different from that of the Roman Catholics. With the exception of a segment of the members of the Church of England, Protestants were largely in favour of common schools for children of all denominations. The theory was that common schools would promote harmony within the community and integrate or assimilate segregated elements. Protestants did not share the Catholic attitude towards clerical control of education because Protestant churches were controlled by the laity not the clergy.[4] Finally, there was a fundamental difference between Protestants and Catholics in their attitude to the concept of a common Christianity. To Protestants there were certain basic underlying beliefs which united all Christians, no matter what particular church they attended. Catholics could not accept this hypothesis nor the assertion that Protestantism was merely a different form of the Christian faith equally acceptable in the eyes of God.[5] Thus the religious instruction or observance which the Protestant majority was willing to allow in the common schools was not acceptable to Catholics. Disagreeing on fundamental principles in their approaches to education, Catholics and Protestants were destined to be at odds when the issue arose in New Brunswick.

I

Anglin agreed whole-heartedly with the stand of the Catholic Church. The state could provide for the teaching of the three 'r's, the *Freeman* declared, but could not 'bring people up to the standard which the law of God requires ...' Anglin also questioned the assertion that direct taxation would be the solution to educational problems. He thought such a plan might be efficacious in providing larger and better school buildings, better books, and better teachers, 'but after all, the positive result of this is but reading, writing, arithmetic, &c. – not education; the negative results may be very disastrous.'[6] In the end Anglin was wary of state interference in a matter which he considered to be the concern of the parents and their church.[7] Besides, the existing Irish and American common schools had been turned into machines of proselytism.[8]

At the time of Confederation the structure of New Brunswick's educational system was far from clear. Its basis was an 1858 act which had left much power to local authorites. Efforts at the time to make provincial education entirely secular had failed because aggressive arch-Protestants refused to have religion completely removed from the schools.[9] The irony was that, while the Bible was accepted in the schools, provision was also made for Catholics – 'the Bible, when read in Parish Schools by Roman Catholic children shall, if required by their parents or guardians, be the Douay version ...'[10] Within the framework of this act and under the leadership of Bishop Sweeny, Catholic educational facilities grew markedly, a growth which the *Freeman* took pains to publicize. Catholic leaders were not afraid to ask for increased financial aid from the province. In 1862 Sweeny in private and Anglin in public both made such requests, with Anglin suggesting in the Assembly that denominational grants which had grown up year by year 'should be regulated by some consistent method.'[11] Had this suggestion been adopted, New Brunswick would have had the equivalent of a separate school system. But Anglin did not push the issue, probably because he feared arousing anti-Catholic antagonism in the legislature. Failure to achieve this point, or at least legal clarification of the Catholic position, did not seem particularly important at this time. The actual working of the system in practice was reasonably acceptable.

The schools question played no role in the Confederation struggle in New Brunswick.[12] It was not until after the 1866 elections, at the London Conference, that Archbishop Connolly attempted to improve Catholic education rights in the Maritimes.[13] His efforts, however, were a failure, as Tilley's letter to the reverend editor of the Baptist *Religious Intelligencer* indicated.

Denominational schools can only be established in Nova Scotia and New Brunswick by the vote of the Local Legislature, as for Canada, we have allowed their delegates to arrange matters to suit themselves.[14]

As well as indicating the regional nature of the Confederation agreement, this statement showed that Tilley did not consider denominational schools to be in existence in New Brunswick. Anglin's interpretation of the situation at the time of Confederation was much less clear, as a lengthy *Freeman* editorial of 8 August 1867 demonstrated. It regretted that Catholic minorities did not have the same rights held by the Protestants of Quebec.

We all know what the state of the Catholic minority is here; how studiously their wishes have been disregarded; how little of right or justice they have ever enjoyed; and how grossly they were insulted when, a few years ago, in reply to the expression, in the very mildest manner, of their desire to have a separate school system introduced, as far as practicable, the law was so altered as to require in effect that every school in the Province must be a Protestant school; that in every school receiving public assistance the Bible must be read daily. It was graciously conceded to Catholic prejudice that they may use a Douay Bible, but then it must be without note or comment. No such edition of the Bible has yet been printed. The law was obsolete almost as soon as it received the assent; but the intolerance, the bigotry and the insolence which caused it to be passed are not less palpable.

Obviously in 1867 Anglin recognized that the intention of the 1858 School Law had not been to create Catholic schools, much less to give them permanent public support (which would have made them separate schools). True, special grants for Catholic schools had from time to time been wrung from the government, but even these niggardly sums had aroused great antagonism among some segments of the Protestant population. Strangely enough, Anglin seemed to ignore his writing about the 1858 law when he came to examine the situation under the BNA Act. Section 93 of that act specifically stated that only those rights and privileges for denominational schools which were in existence 'by law' at the time of the union would be safeguarded. Anglin seems to have been confused between what was lawful because it was not illegal and what was lawful because it had legally been declared so. On the one hand, he recognized that no act had ever declared denominational schools legal; on the other, he was convinced that the fact that the existing Catholic schools received legislative grants, and were never declared unlawful under the terms of the 1858 act, made those schools legal under the law. Such a conception led him to make a statement which events were shortly to disprove.

The Confederation Act does one thing at all events. It secures to the minority the paltry grants they have hitherto received and such other rights and privileges as they have been permitted to enjoy, and no change can be made in the law without their consent. This enables them to draw attention to the defects of the existing law and to agitate for an amendment of that law without incurring the risk of losing the little held by what was little better than sufferance. When four or five years ago they asked for an amendment, they brought on themselves new insults and indignities. Now they can boldly appeal to whatever of honesty, good sense and fair play exists in the country.

The *Freeman* went on to appeal, in moderate tones, for understanding for the Catholic position on the education question, and then put forward its plan for solving the problem.

Let it be open to any denomination that chooses to establish schools where it can, under supervision and controul of the Board of Education, the minimum number of pupils in each case to be fixed by the Board according to circumstances, and not according to any arbitrary rule. Let the Board insist that the secular education shall in these, as in all other schools, be fully up to the standard it deems necessary; but let it stop there and interfere no further nor attempt to meddle with the religious education of the pupils. In districts where no more than one efficient school can be maintained, care should be taken that the faith of no pupil should be tampered with; that the feelings of none should be hurt; that the school should be equally free and acceptable to all.

The first indication that a new school law would be presented to New Brunswick appeared early in 1870 when a draft bill was published. In three extremely long articles the *Freeman* presented a 'synopsis' of the chief terms of the projected legislation. Non-sectarianism was not a part of the bill, and the *Freeman*'s objections were to the great power which would be held by the Board of Education and the Superintendent and more especially to the main principle of the bill – direct taxation.[15] While the bill was not presented in the 1870 session, it was clear that it soon would be. In the summer of 1870, however, the *Freeman* detected a new note being introduced into the question.

The *News* is trying to get up an agitation on the School Question, in order to enable the Local Government to reorganize or to cover themselves, when they fall, with a decent cloak.[16]

Once again, the *Freeman* suspected, religion was to be used for political ends in New Brunswick. The *News* was now advocating common schools which 'would bestow on Protestant and Catholic children precisely the same privileges, and would interfere with the faith and rights of neither.'[17] The *Freeman* thought such a view ludicrous.

Now a school must be either Catholic or Protestant, or Godless or Infidel. The *News* does not tell us which of these it will deign to impose upon the people. We know it would not tolerate Catholic schools. We suppose it would not openly avow itself an advocate of Infidel schools. We will not pretend to say whether it is an advocate of Protestant or of Godless schools. The latter would be most unacceptable to many sincere, earnest Protestants. Catholics, of course, could not be expected to be content with either, even though the *News* may think they should.[18]

There were at least two things wrong with such a system. In the first place, the majority could not justly determine the conscientious convictions of a minority.[19] Second, Anglin felt that the state should not interfere in education after secular instruction had been supervised and paid for.[20] A lull followed this brief flurry of interest in the summer of 1870, the lull before the storm.

The government which met the New Brunswick Assembly in 1871 was weak, but shortly after the session began a most unexpected coalition took place between George King and G.L. Hatheway. The base on which this government had been founded was a commitment to the School Bill,[21] which was brought forward with little delay. At first, opposition to the 1871 act was concentrated on the taxation principle and therefore was not centred on the Roman Catholic population except for the fact that the *Freeman* had always been one of the major sceptics of this system. As the debate in the Assembly continued, however, it became apparent that a non-sectarian clause would be added to the bill. Fear of this happening caused twenty-two petitions in favour of denominational schools to descend upon the legislature. But apparently the opinion of 5,281 persons, representing a Catholic population composing two-fifths of the provincial total, meant nothing to the legislators.[22] Section 60, which was passed by a vote of twenty-five to ten, declared that 'all Schools conducted under the provisions of this Act shall be non-sectarian.' To the *Freeman* this was the final blow. The bill had been bad enough before, giving, as it did, immense power to a board of education, the members of which gave Anglin little confidence that justice would be done for the Catholic population.[23] But the *Freeman* objected even more strenuously to any move which would have forced non-sectarian schools upon Catholics. It claimed that what newspapers like the *Religious Intelligencer* claimed to be freedom of conscience was a very strange freedom.

Its conscience cannot be satisfied with merely being left at liberty to think and judge and speak and act for itself; it must also have the right to harass, oppress and outrage others.

Catholics did not want anything outrageous, Anglin stated, just fair play.

All the Catholic petitions ask is that they be allowed to employ in support of their Schools the money which the advocates of the new system say they shall pay by way of direct taxation, and they are willing that the State shall exercise the strictest supervision over their Schools in all that relates to secular education: the only education which the State professes to give; the only education for which it professes to raise money by taxation.[24]

Anglin was very bitter. He believed that the whole issue had arisen because the provincial politicians knew that an anti-Catholic campaign would strengthen their position with the electors and remove the sting of increased taxation.[25] Anglin knew what would happen if the issue became divided along straight Catholic-Protestant lines, and he tried to argue that the contest of the day was not between Protestantism and Catholicism but between 'Christianity and Rationalism and Infidelity in all its phases.'

For the propagation of Infidelity no better engine could be devised than the Common School system which excludes religion altogether and puts it out of view, thus inevitably creating in the minds of the young the impression that religion is of little or no importance in the real business of life, and leading to indifference and latitudinarianism out of which Infidelity is sure to grow in most cases.[26]

As the bill did not go into effect until the beginning of 1872, however, there was little to be gained in a public campaign during the summer and fall of 1871. In fact, during November and December Bishop Sweeny attempted to make accommodations to the new system but the authorities refused to adopt any of his suggestions which would have enabled the Catholic schools in Saint John to continue to operate under the new law.[27]

On 1 January 1872 the Act Relating to Common Schools came into effect. Efforts to make the law acceptable to Catholics had failed. To maintain Catholic schools Catholics would have had to support them above and beyond the compulsory taxation for the common schools, a great infringement upon human rights and liberty, Anglin argued.[28] It was either submit or resist. To the *Freeman* the choice was obvious.

They will use every means their constitution places within their reach to obtain redress. They will never cease to proclaim to the people of the other Provinces the great wrong done to them; never cease to expose before the world the truculent bigotry of which they are the victims; never cease to appeal to the justice and sense of fair play of the truly liberal and enlightened amongst the people of this Province, and ultimately they know religion and justice will triumph. The struggle may be long, the wrong done them may for a time be rendered more intolerable; but they are not the people to be deterred by difficulties or wearied into indifference by the length and the apparent hopelessness of a contest in which their duty to God and their children requires them to engage.[29]

172 Timothy Warren Anglin

The issue, therefore, was whether Catholics would be forced to support a school system of which they disapproved.[30] By April 1872 it was clear that the school system was not operating very successfully. The report laid before the Assembly at that time showed that while 731 school districts had complied with the terms of the law, 571 districts had not.[31]

In the meantime the Catholics of New Brunswick had looked outside the province for assistance. As early as June 1871 two petitions had arrived in Ottawa requesting that the New Brunswick School Act be disallowed.[32] Both petitions used the term 'separate schools' to designate the Catholic schools which were in existence in New Brunswick at the time. This was an unfortunate mistake, for the term meant something entirely different to Canadians than the petitioners had intended. From the very beginning the Minister of Justice, Sir John A. Macdonald, must have considered the claims of the New Brunswick Catholics highly pretentious and erroneous. From a Canadian viewpoint the New Brunswick school system had never given any recognition or support to separate schools. It was a bad start for the Catholic cause and one which may have had continuing repercussions. On 5 October Anglin himself appealed to Macdonald. He asked him to read an article which had appeared in that day's *Freeman* entitled 'Is the School Law Valid?'[33] The argument used by the *Freeman* was very complex. It claimed that one section of the 1858 act had provided that the schools should be, as far as possible, religious and denominational. That section had stated:

Every Teacher shall take diligent care, and exert his best endeavours to impress on the minds of the children committed to his care, the principles of christianity, morality and justice, and a sacred regard to truth and honesty ... but no pupil shall be required to read or study in or from any religious book, or join in any act of devotion objected to by his parents or guardians; and the Board of Education shall, by regulation, secure to all children whose parents or guardians do not object to it, the reading of the Bible in Parish Schools – and the Bible, when read by Roman Catholic children shall, if required by their parents or guardians, be the Douay version, without note or comment.

Anglin argued that it was nonsense to claim that Christian principles could be impressed upon the minds of children without teaching them the doctrines of some denomination. Then too, he asserted, the old act, by putting in clauses for the protection of the minority in a district, recognized that religious instruction would not be merely oral, but also accepted that 'religious books calculated to assist the teacher in impressing the principles of Christianity and a love of the Christian virtues on the minds of his pupils' might be used. Similarly the act contemplated 'that there shall be in the Parish Schools acts of devotion at stated times and not merely such prayers and acts as pupils of all denominations may be expected to participate in without objection, but such prayers and acts as may properly be objected to by the parents of a minority of the pupils.' This all proved that the New Brunswick school system had been denominational.

The school in which Christian principles – that is Christian doctrines – are impressed upon the minds of the pupils; in which due care is taken to imbue the pupils with the spirit of Christianity and to create in them a love of Christian principle: in which text books and leading books of a religious character, such as the parents of the minority may reasonably object to on conscientious grounds are used regularly and by authority of law, in which prayers and acts of devotion of what we may call a denominational character are used by authority of law – that school must assuredly be a denominational school – Catholic, Protestant, Episcopalian, Presbyterian, Methodist or Baptist, as the people of the district in which it is established belong to one denomination or another.

In fact, throughout the province there were hundreds of parish schools, receiving normal state grants, in which the Catholic catechism was taught, Catholic books read, and Catholic devotions practiced. The act of 1871 prevented all these, and therefore by the terms of section 93 of the BNA Act was illegal and ought to be disallowed.

The case was well argued although it was open to dispute and certainly not universally accepted. It was based on the letter of the law and open to the charge of being semantic reasoning which did not accurately represent the underlying thesis of the act of 1858. For one reason or another, those who were called upon to pass judgment on the legality of the 1871 legislation gave the argument short shrift. They were only willing to accept explicit, not implicit, recognition of denominational schools in New Brunswick at the time of Confederation. This most certainly was Macdonald's view when he paid no heed to Anglin's argument. Macdonald would not recommend that the act be disallowed either on the ground that it was unconstitutional or on the ground that it detrimentally affected the interests of the Dominion in general.[34]

If Macdonald would not take action, perhaps the House of Commons would. On 29 April 1872 Auguste Renaud, the French-born farmer who represented the New Brunswick constituency of Kent, moved a resolution asking that all papers relating to the New Brunswick schools question be presented to the House. Anglin took the opportunity to make a very lengthy speech 'to enable,' as he said, 'the House to understand fully the case these papers would present.' He analysed the situation under the 1858 act and demonstrated the legality of Catholic schools under this law. He then gave the history of the issue in detail. For the special benefit of Quebec representatives he spoke of the unjust position in which the Acadian areas of New Brunswick were placed not only by the 1871 act but also by the continual failure of the province to provide a teachers' training school for French-speaking teachers. He spoke in justification of religious education and concluded by appealing on behalf of the Catholics of New Brunswick 'to the French inhabitants of Quebec, to Catholics of all nationalities in every Province of the Dominion and to all sincere, liberal, fair-minded Protestants for sympathy and aid in the life and death struggle in which they have been compelled to engage.'[35]

The Commons debate resumed on 20 May when John Costigan, the Irish Catholic representative for Victoria county in New Brunswick, moved a resolution asking that the Governor disallow the New Brunswick Common Schools Act of 1871.[36] Anglin's main effort on 20 May, as he told Bishop Rogers, was to point out that, however important the legal aspects of the question might be, parliament would be 'recreant' should it allow 'a law so unjust and oppressive and insulting' to remain in operation.[37] Events occurred so rapidly that Anglin was obliged to write to Rogers two days later to keep him abreast of developments. Apparently Costigan's motion won considerable sympathy and embarrassed the government, especially since Sir George Cartier and Hector Langevin spoke against the resolution. Anglin reported that he had probably made Sir George an enemy for life by singling him out in debate and putting 'his share of the responsibility for our sufferings in its true light.' A government representative then went to Costigan proposing an amendment which the government would support. Anglin was not sure of the exact wording, he reported, but he thought that the amendment would request the Queen to place New Brunswick Catholics in at least as good a position as before the passage of the 1871 act and possibly equivalent to the position of the minority in Quebec. The actual amendment proposed by P.-J.-O. Chauveau, the Quebec Premier and Minister of Education, did not satisfy Anglin. He doubted that it would be sufficiently clear to call for a change in the BNA Act to provide for minority educational rights 'to the same extent as if such rights, advantages and privileges had been duly established by law'[38] at the time of union. Neverthless, Anglin concluded that it would be better than nothing, 'as at all events it would give us a basis for future action ...' Anglin recognized, however, that 'many of those who professed to be with us would gladly avail themselves of any pretext for deserting us ...'[39] Indeed, before Chauveau's motion of 22 May could be fully debated, Albert Smith asked that the New Brunswick members be given time to consult together. A week's adjournment was granted.[40]

Events continued to move swiftly. On 25 May Tilley handed in his resignation because he feared complete political destruction if he supported or even remained silent on Chauveau's amendment.[41] His attitude was supported by other Protestant representatives from New Brunswick. Led by Smith, they held several meetings and prepared a protest which was aided by mounting agitation in both New Brunswick and Nova Scotia, for Chauveau's amendment applied to both provinces.[42] On 28 May, Anglin learned that the government was about to break its agreement with the Catholic representatives of New Brunswick. The promise to support Chauveau's motion would not be kept; another amendment would be proposed. In order to prepare for this Cartier met with his supporters in his home, at which time he apparently was able to win sufficient, if grudging, support for the government's plan. The Rouges, on the other hand, agreed to give full support to Costigan, Renaud, and Anglin. Even the Grit caucus decided to assist them as long as Macdonald would not be able to take advantage of what they said or did.[43]

By the evening of 29 May the manoeuvrings had been completed, and the debate resumed. A.J. Smith spoke first. He argued that the school bill was legal in all respects, but he laid emphasis upon the constitutional question in another sense. He claimed that Chauveau's amendment would change the constitution without the consent of one of the parties to the Confederation compact, New Brunswick.

He said that the Canadian Parliament being strong may coerce and crush and whip into submission the Province of New Brunswick which is weak and feeble, but they could not destroy the spirit of resistance which the passage of this resolution would excite ...

What would be legitimate, however, would be an expression of regret that the act had been passed. Other speeches followed, among them Costigan's cry of betrayal by the government. Although excitement caused Anglin to be ill,[44] his speech became very passionate when he took up Smith's argument.

When Mr. Smith appealed to the House to spare the majority, did not the House know that the minority were ground to dust by the majority? He said that the House might coerce the majority; did not the majority coerce the helpless Catholics? – that the House might crush the majority; did not the majority at that very moment ruthlessly crush to the ground the Catholic minority? – that the House might whip the people of New Brunswick into submission; did not that same majority now wield the whip most relentlessly, deaf to the cries and remonstrances of their Catholic victims? ... when they now whined for what was called their rights, was it not the right once so loudly claimed by slave-owners – the right to wallop their own niggers without let or hindrance? He appealed on behalf of those who were indeed weak, who were indeed powerless, who were indeed suffering. He did not ask for them any privilege, any right to injure or offend, to rob or oppress others, but plain, simple, manifest justice, the right to use their own money to give that education to their own children which they conscientiously believe it to be their duty to give.

Eventually the votes were taken. Chauveau's motion lost 34 to 126; Colby's amendment, expressing regret that the act was unsatisfactory to a number of New Brunswickers and hoping that the law would be amended 'to remove any just grounds of discontent that may now exist,' passed 117 to 42; and finally the House accepted Alexander Mackenzie's motion in favour of seeking legal opinion from across the ocean.[45]

Obviously the issue of Catholic schools had not yet been solved. Yet some headway had been made. Almost all the speeches in the Commons had indicated disapproval of the situation in New Brunswick, and the weight of public opinion might have some influence with provincial politicians and the press. At any rate there was now a base from which further appeals might be made to Ottawa.[46] Nevertheless, with June expired the time period in which the School Act might have been disallowed.[47]

II

In the meantime the schools question was proving to be of political use not only to provincial politicians but also to Anglin himself. An election was to be held in the summer of 1872 and there were indications that Anglin might expect strong opposition in Gloucester. One possible contender, and a formidable one, was Kennedy F. Burns, a provincial representative for the constitutency, a prominent Catholic, and a successful businessman. He wrote to Bishop Rogers, Anglin's old antagonist at the time of Confederation, to enquire whether his candidacy would meet with the bishop's approval. The bishop's reply was most interesting. He acknowledged the clash of opinion which had occurred in 1866 and admitted that he could not have recommended Anglin to the electors of Gloucester in the 1867 election had he been in the province at the time. However, the letter went on to say that Anglin was performing capital service for Catholics in the matter of New Brunswick schools and that he did not wish to lose Anglin's services in the Commons, especially considering the fact that the present Dominion government could not claim gratitude for its role on the question. 'Such being the present state of things,' the Catholic dignitary announced, 'I would not like to see Mr. Anglin opposed by any respectable Catholic whom I esteem in the coming election for the Dominion Parliament.'[48] In order that there be no misunderstanding about his present attitude towards Anglin, the bishop circulated copies of this letter to the priests in the county.[49] In a Catholic county like Gloucester Anglin's election was assured. During the 1872 election campaign Anglin refused to mix party politics and the schools question in public. 'I felt it to be my duty,' he said, 'to hold myself aloof from all party movements lest anyone should be able to say that I wished to make the School question subserve the interests of my party.'[50] Of course, one might think that it was as much for the sake of the Liberals as for the sake of the schools question that Anglin wished to keep the two separate. As for Anglin's own candidacy in Gloucester, he did not manage to escape a contest, as he had hoped, but he received 1436 of the 1777 ballots cast.[51]

Elections out of the way, Anglin was able to turn to other things. Perhaps most important was the fact that he had to revive the *Freeman*. 'It had,' he confided to Bishop Rogers, 'become very flat and stale during my long absence. There is now so much competition in the business that it requires the closest attention to keep a newspaper fairly up in public estimation.' He could not afford to let the *Freeman* go down 'even for the chance of attaining political distinction.'[52] Circulation figures from an 1873 newspaper directory show that Anglin did indeed have worries. His weekly edition had about 600 subscribers while the tri-weekly had 720. Even though the circulation of the *Freeman* probably fluctuated greatly, these were sorry figures compared to those of the *News* and *Telegraph*, which claimed a circulation of 5,000 and 8,000 respectively for their weekly editions alone.[53] While working on this problem Anglin was also able to return to the schools issue.

The 1871 act required financial support. In many places in the province, however, the necessary assessments had not been made. In Saint John, Anglin felt, they had been made illegally. The *Freeman* advised those who opposed 'Godless' schools not to pay that part of their assessment which went to those schools.[54] As a result legal cases soon reached the New Brunswick Supreme Court. At the same time, of course, the cases of the federal and provincial governments and the Catholics of New Brunswick were being prepared for submission to the British Law Officers according to Mackenzie's motion in the Commons. Anglin played a significant role in preparing the Catholic case in both instances. To his mind the case was really quite simple:

A school in which the teacher and pupils are Catholic; in which the work of each day is opened and closed with prayers peculiarly Catholic; in which the Catholic Catechism is daily taught; in which the class books are those published by Catholic authority, almost every page of these books inculcating some Catholic doctrine or presenting some Catholic idea – is not such school Catholic – denominational?

Such schools had existed and had received provincial grants; the 1871 act deprived Catholics of lawful rights under the 1858 law; the 1871 act was therefore illegal under the terms of the BNA act.[55] But Anglin found it hard to convince others of the correctness of his views. In a letter to Bishop Rogers he confessed that he was finding it difficult to persuade even the lawyers presenting the Catholic case that 'denominational' schools had existed under the old system.[56]

The legal machinery lurched slowly forward. In November Macdonald wrote to Sweeny directing the bishop to send to him any comments he might wish to make on the case for transmission to the Law Officers. The case finally submitted showed Anglin's imprint, but Mr Duff, the lawyer retained by the bishop, felt that something was lacking in the argument.

Mr. Duff thinks it would be well in order to prove that the right the perpetuation of which we now claim is no abstract right dug out of the old law to serve our present purpose but that it was an actual living right which we fully enjoyed in practice.[57]

Details and facts were required, and Anglin must have realized that all this would take time and delay the Catholic submission. He was to find out later how unfortunate this delay was for the Catholic case. On the other hand, the New Brunswick government managed to get its submission in by February 1873. When Anglin saw the argument, he was pleased: 'It is as feeble and as flimsy as we could have wished it to be.'[58] Anglin's difficulty was that the judges did not agree with him. In the appeal test case brought before the New Brunswick Supreme Court, *Ex parte Renaud and Others*, the judges decided that the 1871 school law was constitutional although they would not state their views on the legality of assessments.[59] The *Freeman*'s comment on this decision was one of restrained disapproval:

A careful analysis will show that the judgment really rests on the assumption that there can be and there are 'principles of Christianity which are of general application, interfering with the peculiar religious views of none; doctrines, precepts and practices which all Christian people hold in common, and which are not the dogmatic teaching or tenets of a particular denomination or sect.'

Upon this egregarious fallacy, we repeat, the judgment does in reality wholly rest.[60]

But it was clear that, if it came down to this question, Anglin and the New Brunswick Catholics would never win their case in front of non-Catholic judges.

When Anglin arrived in Ottawa for the 1873 session of the Commons where the next skirmish of the battle on the New Brunswick schools question was to take place, he was both distracted and morose. Less than a fortnight before personal tragedy had struck. On 22 February, at 2:30 in the morning, the Anglins' youngest daughter, Maggie, died at the age of fifteen months and fifteen days. Only half an hour later their other daughter, Mary Ellen, nearly four, also died of whooping cough.[61]

The blow it pleased Providence to allow to fall upon us was very severe and it will be long before we cease to feel its bitter effects although we strive to submit as we should to God's Holy Will.[62]

What made this double tragedy even worse was that in late 1872 or early 1873 an infant son had also died.[63] In their mourning the Anglins did not, of course, attend the social functions of Ottawa during the 1873 session.[64] In fact, everything seemed to conspire against Anglin to make his life miserable. Even the train carrying the MPs to Ottawa was involved in an accident.[65] As a result Anglin was crotchety and took out his frustrations on his employees at the *Freeman* office back in Saint John who could not read his atrocious writing and consequently made mistakes in copying the reports of 'T.W.A.'[66] In this solemn, ill-tempered mood Anglin turned with a vengeance to his work. There were several special issues which aroused his concern. The first, of course, was the schools question.

The judgments in the assessment cases in New Brunswick which had relied upon the legality of the mode of assessment – rather than the 1871 school law itself – had in many cases been favourable to Catholics who had refused to pay the school tax. This led the New Brunswick Assembly to pass new regulations about these taxes to be applied retroactively. Anglin was not dismayed by these new regulations. They would provide a means of bringing the subject to the floor of the Commons, he confided to Bishop Rogers.[67] He was also encouraged by the apparently more determined attitude of the Quebec members, especially the newly elected ones.[68] But the government, he was sure, desired that this embarrassing question not be agitated. Its members would argue that no action ought to be taken until the Privy Council had made a decision on an appeal case, *Maher vs. Town Council of Portland*, which was to come before it.[69]

On Thursday, 3 April, Anglin requested that copies of all acts passed in the recent session of the New Brunswick legislature, especially the new regulations relating to schools, be brought before the House. Anglin stated that it might be necessary to ask the House to request that the Governor General disallow the assessments legislation.[70] Compliance with this request could not be instantaneous. In the meantime the New Brunswick school papers were tabled in the House on 15 April. It was shown therein how the British Law Officers had viewed the case, and also how the Canadian government had handled the whole affair. Before inviting either party in New Brunswick to send remarks on the Dominion government's case, Macdonald had forwarded that case to the Law Officers via the Colonial Office. Without waiting for further information the Law Officers had, by the end of November 1872, concurred with Macdonald's opinion;[71] 'and this they base mainly, if not entirely,' Anglin complained, 'upon the assumption that the Catholics believed the School Act to be unconstitutional because they formerly received Special Grants for Schools, of which they have been deprived since the passing of the Act of 1871.' The Law Officers had asserted that the 1871 school act was *intra vires* and that no appeal to the Governor General and the Dominion parliament for remedial legislation would be proper. When the comments of the New Brunswick government were sent to Ottawa, they too were transmitted and the Law Officers, of course, reiterated their opinion. Finally the Catholic case was forwarded to the Colonial Office, but it was not even submitted to the Law Officers. Kimberley, the Colonial Secretary, thought it useless to trouble the Law Officers further unless the Canadian government made a special request. Only on 13 March, the day after Honoré Mercier had moved that the relevant papers be tabled, was such a request made, and it was made only for its political utility apparently, as no one expected that the Law

Officers would change their minds now. 'The *probability* that any argument would cause the Law Officers to change an opinion twice given,' the *Freeman* concluded, 'seems very small.'[72]

As the New Brunswick schools agitation continued, it must have become clear to Bishop Rogers and Bishop Sweeny, who were in reality the leaders of the campaign, that Anglin was not the best man to direct their efforts in the Commons. Undoubtedly they desired his assistance, especially in organizing things behind the scenes, but it seems probable that the bishops were coming to the conclusion that it would be better to work through a supporter of the government, such as John Costigan, than through Anglin, a prominent opposition MP, whose strenuous forwarding of the question in the House could not fail to have the appearance of party antagonism. Certainly Anglin was not reticent to use the schools question as a whip to lash the government. Anglin himself probably realized that it would be better if he took a back seat on such matters as formulating resolutions. After all, he could still speak on motions. In any case, from this point in time others held centre stage in the House of Commons on the schools question.

On 17 April, when Anglin asked Macdonald if he had received copies of the New Brunswick acts, Macdonald replied in the negative. This seemed strange as he had promised two weeks before that he would make a special request. 'T.W.A.' considered this sheer neglect and evasion.[73] On 5 May Macdonald as last produced the legislation passed in the recent session of the New Brunswick parliament. About a week before this Bishop Sweeny had gone to Montreal to confer with the Quebec hierarchy. It was reported to Costigan by Hector Langevin, Cartier's successor, that Sweeny did not wish the question pushed. When Costigan sought confirmation of this information, the bishop replied by coming to Ottawa. There he managed to win promises of support from the Rouges and even from the Grit leader, Alexander Mackenzie, whom Anglin had introduced to the bishop. But Sweeny could get no satisfaction either from the Catholic supporters of the government or from the hierarchy in Quebec and he returned to Saint John leaving the schools question in a state of uncertainty. The inability of the Bishop of Saint John to make satisfactory arrangements for political action made things difficult for Anglin and Costigan. It had been understood that they should not take any further steps as Bishop Sweeny felt that it was politic to wait until the next session. Therefore, Anglin stated, he did not feel he could even move that the assessment legislation be disallowed. He was willing to do whatever the bishops thought best, although he admitted that he would find it personally embarrassing to allow the matter to drop.

He was convinced, too, that some of those who had frightened Sweeny would be forced to help if the question were pushed to a vote. Most important of all, Anglin recognized, was that the active cooperation of the Quebec bishops be secured. Without that the prospects were dismal – 'when so many Catholics play us so false it is hard to work effectually.'[74]

A second Sweeny visit to Ottawa proved just as unsuccessful as the first, but this time the bishop pushed Costigan to move that the tax laws be vetoed.[75] On 14 May Costigan moved the necessary resolution in the form of an amendment to a motion for the Commons to move into a Committee of Supply, and the debate went into high gear. Macdonald made the question a quasi-open one, in order to deprive the Grits of a pretext for voting for the resolution, Anglin believed. Yet when the vote came, the Grits did not desert Anglin and his cause. Nor did the Rouges. Most important of all, nor did the Bleus. It was a great victory.[76] Excitedly Anglin telegraphed the news to Rogers: 'Resolution disallowance School acts last session carried – majority thirty-four.'[77]

This turn of events placed Macdonald in a very difficult position. As the *Freeman* put it, 'Sir John is now bound to advise the Governor to do that which, he says, will tear our Constitution to tatters, &c.'[78] Macdonald's way out was to advise the Governor General to apply to Her Majesty's government for instructions.[79] As a sop to New Brunswick Catholics he promised to ask parliament for an appropriation to defray the expenses of an appeal to the Judicial Committee of the Privy Council.[80] While Macdonald thought the action of the House of Commons was out of order, Anglin believed that the government was responsible for the actions of the Governor. If the government could not, in good conscience, carry out the wishes of the Commons, then it should resign.

They take no such position, but pretending to guard the Constitution they abdicate their own constitutional position as the advisers of the Governor; invite unconstitutional action on the part of His Excellency, and trying to steer a middle course they give cause of offence to all parties, satisfying none ...[81]

Of course, if the Commons had been willing, it could have voted down the government for failure to carry out its wishes, and the government could have been overthrown. But, as Anglin told Bishop Rogers, the Quebec bishops 'for some reason I can not understand or even imagine' did not use their influence among the Quebec representatives at Ottawa. Anglin was certainly unimaginative if he really could see no reason for this. In the first place, it was unlikely that French Canadians in Quebec could view federal

TOP LEFT T.W. Anglin, 1872 / Public Archives of Canada PA 26338

TOP RIGHT T.W. Anglin, 1881 / Public Archives of Canada PA 26669

BOTTOM Alexander Mackenzie / Public Archives of Canada C 10460

TOP LEFT John Costigan / Public Archives of Canada PA 26701

TOP RIGHT Edward Blake / Public Archives of Canada C 3833

BOTTOM The Great Fire in Saint John, 1877
Canadian Illustrated News (Montreal), 7 July 1877, p 13
Public Archives of Canada C 35930

Thomas D'Arcy McGee
Public Archives of Canada c 6109

Bishop John Sweeny / Public Archives of Canada PA 31488

disallowance of a provincial education act with equanimity, for such federal action would pose a threat to the autonomy of any provincial educational system, including that of Quebec. Second, the Catholic hierarchy of Quebec had long favoured the Conservatives, and now Macdonald's lieutenant in Quebec was Hector Langevin, the younger brother of the Bishop of Rimouski. The bishops were not anxious to turn out the government. In fact, they strongly urged that no further action be taken on the question for the present. Anglin was perturbed:

This of course prevents our moving and indeed we could not hope to move successfully when in all probability Mr. Langevin who has worked against us with all his power is armed with similar telegrams which would seem to justify the Government Catholics in opposing any resolution we may move. I hope their Lordships' decision will prove to be for the best, but it is hard when victory seemed so certainly within reach to have it thus snatched away. The resolution which seemed so glorious a triumph will now have no practical effect.[82]

The Quebec hierarchy had saved Macdonald at the eleventh hour. With the end of 1873 session thus passed the best chance of New Brunswick Catholics to receive redress of grievances from the House of Commons.

III

The New Brunswick schools question had disrupted the government to no small degree during the 1873 session. For the Conservatives there was another most disconcerting issue raised in the same session. That issue was the Canada Pacific Railway Scandal.[83]

On 2 April the Commons rejected a proposal that an enquiry be made into Lucius Huntington's charges over the Canada Pacific Railway. Anglin's report to the *Freeman* was not sparing in its criticism; he spoke of men sacrificing honour, character, honesty, and reputation in support of the government.[84] On 17 April James MacDonald, the member for Pictou, rose in the House, condemned the *Freeman*'s writings, and then moved that the article 'is a scandalous, false and malicious libel upon the honor, integrity and character of this House, and of certain Members thereof; and that the said publication is a high contempt of the privileges and of the constitutional authority of this House.' There was little question that the *Freeman*'s report had been excessive, but this was hardly unique in the journalism of the day. It is unlikely that, if Anglin had been a less important and less vocal critic of the government, the libel charges would have been made. In most particulars the debate which followed MacDonald's motion was unexceptional. Anglin was attacked by the premier, Charles Tupper, and others and was defended by Reformers including Mackenzie, Huntington, and David Mills. One interesting incident occurred when Anglin rose and the Speaker asked the House that he be allowed to make an explanation. But, after consulting with some of his allies for a few moments, Anglin resumed his seat and remained silent. His political friends obviously knew Anglin's headstrong nature and urged him to keep his seat before he made any remarks which might put him in serious trouble. The resolution passed by a majority of twenty-six but no move was made to expel Anglin from the House. Had it been possible to goad Anglin into making an outburst in the House, he might well have been expelled. As it was, MacDonald's action merely drew attention to the power of the *Freeman* and aroused sympathy for one who seemed to be the victim of oppression by the government majority.[85]

The first session of the second Dominion parliament saw the beginning of Anglin's involvement with the issue of the Pacific Scandal, but not the end. During the summer Anglin time and again wrote about the subject in the *Freeman*. Mackenzie was grateful. 'Your articles,' he said, 'are being copied in our Western papers and are doing an excellent service.'[86] Indeed, while others held the spotlight in the Commons in the summer and autumn of 1873, there was no question that Anglin played an important role in the agitation over the Pacific Scandal.[87] Over the past six years he had earned a prominent place in the ranks of the opposition, and when the downfall of the Macdonald government came in early November, it seemed probable that Anglin would be a member of the new cabinet which Alexander Mackenzie was called upon to form.

When the membership of the new administration was announced, however, Isaac Burpee and Albert Smith were the two New Brunswick cabinet representatives. And that is exactly what they were – New Brunswick representatives. They were chosen by a caucus of New Brunswick members who were willing to support the government and who forced their selections upon Mackenzie.[88] Anglin was unhappy about this turn of events. He thought that Mackenzie would have been wiser to select 'the most able and reliable of those who worked with him' and present the cabinet as a *fait accompli*. Such a cabinet would have been supported in the House of Commons without much difficulty.[89] But why had the New Brunswickers in Ottawa not chosen Anglin? The answer to this question is that Anglin's role in the school question had made him too hot to touch. The representatives claimed that public opinion in New Brunswick would not support a government of which Anglin was a member. This attitude may have been a thin veneer for personal ambitions or anti-Catholic biases, but the fact was that these men informed Mackenzie that, if Anglin were chosen, they would withdraw their support from the government.[90] Mackenzie himself wanted Anglin in the inner circle. 'I would have been glad,' he confided to Brown, 'to have Anglin in but I could not pacify N Brunswick and had to have him out of the arrangement for the present.'* The Dominion press was surprised to find that Anglin had not been named to the cabinet. While one must note the political ends the various newspapers served, the consensus was that Anglin had been ill-used. Even the *News* made this clear:

Mr. Anglin had an unmistakable claim to a seat in the new Cabinet. There are very few men in it of equal ability, and only two or three men of equal service to the late Opposition. We have always been at political warfare with Mr. Anglin, and probably always shall he. But for all that, we must say that he has received the worst of treatment from the men whom he has served so zealously.[91]

If Anglin was too dangerous within the government, he would be even more dangerous in the opposition, and the Reformers sought to placate him in other ways. Mackenzie gave him personal assurance that some patronage appointments would be looked after.[92] It was also taken for granted that the *Freeman* would be the government's chief organ in New Brunswick, a role which promised support for the newspaper.[93] Anglin became a stockholder and a director in the Royal Canadian Insurance Company, whose president was John Young, a prominent Liberal MP from Montreal West.[94] Apparently Anglin was also offered the posts of Speaker of the Senate and the Chief Commissioner of the Railways but he turned down both of these posts because he did not want to desert the schools question in the Commons, the issue which caused his exclusion from the cabinet in the first place.[95] Sometime before the new year, however,

* George Brown Papers, vol IX, Mackenzie to Brown, 13 Nov. 1873. Mackenzie had made efforts to change the views of the New Brunswickers regarding Anglin (see Rogers Papers, Anglin to Rogers, 21 Nov. 1873). Even in a letter to Charles Burpee (Isaac's uncle) Mackenzie recognized the justice of Anglin's claim to a cabinet seat, and stated that he had told him that, when circumstances changed, 'we would all be willing to do him justice' (see Mackenzie Letterbooks, vol III, Mackenzie to Burpee, 4 Feb. 1874).

Mackenzie made another offer. This time he suggested that, if Anglin agreed, the Speakership of the House of Commons would be made available to him.*

Anglin's failure to receive a cabinet post and his discontent with the new government's apparent position on the schools question did not lead him to oppose the government. Throughout the late fall and early winter of 1873–4 the *Freeman* consistently supported the administration, particularly during the general election held in January. Anglin rationalized that a Reform victory would aid in the schools campaign.

I think it would be folly for us to quarrel with them if we can avoid it. The leading men are pledged by their votes of last Session to do all in their power to obtain justice for the Catholics of this Province and to that we should try to hold them even if thereby we only secure their help at the next Local Elections. Dr. Sweeny is afraid that the Govrnt will be too strong and that if so strong they may treat us unfairly. They certainly cannot treat us more unfairly if they are strong than they are ever compelled to do under the pressure from the New Brunswick members, I can hardly imagine that we can suffer from their being relieved from that pressure and therefore I am inclined to think that it will be to our benefit to have them stronger than they are at present if they are to exist at all.[96]

Anglin's own re-election was the easiest contest he had ever encountered: he won by acclamation.[97] When the House of Commons met on 26 March 1874, it seconded his constituents' confidence by naming him Speaker of the House.[98]

Anglin's acceptance of the speakership raises the question of motive. In November he had said that he 'could accept nothing' for himself because he had to continue to press Catholic claims on the schools issue, in spite of his fears that the time for successful agitation on the question in the Commons had passed.† In order for him to accept a post one of two things had to

* 'Letters of the Hon. Alexander Mackenzie to Hon. A.G. Jones, 1869–1885,' *Report of the Board of Trustees of the Public Archives of Nova Scotia, 1952*, Mackenzie to Jones, 6 Jan. 1874. Although the letter does not make it absolutely clear, it also appears that Mackenzie offered to Anglin the first cabinet position available.

† Rogers Papers, Anglin to Rogers, 21 Nov 1873. In later years Onésiphore Turgeon claimed that Anglin in his Gloucester election victory speech had promised 'qu'il n'accepterait aucun poste dans le gouvernement, aucune position d'honneur ou d'émolument quelconque avant d'avoir réglé la question des Ecoles à la satisfaction de la minorite catholique du Nouveau-Brunswick' (see Turgeon, *Un Tribut*, p 20). As no newspaper account of this speech seems to be available today, there is no direct contemporary evidence to support or disprove Turgeon's statement. Other evidence suggests that Turgeon's memory played

happen. Either the schools question had to be settled, or the directors of the agitation – the New Brunswick bishops – had to relieve Anglin of his responsibilities in Ottawa on the matter. The first possibility did not materialize, although Mackenzie gave evidence of a helpful attitude.[99] What did happen was that Rogers and Sweeny both urged Anglin to accept the position offered him. Indeed, the bishops had already begun to relieve Anglin of leadership responsibilities during the 1873 session. As well, Anglin was himself convinced that his acceptance would not hurt the case of the New Brunswick Catholics to any appreciable extent.

I have accepted the Speakership which I told you Dr. Sweeny wished very much I should take and which your lordship also thought it well I should take. It may be that as you and my friends say I should be able to do more in that position than I would as an independent member. It may be that my seeming to stand aside will help to a settlement of our School question. At all events should it be necessary I can resign at any moment and go back to my old place and thus do my share in the fight.[100]

It is probable that the bishops recognized that Anglin merited some recompense for his parliamentary labours and did not want to see him give up a fine opportunity for advancement. There were others, such as John Costigan, who could carry on the fight. Anglin, they felt, would be able to do more for the cause as Speaker, even though, or perhaps because, his voice would be silenced. In accepting the Speaker's chair, therefore, Anglin was not betraying New Brunswick Catholics. And so it happened that Anglin became the first and only Speaker of the House of Commons from New Brunswick.[101]

tricks on him. By the time Anglin was returned for Gloucester, Mackenzie's offer had been in his hands for at least a month. It is probable that he had already made up his mind to accept the position, and in any case it is most unlikely that he would have made such a statement had he any inclination whatever to take the post. One suspects, then, that Turgeon misconstrued Anglin's remarks.

10

First Commoner, 1874-8

From 1874 to 1878 Ottawa was a second home for the Anglin family. In those days the Speaker had housekeeping quarters in the parliament buildings. One result of this arrangement was that Mary Margaret, the Anglins' seventh child, became, on 3 April 1876, the only person ever born in the parliament buildings of Canada. Mrs Anglin, like her husband, was energetic and talented. Her family duties did not prevent her from becoming an accomplished amateur actress and singer, according to the testimony of Lady Dufferin herself.[1] Indeed, the head of the household was having to share the limelight not only with his wife but also with his two oldest boys who were showing that the good educational atmosphere in the Anglin home was having an effect.[2] In fact, with the exception of the terrible memory of three dead children and a fire which destroyed their Saint John house and most of their belongings in September 1874,* these were good

---

* At the time of the fire Anglin had been in Gloucester and his wife and some of the children in St Stephen, leaving the male servant and 'one of the younger members of the family' in charge (see *Freeman*, 26 Sept. 1874). Anglin's insurance coverage was estimated to be $14,000 (see *Morning News* [Saint John], 25 Sept. 1874), but Anglin confided to Bishop Rogers that his loss was much greater than his coverage (see Bishop James Rogers Papers, Anglin to Rogers, 2 Dec. 1874 in UNBA). While a new house was being built on their lot, the Anglins boarded at the Victoria Hotel in Saint John (see *McAlpine's Saint John Directory, for 1875–76* ... [Saint John, n.d.], p 37). That the Anglins had a man servant and, at times at least, a cook (see *Freeman*, 23 Sept. 1878) is interesting, given the fact that one historian views the delineation between the middle and working classes in the nineteenth century 'in terms of keeping or not of servants' (see J.F.C. Harrison, *The Early Victorians 1832–1851* [London, 1971], p 110).

years for the Anglin family. Above all, they could enjoy the prestige of Anglin's position as Speaker of the House of Commons. In March 1874, of course, it was not known what kind of Speaker he would make. But Anglin himself must have reflected at times about the irony of the situation. Here was he, an old anti-Confederate, the First Commoner of the Dominion of Canada.

I

The first task of the 1874 session was to choose Anglin as Speaker. Normally the selection of the Speaker is a perfunctory sort of thing. This was not quite the case in 1874, for after Anglin had taken the Speaker's chair, Sir John A. Macdonald rose to express his surprise that Luther Hamilton Holton, a prominent Liberal whose interest in and knowledge of parliamentary procedure was great, had not been chosen. But the Tory leader acknowledged that Anglin's industriousness and intelligence ought to make him a satisfactory Speaker.[3] He may have doubted the newly elected Speaker's vow that he hoped 'to prove himself worthy of the honour by acting and conducting the debates with the strictest impartiality and regard for the rules of the House,'[4] but he did not suggest that Anglin's well-known partisanship or even his editing of a public newspaper made him unsuitable for the position. In any case, Macdonald did not really expect impartiality from Speakers.[5] Comments made by observers off the floor of the House were more forthright. The *New Brunswick Reporter*, for example, thought it 'strange ... that the man who a few months ago was publicly censured for insulting the dignity of Parliament, should now be raised to the position of First Commoner, and conservator of that very dignity which he outraged so recently.'[6] The Conservative Ottawa *Citizen* hoped that Anglin would, while Speaker, 'obliterate from public memory the stains left upon his reputation by the records of the Dominion Parliament.'[7] More serious criticism came from the Ottawa correspondent of the *Canadian Illustrated News*, who pointed out that Anglin knew no French.* Yet despite these criticisms and the belief of many journalists that the government had given the speakership to Anglin not only to compensate him for not receiving a cabinet post but also to silence him on the schools ques-

---

* 'Chaudiere,' 4 Apr. 1874, in *Canadian Illustrated News* (Montreal), 11 Apr. 1874. This became painfully obvious in 1877 when Anglin was forced to admit that he could not read the opening prayers to the House in French because any attempt to do so would be 'ludicrous' (see *Canada: House of Commons, Debates, 1877*, p 94 [19 Feb.]).

tion,[8] there was recognition of Anglin's talents in the opposition press. 'Mr. Anglin,' wrote the *Citizen*, 'is a man of considerable ability, affable in his manner and courteous in his disposition.'[9] Government organs, arguing that Anglin's election as Speaker rectified the outrageous treatment he had received from a vindictive majority in the Commons some ten months earlier, praised Anglin to the skies.[10] The Toronto *Globe*, for example, assured its readers of Anglin's suitability for the position in no uncertain terms:

Mr. Anglin is a man of great dignity and force of character, and is far above the suspicion of swerving a hair's breadth aside from what he deems right. His decisions cannot fail to command respect from both parties.[11]

Contemporary newspapers favourable to Anglin were, of course, as heavily laden with party prejudices as those opposed. But one cannot say that Anglin received an unfavourable reception from either the politicians or the press when he became Speaker.

The 1874 session gave Anglin a baptism of fire. From its beginning the name of Louis Riel caused great turmoil, for Riel came to Ottawa before the session and was administered the oaths for elected members of the Commons by Mr Patrick, the Clerk of the House.[12] Riel's 'audacity' roused the temper of Mackenzie Bowell, the Orange leader. With A.J. Clarke, the Attorney General of Manitoba, as his prize witness, Bowell attempted to prove to the House that Riel was a fugitive from justice and ought therefore to be expelled from the Commons, in spite of the fact that he had never occupied his seat. To maintain order and to keep the examination within proper bounds was a very difficult task, and Anglin's fledgling efforts were not very successful. In fact, as the investigation dragged on and as members became weary and desired an end to it all, Anglin was forced to turn the problem over to Holton and A.-A. Dorion for them to decide. Perhaps Anglin was not as incompetent as this might make him appear, for they did not come up with a solution either, and both the inquiry and the debate went on.[13]

Controlling the House was never an easy task. Members of the Commons were not noted for their decorum and Anglin can hardly be blamed for their undignified outbursts.[14] Still, Anglin was not very impressive, a fact which he himself later admitted to Archbishop Lynch of Toronto:

I was really quite unprepared for the discharge of the duties as it was the one position in public life which I never dreamt of occupying but I have endeavoured by hard work to make myself acquainted with the duties and by endeavouring always to do what is right I hope to deserve the approval of all whose esteem is worth having.[15]

His efforts bore fruit towards the end of the first session and carried over for subsequent meetings of parliament. At the end of the first session both the Toronto *Globe* and the Ottawa *Free Press* paid special tribute to Anglin's ability as Speaker.[16] In the following sessions Anglin's decisions as Speaker became thoroughly conclusive and authoritative. Because they were firmly based in parliamentary practice, which Anglin learned to cite chapter and verse,[17] there was little disputation of them.[18] In fact, Anglin often carried his display of knowledge to extremes.

A ruling should be brief, clear as crystal and final as fate. One superfluous sentence spoils its effect. Mr. Anglin utters many superfluous sentences ... He explains, expostulates, nay even argues from his seat.[19]

Generally speaking, he allowed a free rein to debate, giving considerable latitude for discussion, even of his own rulings. While he certainly tended to side with the government, he was not noted for partisanship in his rulings;[20] even opposition MPs seldom complained.[21] This was no mean achievement, for Anglin certainly retained strong political views. Yet it was essential for the effective functioning of the Commons that its Speaker apply the rules of the House without party bias. In performing this important task Anglin succeeded admirably. Indeed, once he had 'learned the ropes,' Anglin's greatest problem was that he found the job rather tedious and uninteresting.[22] As he later related, 'I had always regarded the Speakership as most irksome and unpleasant, and with my habits ... accustomed as I was to take an active part in the business of the House – I felt the occupancy of the Chair would be for me a particularly unpleasant position.'[23] By and large, however, Anglin made an acceptable, if not brilliant, Speaker.

The duties of the Speaker did not end when he left the chair for the day. He was responsible for expenditures made for the House of Commons in much the same way that ministers are in charge of the expenses of their departments, and like most cabinet ministers he often felt the pressures which the control of patronage brought.[24] Anglin also found that he had to keep a close watch on House employees. During the 1878 session he checked up on some clerks, found them 'disporting about' on the streets, and fired them forthwith.[25] On the other hand, he was not a heartless taskmaster for those who did a good job, such as H. Hartney, one of the clerks of the House. 'Why is it,' Anglin queried in a letter written from Saint John 'that you do not take a few weeks holidays and escape from the dreadful heat of Ottawa. You attend so assiduously to your duties that you certainly are entitled to some recreation. I would be glad to learn that you have arranged matters as to be able to get away for a time.'[26]

Being Speaker brought Anglin certain social rewards. As First Commoner he was one of the leading citizens of the Dominion. From state receptions held by the Governor General and the Countess of Dufferin at the opening of parliament to dinners and balls sponsored by the prime minister, the Anglins took a prominent position.[27] Mrs Anglin, in her early thirties and reputed to be 'one of the most beautiful women of the capital,'[28] undoubtedly drew more attention than her husband at such affairs as the 1874 Citizens Ball in Ottawa when she wore a dress of white silk, trimmed with black lace and ermine, and a head dress of violet and white flowers. But Timothy probably received at least passing notice when dancing the opening quadrille on that occasion.[29] The Anglins also did a good deal of entertaining in their quarters in the parliament buildings.[30] On occasion the guests included prominent overseas visitors such as O'Connor Power, MP from Mayo.[31] Indeed, as Speaker Anglin gained not only national recognition but also a limited amount of publicity outside Canada; for example, a biographical sketch and photograph of Anglin appeared in the New York publication *McGee's Illustrated Weekly*.[32] In terms of increased prestige, therefore, the speakership was a significant post. Since Anglin seems to have been very anxious to achieve 'success,' the recognition he received as Speaker must have been gratifying.

II

Anglin's Speakership was complicated by the fact that this was not the only phase of his life. He was as well the representative for Gloucester, a prominent Liberal, a newspaper editor, and an Irish Catholic leader.

As the representative for Gloucester and as one in whom the government had confidence, he was looked to for patronage. Anglin was not reticent to press the claims of his political supporters and friends in response to their pressure upon him. Indeed, most of the letters which passed between Anglin and Mackenzie in these years dealt with patronage matters.[33] As a member of the Reform party Anglin lost little of his prestige during this period. His status in the Reform ranks accounts for the fact that he continued to be considered as a possible recipient of a cabinet post.[34] Such a move seemed logical, particularly in the summer of 1877 when Anglin had resigned the Speakership for reasons which will be examined later. It is difficult to know why he was not offered a cabinet position except that neither Anglin nor Mackenzie wanted to give the opposition the satisfaction of saying that they had forced the government to drop its Speaker. The significant point, however, is that it was assumed that a man was equally well suited to be either a cabinet minister or the Speaker. It was apparent that the Speaker did not have to show any detachment from partisan politics.

Any supposed neutrality of the Speaker on political matters was reduced to an absurdity in the columns of Anglin's *Freeman*. Of all the Speakers of the Canadian House of Commons, Anglin was the only one to have been an active journalist,[35] and by means of his newspaper he made his views known far and wide. The *Freeman* remained one of the strong arms of the government. Although it demonstrated independence on certain points,[36] the *Freeman* found little to oppose and much to support where the government was concerned. This public enunciation of his opinion meant that the Speaker's newspaper became subject to criticism on the floor of the House even while Anglin was in the chair.[37]

Finally, Anglin was an Irish Catholic leader. It was probably fortunate for him that there were rather few political issues during this period which directly concerned Irish Catholics. True, Anglin did write to the Minister of Justice in two judicial cases where Irishmen were involved.[38] And, to be sure, events in and about Ireland continued to occupy Anglin's attention. In 1872, for example, he felt himself obliged to write a series of lengthy and remarkably learned articles for the *Freeman* combatting the interpretation of Irish and Catholic history which the eminent historian James Anthony Froude had expounded while he was lecturing in the United States.[39] In Canada itself it was of considerable concern to Irish Catholics that, although they numbered perhaps one-seventh of the population of the Dominion, only seven had been elected to a federal House of 206 members.[40] Such an anomaly ought to be corrected 'if only,' said the *Freeman*, 'to give so sensitive a people substantial proof that they enjoy perfect, civil and political equality in this country, practically as well as theoretically.' Part of the problem was that in no constituency did Irish Catholics hold the majority of the votes, and in many places a hearty prejudice against them made it most difficult to get an Irish Catholic elected.[41] What was the answer to this problem? A form of proportional representation might help, thought the *Freeman*, but its support for this scheme was lukewarm.[42]

Putting pressure on party leaders was no real answer, for they did the best they could, considering the attitude 'of the more ignorant and prejudiced who unfortunately form so large a proportion of the rank and file of both parties.'[43] In any case group politics were not normally advisable.

The cause must be weighty and important indeed, and the necessity great and manifest which would justify the dividing up of the Canadian body politic, so that instead of the people with interests in common we should become a set of associations, Catholic and Protestant, Irish, English, French and Scotch.[44]

The only answer which the *Freeman* could offer was the solution that time alone could bring – a change in attitude.

It would be indeed a great change for the better if, when only political questions are at issue, the constituencies would not stop to ask what the religious tenets of any candidate were, and if a Catholic candidate could reasonably hope to gain the confidence of a Protestant majority by proving that his aims were high and statesman-like and his tone lofty.[45]

The views Anglin had expressed to the St Patrick's Society of Montreal in 1867 obviously had not changed much. None of the issues which related to Anglin as an Irish Catholic leader created much problem for Anglin as Speaker except one – the New Brunswick schools question.

III

The schools question provides the best example of Anglin's difficulty in being both Speaker and a politician-editor with a strong interest in a particular issue. While the schools question can legitimately be viewed from this angle, in the context of Anglin's life as a whole it would be erroneous to give it such a narrow focus. After all, the question of Catholic schools involved Anglin long before and long after he was Speaker of the House of Commons.

Between the end of the 1873 session and the beginning of the 1874 session Anglin viewed, participated in, and reported developments on this issue. During the summer and fall of 1873 local authorities in New Brunswick had stepped up their campaign to collect unpaid school taxes, even before Lord Kimberley, the Colonial Secretary, decided in late June that the assessment acts were legal and that the House of Commons had no power to disallow them.[46] Refusal to pay was met with seizure of property followed by public auction. Officials were particularly zealous in cases of prominent Catholic leaders. Anglin had twelve reams of printing paper confiscated, while his friend Dr Travers lost a family carriage.[47] Things were carried to extremes, however, when Father Michaud, a Saint John priest, was arrested in broad daylight on Prince William Street, one of the main thoroughfares in the city. He had failed to pay a sum of $4.80, an amount which the *Freeman* claimed could have been obtained by seizing books or other property. For a time violence threatened to erupt, but when Michaud's tax was paid anonymously, the city quieted, though not without a residue of bitterness.[48]

Yet there were also more encouraging developments. Perhaps most important in the long run was the fact that Father Dunphy, the parish priest in Carleton, just across the Saint John harbour, had managed to come to an acceptable compromise with the school board trustees. It was agreed that the teachers in the Catholic Boys' School would be Catholics, selected and approved by Father Dunphy; books to which he objected would not be used; and religious instruction would be given every day after a fixed hour.[49] In other respects the school would be the same as other common schools. This compromise pointed the way out of the educational quagmire in which the province found itself. Unfortunately the problem was more complex elsewhere. In Saint John itself Bishop Sweeny was especially concerned to retain the excellent services of the Christian Brothers, but this undertaking, apparently, no board of trustees could grant under the existing regulations. In any case the Saint John trustees had refused to give any substantial concessions when the bishop had approached them in the fall of 1871, and there was no reason to think that they would be more amenable now. In late September 1873, however, another propitious development took place. Bishop Sweeny, without having to take the initiative, met with members of the provincial government to discuss the problem.[50] While nothing was solved, the fact remained that a few hesitant steps had been taken along the path of conciliation. During this period the *Freeman* cautioned those Catholics whose tempers were wearing thin not to go beyond constitutional tactics.

Those who wish to see justice done must address themselves to the good sense of their Protestant neighbours and endeavour to satisfy them that they have been grossly deceived by those whose statements they have too readily accepted as true, and to show them that Catholics ask only what is fair and right, and what all Protestants who value religion should freely accord.[51]

To further this object the *Freeman* continued to enunciate the Catholic position as clearly as possible.[52]

As Anglin took the Speaker's chair in the Commons his attitude towards action in the House on the schools question became more conservative. He now owed something to the party which had placed him in his post, and he acted in much the same way as had Cartier and Langevin when the interests of their party had been at stake. John Costigan and L.-F.-R. Masson, of course, were not concerned that the government might be embarrassed and pushed forward the issue with vigour. Because Anglin was no longer available for the parliamentary battle, Costigan took over undisputed leadership of the question in the Commons. He wanted to press the question in spite of the fact that the Judicial Committee of the Privy Council had not yet handed down its decision.[53] Anglin's influence, felt behind the scenes, was still considerable. In his view, the fact that New Brunswick Catholics had accepted the $5,000 grant to cover expenses in their appeal to the Judicial Committee obligated them to take no action in the Commons before the result of the suit was known.[54] Moreover, he claimed, it was unfair of Masson to blame the government for not giving effect to the Commons' resolution calling for disallowance of the assessment acts. The Colonial Secretary, Anglin pointed out, had declared that the Commons had no right to take such action, and while Anglin believed that Lord Kimberley was entirely wrong in his interpretation of the constitution, one could not expect the Governor General to act in complete disregard of the instructions he had sought at the urging of Macdonald. The situation would have to be clarified.[55] Bishop Sweeny agreed. He came to the conclusion that walking softly was the prudent course to take, and he suggested to Costigan that he ought to consult with friends in Ottawa, 'especially Mr. Anglin who, with yourself, has the best knowledge of our position ...' He feared that pressing the issue in the Commons under the circumstances might alienate support. Better to wait until the Judicial Committee had spoken.[56] Costigan dutifully dropped the matter in the House.

In the interim between the 1874 and 1875 sessions of parliament there were several significant developments. First, the 1874 New Brunswick provincial election demonstrated that Catholics would not be able to improve their position politically, as federal politicians had often suggested.[57] The *Freeman* considered thirty-six of the forty-one elected members to be No Popery men 'pledged to refuse justice to the Catholics of the Province.'[58] Hard on the heels of this electoral defeat were further disheartening developments for the opponents of the New Brunswick school system. In a nice effort to collect the school taxes these were now lumped together with other taxes.[59] Those who refused to pay school taxes now had to refuse to pay all taxes, a move calculated to remove any sympathy which Protestants had shown the previous year. But even this became unnecessary when the Catholic argument in the test case which had been appealed to the Judicial Committee was dismissed.[60]

The events which demonstrated the impossible situation existing in New Brunswick occurred in Anglin's own constituency in the small Acadian fishing village of Caraquet. There, early in 1875, a tiny minority of English-speaking Protestant residents attempted to establish a school which would have necessitated taxing all the inhabitants. Not surprisingly trouble erupted. Several disturbances occurred, perhaps meriting the term 'riots'; eventually developments took an ugly turn and two men died.[61] These unfortunate incidents shocked all New Brunswick. Anglin, as might be expected, claimed that they showed the necessity for the government to make amendments to the school laws to make the system acceptable to Catholics. In the eyes of the editor of the *Freeman* the real violence had been perpetrated by the enactment of unacceptable school legislation.[62] Other New Brunswickers agreed with Anglin in thinking that something must be done.[63] Possibly some meaningful progress might now occur within the province; it was certain that efforts would be made in the House of Commons to improve the situation.

Anglin was quietly working behind the scenes in Ottawa. He gathered impressions, canvassed opinions, reported developments to the New Brunswick bishops, and arranged visits between government leaders and Catholic dignitaries such as Bishop Sweeny.[64] Sweeny had full confidence in Anglin, urging Costigan to consult the Speaker on the question early in 1875.[65] Costigan, however, was not anxious to do this, and Sweeny conceded the point:

I requested you in my letter to consult with Mr. Anglin, on account of his intimate knowledge of every circumstance regarding the vexed question in this Province, but I suppose, from what you say in your letter, that his position and occupations as Speaker will prevent him from taking an active part in the matter.[66]

What was evident from this comment was not that Anglin could play no role, but rather that Costigan would have nothing to do with him. The two Irish Catholic New Brunswickers were on different sides of the political fence, and Costigan was not about to give his competitor a part to play.

On the evening of 8 March Costigan presented a motion that an address be presented to the Queen, requesting an amendment to the BNA Act to the effect that Catholics in New Brunswick be granted the same educational rights as the minorities in Ontario and Quebec.[67] The government did not wish to support such a clear statement of policy and managed to have the House adjourned.[68] During the next two days supporters of the government hammered out a compromise consisting of two amendments to Costigan's resolution. The first, to be moved by Mackenzie, would express the opinion that imperial legislation on the Canadian constitution 'would be an infraction of the Provincial Constitutions, and that it would be inexpedient and fraught with danger to the autonomy of each of the Provinces for this House to invite such Legislation.' The second amendment, to be moved by J.-E. Cauchon, would request that the Colby motion of 1872 be brought to the attention of Her Majesty, requesting that she use her influence with the New Brunswick legislature to bring about modifications which would remove grounds of discontent.[69] The exact meaning of Mackenzie's resolution was questioned. Did its acceptance mean that hereafter the House would reject any attempt to have the constitution changed? Anglin claimed that such was not the case; that Mackenzie had assured his supporters on this point.[70] Because of uncertainty on the question, however, many MPs consulted with Bishop Sweeny, but he was as indecisive as they. 'He told them in effect,' Anglin later reported to Bishop Rogers, 'that if the resolutions taken together would not preclude future action he thought it would be better to accept them but to consent to nothing that would fetter their future action.[71] This was no help. When it came to the vote, Costigan and other opponents of the government opposed the amendments on the ground that Mackenzie's precluded any further appeals to the Commons. Catholic supporters of the government took the other side. Catholic MPs split along party lines and the government carried the day.[72] Party politics undoubtedly played a part, but this was a case in which men differed in their attempt to carry out the bishop's wishes.[73] After the passage of these amendments a motion was made to appoint a committee to draft an address to the Queen. Costigan moved an amendment which would have asserted the right of the Commons to seek amendment of the BNA Act if redress of Catholic grievances did not occur as a result of the amended resolution. This initiative was objected to, and Anglin must have wished that someone else was in the Speaker's chair. Obviously he wanted to keep open the possibility of further action by the House. Yet was not such an amendment unnecessary? Would it not create great difficulty for the government? Was it not also a substantive change from the motion? His decision, as difficult as it may have been, was clear.

The House has ordered an Address within a certain scope, and I do not think it is competent now to make a motion asking the House to depart from the Resolution which it has just affirmed.[74]

While the entire episode showed the weakness of the position and leadership of Bishop Sweeny and the ingenuity of the Mackenzie government, Anglin was reasonably satisfied. In the first place the passage of Costigan's resolution 'would accomplish little unless the govrnt earnestly endeavoured to induce the Home govrnt to give them effect,' and it was clear that this could not be expected. With the passage of the amendments, however, a large majority of the new House of Commons had expressed its sympathy with New Brunswick Catholics, 'and if the Queen's intercession failed and her advice was ignored the Parliament which had gone so far could not consistently refuse to go further and assist us in wresting Justice from those who disregarded all considerations but the gratification of their own bigotry.'[75] As for the Queen's intervention, Anglin was pessimistic about its effect; in New Brunswick, once the No Popery cry was raised, 'reason is blind and justice is forgotten and the one passionate desire of the masses is to trample Pope and Popery in the dust.'[76]

If Anglin thought that nothing could be accomplished on the provincial level, he was wrong. During the summer of 1875 Kennedy Burns, MPP for Gloucester, and a small band of legislative associates approached the provincial government with a set of propositions. They asked that members of religious teaching orders be accepted on the certificate of their superiors; that children be allowed to attend schools outside their own district; that books prescribed by the Board of Education but found to contain objectionable passages would not be compulsory and would be replaced; and that religious instruction be allowed after school hours and regular school hours be shortened in order that such instruction might be given.[77] The government's answer was long delayed, and when it did come, it was unclear what the practical results for Catholics would be. First, the Christian Brothers and Sisters of Charity would not have to attend a teachers' training school but they would be required to undergo examination before receiving their license; whether such examination could be taken at their place of residence was not specified. The second point – attendance at schools outside the district – was left up to the local trustees. Books containing objectionable passages were to be edited rather than replaced. Finally, the Government expressed its view that, depending on local circumstances – that is, in Catholic-owned schools – it would be possible to give religious instruction after school hours, although it made no mention of shortened school hours. Further than that the government could not go:

It is obvious that if the Trustees be required to allow the teachers to give denominational instruction after school to the pupils assembled for public purposes under the authority of the School Act, the direct tendency of such a provision would be to render the selection and appointment of teachers a matter to be determined rather by their denominational views than their fitness to discharge the specified duties required of them, during school hours.[78]

What all this actually meant could only be determined by the local trustees. The government's stand had thrown much of the responsibility on the trustees; while this was not as acceptable to Catholics as an agreement on a province-wide basis would have been, at least the way was now clear for more arrangements such as the Carleton agreement of a couple of years before.

In the meantime the Commons' resolutions had been submitted to the Colonial Secretary and Anglin urged Edward Blake to do all that could be done. 'The despatch expressing the Queen's wishes can not be too strong,' Anglin told the Minister of Justice, 'and it should if possible be sustained by private instructions conveyed to the Local Govrnt.'[79] Not until December 1875 did Anglin learn from Mackenzie what Lord Carnarvon's response had been.[80] His despatch virtually prohibited any future appeal for constitutional change on the question, undoubtedly much to Mackenzie's delight. In fact, while Carnarvon himself expressed the hope that changes might be made in the New Brunswick educational system, he did 'not feel himself at liberty even to advise Her Majesty to recommend anything to the local authorities ...'[81] Anglin was not pleased. If the expression of sympathy had been in the Queen's name rather than in Lord Carnarvon's, it might have done some good. As it was, he told Bishop Rogers in sending him a copy of the confidential despatch, the provincial government would just laugh at it.[82]

The situation had now become desperate. No hope of redress from the federal government could be entertained. Anglin confessed that he was at a loss to know what should be done next. He could only hope that Bishop Sweeny and Bishop Rogers would be able to come up with some viable plan of action.[83] The bishops did the only thing they could; they gave up the fight on a province-wide basis. Early in January 1876 Bishop Rogers announced this change in a bitter letter sent to the priests in his diocese. No longer was the establishment of schools under the school law to be opposed. In each district Catholics were to strive for the best terms they could obtain from the local trustees.[84]

The problem was not resolved immediately. Even as late as December 1876 Bishop Sweeny's carriage was seized for non-payment of taxes. Not until March 1877 were the Catholic schools of Saint John finally placed under the control of the Board of School Trustees, under conditions which the Sisters of Charity would, but the Christian Brothers would not, accept. The Brothers, who had done so much for education in Saint John, were forced to leave the province because their superior would not agree to their being examined by the Board of Education before being given a license, even if such examination took place at their own house. In other respects the settlement reached was reasonably acceptable to Catholics.[85] Once Saint John had come to terms, other areas which had not yet reached a solution rapidly followed.[86] At last the question was settled – settled, according to Bishop Rogers, 'by utter defeat on our part with everything lost except honour.'[87]

Was the failure of New Brunswick Catholics to receive redress of grievances on the education issue Anglin's fault? Had he betrayed the Catholic cause by playing party politics and accepting an office which prevented him from wielding a weapon on the Ottawa battlefield. Onésiphore Turgeon, as noted previously, believed the answer was 'yes.' The opposition press argued in 1874 that Anglin had been made Speaker because the government wished to remove him from active advocacy of the Catholic case. Whether or not this was the primary intention of the government, the fact remains that Anglin's acceptance of the Speakership muted his voice most effectively. Yet it is difficult to place very much blame on Anglin. The bishops themselves had agreed to his elevation to Speaker. Moveover the House of Commons was a political arena, and one had to play the game if one wished to accomplish very much. In working quietly behind the scenes Anglin was wielding as much influence as he could. Had he resigned as Speaker in 1875, for instance, he would merely have isolated himself from the government and done the cause of Catholic schools in New Brunswick little good. Anglin did not betray that cause. But because it could be argued that he had, and because there was little evidence before the public that he was working at all on the matter, Anglin found it extremely difficult to appear to champion Catholic interests while he occupied the Speaker's chair.

IV

Another significant problem demonstrated the difficulty of being Speaker and a politician-newspaperman at the same time: the matter of Post Office printing. During the Macdonald administration Post Office printing for the Maritime provinces was done at or through newspaper offices in the region. When the new government came to power in 1873, the Postmaster General, D.A. Macdonald, took this patronage away from the newspapers that had enjoyed it and gave it to papers which had supported the Reformers. At first two-thirds, and later all of the New Brunswick printing for the Post Office was sent to the *Freeman*.[88] For the next two years this practice continued, the work amounting to $8,000 in 1874 and $10,000 in 1875.[89] When Lucius Seth Huntington became Postmaster General late in 1875, he became aware of what he considered to be an anomalous situation, drew it to the attention of the cabinet, and subsequently directed that no more printing be done at the *Freeman* office. Henceforth all Post Office printing would be done under contract in Ottawa.[90]

It was logical to assume that the *Freeman* had entered into an agreement or contract with a government department and that therefore for over two years Anglin had been violating the Independence of Parliament Act. It was also logical to think that the *Freeman* had been given this patronage in order to propitiate Anglin for not receiving a cabinet seat and a higher salary than that of Speaker. The *Freeman* denied any corrupt bribe, and Anglin maintained that no contract or agreement had ever been made. Had such contract existed, claimed Anglin, 'the Government would not so summarily have transferred it all to Ottawa ...'[91] The *Freeman*'s defence was weak. Its editor may have been convinced that he was not violating the Independence of Parliament Act, but his conscience must have told him that his position was only legally correct. Six years before he had been quite righteous about such matters.

The Act to preserve the Independence of Parliament, which was passed at the close of the Session, is very far from being what it ought to be were the real object the exclusion from the House of Commons of all persons who, through the action or connivance of the Government, receive a share of the public revenues.[92]

The issue did not reach serious proportions in the House of Commons until 1877.[93] That session was long and bitterly fought, and Speaker Anglin did not help matters by his continual interruptions and long explanations, at times almost entering into debate.[94] It was a difficult session to handle, and on one occasion Macdonald accused the Speaker of cheating the opponents of the government of their rights.[95] Two days later, on 7 April 1877, Mackenzie Bowell moved an amendment to the House going into a Committee of Supply that it was 'inexpedient and improper' for the government to enter into 'agreement or contract' by which public funds were to be paid to a member of parliament, specifying Anglin as the one who had so contravened the Independence of Parliament Act. That the amendment was directed as much against the government as against the Speaker is unquestionable. Charges that Anglin had violated the act could have been brought before the Committee on Privileges and Elections at any time. But by moving this amendment the Liberal-Conservatives were able to attack the government without either giving Anglin an opportunity to explain anything or allowing the Government to move a sub-amendment, as this was impossible when the House was going into a Committee of Supply. The government's response was to regard the amendment, even if it passed, not as a want of confidence motion, but merely as a censure of the Speaker. Sir John A. Macdonald berated the government for attempting to shield themselves by sacrificing Anglin whom, ironically enough, he eulogized for the dignity and impartiality with which he had presided over the House.[96] Macdonald was after bigger game than Anglin; he wanted to bag the entire government.

The issue was one which was debated throughout the nation. Conservative newspapers, such as the Toronto *Mail* and the Ottawa *Citizen*, presented column after column in an effort not merely to denounce Anglin but also to build up a case against Mackenzie's government.[97] The Reformers had come to office riding the wave of the Pacific Scandal, and now the Conservative organs had a hey-day, saying, in effect, 'the Reformers are just as corrupt as the Conservatives.' Government papers, such as the Toronto *Globe* and the Ottawa *Free Press*, also played the party game, arguing that the government had acted correctly in the matter and that Anglin had operated according to established practices and had certainly not been bribed to support the government.[98]

In the debate in the House on Bowell's amendment Macdonald, Blake, Mackenzie, Huntington, Costigan – all had their say; almost everyone but the man most directly involved, Anglin himself. No one in the House seemed much concerned with what happened to Anglin's name. The Tories were out to blast the Grits and the government was out to protect itself. Anglin was caught in the crossfire. When the amendment was defeated, the question was referred to the Committee on Privileges and Elections. Ten years later Anglin claimed that this had been done at his suggestion and in order to clear his name.[99] At least it gave him an opportunity to defend himself.

In giving evidence before the committee Anglin answered the charge that the printing had been compensation for not receiving a seat on the cabinet. He claimed he had advised Mackenzie at the time of the formation of the cabinet that he had no claims upon the government but that he had confidence in it and would give it a general support.

There was not a single word said during all that time about my getting any benefit or advantage from the change in the Government, or of my getting any compensation for not becoming a member of the Government.

He denied that a contract or anything resembling a contract had ever been made. Unsolicited, D.A. Macdonald had simply informed Anglin that the Post Office printing for New Brunswick was to be sent to the *Freeman*.

There was nothing said that any ingenuity could possibly convert into the semblance of a contract or agreement. I did not imagine that the Postmaster General was bound in the slightest degree to send me any work he pleased to withold, or that I was bound to do any work he sent. I did not imagine at all when he told me this that there was in this transaction or would be in it the slightest violation of the Independence of Parliament Act.

Whether the other members of the cabinet had known about these dealings Anglin was not sure, but he presumed they did as it was a perfectly open transaction. In general, his testimony continued, his business man had looked after the matter. Work came to his office from day to day 'without my ever knowing that a single order would succeed it or not.' And, in fact, one day the orders did stop 'without a word of warning being given me by the Government ...' The care with which Anglin had acted was clear in his response to his foreman in reply to an inquiry from the Inspector in Saint John whether Anglin would agree to a specified price list:

I said to him, 'Take care and do not, on my behalf, agree to anything; simply state to the Inspector that you have examined the scale of prices, and that you think them fair and reasonable.'

If this did not amount to an agreement, it was at least an understanding in regard to prices. Yet this was not the same as having a contract or an agreement that work would come to the *Freeman* office. Anglin's evidence before the committee showed that he had acted in accord with the law and precedent. He also pointed out that there were a number of gentlemen who had sat in the Commons since Confederation who had been intimately connected with newspapers which received government advertising. Nothing had ever been said to indicate the illegality of this, Anglin claimed.

These things, I have no doubt, had their influence on my mind, so far as to cause me never to suspect for a moment, that I was committing any violation of the Independence of Parliament Act; and as I knew that I had done nothing dishonourable, I never really felt that there was anything to be ashamed or afraid of in this transaction; I never thought that the work was sent to me because I happened to be a member of Parliament. I was satisfied that if I ceased to be a member of Parliament the work would have been sent to me, and I believe that under such circumstances I could possibly in a great many cases have insisted upon getting what my foreman said were more reasonable prices than were allowed. Of course my position as a member of Parliament would prevent me at all interfering between him and the Department in matters of that kind.

Anglin concluded his statement by summarizing his position and ended on the following note:

Whether it was expedient or inexpedient that this work should be done by a Member of Parliament is, I think another question altogether. I would be myself prepared to say, I think, that if I had an opportunity of voting on the question now – having had more time to give to the consideration of it – I would vote that it is inexpedient, and I do not know but that I would not go so far as to say it is improper. But as to there being anything improper in it under the circumstances, as they existed, this never occurred to me; there was nothing dishonourable or dishonest in the transaction ...[100]

Anglin's legal position was good; his moral position was not. To accept his statement that he had not thought that he had violated either the letter or the spirit of the Independence of Parliament Act is most difficult. In the extraordinary care he took to maintain his legal position on the question one can see that he realized that he was treading on dangerous ground. The fact that others had done almost the same thing could not excuse him. He had spoken in high moral terms and had judged others by this standard; if one is to judge him by his own standard he must be condemned. One cannot but think that he realized that he was standing on the letter of the law rather than on right and justice. Had the printing been given to the *Freeman* as partial recompense for Anglin's exclusion from the cabinet? It seems clear that Anglin did not solicit it directly, nor did the matter enter his correspondence with Blake or Mackenzie. The most reasonable hypothesis might be stated as follows: Postmaster General Macdonald, himself a Catholic and undoubtedly aware that it was 'Protestant bigotry' on the New Brunswick schools question which kept Anglin out of the cabinet, sympathized with Anglin; when the opportunity arose to do something for the editor of the *Freeman*, he did so on his own initiative, neither Anglin nor the government being directly involved. That the printing did promote Anglin's acceptance of the government seems likely, however, and so the interpretation comes full circle.

Fortunately for the country and the purity of parliament, but unfortunately for Anglin, the Committee on Privileges and Elections decided to reverse practice and precedent. Following Blake's lead it asserted that 'said precedent and practice are erroneous, and that according to a true construction of the Act for securing the Independence of Parliament, the transactions in question did constitute disqualifying contracts.'[101] His election, the committee declared, was void. But for Anglin's sake and the sake of the smooth functioning of the Commons, this report was not brought down to the House until the session ended. However, Anglin knew that it was essential to resign his post and seek re-election in Gloucester before the next session met, at which time he could be re-elected Speaker.

Opposition to Anglin's re-election in Gloucester was more vociferous than he had ever encountered before. Anglin thought it was 'in some respects the most unpleasant election I ever ran or took part in ...'[102] Yet a strenuous five-week campaign enabled him to overcome disappointed office seekers (and even some office holders) and a nationalist-oriented segment of the Acadian population and be re-elected by a majority of more than 200 votes over his opponent, Onésiphore Turgeon.[103] Anglin could now be re-elected Speaker, or so he expected.

Thinking that his political problems had been solved, Anglin devoted the rest of 1877 to re-establishing the *Freeman* after the Great Fire in Saint John and to recuperating from an illness which kept him in a weakened state for a number of weeks.[104] Early in January 1878, however, Mackenzie notified Anglin that the Clerk of the House, Mr Patrick, was doubtful whether he could allow Anglin's name to be put forward for renomination to the Speakership. Patrick was convinced that the Speaker had to announce the results of special elections and that therefore another person would first have to be elected Speaker in order that the Gloucester results could be announced.[105] Anglin's response to this information was to for-

"WAITING FOR A DEAD MAN'S SHOES."

'Waiting for a Dead Man's Shoes'
by J.W. Bengough in *Grip* (Toronto), 2 June 1877
Provided by the Thomas Fisher Rare Book Library,
University of Toronto

ward his own case. The main thrust of his argument was that according to Canadian practice the Clerk could administer the oath; anyone who had taken the oath and had been duly elected could sit in the House; and anyone who legitimately held a seat in the House could not be restricted from any of its privileges. He then proceeded to cite a number of precedents which showed that his contention was solid.[106] Nor did it hurt his cause that Luther Holton and George Brown agreed that he had a right to stand for re-election.[107] Mackenzie, therefore, was well prepared when Sir John A. Macdonald objected to Anglin's nomination as Speaker. The Conservative leader found his arguments were no match for those of his fellow Scotsman and, although the issue was pushed to a vote, Anglin was re-elected by a vote of 116 to 53.[108] Anglin thus became the only Speaker of the Canadian House of Commons to be unseated for corrupt practices and re-elected during the life of a single parliament. Undoubtedly this action was a necessary face-saving device for the government and essential for Anglin's future as a politician. But it hardly benefited the dignity and respectability of the House and its Speaker.

V

Anglin had mentioned in his evidence before the Committee of Privileges and Elections that he had found the Speaker's chair rather confining as he was used to taking a prominent role in debate.[109] It would appear that he decided not to be silenced during the 1878 session. The particular discussion which drew him out was the Scott Act which provided for local option on the issue of prohibition.[110] As far as Anglin was concerned the only antidote for drunkenness was religion, 'which alone can elevate, purify and strengthen the soul of man and enable him to overcome his evil propensities ...'[111] Prohibitory legislation was unworkable and unjust, and the experiment in New Brunswick twenty years before had proven it, Anglin believed.[112] It was not surprising, therefore, that Anglin should oppose the Scott Act, but the manner in which he did so was rather startling. As soon as the House had resolved itself into a Committee of the Whole, Anglin stepped around the Clerk's table and told the ministerial benches he had something to say about the Bill.

The face, flushed with feeling, the voice trembling with passion, and the aggressive attitude, sent a thrill of expectation through the House, and the silence was intense. He continued, raising his voice and looking angrily towards the Premier:

'*I regard it as of the most injurious and pernicious character* that can possibly be conceived, and also of *the most tyrannical character.*

Yes, he said, tyranny more gross than this had never been attempted. No one had the right to tell another what he could eat, drink, or wear. The bill would be productive of great evil – riot, tumult, and confusion – and in addition it would cause the government to suffer politically.[113] Obviously Anglin felt strongly about this question, but it is likely that his over-reaction was caused in part by the strangeness of his position, for he had not taken part in debate before while he was Speaker. The ministry was made extremely uncomfortable and rather angry by this outburst.[114] But Anglin had ruffled feathers before and he would do so again. His forthright statement even won him plaudits.[115] At least no one could say that he was a tame follower of the government. Anglin's first incursion into debate when the Commons was in Committee of the Whole did not deter him from doing it once again the following day. On this occasion, however, he merely suggested that a Bill for the Better Prevention of Violence be stiffened by allowing shops and houses to be searched for weapons, a suggestion which was, with modifications, accepted.[116] For the Speaker to discuss issues brought to the floor of the House was most unusual, and Anglin refrained from doing so again during the rest of the session. Still, these two speeches probably relieved some of the boredom of the session.[117]

Anglin could not say, however, that the conclusion of the session was boring. On the last day of the third parliament of Canada, while the Commons was waiting for the Black Rod to summon it to the Senate, Donald Smith got into a heated argument with Charles Tupper and Sir John A. Macdonald. Anglin, seeing no prospect of silence, signalled the Sergeant-at-Arms to admit the Black Rod. Smith kept on talking until the Black Rod interrupted him. No sooner had the House been informed of His Excellency's 'pleasure' than Macdonald cried, 'Donald Smith is the biggest liar in Canada.' Smith replied in kind. As both sides spilled out onto the floor of the House, the prospect of blows seemed so great that Anglin ordered the Sergeant-at-Arms to clear the way and arrest the men involved. But they were pulled apart and, as they had not yet been named, no arrests were made. After the Speaker, the Clerk, the Sergeant-at-Arms, and a handful of members left the House, the tumult continued, peace being maintained only through the hard work of the Deputy Sergeant-at-Arms.[118] It was a fitting prelude for the battle to follow – the 1878 general election. Anglin knew that he retained the title of Speaker until the next parliament opened. He may well have suspected that he would never again have to preside over a debate in the House of Commons. What he could not have known or suspected was that he was leaving the most significant office he was to fill in his career.

11

Perspectives, 1874-8

Certain issues which arose between 1874 and 1878 were not particularly relevant to Anglin as Speaker but were very important to Anglin in other aspects of his life – as a Canadian, as an Irishman, as a Catholic, as a politician, and, of course, as a man whose children would be heirs to the world he and his generation left behind. His views on these issues, though generally in line with opinions expressed earlier in his life, were also shaped by increasing age and high position. In other words, Anglin's basic conservatism was very apparent between 1874 and 1878.

I

In the first place Anglin was living another chapter in the mythical autobiography 'The Making of a Canadian.' The country formed in 1867 was gradually winning his heart. By 1872, as we have seen, Anglin had come to accept Confederation, and this acceptance did not diminish as time went on. Even the New Brunswick schools question did much to make Ottawa rather than Fredericton the prime object of his loyalty. In 1877, when Anglin learned that some persons were attempting to establish a 'Canadian National Society' in Montreal, he printed the following statement in his *Freeman*:

We have already in this pretty well organized Dominion a national society to which all Canadians do actually and really belong, and this is the only Canadian National

Society that can exist in Canada. To call any other association than the Canadian people, so organized, a Canadian National Society, is a misnomer.[1]

Anglin, like many others, demonstrated Canada's power to produce patriotism and loyalty.

A non-vociferous anti-Americanism was one ingredient of this patriotism. Annexation was unthinkable. The government of the United States, the *Freeman* claimed, had for some years been 'the most wasteful, extravagant, and in many respects the most inefficient perhaps in the world.'[2] Annexation to the United States, a society pervaded by corruption and 'sapped and undermined by Divorce and Foeticide,'[3] would now bring few material benefits and many troubles and burdens, 'and there are few thinking men who would prefer the constitution and form of government to our own ...'[4] Even Canada's position in the Empire had become acceptable to Anglin. In 1872, when the Treaty of Washington was passed, he had been convinced that there was little chance that the imperial connection could be maintained in its existing form. Yet it soon became apparent that a new trend away from separatist sentiments was beginning to make its appearance in Britain.[5] Anglin, though initially considering this change to be motivated by selfish reasons, welcomed it. He acknowledged that Canada's position in the Empire, when logically considered, did seem anomalous.[6] Yet in practice 'it suits us and our present position pretty well,' and Canadians desired no change for the present at least.[7] Contrary to his expectations, but quite to his liking, the imperial connection strengthened immeasurably in the years following the Treaty of Washington.

The people of Canada ... are at this moment more devotedly attached to the Empire than ever they were, because they know that as part of the Empire they enjoy all the liberty it is possible for them to enjoy in their present circumstances, because they prefer the form of government and political institutions under which they can enjoy so much liberty to all other forms of government, and because the Empire, while it protects them without cost, places no obstacle in the way of their prosperity. England, on the other hand, desires to retain Canada because it gratifies her pride of empire, because she sympathizes with a people who are of her own nearest kindred, and because the connection costs her nothing, and is materially beneficial, the colonist being the best customers for her manufacturers.

Above all, the connection provided some protection against the United States, for Anglin was not convinced that Canada had nothing to fear from that quarter. 'The ambition of powerful peoples,' he wrote, 'the exigencies of political parties, the folly or frenzy of rulers or legislatures have caused war in the past and will cause wars in the future, and Republics are by no means the least insolent or aggressive.'[8] The fact that such a comment was at odds with his statements when defence expenditures were being considered did not seem to bother him.[9] All in all Anglin was happy with his adopted country – if only sectarian strife could be eliminated.

II

As an Irish Catholic Anglin had always disapproved of the Orange Society, its incorporation, and its 12 July marches.[10] None of the latter had taken place in Saint John since the fatal confrontation of 1849, and for the most part peace and relative harmony had prevailed in the city. This satisfactory state of affairs came to an end in the 1870s, for that decade witnessed a revival of religious and ethnic strife in North America as exemplified by the famous Guibord affair in Quebec and the Orange-Catholic riot in Toronto in 1875.[11] It is difficult to say why such a development came about, although the revolutionary experiment of the Paris Commune in 1871 and the resulting conservative backlash probably created the general ideological framework. Moreover, the economic stagnation which began to settle on Canada in 1873 was not conducive to social harmony. Whatever the causes, however, the 1870s witnessed a resurgence of militant Orangeism.[12] In 1876 the Orangemen of Saint John, under the leadership of Edward Willis, MLA and editor of the *News*, decided to march. The *Freeman* expressed disapproval, and asked Orangemen to change their minds:

Since that terrible conflict at York Point 27 years ago no demonstration of this kind has ever been made in St. John. The memory of that dreadful day had almost died away, and although there have been many exhibitions of religious intolerance at elections and in other ways, nothing has been done to provoke ill feeling on any side, and blessed peace has prevailed all around. We hope that the Orangemen, if they ever entertained any such idea, will, for the sake of the public peace, and to prove their kindly feelings and good will towards their neighbours, abandon it. They would thus achieve a greater triumph than any marching in procession can afford them, and earn the thanks of all their fellow citizens.[13]

To this the *News* reacted angrily, telling its readers that the *Freeman*'s words constituted a threat to Orangemen; it suggested that the *Freeman* 'address its counsels not to the men who have no intention of breaking it [the peace], but to the parties whom it may suspect of violent purposes.'[14] Anglin denied that his words could be construed as a threat. The *Freeman*, he said, had always discountenanced public processions, especially those insulting or offensive to a segment of the population. The Irish Catholics of Saint John had not had St Patrick's Day parades, and even the Catholic Temperance Societies had been persuaded by the bishop to take the shortest routes and carry no banners as they processed to the cathedral. Catholics had given no offense to anyone; why should they be subjected to any? Yet, whether Orangemen realized it or not, there was a very deep insult to Catholics in the celebration of 12 July, which commemorated a defeat of Irish Catholics – a defeat 'which deprived the Catholics of whatever religious and civil rights were left them after a struggle of centuries; took away what remained of their properties, and made them paupers, aliens, Helots in their own country ...' In view of this the *Freeman* could only reiterate its position:

Should the necessity be forced upon us, we shall do all in our power to induce those to whom such processions are an offence to prove themselves good citizens, peaceful, forbearing, patient and law-abiding, but at present we appeal to the Orangemen and beg of them to show that they can forego, for the general good, and for the sake of peace, harmony, and good will, any gratification such an exhibition may, under other circumstances, afford them.

Let us have peace.[15]

But Willis and the Orangemen would listen to neither the *Freeman* nor the mayor and the sheriff.[16] The *Freeman* proved as good as its word: 'It now becomes the duty of well disposed citizens of all classes and denominations,' it propounded, 'to do all in their power to preserve the peace.' In most serious tones it urged Catholics to ignore the insult which was offered them and warned that even a single small incident could lead to riot and tumult. Not only should the steady, quiet, and orderly keep a guard upon themselves and their families, but also they should use all their influence with the more excitable and easily provoked members of the community and if possible to induce them to keep out of the way completely. In conclusion the *Freeman* gave its Catholic followers a challenge; a challenge to turn the other cheek.

It will be a great triumph for the Catholics of St. John if on that day no man or woman or boy bearing the name of Catholic interfere in any way with the procession and excite ill feeling as it deserves. Every Catholic householder, every well educated Catholic young man, every Catholic who respects his religion and who wishes to prove that he knows what his duty to the country is, and that he means to do it, will on that day and on all preceding days do all in his power to allay irritation, to calm excitement and to preserve the peace.[17]

Despite the abuse it received from the *News*,[18] the *Freeman* repeated its advice on the day before the march and passionately urged that peace reign supreme.[19]

Amazingly, peace was maintained almost entirely. There were only two casualties – one an innocent bystander shot in the leg by a stray Orange bullet, the other an Orangeman who blasted his own leg in his haste to draw a revolver out of his pocket. Apparently the only Irish Catholic arrested, but even then held only briefly, was Ellen Cain, an old apple woman, who threw a chunk of wood and them tried to get at Willis. Considering the circumstances, everything passed off quietly. Little thanks, however, was due to the marchers. Most of them had proceeded on their way armed with revolvers and were quick to brandish them. The parade route chosen had gone through York Point, an area populated almost entirely by Catholics, where the streets were very narrow, and where twenty-seven years earlier lives had been lost and men had been maimed.[20] Above all, the attitude taken by Willis's *News* to the potential danger the parade had posed to the peace of the community was quite incredible:

There was not the ghost of a chance that any attempt would be made to deter them [the Orangemen] from marching over the route they had chosen. It was foreseen, of course, that individual quarrels might arise during the day; that it might become necessary to arrest, kick or shoot some misguided disturber of the peace; that an individual in the procession might be injured by accident or shot by a concealed murderer, but what of that? Are men to listen to the voice of cowardice, to give up their cherished rights (and abstaining, under menace, from exercising a right is giving it up) because a head may be broken?[21]

Obviously the *News* was no longer the same paper to which Anglin had written in 1849 after the disaster at York Point.

The *Freeman* was duly thankful that peace had been preserved:

Thank God those people were patient; that they respected the laws of the country, themselves and their religion, and treated this demonstration precisely as they should always treat all such demonstrations.

Although the injury of two men, the insult to Catholics, and the general anxiety were too high a price to pay, nevertheless the parade had brought some good. It had demonstrated that Catholics 'could rise superior to ... insults and provocation, and conduct themselves so peaceably and calmly as to win the admiration and respect of their fellow citizens.' Second, the poor turnout of marchers had shown 'that few of the Orangemen of the city and Portland approved of the demonstration, sympathized with the Grand Master, or wished to revive old quarrels and causes of difference, or to offend or annoy their Catholic neighbours.'[22] Anglin had cause to be proud. In 1849 he had not had any influence among the Irish Catholics or their neighbours in Saint John. By 1876 he had exercised considerable influence for a long time. He had always advised moderation, legality, and non-violence. His leadership, not only during June and July 1876, but also during the many years in which he had instilled his philosophy in his followers, was undoubtedly one of the major factors which made the results of the Orange parades in Saint John in 1849 and in 1876 so different.

III

A new form of group antagonism, also involving Irish Catholics and their leaders, was emerging in the third quarter of the nineteenth century. The problems created by industrialization and the strife between capital and labour opened up the whole area of social justice as it never had been before.[23] Labour organization and social action were, in fact, two parts of the same puzzle, and an individual's attitude on one was often reflected in the other.

As an industrial society emerged in North America, primarily in the United States, it became obvious that everything was not for the best in the best of all possible worlds. Surely, many began to think, it was not necessary to have unemployment, filthy and disease-ridden tenement houses, at times virtual starvation, sixteen-hour work days, and unsafe working conditions, in the midst of so much wealth. Was the solution to these problems to be found in labour unions? American Catholic leaders gave an uncertain answer to this question. On the one hand the mass of American Catholics were wage-earning immigrants and stood to gain from advances made by unions. On the other hand, because they were a religious minority they were subject to prejudice, and it seemed necessary to make some efforts to mollify the majority. It was a matter of learning how to 'champion the cause of the poor without endangering the public interest or the common good,' and to 'oppose socialism without negating or ignoring the claims of social reform.'[24]

Like Alexander Mackenzie and George Brown, leaders of the so-called Reform party, Anglin was no social reformer. As a puritanical moralist of the Catholic faith he was not very sympathetic to the foibles of human nature. Thus while Anglin was outraged by conditions in the police cells in Saint John,[25] he had little pity for those the police court served. Indeed, he was a 'law and order' advocate, charging the Saint John police force and the chief of police with 'absolute worthlessness' because of their ineffectiveness in hunting down criminals 'as terriers hunt down rats.'[26] Corporal punishment for crime raised few humanitarian scruples in Anglin, his attitude being that it 'served them right.'[27] On the other hand Anglin always supported the annual campaigns to provide winter relief for the destitute or money for orphanages.[28] He also spoke about the Lazaretto at Tracadie and urged that 'if it was possible to rid this country of it [leprosy], no pains or expense should be spared to effect that object.'[29] But these examples of Anglin's concern for social welfare were overshadowed by his retention of a *laissez faire* philosophy.

In America we are nearly all hard-working toilers; comparatively few are wealthy, and comparatively few who are industrious, sober and frugal are condemned to live in penury, in dark cellars or crowded tenements. We would wish to see the men who work, the wealth producers, enjoying their full share of the world's work, and we would be sorry to see capitalists increasing their wealth by grinding the faces of the poor, or overtaxing the muscles or brain of the working man, or depriving him, through the force of law or usage or of circumstances, of fair remuneration for his labour; but this idea that the condition of the working classes can be improved by pulling down all who are called wealthy to their own or any other level, is most dangerous to society, and to the best interests of the working men themselves.[30]

Yet, despite his commitment to a free enterprise system, Anglin sympathized with the efforts of workers to improve their position. Unlike many other middle-class Canadians, he did not oppose labour organizations.[31]

The early development of unionism in Saint John is a prominent feature of that city's history. Perhaps most notable of all is the fact that trade unions were allowed to operate in the city with little public opposition until the 1870s.[32] One reason for this was that until this decade the New Brunswick economy was expanding in spite of periodic and disastrous depressions. Second, the industrial revolution had barely begun before that time, and the conflict between capital and labour was not developed. All a clerk in Newcastle wanted in 1859, for example, were some public holidays other than Sundays so that he would be able to shoot rabbits.[33]

Even before the conflicts of the seventies Anglin took a moderate stand on labour disputes, though he did not think that strikes were advisable:

Strikes are always objectionable, because of the loss of time and money they cause, and of the ill feeling which they too often engender, and they should never be resorted to except in the last extremity – when right is clearly on the side of the workmen, and all other means of getting justice have been tried in vain.[34]

Anglin's attitude was in line with his general approach to political leadership – urge those in authority to be just and convince those he leads to be moderate and law-abiding. In a very real sense Anglin's position on labour disputes was an important part of his effort to be an Irish Catholic leader. After all, the labouring class of Saint John was composed largely of Irish Catholics. The names of those on the executive and board of directors of the powerful Labourers' Benevolent Association were overwhelmingly Irish.[35] As the sole organ of the Irish Catholics in Saint John, the *Freeman* was looked to for support by many of the labour organizations. It was there that certain labour meetings were announced and it was there the unions sent notices defending their position in times of trouble. Anglin willingly published such notices and seemed genuinely interested in hearing both sides of a case. He did not, however, give blanket approval to everything the unions did. Nevertheless, of all the Saint John papers, the *Freeman* showed the most consistent sympathy with and understanding of the position of the unions.[36] Nor were Anglin's views static. If anything he developed a more pro-labour attitude as time went on. In 1869, for example, the *Freeman* condemned as a negation of personal liberty unbecoming to North America the non-violent attempt of the Society of St Crispin to force an employer to dismiss a worker who was not a member of the society.[37] By 1875, however, the *Freeman*'s views had shifted as a result of its dealings with several specific disputes.

The first of these episodes occurred in March 1874 when the workers in the steam saw mills met and formed the Millmen's Protective Union. The first draft of their constitution contained some rather militant by-laws concerning wages and working with non-union men. The *Freeman*, unable to support by-laws which seemed 'calculated to take all control of property out of the hands of those who now think they own it,' sought to moderate the workers' stand.[38] The *Freeman*'s arguments may have had some influence with the men, for the union's constitution, as adopted on 6 April, was considerably more moderate.[39] But this did not end the issue. The mill owners took counter-measures against the organization, showing, in the words of the *Freeman*, 'that they can resort to measures quite as extreme in their character as any of which the men are accused, having, it is said, discharged a number of hands merely because they belonged to the Association.' The owners organized themselves into a 'Lumbermen's Exchange' to counteract and, if possible, eradicate the union.[40] Consequently they subscribed no less than $23,000 to be used to give protection to non-union workers and to bring in workers from Maine. The Exchange also formally agreed not to employ union members.[41] The result was the crumbling of the union, and it was only a matter of time before the workers came to terms with the mill owners.[42] The *Freeman* drew certain conclusions from this struggle. In the first place the workers may have been wrong in their militancy, but then the action of their employers had shown what they were up against. The *Freeman* found the attitude of the other papers of Saint John anomalous.

The papers announce that the mill owners of the city and neighborhood refuse to employ men belonging to the Millmen's Society, and have not a word to say in disapproval of such a course. If the workmen combine they are accused of a desire to injure their employers and ruin the trade of the port, but it is entirely different when a body of capitalists unite to deprive a large number of poor men of their only means of earning a livelihood.[43]

It was apparent that, if another conflict between capital and labour arose, Anglin might be more understanding of tough labour tactics, providing that they were legal and non-violent.

Such a conflict arose in the winter and spring of 1874–5. Of all the labour organizations in Saint John, the Labourers' Benevolent Society, a union of stevedores, was probably the most prominent and powerful. Yet the fall and winter of 1874–5 were particularly hard, and great unemployment meant that the very survival of the union was in doubt. Some men, with the encouragement of employers, turned away from the union and found work without its sanction.[44] The *Freeman*'s advice to the Society, under the circumstances, was to take a step backward and 'to cut out or amend everything that tends to create hostility to their society ...'[45] The Labourers' Association managed to survive the winter; some of the men who had strayed were allowed to return; and by March the organization felt strong enough to set $3 per day as the wage rate for the coming season.[46] At the end of April the Society decided to go on strike in an attempt to have only union men employed on all ships in the harbour. At a joint meeting of the Lumber Exchange and the Board of Trade the employers decided to resist this demand and to adopt the same tactics which had proved so successful against the millmen the year before. This time $100,000 was subscribed.[47] Much the same sequence of events occurred, the main difference being that this time the union was not destroyed. The Society did not win, but it did manage to get a tacit agreement from the shippers not to employ non-Society men on ships where union men were engaged.[48] The *Freeman*'s position on this issue was somewhat different than it had been just a year before. It did not now pass judgment on the morality of strike action taken by the Society. Instead of asserting the rights of employers and workers to make mutually acceptable terms, the *Freeman* now pointed out that union members had a perfect right to refuse work. Besides, said the *Freeman*, such action was legal, and 'we do not know that we have any right to advise the labourers any more than to advise the merchants or to meddle in their affairs.'[49] It was unfortunate, however, that labour disputes could not be settled peacefully, that the business of the port was paralyzed, and that hundreds of men were losing wages which they could ill afford to lose. Anglin thought it regrettable that both sides showed a disposition to push things too far.[50]

Thus while Anglin's views on labour conflicts had not changed radically, they had modified somewhat and shifted in emphasis.[51] In 1869 he had stated:

Here, as much as in any part of the world, the supply and demand regulate themselves in this respect [the over- or under-abundance of labour], and usually in favour of labour.[52]

But by the end of 1877 he was saying:

The best mode of establishing and maintaining the proper relations between capital and labour has not yet been discovered, or if it has there is still much to prevent its proper working. The law of demand and supply left to work unaided, has not worked quite satisfactorily.[53]

The key of Anglin's approach to labour disputes can be summed up in one word – harmony. The central theme running through the *Freeman*'s analysis was that both sides in the conflict ought to be moderate, conciliatory, and, of course, law-abiding. The significance of Anglin's position is difficult to assess. On the one hand the *Freeman* was the recognized mouthpiece of New Brunswick Irish Catholics, and in general the Saint John unions did steer away from radical labour politics. On the other hand the *Freeman* was by no means fully acquainted with developments among workers and gave as little coverage to ordinary occurrences in this field as the other papers. Yet the voice of the *Freeman* must have meant a good deal to the labourers. It was the one paper likely to give a fair hearing to the workers and to give publicity to their side. Its editor was the only Irish Catholic of recognized political stature in the city. He also had the ear of the bishop and often represented the latter's views – a fact of some importance to Irish Catholics who were closely attached to their church. If Anglin through the *Freeman* advised moderation, it seems likely that the advice would be given serious consideration. Indeed, the *Freeman*'s position was probably a compromise between the generally conservative attitude of the Catholic Church on the labour question and the more militant views of Catholic workers.[54] As an Irish Catholic leader Anglin had to bring about some accommodation between the two views.

IV

In his attempt to promote harmony in society Anglin became deeply disturbed about the growth of certain trends in the world. While he was able to come to terms with one of these new developments – labour organizations – he fought against others with fervour, becoming increasingly conservative and moralistic.

Evidence of Anglin's changing outlook came in 1874 and 1875, during which time the *Freeman* began to carry a far larger number of accounts of infanticide, atrocious murders, rapes, strange divorce cases, abortions, violent crimes, and anything else which its editor considered depraved. The newspaper became less sympathetic towards the poor souls whom circumstances had trapped and more completely condemnatory. Why did the change take place at this time? There are three possible answers. In the first place Anglin was getting older, and, more important, he was well established by now; after all he was Speaker. Second, he used these examples of depravity and immorality to prove that common schools did not elevate mankind. The schools question was, of course, still a significant issue in 1874-5. Finally, it became increasingly apparent during the 1870s that traditional western society and Catholicism were facing a variety of challenges.

Socialism, red republicanism, communism – they were all the same to Anglin or nearly so[55] – presented one of the gravest threats in Anglin's eyes. 'They appear to be actuated above all,' the *Freeman* said in regard to the red republicans in France, 'by a fiendish hatred of Christianity, and their hatred of social order, as constituted on the Christian basis, is almost as intense.'[56] Anglin certainly did not agree with communist philosophy, which originated, he assured his readers, 'with crazy theorists and idle worthless fellows, who never want to work ...'[57] Anglin could not accept a theory which, to his middle-class mind, denied to 'ability, industry and self-denial ... the rewards now attainable.'[58] For the editor of the *Freeman* the advance of socialism had been promoted by 'a false philosophy, which ... persuades men that there is no God to whom they must answer for their thoughts as well as their actions, and that happiness consists only in what this world can give,' and by governments which attempted, through such instruments as 'Godless' schools, to eliminate religion by treating it as a despicable superstition. The result was 'that for the present religion can do little amongst the classes which furnish recruits to Socialism.' Yet, according to Anglin, religion was 'the only effectual means of eradicating all evil which exists ...'[59] Anglin's perspective on socialism was paralleled by his views on scientific rationalism or, to use the modern term, 'scientism' – the religion of science based on the premise that there is no truth other than that which can be explained and proven by scientific methodology:

He [the scientist] will not allow God himself to tell him anything of His nature or His attributes. Only what the human mind can learn by the exercise of his own feeble powers will he accept as truth, and so he gropes his way ... growing more puzzled and bewildered at every step ... How deplorable it is to see man thus using against God the reason and other faculties with which God has endowed him and endeavouring to find in the wonders of creation proof that there is no Creator, and in the perfection of His laws proof that there is no eternal Lawgiver.[60]

There is no question that Anglin viewed events and developments in the world through religious eyes. He was at a complete loss to account for the conduct of four Indians on Vancouver Island who had turned themselves in to the authorities for crimes committed ten years before. 'They are,' the

Freeman pointed out in bewilderment, 'still heathens,' implying that only a Christian had a conscience.[61] Anglin argued against divorce 'not only because it is subversive of what many believe to be the Christian doctrine regarding marriage, but because it attacks the family which is the very foundation of our political as well as our social system.'[62] By 1877 the editor of the *Freeman* had come to this conclusion:

It is now generally admitted that the great struggle, in which nearly the whole world is engaged, is the contest between Christianity and Infidelity.[63]

Anglin had always felt that religion ought to play a major role in the life of society and individuals, but during the 1870s this became a more and more prominent feature of his thought.

If the struggle of the age was between Christianity and infidelity, it was obvious that one of the battlegrounds would be the political arena, that spokesmen for the sacred and for the secular would take sides, and that there would ensue debates about the issues of church and state in general and the role of clerics in politics in specific. Such debates did indeed develop in Canada during the Mackenzie régime.[64] Given Anglin's views about the direction in which the world was heading, his position in the debates was not surprising. In general he rejected any attempt further to weaken the role of religion in society. On the other hand he was committed to the Liberal Party and did not wish to see its power diminished. In the 1870s it was not always easy to combine these two affiliations: it was claimed that one could not be a good Catholic and be a Liberal; and also that a good Liberal ought to oppose clerical interference in politics. Anglin's response to this double-barrelled attack defined what it meant to him to be a Catholic Liberal (not to be confused with a liberal Catholic).

As far as the issue of clerics in politics was concerned, Anglin had indicated at the time of the Confederation struggles that clergymen, whether Catholic or Protestant, ought to have as much right as anyone else to discuss political questions, to express their views, and to vote.[65] Yet in politics they were just as other men – no more, no less.[66] One was certainly free to disagree with bishops and priests on political matters while still feeling great respect for them personally, reverence for their sacred office, and esteem for their zeal and devotion.[67] Anglin dismissed the Protestant fear that priests used the threat of refusing religious ordinances to those who voted against their wishes,[68] but he also maintained that Catholics 'hold themselves absolutely bound by the decision of the Pope in all matters of doctrine and Church discipline, and obey his decrees in all such matters faithfully.'[69] Unfortunately the line between religious and political matters became blurred in the decade following Confederation. The emphasis, but not the actual content, of Anglin's argument began to shift from the right of Catholics to disagree with their priests on political questions to the right of clerics to participate in political matters.

In the decade after Confederation it became quite clear that Anglin was in the confidence of Bishop Sweeny and Bishop Rogers. His close communication with both of them on the schools question is sufficient proof of this statement. A man with such intimate acquaintance with the clergy of New Brunswick, with whom cooperation seemed to be the general rule, was not likely to see any reason to restrict the influence of clerics. And, of course, 'clerical influence' had greatly aided Anglin's election in 1872 and 1874. Thus when the Saint John *Globe*, in the interests of the Liberals, strenuously criticized the supposed action of the Catholic clergy of Quebec during the 1874 election, the *Freeman* took issue.

The *Freeman*'s response began by recognizing that many clergymen in Quebec had indeed supported the Conservatives. The *Freeman* believed that in taking this stand they were mistaken 'and that they now appear to the rest of the Dominion as supporters of a set of men who have notoriously been guilty of the most gross and flagrant corruption ...' Yet their reasons for so doing, though greatly mistaken, had been honourable.

[They had] confounded the Liberals of Quebec with the Liberals of France, Italy and Germany, and thought they saw proof of the justice of their views in the articles of the *Witness*, and the letters of Mr. Joseph Doutre, and the Guibord case, and many other articles, speeches, and proceedings of men who, unfortunately for the Liberal party in Quebec, profess to belong to that party.

Surely it was no crime for priests to express their opinion. No, concluded the *Freeman*, it was not by attempting to restrict the rights of priests that the Liberals would win the support of the people of Quebec.

They must prove by their acts and language that they are just, honest, upright, fearless and truly Liberal in the best sense of the word, and that they have no sympathy with the infidel party who in Europe disgrace the name of Liberal by warring bitterly against all true liberty, against society and against God. This the ravings of the *Witness* and others must render difficult, but we hope it is not impossible.[70]

For this pronouncement the *Freeman* was labelled an 'ultramontane' organ. It was an unwelcome label, for the *Freeman* claimed that it was merely a modern anti-Catholic epithet. The use of the term was simply an attempt to divide Catholics by saying that some were disloyal to the country because they were loyal to the pope and as such were enemies to all political liberty and progress. To the *Freeman* there was no such true division, or at least this is what it told the Toronto *Globe* in a stern lecture.

It is a mistake ... to imagine that there are any number of Catholics who may be distinguished from other Catholics by the name of Ultramontanes; it is a serious error to assume that the Quebec Tory papers or any other papers have authority to speak for Catholics as Catholics, or that the political opinions or acts of one priest or half a dozen priests are to be regarded as the conduct or opinion of the Catholic church. It is more wise, fair and prudent to treat Catholics in politics precisely as others are treated. The *Globe* would not be willing that the Protestants of Ontario should be held responsible for all that the *Leader* and other papers of that class chose to say in the interest of their party. Yet it would hold the Catholics of Quebec responsible for what the *Minerve* and its associates say. If the *Globe* looked at facts instead of at the electioneering articles in the Quebec Tory papers, it would not find anything to justify warning against the thrusting forward of special claims or pretentions or the exhibition of an agressive spirit. We believe that the *Globe* means to be fair and just, but it should not allow itself to be carried away by senseless cries. And it should be more careful in the use of language when describing the state of parties in Quebec. The word Ultramontane it should eschew altogether.[71]

If the utterances of the *Globe* showed that the position of the Catholic Church was misunderstood, Bishop Bourget's pastoral letter of February 1876 showed that the Liberal Party in Canada was equally misunderstood. For the Bishop of Montreal the label 'Liberal' had the same effect as did the label 'Ultramontane' for many Protestants. Anglin completely agreed with Bishop Bourget's comments about liberal Catholicism and liberalism as it existed in Europe. Men who espoused such beliefs were enemies of Christianity. But, he asserted, there were few such men in Canada and the danger they posed was minute. The bishop had not thought so and had viewed the Reform or Liberal Party of the Dominion as most closely resembling the liberals of Europe; as proof he had pointed to a recent inflammatory speech made by Lucius Seth Huntington during a by-election in Argenteuil. Huntington, the Liberal hero of the Pacific Scandal and now Postmaster General, had been upset by the Guibord affair and at Argenteuil had attacked the Catholic clergy for their interference in affairs of state, maintaining, moreover, that his view was that of the Liberal Party.[72] To Anglin, however, even if Hungtington had really meant 'what his language undoubtedly expresses,' one man's opinion did not represent the government's position. For its part the *Freeman*'s position was quite clear.

If Mr. Huntington's speech, as understood by the Bishop, and let us add, the *Freeman*, expressed the views of the Liberal party, then, assuredly, would it be the duty not only of all good Catholics, but of all who value as they should good government and social order, to do all they could to deprive that party of the power to do such mischief as the Bishop believes is threatened. So also, if the ravings of the Montreal *Witness* could be regarded as any more than the utterances of a little set of bigots and fanatics, Catholics should take the alarm. But in no respect have the party in this country called Liberal as yet shown any disposition to meddle in ecclesiastical matters, to persecute or oppress the Catholic Church, or to diminish the liberties it now enjoys ... Catholics who prize their religion above all else, who would make any sacrifice to maintain the freedom of their Church and the rights of its episcopacy undiminished, knowing both the political parties more intimately perhaps, than the Bishop of Montreal can know them, are satisfied that the freedom and the rights of the Catholic Church, of Catholics, and of all others in Canada, are at least quite as safe under the present Government as they ever were or ever will be under a Government called Conservative – in short that they are perfectly safe.[73]

Anglin rejected, almost instinctively, anything that tended to throw all elements of a particular religious group into one party. He argued that Catholics should not always act together in politics. They should take sides on political grounds. The development of political parties along religious lines was not only unnecessary; it would also prove disastrous and 'inflict incalculable injury on the whole people.'[74]

One of the real difficulties in the whole problem, Anglin complained, was that there was a great deal of misunderstanding among Catholics as well as Protestants concerning the relationship between Catholics and their ecclesiastical superiors.[75] The relationship was not so unusual, according to the *Freeman*.

In religious matters they owe and pay them due obedience. In all matters they owe and pay them reverence and respect. In what are ordinarily called political questions they are as free to think, judge and act for themselves as Protestants should be. In political contests, as in all the affairs of life, men are bound to do what is right, to act in conformity with the will of God and to observe his law. This applies to Protestants as to Catholics, and within this, which must be for all the limit of liberty

– beyond which all is license – the Catholic is quite as free to think and judge for himself as others are.[76]

Obviously, however, this was too simplistic an explanation, for even the *Freeman* realized that religious matters did not always stay outside the political arena. Yet despite this flaw, and the fact that adjustments would have to be made in practice, the statement was essentially valid and worth stating and following.[77]

Throughout the entire discussion of the matter of clerical influence Anglin was in favour of allowing the priest the right to express his own opinions. He rejected any attempt to limit this freedom:

Surely if a priest thinks that to vote for a particular candidate is to vote against religion and society, and therefore is a sin, he should be at liberty to say so, precisely as a Free Trader or Protectionist is at liberty to say, that the man who votes for a candidate holding Protectionist or Free Trade principles will do injury to the country and to himself.[78]

The clergyman had a right and a duty to identify and condemn what was unlawful and sinful, Anglin claimed.[79] To allow the state to say when the refusal of sacraments was acceptable and when it was not was inadmissible. '[T]he refusal of sacraments,' the *Freeman* informed those readers who did not know, 'is a penalty imposed not by the caprice of a priest, but by law – the law of the church ...'[80]

The issue of clerical influence hit very close to home as far as Anglin was concerned during the Gloucester by-election in 1877. Anglin's elections in 1872 and 1874 had been facilitated by the public support of Bishop Rogers. Anglin sought to secure this support once again for the by-election in 1877. The bishop's private response was eulogistic towards Anglin personally but, from Anglin's point of view, unsatisfactory in other respects. 'Whether any suitable action could be taken by me in the event of an election,' Rogers proclaimed, 'I am really doubtful.' He proceeded to tell Anglin that, although he took little interest in party politics, 'my sympathy and judgment were ever in favor of the pro-Confederation party,' and intimated that the now dormant schools question had been the reason he had supported Anglin in the earlier elections. He was also concerned about the matter of clerical influence.

But with the recent court decisions against what they call undue clerical influence in elections, it probably would be impolitic, if not really detrimental to the candidate whom the clergy would support, for them (the clergy) to take any part in the contest – for it would give a pretext to opponents to seek to nullify the election, if the Clergy's candidate were successful.

In short, the bishop concluded, 'these reasons I fear must necessarily force me to confine my action to simple good wishes for your success, should a contest be forced upon you.'[81] Anglin was distressed with this response and he pleaded with the bishop to reconsider the matter. For the bishop to say nothing after having supported him in the two previous elections would be viewed by many as repudiation. He claimed that the court decisions on the question of undue influence had not made it illegal for clerics 'to say that they think a candidate entitled to election either for what he has done in the past or for what there is reason to believe he will do in the future ...' He urged the bishop to at least let it be known to the priests of the county that he had the bishop's approval for past conduct and best wishes for the present election. 'This is not too much to ask,' Anglin concluded, 'and this I hope you will not refuse.'[82] Rogers's response to Anglin's second request was of some assistance but far from what Anglin would have liked. On 24 June he wrote a pastoral letter which explained his attitude to elections and politics and, while vowing that he would not publicly support either candidate in Gloucester, he made it clear that he was not repudiating Anglin. In fact one passage which suggested that a man with ability and experience should be elected was of distinct advantage to Anglin, for his opponent, O. Turgeon, had no legislative experience.[83] Finally the bishop did not prevent the priests from supporting Anglin, and most of them did so.

Strangely enough, Rogers's careful movements did not satisfy Turgeon. After his defeat Turgeon claimed that several priests had used undue influence against him and eventually he brought his complaint to the attention of Bishop Conroy, the papal delegate sent to Quebec to look into the strife which was disturbing the church in that province.* Conroy advised Turgeon to consult with his own bishop and warned Rogers to be very careful in any steps he took. Rogers acted on the suggestion and proceeded gingerly, pointing out to Turgeon that some of the priests had voted for him. The reply satisfied Turgeon and he carried his complaint no

---

* Interestingly enough, Anglin had conversed with Conroy on the subject of clerical influence several times and felt that Conroy's visit would do much good (see Alexander Mackenzie Papers, A.G. Jones to Mackenzie, 25 May 1877; ibid, Anglin to Mackenzie, 23 July 1877; Lynch Papers, Anglin to Lynch, 6 May 1878; and *Freeman*, 27 June 1878).

further.[84] Yet if Bishop Rogers had been concerned about the charge of undue influence before, how much more so now and in the future? With political unrest mounting in Gloucester, the changing attitude of Bishop Rogers was ominous for Anglin's electoral future.

12

End of an Era, 1878-83

Anglin won Gloucester by acclamation in the Dominion election of 1878, his by-election victory in 1877 probably saving him from meeting opposition at this time. Since he had little to do in Gloucester, Anglin's main role during the election was as a newspaper editor. So important a cog in the government machine was the *Freeman* that Isaac Burpee, the Minister of Customs, spent $500 in circulating upwards of 25,000 copies of it during the two weeks preceding the election.[1] Day in and day out the *Freeman* provided the best support for the government that could be found in the province. Anglin turned down invitations to speak in western Ontario, eastern Nova Scotia, and Prince Edward Island on the ground that it was unbecoming for the Speaker to go about 'stumping' the country.[2] An 1877 letter to the premier indicated that fear of embarrassment may also have contributed to his reticence.

I do not quite understand what you say of the expectations of some friends who desire to see me out west. Is it that they wish me to hold meetings on my own account on a small scale after yours are all over – a sort of side show following not accompanying the great show – an exhibition of some special monstrosities &c? I do not see how I could very well undertake an engagement of that kind even if we had no doubt as to its propriety and expediency.[3]

Apparently he did not consider outspoken newspaper articles to be equally unbecoming. In the columns of the *Freeman* he harped away on the most significant issue of the 1878 election, the tariff, and kept up a bold front despite his private recognition that the Reformers were not in very good shape.[4] However most New Brunswickers agreed with his opposition to the Conservative tariff policy. When the ballots were counted, New Brunswick supporters of the Mackenzie government numbered ten, opponents five, with one 'doubtful.'[5] But New Brunswick was not typical of the country. 'New Brunswick alone among the faithless stood faithful. "Among the faithless, faithful only it."' – that was the way a forlorn Alexander Mackenzie put it.[6] Throughout the country at large the government suffered a resounding defeat. Anglin commiserated with his leader.

I feel that I ought to say something but I really hardly know what to say so stunned and stupefied am I by this great disaster. It is hard enough on rich men like Smith and Jones and Burpee who have little to regret on personal or pecuniary grounds. To poor men like you and me who have not worked for money and who have saved nothing the blow must necessarily be more severe no matter how patriotic and unselfish we may wish and strive to be.[7]

As difficult as the adjustment might be, there were even more ominous words from Bishop Rogers. The prelate congratulated Anglin on his personal victory, but then proceeded to speak his mind on party politics. He came down on the side of Macdonald's forces, even rejecting Anglin's comments on tariff protection. The schools question was over and done with, and the bishop could now give rein to his strong predilections in favour of the Tories. 'I only write the above,' he told Anglin, 'in all candor and sincere friendship to you – friendship on account of your personal merits of every kind, not on account of, but in spite of the side of political questions and parties you advocated.'[8] Undoubtedly Anglin the individual cherished this friendship but he was not just a private person – he was also a politician, and a politician needs votes. How long could he rely upon the bishop for effective support under these circumstances?

I

When a government is defeated at an election, it does not usually hand in its resignation immediately. In the interim period appointments of one kind or another are made and desks are cleared for their new occupants. In other words the government acts as its own executor and puts its affairs in order before giving up the ghost. In 1878, however, the first inclination of such prominent Reformers as George Brown and L.H. Holton was to call an early session of parliament in an attempt to force the Conservatives to put their program into effect quickly. Anglin was opposed, for reasons both political and personal.

The idea of calling an early meeting of Parliament appears to me objectionable on many grounds. There is no necessity whatever to justify it. The trouble to members of the House and the cost to the country would be considerable and you could not hope to force your opponents to early action by such means as they could reasonably plead that they are entitled to time to form a government, to get their elections over and to prepare their grand scheme of readjustment. They would merely vote you out and then adjourn to the usual time of meeting in February. If the public service were in such a state as to demand an early meeting the case would be different but as it is not the victors would no doubt pretend to regard such a mode of proceedings as an attempt on your part to embarrass your opponents no matter what the cost to the country. I can not see what we could hope to gain by that course … An early calling of Parliament would cut off my pay as Speaker and this I could ill afford to lose as I have spent large sums in keeping up the *Freeman* for the last year in order that it may do the good work at the Elections which it has done but I would not of course ask you to alter any decisions you may arrive at on that account if I saw that anything could be gained by the country or by the party from an early summoning of Parliament.[9]

Anglin's argument was hardly crucial to Mackenzie's decision. More important was the fact that the government had run out of money and refinancing was necessary. The defeated Liberals could hardly take on that responsibility and so Mackenzie simply handed in his resignation on 9 October.[10] Anglin, therefore, remained Speaker until the House met and chose another. He was *de jure*, but what about *de facto*? Did he retain his powers to appoint House of Commons officials as a 'lame-duck' Speaker?[11]

Anglin sought advice on this question. The answer he received indicated that he did indeed possess his powers until parliament met 'and that the precedents favour your exercise of it.'[12] Unfortunately, however, these views emanated from neither constitutional experts nor the incoming government. Anglin was being advised, in the main, by Mackenzie, and a defeated premier was not the best source for such advice. Yet after giving the matter considerable study, Anglin accepted this advice.[13] His attitude might have made little difference had the issue remained theoretical, but it did not.[14] Several vacancies had arisen in the translators' office and it seemed desirable to fill them before the House met in order to keep the department abreast of its work and to familiarize the new men with their duties. Accordingly, Anglin went to Ottawa in the second week of November 1878 in order to study the qualifications of the candidates. It was arranged that the appointees would commence work on 1 December. So far so good. But then Sir John had not been heard from. On 2 December he made his views known. H. Hartney had gone to him on that day requesting his signature to a warrant for money. Sir John agreed and then, with a sure knowledge of the power of the purse, told Hartney to inform Alfred Patrick, the Clerk of the House, that Anglin's recent appointments were not to be recognized. Patrick, not wanting to jeopardize his position, dutifully informed the appointees that they were not to be employed after all. Anglin wasted little time in writing to the Clerk.

I have just received your letter of December 4th, and I write at once to protest against the interference of the Privy Council or any members of it in the administration of the Department of which as Speaker of the House of Commons I am the head, and to call on you formally not to recognize the authority which, as I learn from your letter, Sir John A. Macdonald has usurped; to undo whatever you have done by his instructions, and hereafter to act only upon the instructions given you by the Speaker. I know that your position is extremely delicate, but I feel it to be my duty to maintain as far as in me lies the privileges and the independence of the House of Commons.

Patrick's reply to this communication indicated quite clearly that he thought that Anglin did legally retain the power of appointment, but now he feared for his job and hoped that Anglin could do something to get him out of the position he was in. On 18 December the Speaker wrote once again, exonerating the Clerk from responsibility and claiming that, if Sir John had objections, he should have directed them to the Speaker rather than placing the Clerk in such an embarrassing position. By the day before Christmas Patrick was accepting Macdonald's view of the powers of the Speaker and seemed to be claiming the right to make provisional appointments under the circumstances. Anglin disagreed, of course, and told Patrick to pay no attention to Sir John's commands. Even here, however, the matter did not end. In January Anglin attempted to have promotions made in the Department of Private Bills to fill a vacancy. Anglin's plan was simple – promote the three members of the department and make other adjustments to take up the slack, rather than make a new appointment. He must have expected that this arrangement would be vetoed by the government, and it was.

This was the position when the House met in mid-February 1879. Anglin was not reelected Speaker, to no one's surprise. But shortly after the session got under way, the member from Gloucester brought up the question of the powers of a 'lame-duck' Speaker. He outlined the tale of the appointments to the House. He explained that he had looked into the question of his powers thoroughly and had found no British precedents, for there the Commissioners for the Internal Economy of the House had authority. In Canada they possessed no such powers. He explained that the Statute of 1868 was fragmentary and inadequate to cover the case, but that it had stated that the man who is Speaker at the end of a parliament should continue to be Speaker for the purposes of that act until a successor is named. The same act gave the Speaker the power to appoint an accountant and to suspend or dismiss any or all of the officials during an interregnum. Anglin argued that such powers implied the right to make appointments. The question was of some importance he concluded, for was this not an infringement on the rights of the Speaker by the executive, and therefore a challenge to the privileges of the House which the Speaker represented? If ministers were to have this power, a bill should be passed saying so.[15]

The premier rose to answer the ex-Speaker. In brief, his view was that no one had the power of appointment. The Speaker's powers in such circumstances were severely limited and the right to dismiss did not mean the right to appoint. The Speaker retained certain limited powers by the Internal Economy Act just to keep things working. Aside from this, when a parliament died, its Speaker did also. Anglin's appointments had been made illegally and were therefore void. It would be unfair to fetter his successor in this way. But, Macdonald concluded, while the act was not very clear and would be clarified, it would not be 'by clothing a defunct official with power.' A few more speeches were made, but the debate ended without the issue being resolved.[16]

In the matter of appointments Anglin had a plausible but not overwhelmingly strong legal case. He claimed, of course, that he was concerned only with the smooth and efficient functioning of the House, and there was something to the argument. Yet surely, one would suggest, it would have been wise to have cooperated with the new government in making the appointments. He could have ensured that the government did not appoint incompetent party hacks because he did have dismissal powers. But Anglin chose otherwise. The Speaker, he claimed, should not be so much 'the creature and slave of party as to be influenced in the discharge of his duty by the manner in which the elections happen to go.'[17] It is difficult to believe, however, that Anglin was acting purely out of a sense of maintaining the independence of the Speaker. Anglin made the batch of promotions in January knowing full well that they would not be accepted – not because they were foolish, but because he was making them he was leaving no position to be filled by a Tory office-seeker. In part Anglin performed this futile task in order to protect the office of Speaker from outside encroachment but also, one must think, for party advantage. He undoubtedly realized that, if the issue could be presented as an overbearing executive encroaching upon the rights of the First Commoner, and thereby those of the House, it had some potential. Yet in bringing the question before the House he cannot be said to have been unreasonable in his party antagonism. But it is unquestionable that party politics had a good deal to do with the whole question. Had not Macdonald himself told Anglin that the best policy was to reward your friends, not your enemies? He had not listened to Anglin's views on patronage; why should Anglin solicit his?

There was one other matter to clear up before Anglin could say a final goodbye to the office of Speaker. Even Macdonald had recognized that Anglin had been the Speaker, at least in name, until another was chosen, and he had incurred expenses on this account. His trip to Ottawa in November had been on House business and his visit to Halifax to greet the new Governor General, Lord Lorne, and the Princess Louise, had been in an official capacity.[18] The Speaker was paid to perform such duties. But to his chagrin Anglin found that the Deputy Minister had given the opinion that he was not entitled to any pay for January and thirteen days in February – about $500. Not surprisingly, Anglin brought the question to the floor of the House, claiming that his predecessors had always been paid until the election of their successors. James McDonald notified him that the matter was being considered and that justice would be done.[19] Anglin undoubtedly got his money as he never again introduced the question in the House. The episode, characterized by annoyance but ultimate satisfaction, was an appropriate summation to his entire experience as Speaker.

II

Leaving the Speaker's seat must have seemed like a release from prison for Anglin. He was opinionated, argumentative, and loquacious. As Speaker he could seldom give vent to these predilections, but during the following four sessions he was without question one of the most significant, and vocal, members of the opposition. He had always attended the sittings regularly, and his years as Speaker had accustomed him to being in the House most of the time. Given his other traits of character and his many years of experience in the House, his excellent attendance made his name appear time and time again in the *Debates*. He was often to be found questioning the statements of other speakers or interjecting with differing opinions. He spoke on all issues, large and small, and seemed to delight in combing financial statements for errors. Perhaps the partial cause of the latter was that Tilley was Minister of Finance and as the sessions went on it became clear that Tilley and Anglin were in a separate category from their fellow New Brunswickers when it came to effectiveness in the House. Anglin's major speeches, such as those on the issues he and other Liberals opposed most strongly, the National Policy and the Canadian Pacific Railway, were gargantuan affairs.

There was nothing unique about Anglin's position on these matters, for most Reformers shared a common perception on the tariff and the railway. Extravagant railroad building with heavy public funding was, they argued, completely irresponsible on the part of politicians. It was mortgaging the future of generations yet to come for the sake of electoral appeal. Moreover, the CPR and the protective tariff did indeed go hand in hand because the increased public debt created by federal subsidies for the railway meant that heavier taxation, usually in the form of the tariff, would be necessary. This course of action was sponsored, of course, by wealthy financiers and manufacturers who were bankrolling the Conservative party against Reformers, the representatives of the ordinary honest citizen who was paying the price of governmental extravagance and corruption. This Liberal perspective was quite in harmony not only with Anglin's views on the particular subject but also with his politico-economic philosophy.[20]

Incredibly detailed, full of figures, yet containing much real meat, Anglin's speeches were effective, even if they justified the stricture passed by one of his contemporaries:

[A] forcible but diffuse speaker, who made long excursions into the by-ways of his argument, seldom delivering a speech within bounds suitable to the time of those whose temporal span is fixed at three score and ten, and whose patience is only good.[21]

A measure of Anglin's significance in the Commons debates is that the entries under his name in the index to the official *Debates* for 1879 took up one-and-a-half columns. Only four men – Macdonald, Mackenzie, Tupper, and Mills – required more space, while Tilley, Cartwright, and Holton required about the same or slightly less. By the last session, held in 1882, this pattern was still holding, although Anglin was not quite so

SCENE FROM THE POLITICAL OPERA, "PINAFORE."
Lord Cartwright, K.C.B.—"I'M THE MONARCH OF FINANCE,
AND WHEN I GET A CHANCE,
I'LL ASSAIL TILLEY'S TARIFF (WHATE'ER IT BE) WITH TAUNTS——"
Chorus of Political Relations.—"AND SO WILL HIS SISTERS, HIS COUSINS AND HIS AUNTS!"

Scene from the Political Opera 'Pinafore'
by J.W. Bengough in *Grip*, 1 March 1879
Provided by the Thomas Fisher Rare Book Library,
University of Toronto

prominent, according to this rough test. Anglin's skill at debate, as he sat up there in the second row to the Speaker's left (playing middle linebacker behind the big front six of the Liberals – Laurier, Huntington, A.J. Smith, Cartwright, Mackenzie, and Holton) was more than acceptable.[22] He was quite good at repartee though seldom witty. In any case Mackenzie was very pleased with his Irish colleague. 'Anglin did capital work all through the session speaking and writing,' he confided to Alfred Jones after the end of the 1879 session.[23] To the London *Advertiser* there was 'perhaps no man in Parliament more capable of discussing public questions than Mr. Anglin ...[24]

There was a particular type of public question which was of special concern to Anglin. He was not simply a Liberal politician and newspaperman; he was also an Irish Catholic spokesman. As such he had duties to perform both inside and outside the House of Commons. Anglin's style of

'Taking the Bull by the Horns,' or
The 'Noble Attitude' of the Opposition
by J. W. Bengough in *Grip*, 29 January 1881
Provided by the Thomas Fisher Rare Book Library,
University of Toronto

leadership outside the Commons was seen on the occasion of the visit of the Governor General and Princess Louise to Saint John in the summer of 1879. Prior to the visit a reception committee was set up and Anglin was one of a large number named to it.[25] When the committee met it considered whether there should be a procession and if so what kind. For some time those present debated back and forth whether or not the Orange Society should be invited. Eventually it came to a vote whether a procession should he held at all and the majority favoured having one. At this point Anglin rose and asked the indulgence of the meeting. He stated that he had remained silent until this point as he wished the Protestant gentlemen to settle the question themselves and he had hoped that they would do so satisfactorily. But now, he continued, it seemed very likely that the Orange Society was to take part in the procession. The *Freeman* recorded the rest of his brief speech.

He bore no ill will towards that Society or any of its members, but it was a Society established for the exclusion of Catholics from the enjoyment of those rights and liberties to which they are entitled as British subjects. This has often been denied of late, but nevertheless it is believed by many, and to these the presence of that body in the procession would be offensive ... He could not accept any share of the responsibility, direct or indirect, of inviting the Orange Society to take part in the procession, or of assigning them a place in it. He spoke only for himself, and the societies, whose members are Catholics, would of course judge for themselves, and act upon their own judgment; but he thought it very improbable that any of those societies would take part in the procession were a place in it given to the Orange Society. No matter what the decision of the Committee may be, he felt assured that the Catholics of the city would do all in their power to show due respect to the Governor-General and Her Royal Highness Princess Louise when they visit St. John.

What veto power! Needless to say a subcommittee which met the following day decided that a trades' procession would be more suitable and later even this was given up as impractical.[26]

Anglin's main method of championing the Irish cause, however, had never been in such meetings, but rather on his own private platform, the *Freeman*. Anglin always made a conscientious effort to give the Irish news to the readers of the *Freeman*. It was essential for Anglin and the *Freeman* to keep abreast of Irish affairs if for no other reason than to maintain Anglin's position as an Irish Catholic spokesman. North American Irishmen demanded Irish news, and papers such as the *Freeman* had to supply it. Indeed, the tremendous interest which overseas Irishmen displayed in developments in Ireland suggested that many emigrants felt they had betrayed the Emerald Isle in leaving her. Anglin himself may have felt this to some extent, for there were often deep emotional overtones in his speeches and writings about Ireland.

In interpreting Irish developments for his readers Anglin operated on four basic premises. He firmly believed that conditions in Ireland were bad, often deplorable. That the Irish and Ireland were unjustly treated was the second tenet of belief. Third, he was convinced that the news reporting where Ireland was concerned was very misleading. Finally, he asserted that the Irish were basically law-abiding and peaceful citizens.[27] But this reduction takes away the vibrancy of the *Freeman*'s writings on the question. In fact, the best articles in the *Freeman* in these years were concerned with Irish matters. On one occasion, for example, Anglin presented a rather atypical definition of 'agrarian outrages.'

The *Freeman* does not deny the prevalence of agrarian outrages in Ireland. For many centuries they have been only too numerous. Again and again were the lands of Ireland confiscated, and their true owners driven to the mountains and to the woods for shelter. Again and again did thousands of those so robbed die of hunger ... In later times these outrages changed their character somewhat, and became 'evictions'. Then, when a landlord, wishing to evade the payment of tithes, or believing pasturage more profitable, or preferring large farms, or desiring to gratify some whim, wished to depopulate a country side, the law enabled him to work his will, and scores, and, in some cases, hundreds of families were driven away to make room for cattle. In the year of the great famine the working of the poor law, introduced a short time previous, stimulated the landlords to clear their lands of people whom they treated as human vermin; advantage was taken of the loss of crops and the impossibility of paying all the rent due to sweep the people off the land. Hundreds of thousands who should have received kind treatment and help when afflicted by Providence were then cast on the road side to perish, by the landlords and the landlords' law. To-day in many places similar outrages are threatened ... Oh yes! agrarian outrages, are, unfortunately, prevalent in Ireland. On the other side there have been offences – outrages also, which are in themselves utterly indefensible, but those who know the country and its laws, and how those laws have been used, must devoutly thank God, who alone could enable so many to bear patiently the grievous wrongs they have endured, that so few of the oppressed sought or desired revenge.[28]

During the late 1870s and early 1880s there was renewed agitation in

Ireland for reform. On the one hand there was a drive to change the land system so that it would be more just and serviceable to the needs of Irishmen. On the other there was a renewed attempt to win some form of self-government for the country. Almost all Canadian newspapers gave considerable coverage to Irish developments, but the Irish Canadian press was, as might be expected, the most deeply concerned. The evolution of the *Freeman*'s views on the nationalistic and land agitation paralleled developments in Ireland. While Anglin was never in the revolutionary vanguard and supported popular moderates in Ireland, the coercion of the Irish in the early 1880s forced Anglin, as it forced the leaders and people of Ireland, into more radical thinking. Still, this was a defensive reaction. Individual or collective acts of violence could not be condoned, but how could one condemn the Irish people for standing up for their rights and for justice? Anglin could not.[29]

Anglin's views on Irish politics had an impact upon his political life in Canada, but not always in expected directions. Anglin tended to compartmentalize his attitude towards the British government, as has been mentioned before. Although he firmly believed that the link with Britain, as it existed, was almost wholly detrimental to Ireland, this did not mean that in the Canadian context England was the enemy. Irish Catholics in Canada might be underrepresented in political life,[30] maligned by the statistical lies of police reports.[31] and suffer other forms of prejudice, but, the *Freeman* claimed, they were at least as well off in Canada as elsewhere.

Irish Catholics complain, and not without reason, that in Canada they are systematically excluded from public positions, and that their religion, and their nationality, often prove obstacles to their success; but they are mistaken if they suppose that in this respect the Irish Catholics in the United States are more favoured, and in some respects Catholics are treated with greater injustice than in Great Britain itself or any of its colonies.[32]

Thus, Anglin asserted, the Canadian Irish were thoroughly loyal to the Dominion while still remaining loyal to the land of their birth.[33]

There were ways in which the Canadian Irish could aid their suffering brethren in Ireland, particularly during the food crisis of 1879–80. Collections taken throughout Canada provided some effective relief. The Irish of Saint John did not have much money to spare after the disastrous fire of 1877, but they did their part.[34] At the instigation of John Costigan,[35] the federal government announced in the Commons in 1880 that it also intended to make a donation. As soon as he heard this Anglin rose to his feet, urging the government to act quickly and showing, by reference to some of his own experiences in the Great Famine, the necessity for immediate action.[36] Not until a week later, however, did the matter come to the floor of the House. Macdonald announced that $100,000 would be sent for the relief of the famine victims of Ireland. Anglin's was the first major speech in reply. He acknowledged that he was rather disappointed that the amount was so small as he had hoped that the sum of £50,000 sterling that had been mentioned earlier would be the figure.

I was led, by the language of the [Throne] Speech, to expect that a larger amount than this would have been voted for the relief of Ireland by this Parliament. We are asked to give, not out of our poverty, but out of our abundance, for the relief of people, hundreds of thousands of whom have, for many weeks, been on the very verge of starvation, and who are to-day suffering from the want of food. It was to be the gift of a great nation, stretching from the Atlantic to the Pacific, to another nation forming part of the same Empire, whose people are the kith and kin of a large number of the people of this Dominion, and for whom we feel all the sympathy we possibly could feel for a kindred suffering people.

But then he admitted that it would be ungracious for 'one who, though a Canadian, still regards himself as an Irishmen,' to complain of any gift 'that is graciously offered.'[37]

The Irish question came up again in the 1882 session – the pre-election session – once again introduced by John Costigan. On 6 March he notified Macdonald of his intention to introduce resolutions supporting Home Rule for Ireland.[38] He told the premier that he would take the earliest opportunity of submitting them for his perusal and that suggestions 'calculated to make it acceptable to yourself and colleagues thereby ensuring its adoption by the House' would be cheerfully received.[39] The background of the resolutions which Costigan submitted to Macdonald was very interesting. Costigan had approached all the Irish members of parliament and invited them to attend meetings to draft resolutions. In Anglin's case it had been rather difficult as the two New Brunswickers had not been on speaking terms for some time. Nevertheless, 'he was invited to our meeting,' Costigan later said, 'and from his well-known ability and prominence we had him named upon our committee to frame these resolutions.' But Anglin neither came to the meetings nor served on the committee.[40] Why Anglin refused is a difficult question to answer. Undoubtedly his personal antagonism towards Costigan had something to do with his decision; unquestionably he knew that Edward Blake was also preparing resolutions on the question.[41]

and he probably wished to cooperate with his leader just as Costigan did with Macdonald; and possibly he felt that the committee called together by Costigan could never draft resolutions to his liking or that, if it did, the government would not give them the necessary support. Anglin probably thought that he had nothing to lose by staying aloof. If the resolutions adopted by the committee were satisfactory, he could support them; if not, he could attempt to amend or oppose them. In any case his freedom of movement would not be curtailed. It was not a very heroic course of action but it may have been politic.

Macdonald found Costigan's resolutions too strong and he amended them, or, as Blake said, he emasculated them. He also made arrangements with Costigan that the resolutions should be moved while the House was going into Supply thereby precluding the possibility of amendments.* The resolutions as they now stood began by professing that the Canadian Irish were among the most loyal and contented of Her Majesty's subjects. It went on to say that, because of the discontent in Ireland, Irish emigrants shied away from Canada on account of their 'feelings of estrangement towards the Imperial Government.' It expressed the view that Canada could not afford to lose such a large proportion of emigrants and hoped that, as Canada had prospered under a federal system, some form of the latter would be extended to Ireland 'if consistent with the integrity and well being of the Empire, and if the rights and status of the minority are fully protected and secured ...' The Irish would then be able to accept the British

---

* Pope, *Memoirs of Macdonald*, pp 228–9; J. Pope, *Correspondence of Sir John Macdonald* (Toronto, 1921), pp 287–9 (Macdonald to Lorne, 2 May 1882); and *Freeman*, 29 Apr. 1882. In a letter to Lord Lorne Macdonald claimed that Costigan forced his hand in the first place by telling Macdonald that if he (Costigan) were not allowed to introduce resolutions, then Anglin would. Moreover, the premier defended introducing the revised resolutions when going into Supply on the ground that, if it had been possible to move an amendment, Anglin would have introduced one which would have brought in the original resolutions (see Macdonald to Lorne, 2 May 1882, quoted in Pope, *Correspondence of Macdonald*, pp 287–9). Macdonald was obviously playing politics and using supposed pressure from Anglin to make it appear that the government had moderated the resolutions as much as was possible. Macdonald knew, probably better than anyone else, the political value of passing such resolutions but he did not want to appear to be a calculating politician to Lord Lorne and other British officials and so made rather free use of Anglin as a 'threat.' Professor MacNutt's account errs when it asserts that Anglin was the leading figure in the Irish caucus (see MacNutt, *Lorne*, p 164); Anglin did not even attend its meetings. Moreover, I have found no evidence to confirm MacNutt's assertion that in 1881 Anglin 'had been deterred from introducing resolutions of a violent nature in favour of Home Rule' (ibid, p 163). Anglin's critical comments in the 1881 session of the Commons related to Canada's 1880 gift to Ireland (see *Commons Debates, 1881*, pp 1218–20 [4 March]).

connection and they would not hesitate to emigrate to Canada. The final clause expressed the hope 'that the time has come when Your Majesty's clemency may without injury to the interests of the United Kingdom be extended to those persons, who are now imprisoned in Ireland charged with political offences only, and the inestimable blessing of personal liberty restored to them.'[42] When these resolutions were introduced on 20 April, no one stood to speak for some time. At last Blake rose and gave a long and quite magnificent speech which expressed disappointment with the resolutions, detailing Irish rather than Canadian reasons for granting Home Rule.[43] Macdonald and others followed Blake. Towards the end of the debate Anglin rose. 'Mr. Speaker,' he said, 'I find, Sir, that it is entirely unnecessary for me to make a speech on this subject.' It was a good thing, for he proceeded not to make a speech for close to an hour! His main points were three in number. He thought that, if the House felt that Ireland was entitled to Home Rule, it should say so simply and directly without the 'ifs' and 'buts' which the resolutions contained. He disliked the part of the resolutions which called into doubt the good faith of the Irish people by saying that it hoped certain things would be done 'if the rights of the minority are fully protected.' The Protestant minority, he claimed, had always been treated well.* Finally, he disliked the last clause because asking for clemency assumed guilt. All that the imprisoned wanted, and all that anyone should want, was that they receive a fair trial. But he would certainly support the resolutions even if they were somewhat defective. He added:

I am glad to find that a better sense of the condition of things in Ireland is prevailing; I am glad to find, as the hon. member for Vancouver (Mr. Bunster) said, that prejudices which came with the mother's milk are gradually disappearing. We are learning to appreciate and understand each other more thoroughly, and to find that if one man is a Protestant and another is a Catholic, one an Episcopalian and another a Presbyterian, it matters little, that every man should act and think for himself, and that notwithstanding these differences we ought to combine in all that relates to us as a people, by having one heart, one mind, one thought, and one vote.[44]

As 'cabin'd and crib'd' as these resolutions were, they did not sit lightly

---

* John Wallace, who represented York constituency in New Brunswick, scored a debating point by mentioning that it had not been long since Anglin had wanted protection for the minority of New Brunswick (see *Commons Debates, 1882*, p 1066 [20 Apr.]).

The Irish Pie
by J.W. Bengough in *Grip*, 22 July 1882
Provided by the Thomas Fisher Rare Book Library,
University of Toronto

with the Colonial Secretary and the British government. The timing was very bad, for only four days after the Senate had passed the resolutions, Lord Cavendish, the new Chief Secretary for Ireland, and his Secretary, Thomas Burke, were murdered by members of an extremist movement.[45] Lord Kimberley politely told Canadians that it was not their place to be petitioning on Irish affairs.[46] Privately he was less polite.

> The people of this country have shown wonderful calmness under immense provocation, but they are not in a temper to be trifled with by anglers for Irish votes at elections for Colonial Legislatures.[47]

To the *Freeman* this response was flatly ridiculous. As imperial subjects Canadians had an interest in the good government of the entire Empire. Of more particular concern was the emigration difficulty. And surely Canada had a right to speak out on a problem which had more than once caused armed clashes on her border, many an anxious moment, and considerable expenditure of money. Finally, Canada had a right to speak from its experience on the benefits which a federal system could bring.[48] Under the circumstances, however, there would be no reform for Ireland for a few years at least. The assassinations had ensured that.

III

Anglin's performance on these Irish questions was satisfactory. He defended the Irish cause and was seen to be in the vanguard for Irish reform. Yet at the same time it was Costigan who was initiating things in the Commons and, because he was a Conservative, was able to get something of value through parliament. As a Conservative Costigan was also in a better position to supply patronage than Anglin. Thus by the 1880s Costigan was able to challenge Anglin's hegemony as an Irish Catholic leader.

The rivalry between Costigan and Anglin went back at least as far as the New Brunswick schools question, but it was not until the late seventies and early eighties that Costigan began seriously to challenge Anglin's position in the Irish Catholic community. In 1877, both in the House of Commons and during the Gloucester by-election, Costigan accused Anglin of dereliction of duty on the schools question.[49] 14 January 1881 saw their first major confrontation in the House of Commons.[50] The exchange was not particularly edifying but it did serve notice that Costigan had been a political apprentice long enough; from now on he would strive to be a leader.

Macdonald was not one to overlook such a performance. He was probably even more impressed with the cooperation Costigan gave him on the Home Rule question a year later. Finally, in 1882, pressure was put on the federal government to appoint a Catholic to the New Brunswick cabinet seat which had been vacant since R.D. Wilmot had resigned in 1880 to become Lieutenant Governor.[51] On 23 May 1882 John Costigan became Minister of Inland Revenue. What would be the repercussions for Anglin? The newly established Conservative newspaper in Fredericton, the *Capital*, answered the question.

We are disposed to think that his appointment will seriously effect [sic] Mr. Anglin's following in this Province. Our Irish people are singularly loyal to their leaders, as a general rule, and no man knows this better than Mr. Anglin; but if leaders persist in striving to lead people where they do not want to go, they must take the consequences. The Irish voters are beginning to see that if they wait till they have Mr. Anglin to represent them in the Cabinet they will have to wait a long time ...[52]

Even more ominous for Anglin's political future was the public congratulatory note sent to Costigan by Bishop Rogers. In part it read:

Again tendering you my felicitations and best wishes for your success in your new office, and the assurance of my sympathy and good will towards the Government of which you are now a member and of which you were in the past a faithful supporter.[53]

In the Conservative cause Bishop Rogers was not so chary of 'clerical influence.' If Rogers's political views had not been known before, they were certainly no secret now.

Aside from the competition that Costigan was offering there was another factor which was undercutting Anglin's political strength. Gloucester was, of course, overwhelmingly Acadian and during the late seventies and early eighties Acadian nationalism began to emerge among the French-speaking inhabitants of the Maritimes.[54] This revival took various forms, but from the perspective of Anglin's career the development of Acadian political assertiveness was the most important. Anglin had never championed the Acadian cause as he had the Irish, but he had always spoken well of his co-religionists and had supported their efforts at self-improvement. During the 1870s he complained strongly about the educational difficulties under which the Acadians laboured, particularly the fact that there was no training school for French-speaking teachers and that school inspectors not only did not understand the French language but also attempted to discourage its use.[55] Indeed Anglin was not opposed to the development of Acadian nationalism itself: 'A profound, but reasonable national spirit, inasmuch as it fosters self-respect and self-reliance, stimulates a people entering on the march of improvement ...'[56] He was pleased to see that the Acadians were coming to grips with modern society even though he believed that considerable effort was still required 'in order that in the professions, in trade, in agriculture, in mechanics, &c., they may become all that so large a portion of the population should be.'[57] Nevertheless, Anglin became concerned about the developing tendency of Acadians to adopt group politics and he cautioned them that one such combination would lead to other group combinations.[58] It is possible, of course, that Anglin was more concerned about his political position than the potential threat such combinations posed for the Acadians.

The Acadian renaissance did put Anglin's political career in jeopardy. The yoke the Acadians had to discard was English dominance,[59] and Anglin was, after all, English-speaking and an outsider at that. Acadian dislike of English control was surely part of the campaign to oust Anglin, a campaign which had been building since the mid-seventies. Antagonism developed between the Irish Catholics and the French Catholics, reaching a high point in 1882 when Bishop Rogers charged that the Collège Saint-Louis was ignoring English instruction and its Irish pupils and withdrew his patronage of the school.[60] The *Freeman* attempted to bridge the growing gap in the Catholic ranks but it was a futile effort.[61]

By the time of the 1882 election Anglin's hold on Gloucester was rather tenuous. His annual visit to the constituency had never accomplished sufficient political fence-mending.[62] That opposition to Anglin was increasing could be seen in a resolution passed by the Gloucester Municipal Council on 21 January 1881 in support of the CPR contract which Anglin had denounced:

We consider it behooves every honest, loyal lover of his country to give his warm support to the Government in this matter and frustrate the objects of factious opponents who are only trifling with the best interests of the country.[63]

Certain elements in the county had grown tired of finding their representative in the ranks of the opposition, for this provided little scope for patronage appointments and government favours to the constituency. Even during Mackenzie's regime Anglin had found it impossible to meet the demands for positions and therefore alienated some of his supporters.[64] The difficulty of Anglin's position was shown by the silence which greeted his arrival at Bathurst for the start of the campaign.[65] His political organization was in a deplorable state.[66] Until the 1882 campaign local priests had named his canvassers but this time they seemed reluctant to act.[67]

Facing Anglin were not one, but two opponents, both supporters of the government. The dual opposition of K.F. Burns and O. Turgeon appears to have been less an accident than the result of a Conservative plan to defeat Anglin. The Conservatives apparently realized that Anglin's support was such that, if his opponent were French-speaking, Anglin could take some of the Acadian vote while retaining the solid support of the English; the same, in reverse, was true if Anglin faced an English opponent.

In this emergency keen Conservative managers concluded that their best chance would be in a three-cornered election, with a French candidate to take off a section of Mr. Anglin's French vote. Mr. Turgeon was ready to take the field as an independent, and thus the contest was run.[68]

During the campaign itself Burns concentrated on the view that the country should elect one of its own residents and a member of the party which would unquestionably win the election; he pointed out as well Anglin's apparent failure to promote the projected Caraquet Railway.[69] Aside from his political prestige as an MLA, Burns was 'the greatest employer of labor in Gloucester,' a factor which Anglin thought crucial.[70] Onésiphore Turgeon, born in Quebec but by 1882 an important Acadian nationalist who had attended the 1881 Acadian national convention,[71] had carried on a running battle with Anglin since the 1877 by-election.[72] In 1882 Turgeon concentrated on the Acadian vote and was aided by public letters and telegrams from Sir Hector Langevin.[73]

Anglin made a valiant attempt to defend his record and to rescue his seat but the situation was out of hand.[74] Bishop Rogers was of little help. Anglin had approached the bishop on his way to Gloucester and asked for a word of approval. Rogers's reply to this request was an open letter to the Right Reverend T.F. Barry in which he expressed his warm admiration for Anglin's merits and made the statement that he would 'regret his absence from the House of Commons ...' However, he acknowledged that his political sympathies lay with the party to which Anglin was opposed and he concluded his letter by saying that each elector should vote 'for the Candidate of his own free choice, according to his own free conscience and for which he is accountable to God.'[75] In short, the bishop offered anything but unqualified support for Anglin. The election was an ignominious defeat for Anglin at the hands of Burns. Even Turgeon won more votes than Anglin. The reactions to Anglin's defeat were varied. Tilley did not gloat; he merely commented that, combined with that of Smith, Anglin's defeat was a great blow to the opposition party.[76] Alfred Jones felt sorry for Anglin more than for any of the other Liberal leaders who had gone down to defeat, and the list was formidable.[77] The *Sun* considered that the defeat of Smith and Anglin marked the end of an epoch in New Brunswick political history.[78] John Thompson, although a Conservative, felt strongly enough to write Anglin a note expressing his regret.[79] And an anonymous correspondent of Macdonald's felt that the Prime Minister should do a generous deed and offer an appointment to Anglin.[80] Anglin's own reaction was one of disappointment; despite the obvious signs defeat still came as a shock and surprise.[81] Yet he resolved to make the best of it.

I hope to find in the happiness of home and in more constant association with my family from which of late I have been too much separated compensation for the loss of public position and political honours and consideration which I never valued very highly.[82]

IV

The 1870s and 1880s witnessed the decay of New Brunswick's traditional wood-based economy. As a result, Saint John, the chief export centre of the province, had to struggle merely to keep itself from falling behind.[83] To the *Freeman* the causes of this stagnation were easy to discern: Confederation in the first place and the National Policy in the second were the culprits.[84] It may have been pleasant for Anglin to say 'I told you so,' and this he did frequently, but it was rather meagre recompense for the fact that the prospects for the *Freeman* were growing ever more dim.

In 1877 the *Freeman*'s office and its contents had been destroyed in the Great Fire of 20 June,[85] only the account books, subscription list, and a few files of the *Freeman* being saved. But at this moment Anglin's by-election committee in Gloucester had put in an urgent call for his presence, and he had been forced to leave Saint John without making any arrangements for the paper. With the publication of the *Freeman* unavoidably suspended, Anglin decided to take a little extra time in making preparations for its reappearance. It was to have a different business organization and to appear daily.[86]

It had been difficult for Anglin to control the *Freeman* while he was in Ottawa several months of each year, and when he became Speaker it became impossible for him to send reports of parliamentary debates signed 'TWA.' Nevertheless it is clear that he continued to send the lead editorials; some of these were really reports of debates, but others, perhaps most, dealt with particular topics which came up in debate. By 1877 the *Freeman* seemed to have overcome some of the difficulties of communication. Either the mail service had improved or Anglin had taken to sending his lengthy articles by telegram. Anglin's evidence given before the Committee on Privileges and Elections also showed that by this time Anglin's involvement in the business side of the newspaper was minimal. It seemed feasible, then, for Anglin to give up in name as well as in fact the business side of the operation and to concentrate on editorial writing for the daily edition. But it would not be an easy thing to do, Anglin confided to Bishop Rogers:

Owing to the extraordinary opposition in the business developed of late years by the extraneous support given to other papers by Railway speculators willing to spend freely to promote their schemes and by political partizans willing to purchase support for their friends the cost of publication was greatly increased and the revenue diminished or kept down. The devotion of so much space in the Freeman for so long a time to the School question hurt its circulation even with Catholics – perhaps quite as much with them as with others and the late Parliamentary decision prevents my publishing a single government advertisement. The fire was so destructive that I saved nothing of the plant or stock and my insurance is scarcely sufficient to pay for a new press. I have some idea of putting the publishing part of the business in the hands of young men who I think could work it up again and make the property valuable continuing myself the chief editorship so that the paper would lose none of its usefulness. The general ruin caused by the fire which has crippled nearly all the leading Catholics of the city makes this more difficult than it would have been if I alone had suffered. The Catholics of this Province I suppose could not afford to lose the *Freeman* altogether yet to tell the truth they have never done much to support it.[87]

Not until 29 August 1877 did the first edition of the daily *Freeman* appear. The change in business management had indeed taken place. Anglin was apparently now on a salary, for the *Freeman* claimed that in any work done in its office 'the editor of the *Freeman* has no pecuniary interest whatever.'[88] How badly Anglin was hurt by the 1877 fire is difficult to gauge. On the one hand his insurance benefits were inadequate.[89] But on the other hand he must have received something in return for handing over the business part of the operation. Moreover, one would estimate that as a salaried editor of a daily newspaper he must have received upwards of $2,000 per annum. By some means, at any rate, Anglin was able to purchase debentures valued at approximately $12,000 by 1883.[90] However much Anglin lost in the fire, he was certainly not reduced to penury. Indeed, he was sufficiently solvent to be able to purchase a Hoe press and a quantity of material from New York, a portable steam engine built by Burrell, Johnston and Company of Yarmouth, and type from the Millar and Richard foundry in Toronto in reestablishing the *Freeman*.[91] Before long the *Freeman* was taking its accustomed place among the Saint John papers. In part this was because of Anglin's 'unquestionably high abilities as a journalist,' as the *New Dominion and True Humorist* put it,[92] but it was also because of the *Freeman*'s ability to stir up the other papers.

The St. John *Freeman* seems to possess a faculty of exciting most intense combativeness in the breasts of its city contemporaries. Before the great fire every second editorial article in most of the other papers was devoted to the *Freeman*. For several weeks after the fire, the latter journal did not appear, and there was a lull in the references to it. Suddenly it took its place again; and now there is nothing but *Freeman* once more. We have looked over the issues of the F. and detected nought in its pages that would excite the ire of anybody; but lo! and behold! next morning's papers would be full of the *Freeman* and its apparently innocent, but always straightforward utterances. What is the mystery?[93]

The effort to rejuvenate the *Freeman* was no huge success. The *Freeman* lasted as a daily for a little over a year – long enough to be of great service in the 1878 election. On 2 November 1878 it announced that it would be discontinued, although the *Weekly Freeman* would be published as usual. Shortly after, the *Freeman*'s office was moved to a different and presumably, less spacious location on King Street, over Bardsley's hat shop.[94] Bishop Sweeny himself got into the act and urged his parishioners not to allow the *Weekly Freeman* to follow the same path as the tri-weekly and daily editions.[95] But even this did not seem to help. On many occasions the *Freeman* had to appeal to its subscribers to pay their debts.[96] Its yearly prospectus always included the hope that its readers would help increase its circulation.[97] But by 1881 the *Freeman*'s circulation was only 750, compared to 4,000 for the daily edition of the *Evening Globe*, and 5,000 and 3,800 for the weekly editions of the *Telegraph* and the *News* respectively.[98] This was not surprising, for papers such as the *News* and the *Sun* contained showy advertisements and presented a much more modern face to their readers than did the *Freeman*. Yet the editorials of the *Freeman* were head and shoulders above those of its rivals. They contained thought and commitment. Almost always they had something important to say. Their length was their one great fault. But the newspaper business, like many other facets of the Canadian economy and society, was becoming more complex. The age of the one-man newspaper was very nearly at an end. Organization and specialization were required now. Even after his electoral defeat Anglin was able to do little for the *Freeman*. Some of the New Brunswick Liberals scraped up enough money to pay him a yearly salary of $1,600,[99] but the paper was simply not a paying concern.[100] On 12 May 1883 the *Freeman* announced that its editor of over thirty years was severing his tie with the paper.[101]

Anglin was moving to Toronto. There were no longer many reasons, aside from sentiment, for him to remain in Saint John. His services as a mediator between the Irish Catholics and the rest of the Saint John community were no longer necessary. Both the community and the Irish had grown accustomed to each other and, in spite of occasional outbreaks of hostility, had little reason to fear each other. The 1876 Orange parade had demonstrated that. Anglin had played an important role in bringing matters to this point, but his success inevitably diminished the need for him to function as a conciliator. Moreover, his political career in New Brunswick seemed to have come to an end and the *Freeman* was gasping its last breaths. He was bored. Giving occasional lectures to the Irish Friendly Society and to the New Brunswick Total Abstinence Union did little to relieve this feeling.[102] Thus Anglin resolved to sell his house[103] and take his family, which had been increased by three (a girl and two boys) since he had left the Speakership, to a place where prospects looked brighter.

He was not to leave the city unheralded and unsung however. Anglin had been an integral part of the city's life for a third of its one-hundred-year existence.[104] The two receptions which were held in his honour were fitting comments on his career. On 9 May there was a large meeting of Catholics at St Malachi's Hall to thank Anglin for the services he had performed for them and wish him well in his future endeavours. Bishop Sweeny himself took the chair and expressed his view that there was no public man in the Dominion for whom he had more respect.[105] And the following evening the Liberals of Saint John held a farewell banquet for Anglin.[106]

But perhaps most fitting of all was the fact that the *News* devoted its lead editorial article to Anglin's departure – the *News*, the very paper in which Anglin's anonymous letter had appeared in 1849; the paper in which the

Freeman's first prospectus had been carried; the paper which for so many years had been on the other side of the political fence from the *Freeman*. Its article acknowledged that Anglin, though not having the genial temperament of most Irishmen, had served the Irish Catholic community to the best of his ability. It did not know what the future held for him but it did know that it would miss him.

We are among those who regret the removal of Mr. Anglin from St. John. He had grown to be quite an institution here. We shall miss him greatly as a journalist. It is true we have often been in conflict with him. But for all that we are sorry to lose him. He has peculiarities of temperament, sentiment and manner, and these may render his path in the future, as it has more or less in the past, somewhat difficult to travel. There can, however, be no question as to his ability, and it is many-sided. He has a strong intellect, a clear and simple style as a writer, is a fluent and forcible speaker. He acquitted himself well in the Commons Speakership. He is fitted to make his mark anywhere.[107]

13

Wordly Travail and the Ultimate Escape

1883-96

Anglin's reasons for moving to Toronto were several. In the first place, to move from Saint John to Toronto in 1883 was to leave stultifying stagnation for exhilarating expansion.[1] Anglin found it congenial to come to 'a growing thriving place where ... the people generally are full of confidence in the future and there is little of that despondency which one meets everywhere in St. John.'[2] There was a more particular reason, however, for Anglin's move. His importation into Ontario seems to have been part of a grand Liberal strategy, developed by Edward Blake, to woo the Ontario Irish Catholic voters to the federal Liberal Party. The Liberals hoped that Anglin's prominence and prestige would enable him to win as many votes among Ontario Catholics for the federal Liberals as Oliver Mowat's provincial Liberals seemed to draw from that segment of the population.[3] The means adopted to achieve Liberal ends were familiar and natural to Anglin. He was to be a newspaper writer. On paper the plan sounded reasonable; in practice obstacles to its success proved insuperable.

In February 1883 Blake sent a secret circular to prominent Ontario Liberals about his plans for bringing Anglin to Toronto to take over the *Tribune*, a Catholic weekly which supported the Liberals.[4] After stating that Anglin had agreed to the idea 'provided moderate and satisfactory financial arrangements' could be made, Blake appealed for financial support for the endeavour over a five-year period. He made it clear that, although he hoped the paper would pay its way, the project ought to be considered a political rather than a commercial investment. This appeal to political philanthropy received an adequate response and Anglin packed his bags. However, the *Tribune* was a Catholic paper as well as a Liberal one, and even before Anglin left Saint John, Bishop John Walsh of London, Ontario, reminded him that the push of the party would be balanced by the pull of the church. The bishop wrote that of course he expected Anglin to produce a first-rate journal, not like some of those 'so called Catholic' newspapers whose 'Catholicity was but the sugar-coating to the political nostrums which for base sordid motives they administered to their readers.'[5] In the middle of May 1883 Anglin took over the reins of the *Tribune*.[6]

As useful as Anglin's labours on the *Tribune* might be to the party, the Liberals did not consider that his considerable energies would be utilized to capacity merely overseeing a puny weekly paper when there was a giant Liberal daily paper that needed help, the Toronto *Globe*. The *Globe* was one of the great success stories of nineteenth-century Ontario Liberalism. Even the death of its founder, George Brown, in 1880 had not seriously disrupted its fortunes, and in 1882 the *Globe* could boast an average weekly circulation of over 50,000. A paper of this magnitude was no one-man show. A myriad of typesetters, office boys, reporters, and editors were required, and the pen of an experienced Liberal journalist could be put to good use. Thus Anglin became an editorial contributor to the *Globe*. And while Anglin was employing his talents for the Liberal cause, everyone expected that the Liberals would try to find a seat in the House of Commons for him.

I

At first the Liberal plan seemed to go well. Anglin received a marvellous welcome in Toronto. During his first two days in the city he had visits or conversations with a variety of individuals including Oliver Mowat, the Liberal Premier of Ontario; two of Mowat's top lieutenants, A.S. Hardy and C.F.Fraser; Goldwin Smith, Toronto's intellectual devil's advocate; and John Joseph Lynch, the Catholic Archbishop of Toronto.[7] On 5 June a complimentary banquet was held for the newcomer by some 250 Liberal supporters. Anglin made a fine speech describing his political evolution. Why had he turned to the Liberals after Confederation? The answer was that he had found the Liberal Party to be the party of principle and 'pure devotion to country,' whether in or out of office.

They believe that government should be for the good of the whole people; that justice, truth, and right ought to be the guiding motives in every public transaction, as in every act of private life; and that under no circumstances would the people be justified in swerving a hair's breadth from those principles.

He predicted a great future for the Liberal Party so long as religious and ethnic prejudices were banished forever.

It is absolutely necessary that we stand together upon the basis of equal rights, and perfect justice, and thorough fair-play between denomination and denomination, between race and race, between sect and sect, that we may be in reality as we are in name, one Canadian people.

Anglin did not doubt this would be accomplished but he did express a fear that the grand reception he had received indicated that more was expected of him than it was in his power to perform. He promised, however, to work hard and to do his best. He also proclaimed his intention of becoming a good Ontarian by defending the province 'against aggression from any quarter.' Once again Anglin showed the same willingness and ability to adapt to changing conditions that he had demonstrated in becoming a New Brunswick patriot in the 1850s and in accepting Confederation. The speech staked Anglin's claim to the position of federal Liberal leader of the Ontario Irish Catholics. It also introduced a hint of realistic scepticism about how much he would be able to accomplish.[8]

Anglin's reception was not, of course, wholly favourable. The *Mail* dragged out all the old stories which might damage his reputation – his supposed Fenian connections in 1866, his 'libellous' *Freeman* article of 1873, the violation of the Independence of Parliament Act, and so on. Indeed, a delightfully malevolent, though inaccurate, poetic description of the Anglin banquet appeared in the *Mail* of 6 June 1883.

THE ANGLIN DINNER

(Respectfully dedicated to the delighted hosts who did themselves the honour to entertain a man who is, perhaps, not quite a traitor, but a very representative Grit.)

A Kestrel hustled out of his nest,
Was kindly invited out to the West,
By the kites and crows, and others like those,
Who wanted an ally against their foes.
And to celebrate their complete alliance,
And to bid the enemy stout defiance,

They got up a feast of assorted scraps
With a motley crowd of queer-looking chaps;
Birds of all feathers, and various smells,
Sixpenny statesmen and half-guinea swells,
On the edge of reluctant society danglin',
All to do honour to Timothy Anglin.

II.

A Bird called 'Blake' with a streak of Vulture,
Quite free from ornithological culture,
Whom Timothy cursed from claws to pate
When he turned him out in seventy-eight,
Was present to toast and praise the Pope
(Instead of the family wish for a rope),
And to offer a bone that (without invention)
Would not be exactly a bone of contention
To the immigrant Kestrel out of a Job,
And ready 'most anyone's shilling to fob;
And thus they hoped to prevent a janglin'
Of notes at the dinner for Timothy Anglin.

III.

An Owl called 'Mowat' was there that night
Much to the Kestrel's dear delight;
For the Owl had screeched at the Kestrel's tribe,
And the latter had bought him with a bribe;
They hated each other, but that was nought,
For one was sold and the other bought,
And each to each was the dearest brother
For one was just as base as the other.
So 'Mowat' was just as civil as 'Blake'
For the featherless Kestrel's pauper-sake;
And all of them joined in maulin' and manglin'
The feast in honour of Timothy Anglin.

IV.

They cursed the Pope, and they blessed the Pope;
(So nobody can object, we hope)
They quite forgot to honour the Queen,

For Timothy hates a loyal scene;
Blake gave some things from the 'Rights of Man,'
Edgar some verses that wouldn't scan;
And Cook had recently stumbled across a
'Bully good thing of O'Donovan Rossa';
They shouted when they began to stagger
For all good fellows who bear the dagger;
They drank in honour of dynamite;
They cursed the Union out of sight;
And under the table, too full for wranglin'
They finished the feast for Timothy Anglin.[9]

That Anglin should receive a hostile welcome from one segment of the Toronto community was not surprising for he had become involved in political affairs in the city with alacrity. He had always been concerned with government corruption, and in the *Globe* of 1 June an article appeared under the title 'A SECOND PACIFIC SCANDAL' in jumbo-size print. This was the not very famous 'Section B' or 'Shields' scandal. What the article did, as the *Globe* said the following day, was to impeach 'the Government of the Dominion before the people of Canada of having been guilty of trafficking with public contractors to procure election funds, and of having proposed and arranged to reward the contractors by improper concessions.'[10] That Anglin had been the leading scandalmonger was evidenced in the fact that John Shields, the contractor implicated, initiated, on 15 June, a libel suit against Anglin, along with J.D. Edgar and the Globe Printing Company.[11] In fact the case was never prosecuted. But it was not until January 1884 that the case was dismissed and by that time the season for making political hay from the issue had long since passed.[12] Stifling any discussion on such topics was exactly what the government wanted, as can be seen in a letter from Macdonald to Senator John O'Donohoe concerning a *Globe* article printed late in June 1883. 'The article is obviously Anglin's,' Macdonald wrote. 'It was written for the purpose of drawing you into a discussion and you ought not to be "drawn."'[13]

It is clear that Anglin's influence on the *Globe* between 1883 and 1887, the period in which he was a contributor, was considerable because the *Globe* modified its attitude towards Catholic and Irish questions during this period. Only between 1883 and 1887 did the *Globe* show strong sympathy for Catholics.[14] Of course, Anglin was not solely responsible for this change in attitudes, for the *Globe*'s employment of him showed that at the

Waiting for the Judge and Jury
by J.W. Bengough in *Grip*, 23 June 1883
Provided by the Thomas Fisher Rare Book Library,
University of Toronto

beginning of the period the board of directors wanted his views. Nevertheless, the board supplied only the opportunity for Anglin to influence the paper's policy; that he did so was a measure of his capabilities and persuasive powers.

One area in which Anglin made his mark on the *Globe*'s policy related to the matter of clerical influence. A far cry from the attitude of the 1870s, by 1884 the *Globe*'s articles were so closely in accord with Anglin's known views that he may well have written them himself.[15] The same might be said about the *Globe*'s position on the Irish question, for the views expressed by the *Globe* closely paralleled those propounded by Anglin in his *Tribune*, in speeches he made at various Irish nationalist meetings in Ontario, and in an 1883 memorandum which he submitted to Lord Lorne at the Governor General's request.[16] The lengthy submission to Lorne, in what Anglin himself admitted was 'wretched writing,' was a comprehensive analysis of the Irish question. He began by suggesting that the reason for the failure of the various remedial measures for Ireland was that the legislation had been 'too little, too late.' In essence, Anglin claimed, the solution to the Irish problem required an entire shift in emphasis.

If the Imperial government really desire to put an end to all ill feeling to all desire of separation and to the agitation so often renewed and to establish perfect good will and harmony between the two peoples they must strive to ascertain rather how much of self government and how much of legislative independence can be allowed to Ireland, with safety to the Empire than how little will serve to keep Ireland quiet for a time.

In practical terms he favoured Home Rule in the fullest sense. Not only would this be simple justice for Ireland, but also it would promote harmony and unity in the Empire. He foresaw certain difficulties, but was sure that they could be worked out. He was confident, for example, that neither minority rights nor property rights would be imperilled because in the one case Irish Protestants had always been treated justly by the majority and in the other because 'the Irish are in reality a Conservative people and hold the rights of property sacred.' He believed that an Irish legislature ought to possess the widest powers:

The Irish Legislature must have the right to deal fully with everything essentially Irish with civil rights and property in the fullest sense, with education municipal affairs with the relations of landlord and tenant and all other questions affecting the tenure transfer and transmission of property with the construction and management of Railroads and all public works and improvements within the Island or on its coast saving only the Imperial authority with respect to works of defence &c.*

Throughout the period from 1883 to 1887 the *Globe* strongly supported Irish Home Rule, although the year before Anglin had come to Toronto the *Globe* had apparently asserted that Home Rule would result in 'civil war, anarchy, and the oppression of minorities.'[17] The change in attitude must be attributed to Anglin as well as to the Liberal leader, Edward Blake.[18]

In other ways and on other subjects Anglin made his weight felt on the *Globe*. He was, for example, one of the forces pressing the *Globe* to sympathize with the Métis and to favour clemency for Louis Riel in the aftermath of the 1885 North-West Rebellion, a position the *Globe* eventually adopted in large part, despite a massive display of ambivalence before the actual execution.[19] From Anglin's point of view hanging Riel was unjust and impolitic and likely to create more problems by making him a martyr.

It is not necessary in order to overawe the Métis or the Indians to restore peace or to prevent another insurrection. It may not be well indeed to give him his liberty lest he again abuse it. Probably public opinion is that he should be punished severely. Were he confined in a penitentiary or an asylum for criminal lunatics he would soon be forgotten.[20]

However important Anglin's efforts for the *Globe*, his chief concern was the *Tribune*. It was difficult, he confided to his old friend Bishop Sweeny, not only to 'get up' the paper almost single-handed, but also to try to build up its circulation.[21] By March 1884 the paper appeared twice weekly,[22] but

---

* Lorne Papers, Anglin to Lorne, 12 June 1883. Lorne transmitted the submissions of Anglin and Costigan (ibid, Costigan to Lorne, 18 June 1883) to W.E. Gladstone, the British Prime Minister (ibid, Lorne to Gladstone, 20 July 1883). The most interesting difference in the views of Anglin and Costigan stemmed from the different attitude towards the Canadian constitution held by the two political parties to which each belonged. Costigan, a member of the centralist Conservative party, agreed with Home Rule but also the necessity of an imperial veto over the Irish legislation. Anglin, as a 'provincial rights' Liberal, saw little need for such veto power and thought that, if it existed at all, it should approximate the American president's weak veto power. Lord Lorne did not not agree with either of the submissions and seemed to think that Canadian and American experience showed the necessity of keeping the central power strong and not giving any subordinate legislature sufficient power to threaten the central authority (see Marquis of Lorne, 'Canadian Home Rule,' *Contemporary Review* [Nov. 1883], pp 637–43; and *Globe*, 13 and 14 Nov. 1883 and 7 Jan. 1886).

remained a marginal enterprise. Early in 1885 Blake had to appeal to Liberal supporters for financial assistance for the *Tribune* in spite of the fact that Anglin had already devoted a great deal of his guaranteed salary to the cause.[23] A similar appeal had to be made the following year.[24] By the fall of 1886 Anglin's despondency about the *Tribune* was apparent in a letter to Sweeny.

I think I told you before that the Tribune is not doing as well as it should because the business people even the ultra Liberals do not wish to advertise in a weekly paper. I have to suffer nearly all the loss as my agreement is with a Limited Liability Company whose members think they contributed enough before my time. Few others can be found to render any assistance. Could I receive all I was promised from that source I would soon be out of difficulties but much is due to me there that I suppose I never will get.[25]

Anglin's personal finances were not good either. While he was supposed to receive a salary of perhaps $1,600 to $2,000 a year as editor of the *Tribune*, it is unlikely that he received more than 60 per cent of the total amount due him.[26] As well, Anglin had been unable to sell his house in Saint John or even, apparently, to find renters.[27] He had, of course, the bond investment, which yielded about $800 in interest each year, but failure to sell his Saint John property had forced Anglin to borrow $1100 from Bishop Sweeny when he decided to move to Toronto.[28] After 1883, therefore, Anglin struggled to pay off this debt, but it was not an easy task, for, he told Sweeny, 'college fees[,] school fees[,] clothing and food for so large a family consume nearly all I can earn.'[29] For house rental, taxes, and furniture alone he paid out $525 in the year 1883–4.[30] Nevertheless, by May 1887 he had whittled down his debt to Dr Sweeny to $127.87 without cashing in his debentures.[31]

The Anglins' social life in Toronto provided some satisfaction, for they did make acquaintances and were kindly received.[32] Friends from Saint John also visited occasionally.[33] But the Anglins found few other Catholics at the social gatherings in Toronto to which they were invited. To Anglin this indicated both prejudice against Catholics and the failure of Catholics to work their way into elite social circles in Toronto in spite of their apparent success in business.[34] The fact that the Catholic Anglins were invited indicates the elevated status that Anglin had in Toronto as a former parliamentarian and Speaker of the Commons, in spite of his religion. While the Anglins did not find their social life in Toronto unbearable, it was neither very stimulating nor very comforting.

Perhaps the brightest side of Anglin's life in these years was his family. The two oldest boys, Frank and Arthur, were doing well at St Mary's College, a Jesuit institution in Montreal. Frank received his degree in January 1885 and immediately went into Blake's law office for a three-year period before writing his bar examinations.[35] With five younger children running around the house, the absence of Frank and Arthur in Montreal did not leave the Anglin home empty.

II

It had been expected in 1883 that Anglin would become an active politician as well as a political journalist. Indeed, for a time after moving to Toronto Anglin had been at the forefront of affairs. Liberal leaders in Ottawa missed him at first, and there were rumours that a seat in the Commons would be found for him.[36] From late 1883 to September 1884 he went about Ontario speaking at various Liberal meetings, but his prominence waned rapidly.[37] He was given a good reception and listened to, but he failed to implant himself in the hearts and minds of Ontario Liberals. He may be a Liberal, they seemed to be saying, but he is a stranger and a Catholic at that. He received no seat in the Commons and as a consequence his prominence diminished even further. Blake was criticized for this turn of events for, as a Conservative pamphleteer pointed out, seats had been found for Cartwright and Edgar but not for the Liberals' representative Irishman.[38] The criticism would have been justified had it been aimed at the Reform party as a whole rather than Blake himself. In any case, Anglin's initial efforts to become a practising politician in Ontario met with no success. The 1887 election represented a last chance both for Anglin to reenter politics and for Blake in his plan to win the Ontario Catholic vote.

Throughout 1886 the Liberals and Conservatives made preparations for the forthcoming federal election. In Simcoe North, a constituency which stretched from Barrie to Collingwood, the Liberal organization was in sad shape. The area which composed the constituency in 1887 was a Conservative stronghold made even more Tory by the preeminence of its resident representative, D'Alton McCarthy. As there was little likelihood that a Liberal candidate could win the constituency, the party organization was virtually moribund and North Simcoe Liberals were willing to have an outsider carry the party banner – even a Catholic outsider. In April 1886 a convention of North Simcoe Liberals unanimously nominated Timothy Warren Anglin as Reform candidate at the next federal election.[39] Anglin was not particularly pleased with the offer. He was sceptical about the chances of success and he refrained from accepting the nomination immediately. Not until parliament had been dissolved on 15 January 1887, and Blake had urged him to accept the nomination as there was no alternative constituency available, did Anglin definitely accept North Simcoe's offer.[40] This long delay made a bad situation even worse. Why should Reformers of North Simcoe put themselves out in a nearly hopeless situation for a man who had shown such reticence? Despite the futility of the cause Anglin carried on a vigorous campaign, addressing no fewer than thirty-two meetings.[41] But McCarthy was too firmly entrenched. Anglin lost by over three hundred votes and could take little solace from the fact that he had done no worse than the 1882 Reform candidate. Nor was he pleased with the Liberal Party.

I expected that the party would find me a constituency in which there was a reasonable prospect of success. They appeared to feel very little interest in the matter and certainly took no trouble about it. Mr. Blake was very indifferent or very powerless. He allowed himself very easily I think to be persuaded by those whom he usually consults that the chance[s] in North Simcoe were fair ...[42]

Anglin was justified in his annoyance but surely he, as well as Blake, must have known that North Simcoe was hopeless. Nevertheless the North Simcoe election was a severely disillusioning experience for Anglin.

The Liberal defeat in the 1887 election, and the failure of Ontario Catholics to swing to the federal Liberals,[43] had serious repercussions for Anglin. In the first place federal Liberals had no offices to fill nor patronage to disburse. Neither a cabinet seat nor a Senate appointment awaited Anglin for his years of faithful service. More important, his personal loss in Simcoe North and the inability of the Liberals to make gains in Ontario confirmed what was already pretty clear. It was evident that Anglin was not able to win the Ontario Irish Catholics to the federal Liberals. The Blake plan of 1883 had been defeated and this placed Anglin in a most vulnerable position. After 1887 the whole effort initiated by Blake in 1883 to win the Ontario Catholics through Anglin was abandoned. For Anglin the political guillotine completed its work within the year.

Blake was not unmindful of Anglin's work for the Liberal party. He tried to obtain a Commons seat for Anglin shortly after the election results were known. Blake had been more successful in the election than most Liberals. The leader of the party had run both in West Durham and West Bruce and had won both. Of course, he could not retain both and therefore he wished to open the safer of the two, West Bruce, to Anglin, the party having failed to elect any representative Irish Catholics in Ontario. Blake wrote to a Lucknow Liberal:

Under these circumstances it has been suggested to me that it would be my duty, in the interest of the party, to endeavour to secure a seat for a representative Irish Catholic in the person of Mr. Anglin, who gallantly fought North Simcoe under very disadvantageous circumstances. He is our most prominent Irish Catholic and has, as you know, a deservedly high Dominion reputation. His personal character, his staunch fidelity to Liberal principles, his knowledge of public affairs and his ability, all combine to make him a man whom any constituency ought to be proud to choose.[44]

But even the leader's endorsation did not guarantee nomination. Indeed the safest constituencies are often the most chary of accepting outsiders.[45] Anglin did not get the nomination. He recognized that his chances of ever representing an Ontario constituency were poor.[46]

If Ontario Liberals were unwilling to support Anglin as a politician, it is not surprising that they were unwilling to give further financial support to the *Tribune*. The tale of its demise was part of Anglin's letter of woe to his old friend Bishop Sweeny.

You are aware I suppose that the Tribune has gone down. It never paid its way. As usual many of my subscribers were remiss and many did not pay at all. The mode of doing business here is much more expensive than in St. John as much canvassing is necessary. The business people of Toronto could not be induced to advertise in the Tribune sufficiently and although many of the businessmen are Reformers we got no business from anyone through political sympathy. I made extraordinary exertions to keep it alive until after the elections incurring considerable personal responsibility. Its failure reduces our income considerably. I hope matters will mend somehow but the outlook just now is rather gloomy.[47]

Anglin's prospects went from bad to worse. Blake's illness and resignation removed from the leadership of the Liberal Party the man who had concerned himself most with Anglin's fate, while Richard Cartwright's assumption of supremacy among Ontario Liberals under Laurier's leadership brought into the centre of party circles a man who was eager to take bold steps in terms of policy and personnel.[48] As early as the summer of 1886 Cartwright complained that the *Globe* lacked 'a vigorous slashing writer of the Farrer or Shepherd [sic] type,' and indicated that Edward Farrer would be willing to come over from the *Mail*.[49] Obviously the new

Ontario Liberal leader considered some of the staff of the *Globe* expendable. Anglin's agreement with the *Globe* expired late in 1887 and was not renewed. 'The Liberal party have not treated me very well,' Anglin lamented.[50] For the first time in thirty-seven years, since the winter of 1850–1, Anglin found himself without a newspaper in which he could express himself.

By the end of 1887, therefore, the hopes Anglin had cherished when he came to Toronto in 1883 had been shattered. He was further away from the House of Commons than he had ever been, and the Liberals did not even want to make use of his years of writing experience. The five years in Toronto transformed Anglin from a minor political deity into a political has-been. Had the Liberals been in office in Ottawa, Anglin would have become a senator at the very least. But they were not and he did not. Until his death in 1896 he went from job-hunting to short-term work to more job-seeking. He never again clambered back onto the political merry-go-round from which he had been jostled.

But a man's life, like history in a broader contest, displays continuity amidst change. Anglin's was no exception. He had always been interested in politics; this did not change. He had always been concerned with the role of the Catholic Church and religion in society; he did not lose this concern. He had always been solicitous about Irish affairs; this continued.

III

Leaving the *Globe* did not end Anglin's concern for or efforts on behalf of the Irish cause. In 1892, for example, he wrote an article for a short-lived periodical, *The Lake Magazine*, which interpreted Irish history from a Home Ruler's point of view as well as refuting arguments against Home Rule.[51] In April 1893 he gave a speech in favour of Home Rule back in Saint John.[52] Anglin did not forget the land of his birth even as he approached death.[53]

If Anglin remained involved with the Irish question, he was even more concerned with Catholic questions. At banquets, at cornerstone-laying ceremonies, and at Catholic school exercises Anglin was to be found.[54] He was asked to write the chapter on Bishop Lynch in a jubilee volume celebrating the fiftieth anniversary of the archdiocese of Toronto.[55] He became a trustee on the Toronto Separate School Board in 1888 in a strenuously fought contest, and held the position until 1892.[56] Moreover, he became involved in a minor way with the Manitoba schools question in its early stages. In 1892 he wrote a lengthy letter to the *Empire* which analysed the New Brunswick schools question and asserted that the situation in New Brunswick was still unsatisfactory to Catholics. Catholics of Manitoba, Anglin warned, should not be deluded by those who argued that New Brunswick Catholics were now happy with their common school system.[57] In the same year Anglin published an article which criticized the decision in support of the Manitoba School Act made by the Judicial Committee of the Privy Council and urged remedial legislation by the federal government.[58]

While Anglin remained involved with these issues, his foremost concern between 1888 and his death in 1896 was to locate suitable employment. Not until May 1895 did he find a permanent position. For seven years he appealed to all possible sources for jobs but he managed to obtain only temporary positions with the Ontario government. About the only compensating factors during this difficult period at the end of Anglin's life were the advances made by his family and the interest and value of much of the temporary work he did obtain.

Job-seeking began shortly after the North Simcoe defeat and the demise of the *Tribune*.

The Archbishop is kindly interesting himself and urging Mr. Mowat to provide something. I hope he will be successful as it is not pleasant to feel that you are going back ever so little every day.[59]

The great problem was that provincial appointments under the control of the government almost always had to go to the nominees of the provincial Liberal representatives.[60] The one place that a position could be found for Anglin was on special commissions and in December 1887, just as his agreement with the *Globe* was coming to an end, Anglin reported to Bishop Sweeny that he had been appointed chairman of a Commission on Municipal Institutions.[61] This commission, perhaps a response to a suggestion made by the *Globe* two years earlier,[62] was appointed as a fact-finding body which would collect information from other provinces and other countries about their municipal systems, keeping the Ontario case in mind. The commissioners, Anglin, C.F.B. Johnston, and W. Houston, presented two reports, the *First Report*[63] on 16 March 1888, and the much longer *Second Report*[64] on 20 December of the same year. Both reports were stamped with the Anglin trademark by their thoroughness and comprehensiveness. It was quite apparent that the commission had done its job diligently and vigorously.

Anglin's work on the municipal commission was interrupted by another job which Mowat found for him. On 2 July 1888 Anglin left Toronto for Cincinnati where he remained for more than four months as commissioner in charge of Ontario's mineral display at the Centennial Exposition of the Ohio Valley.[65] Through blistering heat, suffocating smog, and the blaring of bands from the nearby bandstand, Anglin remained at his post from 10 AM until 8 PM one boring dinnerless day after another. Fortunately Ontario's exhibit was good, and Anglin was convinced that it had been a successful enterprise, both in terms of promoting the investment of capital and in opening new markets for Ontario's minerals. As has happened so often to so many Canadians, Anglin found his patriotic pride stimulated by contact with Americans.

It required much effort, indeed, to convince many of this class ['mere sight-seers'], otherwise well informed and intelligent, that Canada occupies so much of this continent that is valuable, that we have so many million acres of fertile lands, that those acres are more productive than the rich lands of the Ohio Valley, that the climate is not of Arctic severity, and above all, that we possess such boundless mineral wealth in Ontario and that all those rich specimens came from that Province.[66]

He did not think that any of the eminent American speakers he heard, such as Rutherford B. Hayes, several state governors, and several other politicians, equalled Canada's best men.[67] These patriotic sentiments, expressed by a former anti-Confederate and one who had been sceptical, at best, about the westward expansion of Canada, cast doubt upon the assertion that during the first two decades after 1867 'truly national sentiments had apparently declined in strength.'[68]

Anglin's attitude towards the work supplied by the Ontario government during 1888 was mixed. It was better than being idle but he wished he had something more permanent. 'Looking to a government for employment is a poor business at best and I often feel humiliated enough,' he wrote Bishop Sweeny, 'but I can not help myself and I suppose I should rather feel thankful for having thus far done so well.'[69] Thankful he might be, for what followed was much worse.

In fact, for a year and a half nothing followed at all. His prestige declined so much that at a Laurier meeting in Toronto in the autumn of 1889 he was not among the many notables who sat on the platform but merely the first-mentioned in the *Globe*'s report of those noted in the audience.[70] Four months later Ontario's Lieutenant-Governor was inquiring if Anglin had the right to retain the prefix 'Honourable' before his name.[71] Things got so bad that Mrs Anglin felt compelled to write privately, without her husband's knowledge, she said, to Sir John A. Macdonald himself, asking the Prime Minister to appoint Anglin to a position. Her letter was pathetic.

I would scarcely venture to appeal to you, were I not encouraged by the generosity & impartiality you have shown in recent appointments of men who were not regarded as your political supporters. It is also painful to me to add my name to the list of office-hunters by whom I suppose you are continually beset – unfortunately circumstances warrant me in asking you to consider my husband in the appointment of the Collector of Customs for Toronto. Our anticipations in removing to this city have not been realized. Mr. Anglin has had for the last two years only temporary employment of an uncertain character. We are glad to have even that – although I can see that anxiety for the future is telling against my husband. We have also several children still to educate and provide for – these are my motives in appealing to you – and considering the twenty-five years Mr. Anglin spent in working conscientiously, as he thought, for the good of his country he has some claim, but it is almost too much to ask such recognition from you.

Christian kindness to one less fortunate than you have been, may however, have its weight.[72]

She should have known that kindness was entirely too much to expect. Macdonald had indicated his policy on patronage to Anglin himself long ago – 'reward your friends and do not buy your enemies.'[73] Yet Anglin's wife made one more effort later the same year. This time the position she wanted for her husband, a position she was sure he would accept, was an appointment to the Senate. But this appeal was likewise in vain.[74]

Undoubtedly it was with a profound sense of relief that Anglin greeted the news in the summer of 1890 that he had been appointed as secretary to a five-man Prison and Reformatory Commission for Ontario.[75] From July 1890 until the commission's report was submitted in April 1891 Anglin was kept busy. He looked up information on European prison systems; corresponded with governments outside Ontario; travelled to the United States and various parts of Ontario; attended the Cincinnati Congress of the National Prison Association on behalf of the commission; and wrote the draft of the report submitted to the Lieutenant-Governor. It was an important report, one which 'merits recognition as one of the outstanding documents in the literature of social welfare in Canada.'[76] It was a topic in which Anglin had long been interested, and, more important, it was a job.

In June 1891 there was another attempt to secure employment for

Anglin, this time by Frank Anglin, the eldest of the Anglin children. His appeal was directed to the new king-maker in Ottawa and a man who might be expected, through regard for Anglin as a man and as a fellow Catholic, to show sympathy – Sir John Thompson. Anglin was still unaware, apparently, that such efforts were being made on his behalf. Frank Anglin freely admitted that his father's political views remained unchanged. Thompson's reply was not encouraging.[77] Once again the Ontario Liberal government came to the rescue; on 19 August Anglin was appointed to yet another commission. However this was an insignificant posting to look into a financial dispute concerning the Township of Proton in Grey County and provided Anglin with merely a short-lived reprieve from unemployment.[78]

It appears that Anglin was now being forced to reach into his financial reserves. His bond investments in Saint John had diminished as the terms of the bonds expired, until in 1892 they seem to have run out entirely. Anglin may well have reinvested some of the capital returned to him but some of it must have gone for living expenses. Yet the fact that he had managed to retain approximately $8,500 in capital reserves until 1892 indicates that Anglin was hardly destitute.[79] In 1888 he had at last been able to rent his house in Saint John, and he eventually found a buyer in January 1892. The price he received – $3,000 – suggests not only that property values in Saint John were depressed but also that Anglin was very anxious to sell.[80] After all, he had paid £1,200 for the property in 1857 and expended a good deal of money in building a new house after the fire of 1874.

Lack of employment remained a worry to Anglin for he still had four dependent children under the age of sixteen in 1892, the year he celebrated his seventieth birthday. Anglin must have reflected on the fact that he was getting older, particularly when he acted as one of twelve pall-bearers at Alexander Mackenzie's funeral on 20 April 1892.[81] Mrs Anglin too was worried. She wrote to Thompson pleading with him to select her husband for a federal commission on prisons, an appointment Anglin had requested. Of the several reasons for such an appointment which she presented in her appeal, probably the most important from her point of view was that Anglin was 'a man now in advanced years with a large family to provide for ...'[82] It was, therefore, with real anxiety that Anglin wrote to Bishop Sweeny in August of that year.

I have not earned a dollar for nearly six months and although I have repeatedly applied to Sir Oliver Mowat for employment I see little prospect of obtaining any. Promises which he made to the late Archbishop and to myself some years ago he shows an unwillingness to keep and I have reason to feel that in his eyes and perhaps in the eyes of his colleagues I am not regarded as being of so much importance as I was supposed to be when I was invited to come to Toronto.[83]

In such circumstances Anglin was interested in returning to the places where he had won fame – New Brunswick and the House of Commons. He had never lost his interest in politics although his public role had been severely restricted since 1887. But he continued to be an informed observer of the Canadian political scene and had been mentioned as a candidate for Saint John in the 1891 election.[84] That possibility had come to naught but Anglin thought he saw a golden opportunity when he heard that Edouard Léger, MP for Kent in New Brunswick, had died. Anglin immediately wrote to Bishop Rogers and Bishop Sweeny asking for their active support.

My position at present renders it very desirable in a merely personal point of view that I should if possible *obtain a seat in the House of Commons* and it would be much better in every way that I should not be under an obligation for such seat to any political party but should be absolutely free to take such course as duty and the interests of Catholicity may require. It was my good fortune while in Parliament to be free to do always what I thought right as I never owed anything to party and this position gave me an amount of influence I could not otherwise have enjoyed. The decision in the Manitoba School case may lead to serious complications in the near future and even to a breaking up of the old parties neither of which is very coherent just now. Should trouble arise or should any questions gravely affecting Catholic interests come up for discussion in Parliament would it not be well that the Catholics of New Brunswick had some one authorized to speak for them who knew something more of such subjects than is known by any of the present representatives of Catholic constituencies in that Province?

Catholic interests in the largest sense seem to be but poorly represented in the present House of Commons. Sir John Thompson is the only one in the House of Commons capable of dealing with any grave Catholic question even tolerably well and he appears to be in an awkward position now.

But while I think that is of some importance, from a Catholic point of view that I should return to Parliament I do not wish to put out of view the fact that I am impelled very largely by reasons purely personal to solicit your assistance in being elected for Kent.[85]

Anglin wanted the bishops to pass on the word to the priests who were then to get up requisitions for Anglin's candidacy. In this way it might be possible to develop such a groundswell of support as to render a convention unnecessary.[86] In other words Anglin wanted to re-create the situation of

1867. This time, however, Bishop Rogers was on the spot rather than in Europe and Anglin learned from Dr Sweeny that the difficulties were almost insuperable.[87] It was most unlikely that Rogers would be willing to help Anglin, a Reformer, in his endeavour. But also, it had been a decade since Anglin had resided in New Brunswick and even then he had been connected with Saint John and Gloucester, not Kent.[88] It was hard for Anglin to realize it, but he was past his prime.

On 24 April 1893 another commission of which Anglin was a member handed in its report.[89] The Municipal Taxation Commission had been established in response to the agitation aroused by the 1892 Assessment Act which had asserted that real and personal property were equally liable for assessment for municipal purposes. The commission was a fact-finding one, and while its findings were not wholly without pointers as to the direction legislation should follow, it presented no recommendations. This may have been the reason for a twenty-two page *Supplement* presented by Anglin himself, for the *Supplement* came closer to drawing conclusions than did the factual main *Report*. What Anglin's submission amounted to was a rejection of Henry George's theory of the Single Tax;[90] a reiteration of his conviction that real estate assessment should be calculated on the actual value of the property rather than on a percentage of that value; a recognition that the problem of devising a system which would adequately tax personal property had not been solved; and a defence of the exemption of certain classes of property – such as religious and charitable institutions, city property, provincial and federal property – from taxation in the Ontatio Act. This was all presented with considerable erudition, Anglin displaying a knowledge not only of the work of contemporary political economists but also of the taxation systems of the Roman, Turkish, and Egyptian empires.

While these were trying and humiliating years for Anglin, his tribulations do not seem to have worn down his spirit completely. He showed the Liberal convention of 1893 that he retained an independent mind and was not afraid to speak it. The tenth and last policy resolution, introduced very, very late in the evening at the last session of the convention, was one in favour of going to the Canadian people with a plebiscite on the question of prohibition. Those delegates who had remained so late were anxious to conclude the session and cries of 'carried, carried' were heard. Anglin would have none of this. He spoke against the resolution in at least as strong terms as he had opposed the Scott Act of 1878 when he stepped down from the Speaker's chair to enter the debate. He objected to the resolution on grounds of party expediency, for, he argued, holding a plebiscite provided tacit support for prohibition and he thought that the Liberal Party should not become known as a prohibition party. Nor did he think that prohibition was the best means of promoting temperance. This had been proven by New Brunswick's experience many years before.

I opposed Prohibition thirty-five years ago, and I feel to-day as strongly as I did then that I am as true a friend of the temperance cause as those who have forced this resolution upon the Committee, and ten thousand times a better friend of the Liberal party and the Liberal cause.

If the resolution passed he refused to be bound by it.

No set of men have the right, because they happen to be a majority, to prescribe what other men shall or shall not eat or drink or wear, and no legislature has a right to prohibit, under penalties, that which is not evil or criminal or sinful in itself.

The resolution passed, but at least Anglin had the satisfaction of letting the convention know that he thought of it.[91]

After 1893 Anglin almost disappeared from sight. In the summer of 1894 he wrote several letters to Thompson asking to be appointed to a federal commission on reformatories which he assumed was to be established.[92] But he had read the signs incorrectly; no commission was named.[93] Yet Anglin did not throw in the sponge. In February 1895 he was earnestly soliciting Laurier's support in an effort to secure the Liberal nomination for South Renfrew.[94] Someone else wanted exactly the same thing – and that someone was none other than Anglin's own son, Frank. Frank Anglin wrote to Laurier:

I learn with some surprise to-day that my father is thinking of running if nominated and that he has thought also of South-Renfrew. I most certainly cannot allow myself to be put in such opposition to him in any way. He fully deserves anything that the Reform party can do for him. He has – I have not – claims upon the party. So that if his candidature should be acceptable to the party – and if it is felt that his nomination will be in the best interests of the party – I am of course out of the field. But if the need be for *a young man* as I have been told and if it is thought that my candidature will be a greater source of strength I am content to do what in me lies. I cannot and will not in any way stand in my father's light in the matter – but if he is not considered available or suitable – then I am ready to do my best – I leave the matter in your hands.[95]

As this occurrence signified, Anglin's family was growing up. Timothy Jr had taken a position as a clerk while he was still a teenager, and by 1896 he was working as a teller in the Canadian Bank of Commerce.[96] Margaret, though just fifteen years old, had gone to New York in 1892 to study dramatic art after her mother had scraped up the money by secretly selling some prize lace flounces.[97] By 1896, then, only Timothy Jr and the three youngest children, Eileen, Basil, and thirteen-year-old Alexander were living with their parents in their rented house close to the northwest corner of what is now Dundas Street and University Avenue.[98] Anglin seems to have taken more interest in the careers of his two eldest boys than in the younger children, for his letters to Bishop Sweeny seldom mention the others. But perhaps it was merely that they had not yet had time to establish careers for themselves. With Frank and Arthur Anglin was well pleased.

They are both good boys thank God and never cause us any trouble or uneasiness. If they do not succeed the fault I am satisfied will not be theirs.[99]

They did succeed. Arthur followed his elder brother into the legal profession and established himself in the well-known firm of Blake, Lash and Cassells.[100] In 1894 he married the daughter of Justice Falconbridge of the Ontario Supreme Court. But it was the oldest boy, Frank, whose career was the most impressive. He passed his bar examinations early in 1888, became a partner in a law firm with a prominent Toronto Catholic, D.A. O'Sullivan, and when that gentleman died in 1892 he became the senior partner in a new firm, Anglin and Minty.[101] In the same year his father announced to Bishop Sweeny Frank's forthcoming marriage to a Miss Fraser and added:

His income is not yet as large as I hope it will become but he is very industrious and attentive to business and has big expectations which I hope will be realized in good time.[102]

Frank was following in his father's footsteps and assuming all the attributes of a 'representative Irish Catholic.' He was a soloist at St Michael's Cathedral;[103] he wrote letters to newspapers and politicians in opposition to the McCarthyites;[104] he made speeches about 'The Irish in Canada';[105] and he urged the return of separate schools to Manitoba Catholics.[106] Like father, like son: but while Anglin senior's career was on the wane, Frank's was on the rise. In 1895 the two lines met and crossed. Frank, not Timothy, received Laurier's blessing for the South Renfrew constituency.[107]

IV

The years after 1887 were demeaning for Anglin. He had devoted his life to various forms of public service, as a newspaperman and a politician. Yet he was discarded as soon as he was no longer useful. This was hardly unusual in the nineteenth-century world and Anglin was more fortunate than most for he had some financial reserves to fall back on. Yet it must have been a very trying time for Anglin. A proud and highly accomplished man, he was forced to beg for work from Mowat; a man accustomed to arduous and constant work, he had to cope with long stretches of enforced idleness. He had always believed that diligence and correct, prudent living would bring their just reward, and he had attempted to live according to these precepts; yet it now seemed that he might not even be able to provide adequately for his much younger wife and still dependent children.[108]

Yet his life was in no way a failure. He had been conscientious, hard-working, and competent in almost all of his endeavours – as newspaper-man, as politician, as Irish leader and Catholic spokesman, as Speaker of the House of Commons, as commissioner. He had not risen to heights of brilliance, but he was a man respected for his capabilities, determination, diligence, and uprightness. During the second half of the nineteenth century his name was known and his words heard or read throughout much of British North America. His influence on his fellow citizens in his adopted country had not been inconsiderable. As an Irish Catholic leader he had provided an essential mechanism for accommodating the Irish within Canadian society. Moreover, in spite of his fears, he had provided a firm foundation for the careers of his children. He had lived an eventful, in-teresting, useful life, neither unpleasant nor unfulfilling. What more is success?

Happily, there was a moderately satisfactory ending to Anglin's years of anxiety, for in May 1895 he was made Chief Clerk of the Surrogate Court of Ontario, the influence of Frank and Arthur probably being a factor in the appointment. Late that same year he saw service on a Citizens' Committee for Toronto which drafted a report on municipal reform.[109] But in April 1896 he became ill. At the beginning of May he seemed to rally and on the afternoon of Saturday, 2 May, he went out for a drive, to visit Frank. That night he slept well until about 3:30 AM when he suffered a seizure caused by a blood clot in the brain. Mrs Anglin roused the members of the family present in the house and they went to his bedside. Within fifteen minutes Timothy Warren Anglin was dead.[110]

Funeral services were held on the following Wednesday. The pall-bearers were Oliver Mowat, Dr B. Travers, Anglin's old friend who had encouraged him nearly half a century before to leave Ireland and start anew in Saint John, Sir Frank Smith, Justice Falconbridge, Commander Law representing the Lieutenant-Governor, Eugene O'Keefe, B.B. Hughes, and, of all people, Goldwin Smith.[111] The *Globe*'s eulogy was most kind.

Mr. Anglin was a widely-read man, especially in the field of constitutional law and Parliamentary lore, and his decisions from the Speaker's chair have now all the force of honored precedents. Naturally grave and dignified in bearing, he was in more than one way fitted to discharge the duties of the first Commoner.

While stalwart in his political beliefs, he nevertheless took care to be moderate and fair in his course towards political antagonists, and we may feel sure that he left no enemies behind him. As a writer he was well-informed, ready and weighty, and in that role did not forget that we can controvert the opinions of those who honestly differ from us without hitting below the belt. He was a devout member of his church and was esteemed and trusted by all within its fold, and indeed leaves a record for integrity, high attainments and strict observance of a high code of conduct that marks the best citizenship.[112]

This was very nice and largely true, but somehow one cannot but think that when Anglin had written about George Brown at the time of his death in 1880 he had written his own epitaph as well.

He remained to the end the same straightforward politician, the same uncompromising advocate of the right that he had always been, modifying his views only when reason and experience convinced him that they were more or less erroneous, and changing his course only so far as was necessary to keep it in harmony with his convictions ... What he thought he said or wrote always – perhaps too strongly or too bitterly when the heat of the contests in which he was so long engaged affected his judgment – but never obscurely or uncertainly ... His position as the proprietor and editor of a great newspaper sometimes embarrassed him as a politician, because, while others enquired and hesitated, he was absolutely forced to form his opinion quickly, to express it plainly, and to sustain it vigorously, aiming only at what was right, and regardless of mere expediency.[113]

Notes

NOTES TO CHAPTER ONE

1 S.F. Wise, 'Upper Canada and the Conservative Tradition,' *Profiles of a Province: Studies in the History of Ontario* (Toronto, 1967), p 21
2 S.J.R. Noel, 'Consociational Democracy and Canadian Federalism,' *Canadian Journal of Political Science*, IV (1971), 16
3 S.D. Scott, 'Hon. Timothy Anglin sketched. A career with many elements of interest – Mr. Anglin as Editor and Parliamentarian,' Dr Raymond's Scrapbook, vol IX, in NBMA; and *New Freeman* (Saint John), 6 Jan. 1900
4 First Marquess of Dufferin and Ava Papers, Canadian Letters, VIII, 16, Anglin to Dufferin, 9 Sept. 1878
5 W.E. Houghton, *The Victorian Frame of Mind 1830–1870* (New Haven, 1957), pp 242–62
6 Ibid, pp 62, 189
7 *New Freeman* (Saint John), 6 Jan. 1900
8 I. Sclanders, 'Historical Articles,' p 208 (2 Nov. 1948), in NBMA. For information on Anglin's children see the appendix.
9 *Morning Freeman* (Saint John), 8 July 1875
10 Ibid, 16 Oct. 1877. See also ibid, 3 May 1860; and 'Dominion Parliament,' 21 March 1879, in *Freeman*, 5 Apr. 1879.
11 *Freeman*, 26 May 1866. The meeting, one might add, broke up peacefully.
12 M. O'Donovan-Rossa, *My Father and Mother were Irish* (New York: Devin-Adair, 1939), p 61. See also pp 12, 60.
13 Houghton, *Victorian Mind*, pp 137–80
14 Houghton asserts that readers liked their guides to be dogmatic (ibid, p 138).

15 Ibid, p 146
16 *Freeman*, 12 July 1862
17 Alexander Mackenzie Papers, Anglin to Mackenzie, 25 July 1877; and *Canada: House of Commons Debates, 1880*, pp 1030–1 (2 April)
18 Houghton, *Victorian Mind*, p 341
19 Ibid, p 343
20 P.B. Waite, 'Sir Oliver Mowat's Canada: Reflections on an Un-Victorian Society,' *Oliver Mowat's Ontario*, ed D. Swainson (Toronto, 1972), p 23. Probably all important political figures in nineteenth-century British North America were subject to hostile attacks. Indeed, these were a virtual signpost of the significance of an individual. Goldwin Smith, recognized today as an extremely intelligent nineteenth-century political commentator, was frequently berated by those who disagreed with his views (see, for example, A.G. Bailey, *Culture and Nationality* [Toronto, 1972], pp 160–5).
21 'One of Them' to the Editor, *New Brunswick Courier* (Saint John), 20 Dec. 1856; Sir Samuel Leonard Tilley Papers (uncatalogued collection), T.B. Barker to Tilley, 17 Nov. 1859; and ibid, J. Boyd to Tilley, 13 March 1862
22 *New Dominion and True Humorist* (Saint John), 15 Nov. 1873. The real religious bigotry was less that of Anglin and more that of the writer of the comment. See also *New Brunswick Reporter* (Fredericton), 19 Nov. 1873, which stated that 'Mr. Anglin is one of the cleverest men in the Parliament of the Dominion, his constitutional bad temper and hatred of British institutions, being his only bar to political preferment.' However true the comment about Anglin's temper may have been, the criticism of his dislike of British institutions was hardly justified.
23 *News*, 11 May 1883
24 M.O. Hammond and H. Charlesworth, 'History of the Globe' (unpublished manuscript in the *Globe and Mail* library used by permission), pp 153–4; G.W. Ross, *Getting Into Parliament and After* (Toronto, 1913), p 56; J.C. Dent, *The Last Forty Years: Canada Since the Union of 1841* (Toronto, 1881), II, 479; J.E. Collins, *Life and Times of the Right Honourable Sir John A. Macdonald* (Toronto, 1883), p 342; and G. Stewart, Jr, *Canada Under the administration of the Earl of Dufferin* (Toronto, 1878), p 243. The comment about Anglin's wit is an interesting one, for Anglin was not normally noted for this kind of talent.
25 Raymond's Scrapbook, XIV, 28
26 *Freeman*, 6 July 1871

NOTES TO CHAPTER TWO

1 *Morning Freeman* (Saint John), 19 May 1866
2 Anglin Family Scrapbook (copy in the possession of R.E. Anglin, Toronto)

3 *New Freeman* (Saint John), 6 Jan 1900. Among the many books on the Great Famine the most gripping is C. Woodham-Smith, *The Great Hunger: Ireland 1845–9* (London, 1962).

4 See, for example, *Morning Freeman*, n.d., quoted in *Morning News* (Saint John), 18 Feb. 1850.

5 *Freeman*, 18 Nov. 1858. A Nova Scotian Irish Catholic newspaper shared the *Freeman*'s apprehensions (see *Evening Express and Commercial Record* [Halifax], 1 Aug. 1864).

6 *Freeman*, 9 Oct. 1866

7 P.S. O'Hegarty, *A History of Ireland Under the Union 1801 to 1922* (London: Methuen, 1952), pp 284–5

8 Quoted in John J. O'Gorman papers, 'McGee the Irish Patriot,' p 13. See also A. Brady, *Thomas D'Arcy McGee* (Toronto, 1925), p 11.

9 *Freeman*, 5 Aug. 1875. See also *Globe* (Toronto), 6 June 1883.

10 W.S. MacNutt, *New Brunswick: A History 1784–1867* (Toronto, 1963), p 45

11 The most useful secondary sources on the ferment in New Brunswick at mid-century are D.G.G. Kerr, *Sir Edmund Head: A Scholarly Governor* (Toronto, 1954); and D.F. Macmillan, 'Federation and Annexation Sentiment in New Brunswick, 1848–1851,' unpublished Master's dissertation, University of New Brunswick, 1961.

12 The mayor banned similar processions in the future. See 'A' (perhaps Anglin) to Editor, 31 July 1857, in the *New Era* (Montreal), 4 Aug. 1857; and J.F.W. Johnston, *Notes on North America: Agricultural, Economical and Social* (Edinburgh, 1851), II, 143.

13 Colonial Office 384, Emigration Correspondence, LXXXI, 175 (*Eighth General Report of the Colonial Land and Emigration Commissioners, May 17, 1848,* p 15)

14 Ibid, p 175

15 O. Handlin, *Boston's Immigrants: A Study of Acculturation* rev ed (Cambridge, Massachusetts: The Belknap Press of Harvard University Press, 1959), pp 126–7. The entire section (pp 124–44) is a brilliant analysis of the state of mind of the Irish immigrant.

16 *New Freeman*, 6 Jan. 1900

17 *News*, 27 July 1849

18 Ibid, 20 Aug. 1849

19 *Freeman*, 2 Dec. 1871; second and third weeks of November 1872; 7 Jan. 1873; 10 Jan. 1880; and 13 Jan. 1883

20 To footnote all occasions when Anglin was involved in such activities would be pedantic.

21 See, for example, *Globe*, 28 June 1883; 25 June 1884; 11 Oct. 1887; and *Tribune* (Toronto), 4 July and 16 Sept. 1885.

22 *New Brunswick: House of Assembly Debates, 1865*, pp 85–6 (22 May); and *Freeman*, 28 Dec. 1878

23 See, for example, 'T.W.A.,' 7 May 1868, in *Freeman*, 16 May 1868; *Freeman*, 25 Jan. 1877; and *Canada: House of Commons Debates, 1880*, pp 303–5 (27 Feb.).

24 *Freeman*, 17 Jan. 1861

25 Anglin appears to have had a particularly close relationship with Bishop Sweeny, perhaps because the cathedral and the bishop's residence were just a few doors away from Anglin's home.

26 Among the numerous studies of the nineteenth-century Catholic Church see K.S. Latourette, *Christianity in a Revolutionary Age*, vol I: *The Nineteenth Century in Europe: Background and Roman Catholic Phase* (London, 1959); E.E.Y. Hales, *The Catholic Church in the Modern World: A Survey from the French Revolution to the Present* (London, 1958); J.B. Bury, *History of the Papacy in the 19th Century*, rev ed (New York, 1964); and E.L. Woodward, *Three Studies in European Conservatism* (London, 1963), pp 229–344.

27 R.B. McDowell, *Public Opinion and Government Policy in Ireland, 1801–1846* (London, 1952), p 31

28 *Freeman*, 16 March 1869

29 Ibid, 30 July 1868

NOTES TO CHAPTER THREE

1 The 1851 Census for New Brunswick, as reprinted in *Canada: Census, 1870–71*, does not give breakdowns according to place of birth, ethnic background, or religion. Therefore one can only make estimates from *New Brunswick: Census, 1861*, an appendix to *New Brunswick: House of Assembly Journals, 1862*, and from the 1871 *Canada: Census*.

2 M.J. Herskovits, *Acculturation: A Study of Culture Contact* (Gloucester, Mass., 1958), p 10, defines acculturation as comprehending 'those phenomena which result when groups of individuals having different cultures come into continuous first-hand contact, with subsequent changes in the original cultural patterns of either or both groups.' Assimilation is therefore not synonymous with but may be a form of acculturation.

3 The literature on this subject is far from unanimous and there are historians who imply that the process of Canadianization was not a particularly difficult one. See D.C. Lyne, 'The Irish in the Province of Canada in the Decade Leading up to Confederation,' unpublished Master's dissertation, McGill University, 1960, pp 365–75; and J.S. Moir, 'The Problem of a Double Minority:

Some Reflections on the Development of the English-speaking Catholic Church in Canada in the Nineteenth Century,' *Histoire Sociale/Social History*, VII (1971), 63.
4 J.J. Mannion, *Irish Settlements in Eastern Canada: A Study of Culture Transfer and Adaptation* (Toronto, 1974)
5 K. Duncan, 'Irish Famine Immigration and the Social Structure of Canada West,' *Canada: A Sociological Profile*, ed W.E. Mann (Toronto, 1968), p 14
6 Ibid, p 15
7 *New Brunswick Courier* (Saint John), 17 Jan. 1857
8 *The Merchants' and Farmers' Almanack for 1857* (Saint John, 1856), p 27; and *Morning Freeman* (Saint John), 6 Dec. 1860. On 3 Dec. 1859 the *Freeman* was moved to state that the Society 'is not regarded or recognized by the Irish of St. John as the exponent of their opinions or feelings.'
9 J. Fingard, 'The Relief of the Unemployed Poor in Saint John, Halifax, and St. John's, 1810s–1860,' *Acadiensis*, V: 1 (Autumn 1975), 35–6. Further 'vertical' divisions within Protestant groups also emerged.
10 *New Brunswick Reporter and Fredericton Advertiser* (Fredericton), 23 Aug. 1850
11 The value of property in Saint John fell enormously (see *Freeman*, n.d., quoted in *Morning News* [Saint John], 5 Dec. 1849).
12 The bridge was completed in 1853 (see *Courier*, 26 Feb. 1853). In 1856 it was claimed that about a thousand men were employed on the railroad (see *Freeman*, n.d., quoted in *Courier*, 25 Oct. 1856).
13 J. Fingard, 'The Winter's Tale: The Seasonal Contours of Pre-Industrial Poverty in British North America, 1815–1860,' *Canadian Historical Association, Historical Papers, 1974*, pp 65–94
14 D. Roberts, 'Social Structure in a Commercial City: Saint John, 1871,' *Urban History Review*, no. 2–74, p 16
15 Fingard, 'Relief of Unemployed Poor,' p 1; and M.B. Buckley, *Diary of a Tour in America*, ed K. Buckley (Dublin, 1886), p 112
16 The *Freeman*, 26 Sept. 1861, described the industrial development of the Saint John area.
17 As late as 1853 the *Freeman* was complaining of the lack of housing (see *Freeman*, n.d., quoted in *Courier*, 19 Nov. 1853).
18 Roberts, 'Social Structure,' p 17
19 *Canada: Census, 1870–71*, I, 214–15, 316–17, 400–1
20 G. Bilson, 'The Cholera Epidemic in Saint John, N.B., 1854,' *Acadiensis*, IV: 1 (Autumn 1974), 89–90
21 Ibid, pp 87, 89
22 Ibid, p 98; and *Courier*, 24 May 1856

23 *Head Quarters* (Fredericton), 10 May 1855
24 *Freeman*, 10 Feb. 1859. The date of the founding of the Irish Friendly Society is not known. The society's president in 1859 was Anglin's friend, Dr Boyle Travers.
25 *Courier*, 19 Dec. 1857
26 Ibid, n.d., quoted in *Courier*, 24 Dec. 1853. The account in this issue showed that the existence of the Irish fire company was not without its problems. One of the members of the company was taken into police custody when he endeavoured to break through a restraining line at a fire. His colleagues then attempted to rescue him and two police officials were struck. Apparently the assistance of a body of soldiers was required to get the individual initially arrested to the Watch House. See also *Freeman*, 4 Feb. 1860.
27 See *Freeman*, n.d., quoted in *Courier*, 27 Nov. 1852; and *Courier*, 4 Sept. 1852.
28 Peter Aylen might be taken as an example (see M.S. Cross, 'The Shiners' War: Social Violence in the Ottawa Valley in the 1830s,' CHR, LIV [1973], 1–26).
29 E.M. Levine, *The Irish and Irish Politicians: A Study of Cultural and Social Alienation* (Notre Dame, Indiana: Notre Dame University Press, 1966), pp 91–2
30 R.B. McDowell, 'Ireland on the Eve of the Famine,' *The Great Famine: Studies in Irish History 1846–52*, ed R.D. Edwards and T.D. Williams (Dublin, 1956), p 30
31 See Fingard, 'Relief of Unemployed Poor,' pp 11–12.
32 See, for example, *Freeman*, 17 July 1869, and 20 Nov. 1875.
33 Ibid, 7 Feb. 1861
34 Ibid, 30 Nov. 1858
35 Ibid, 27 Oct. 1860. See also ibid, 29 Dec. 1860.
36 'Chief of Police Report,' quoted in *Freeman*, 14 June 1864
37 *Freeman*, 20 Nov. 1858
38 Ibid, 30 Oct. 1860
39 J.R. Harper, *Historical Directory of New Brunswick Newspapers and Periodicals* (Fredericton, 1961). In 1849 the telegraph line from Saint John to Halifax was completed and in 1858 the Atlantic Telegraph cable was laid (see *Courier*, 3 Nov. 1849; and Sir Samuel Leonard Tilley Papers [uncatalogued collection], T.B. Barker to Tilley, 5 Aug. 1858). Both of these developments assisted the newspapers in providing their readers with recent news from outside the colony.
40 *Courier*, 2 Nov. 1850
41 *Freeman*, 8 Jan. 1859
42 *News*, 20 Nov. 1857; and *Freeman*, 16 March 1861
43 *News*, 20 Nov. 1857. Because of this the *News* was convinced that the *Freeman*'s circulation could not exceed 800.

44 See, for example, Henry G. Simonds to Editors, 29 May 1851, in *Courier*, 31 May 1851, in which Simonds accused Anglin of wilfully perverting the facts of a court case.

45 *Freeman*, 1 June 1852, quoted in *News*, 2 June 1852

46 *Freeman*, 18 Sept. 1858; and 9 Feb. 1861

47 C. Ward, 'Old Times in Saint John,' p 160, in NBMA. S.D. Scott, 'Hon. Timothy Warren Anglin sketched. A career with many elements of interest – Mr. Anglin as Editor and Parliamentarian,' Dr Raymond's Scrapbook, vol IX, in NBMA, also gives evidence of Anglin's phenomenal memory.

48 *News*, 26 Dec. 1851, and 9 Jan. 1852; and *Courier*, 10 Jan. 1852. Anglin was paid for this service by a number of Saint John merchants.

49 *News*, 23 March 1855; and *Courier*, 26 July 1856, and 21 Feb. 1857

50 A compositor in the *Freeman* office was reported as going home at 4:00 AM (see *Freeman*, 27 Dec. 1877).

51 For a time during the 1850s the office was located on the north side of Church Street, just off Prince William (see *Freeman*, 14 July 1855), but by 1858 it had moved to Prince William, probably 35 Prince William, where it remained until 1876 (see *Freeman*, 8 June 1858 and 2 Aug. 1862).

52 See F.B. Roe and N.G. Colby, *Atlas of Saint John City and County, New Brunswick* (Saint John, 1875); K.Y. Johnston, 'The History of St. John, 1837–1867: Civic and Economic,' unpublished Bachelor's dissertation, Mount Allison University, 1953, chap 3, pp 11–13.

53 G. Stewart, Jr, *The Story of the Great Fire in St. John, N.B. June 20th, 1877* (Toronto, 1877), p 116

54 *The New Brunswick Almanack and Register, for ... 1864 ...* (Saint John, 1864), p 52. It was cheaper by half to ferry your elephant or camel across the harbour than to take it across the suspension bridge (see ibid, pp 52–3).

55 *News*, 10 May 1850

56 J.W. Millidge, 'Reminiscences of Saint John from 1849 to 1860,' *Collections of the New Brunswick Historical Society*, no. 10 (1919), p 135

57 Ward, 'Old Times,' p 160

58 Quoted in Johnston, 'History of St. John,' chap 2, p 38

59 Anglin Family Scrapbook (copy in the possession of R.E. Anglin, Toronto)

60 Ward, 'Old Times,' p 160

61 Register of Deeds Office, Provincial Building, Saint John, Saint John County Registry of Deeds, vol, H4, pp 571–2

62 This description appeared in an advertisement in the *Freeman* through the latter half of 1860 and on into 1861 when Anglin was attempting to sell the property. He was unable, apparently, to find a buyer.

63 *New Brunswick: House of Assembly Debates, 1865*, p 36 (10 May)

64 *Freeman*, 28 Feb. 1860

65 Ibid, 6 Dec. 1860
66 Ibid, 28 Feb. 1860
67 Ibid, 6 Dec. 1860
68 See the *Freeman*'s comments on the industrial progress of Saint John in the issue of 26 Sept. 1861.
69 Ibid, 18 Jan. 1862
70 Ibid, 17 Oct. 1861
71 Ibid, 29 Nov. 1859
72 Ibid, 2 Feb. 1860
73 Ibid, 21 Jan., 2, 16, 23 Feb., 7 June, 2 Aug. 1860; 25 July 1861; 9 Sept. 1862; 17 Oct. 1867; 7 Oct. 1869; 5 July 1870; 21 Oct. 1871. Sweeny's Catholic colonization program was far from unique in North America (see M.G. Kelly, *Catholic Immigrant Colonization Projects in the United States, 1815–1860* (New York, 1939). D'Arcy McGee was one of the prominent proponents of such schemes in the 1850s (see ibid, pp 210–11; and A.I. Abell, *American Catholicism and Social Justice: A Search for Social Justice 1865 to 1950* [Notre Dame, Indiana, 1963], p 19).
74 Ibid, n.d., quoted in *Courier*, 18 Dec. 1852
75 *Freeman*, n.d., quoted in *News*, 23 March 1853; *Freeman*, 25 Feb. 1860; and *Assembly Debates, 1862*, p 69 (25 March) and pp 88–9 (3 Apr.).
76 Analyses of railway building in New Brunswick during this period are to be found in W.S. MacNutt, *New Brunswick: A History 1784–1867* (Toronto, 1963), pp 325–9, 334–9, 379–82; and A.W. Bailey, 'Railways in New Brunswick, 1827–1867,' unpublished Master's dissertation, University of New Brunswick, 1955.
77 *Courier*, 8 Feb. 1851
78 Ibid, 2 Aug., 13 Dec. 1851; 21 Feb. 1852. See also Sir Edmund Head Papers, vol III, Head to Joseph Howe, 20 Sept., 9 Dec. 1851; and Head to Sir J. Harvey, 2 Dec. 1851.
79 *Freeman*, 16 Feb., 8 Sept., 9 Oct. 1860
80 Ibid, 23 Sept. 1851; and ibid, 13 Oct. 1853, quoted in *Reporter*, 21 Oct. 1853
81 *Courier*, 17 Aug., 21 Sept. 1850
82 *Head Quarters*, 21 Nov. 1855; *Freeman*, n.d., quoted in *Courier*, 15 Oct. 1856; and *Courier*, 10 Jan. 1857
83 On Head's efforts and difficulties see D.G.G. Kerr, *Sir Edmund Head: A Scholarly Governor* (Toronto, 1954), pp 27–36, 58–82; and D.G.G. Kerr, 'Head and Responsible Government in New Brunswick,' *Canadian Historical Association Annual Report, 1938*, pp 62–70.
84 On New Brunswick politics between 1848 and 1854 see MacNutt, *New Brunswick*, pp 315–52.

85 *Freeman*, 20 Sept. 1851
86 See, for example, ibid, n.d., quoted in *News*, 28 March 1853; and *Freeman*,
n.d., quoted in *News*, 23 March 1853.
87 MacNutt, *New Brunswick*, pp 356–7
88 *Freeman*, n.d., quoted in *Reporter*, 6 July 1854
89 See speech in the Assembly by R.B. Cutler as reported in *Head Quarters*,
1 Nov. 1854.
90 Ibid, 9 May 1855. The *Freeman* took very perfunctory notice of the appointment of Charles Watters, a Catholic, to the executive late in 1855 (see *Head
Quarters*, 5 Dec. 1855).
91 Ibid, 21 Nov. 1855
92 *Reporter*, 25 Jan. 1856; and *Head Quarters*, 30 Jan. 1856
93 Meaningful and reliable statistics on liquor consumption in New Brunswick are
virtually impossible to determine. In 1854, 665,905 gallons of spirits and
280,999 gallons of wine were imported into New Brunswick (see Johnston,
'History of Saint John,' chap 4, p 28). As well, 1,079,405 gallons of molasses, a
basic ingredient in the making of rum, were imported (see ibid, chap 4, p 26).
On top of this, actual consumption figures would have to include smuggled
liquor, home brew, and beer and ale. Of course, one would also have to know
how much was re-exported and how much stockpiling of supplies took place in
order to develop meaningful consumption figures. Johnston's account indicates that 1854 was 'the boom year of the fifties.' Thus any attempt to develop
per capita consumption figures and compare them with those produced by a
royal commission in 1895 would be extremely dangerous. One can say only
that the New Brunswick consumption rate in 1854 seems to have been vastly
greater than the Dominion average recorded in any year from 1871 to 1893 (see
F.S. Spence, *The Facts of the Case: A Summary of ... the Report of the Royal
Commission on the Liquor Traffic* [Toronto, 1896], p 19).
94 J.K. Chapman, 'The Mid-Nineteenth Century Temperance Movement in New
Brunswick and Maine,' CHR, XXXV (1954), 43–60. On the relationship of
alcohol consumption and crime see P.B. Waite, 'Sir Oliver Mowat's Canada:
Reflections on an Un-Victorian Society,' *Oliver Mowat's Ontario*, ed D.
Swainson (Toronto, 1972), pp 20–1.
95 See, for example, Uncatalogued Tilley Papers, James A. Davidson to Tilley,
22 Sept. 1858. See also J.M. Clemens, 'Taste Not; Touch Not; Handle Not: A
Study of the Social Assumptions of the Temperance Literature and Temperance Supporters in Canada West Between 1839 and 1859,' *Ontario History*,
LXIV (1972), 144, 145, 148.
96 Chapman, 'Mid-Nineteenth Century Temperance Movement ...,' pp 53–4
97 *Head Quarters*, 26 Dec. 1855

98 P.B. Waite, 'The Fall and Rise of the Smashers, 1856–1857: Some Private Letters of Manners-Sutton,' *Acadiensis*, II: *No.* I (Autumn 1972), 66. See *Courier*, 17 March, 17 Apr. 1855; *News*, 23 March 1855; and *Head Quarters*, 2 Jan. 1856. The *Courier* and *News* supported the government; the *Head Quarters* was opposed.

99 *Freeman*, n.d., quoted in *News*, 19 March 1855

100 *Freeman*, 11 Nov. 1858

101 Charles Burpee Papers, Anglin to Burpee, 18 Feb. 1856, in PANB

102 Ibid. See also *Freeman*, 3 July 1856, quoted in *News*, 4 July 1856.

103 *Gleaner* (Miramichi), 2 Feb. 1856

104 *News*, 26 March 1856

105 See, for example, *Courier*, 3 May 1856

106 A list of thirteen papers opposed to the Governor's action and of five defending his action is found in the *Gleaner*, 14 June 1856.

107 *Freeman*, n.d., quoted in *Head Quarters*, 28 May 1856

108 *Courier*, 28 June 1856

109 The vote on repeal was thirty-eight to two (see *Gleaner*, 26 July 1856).

110 *Courier*, 21 June, 12 July, 6 Sept., 4 Oct. 1856; *News*, 10 Oct. 1856; and *Reporter*, 23 Jan. 1857

111 *News*, 18 July, 10 Oct. 1856; *Head Quarters*, 13 June 1855; and *Courier*, 6, 13 Sept. 1856

112 *Freeman*, 20 June 1856, quoted in *News*, 1856; and *Courier*, 28 June 1856

113 *Head Quarters*, 4 Feb. 1857; *Courier*, 11, 18 Oct., 1856; 28 Feb., 2 May 1857; and *Reporter*, 10 Oct., 28 Nov. 1856

114 *Courier*, 16 May 1857

115 *Freeman*, 23 Apr. 1857, quoted in *News*, 27 Apr. 1857

116 See *Freeman*, 6 March 1860.

117 Ibid, n.d., quoted in *Courier*, 16 May 1857

118 See especially R.A. Billington, *The Protestant Crusade 1800–1860: A Study of the Origins of American Nativism* (Chicago, 1964), p 1; and E.R. Norman, *Anti-Catholicism in Victorian England* (London, 1968), pp 20–1.

119 Uncatalogued Tilley Papers, Boyd to Tilley, 24 May 1858

120 Ibid, Boyd to Tilley, 3 Dec. 1858

121 See C.M. Wallace, 'Sir Leonard Tilley, A Political Biography,' unpublished Doctoral dissertation, University of Alberta, 1972, pp 388–9. On at least one occasion Tilley tried to ensure that Catholics received some of the patronage in the gift of the government (see Uncatalogued Tilley Papers, John Cudlip to Tilley, 14 Jan. 1859).

122 *Freeman*, 16 July 1858. The Know-Nothing Party of the United States was a political organization of strong anti-Catholic and anti-immigrant tendencies which flourished briefly in the 1850s. Planks in the party platform included the

exclusion of foreigners and Catholics from public office and a twenty-one-year residence requirement for citizenship.

123 Ibid, 5 Oct. 1858; 1 Feb., 20 Aug. 1859; 31 Jan., 23 Feb., 30 June, 12 July 1860; 2 March 1861

124 Ibid, 1 Feb. 1859. Anglin was not as unconcerned about the possibility of a Protestant Alliance as this might suggest (see ibid, 5 Oct. 1858).

125 Ibid, 23 Feb. 1860. See also ibid, 17 Jan. 1861.

126 Ibid, 27 June 1857; 11 Nov. 1858; 28 Jan., 9, 16 Feb., 3 Apr. 1860; 12 Feb. 1861. G.E. Fenety of the *News*, a supporter of the government, was also concerned with the paucity of significant legislation (see Uncatalogued Tilley Papers, Fenety to Tilley, 9 Aug. 1858, 12 Oct. 1860).

127 By 1857 the initiation of money grants had been surrendered by the Assembly to the Executive Council (see ibid, Tilley to Gentlemen of Secretary's Office, 5 Sept. 1857).

128 *Freeman*, 11 Nov. 1858; 25 Feb., 3, 8 March, 23 June 1860

129 Ibid, 26 Feb. to 25 Apr. 1861. See also Peter Mitchell Papers, Mitchell to John Haws, 15, 16 March 1861, in UNBA; and Uncatalogued Tilley Papers, Executive Council to Lieutenant Governor Manners-Sutton, 30 March 1861.

130 *Freeman*, 10 July 1858; 9 Jan., 12 Apr. 1859

131 Ibid, 9, 16, 25 Feb., 3, 19 Apr. 1860. See also Uncatalogued Tilley Papers, Boyd to Tilley, 30 March 1861.

132 *Freeman*, 28 June 1860. Further information on Anglin's non-party position can be found in ibid, 1 March, 23 June, 7, 21 July, 8 Dec. 1860.

133 Uncatalogued Tilley Papers, Barker to Tilley, 3 Sept. 1858

134 Ibid, Barker to Tilley, 17 Nov. 1859. Further material on the significance of Anglin as an opponent of the government is found in ibid, Barker to Tilley, 14 Jan., 27 Sept. 1858; 15 March 1860; and Boyd to Tilley, 21 Nov. 1859; 5 Feb. 1861.

NOTES TO CHAPTER FOUR

1 *Freeman*, 5 Apr. 1860. The vast majority of Irish Catholics in the ward would not have been entitled to vote.

2 Ibid, 13 Apr. 1861

3 *Morning News* (Saint John), 17, 22 May, 3 June 1861; *Freeman*, 18, 21 May 1861; and Peter Mitchell Papers, H. Jack to Mitchell, 18 May 1861, in UNBA.

4 *Freeman*, 21 May 1861. See also ibid, 13 Apr., 7 May 1861

5 Ibid, 5 Apr. 1860

6 Ibid, 21 May 1861

7 Ibid, 4 June 1861

8 Ibid, 8 June 1861. The County of Saint John was a single constituency but was entitled to elect four representatives. Electors voted for up to four candidates.
9 The *News*, 7 June 1861, gave these three reasons for his success.
10 R. Kelley, *The Transatlantic Persuasion: The Liberal-Democratic Mind in the Age of Gladstone* (New York, 1969), pp 26–9
11 *Freeman*, n.d., quoted in *News*, 4 July 1856. See also *Freeman*, 1 Oct. 1861.
12 Ibid, 4 Dec. 1860. See also ibid, 9 Jan. 1859; 2 July 1861.
13 Ibid, 26 Oct., 4 Nov. 1858. A detailed study of the New Brunswick franchise is found in J. Garner, *The Franchise and Politics in British North America 1755–1867* (Toronto, 1969), pp 54–72.
14 *Freeman*, 21 Oct. 1858
15 See, for example, ibid, 18 Sept., 19 to 30 Oct., 2, 4 Nov. 1858; 6 Jan., 1 Sept. 1859; 4, 27 Sept., 15 Nov. 1860.
16 Ibid, 2 July 1861; and *New Brunswick: House of Assembly Journals, 1864,* p 104
17 Democracy was not a generally accepted ideology in British North America at this time (see B.W. Hodgins, 'Attitudes Towards Democracy During the Pre-Confederation Decade,' unpublished Master's dissertation, Queen's University, 1955).
18 *Freeman*, 6 Jan. 1859
19 Ibid, 27 Sept. 1860
20 Lord Lorne Papers, Anglin to Lorne, 12 June 1883
21 *Freeman*, 16 March 1869. See also ibid, 12 July 1862
22 B. Menczer, ed, *Catholic Political Thought 1789–1848* (Notre Dame, Indiana, 1962), p 78
23 *Freeman*, 5 Aug. 1875
24 Ibid, 24 Apr. 1862
25 Sir Samuel Leonard Tilley Papers (uncatalogued collection), Boyd to Tilley, 14 March 1862. See also ibid, T.B. Hanington to Tilley, 3 March 1862.
26 *News*, 26 Sept. 1862; and *Freeman*, 27 Sept. 1862
27 On Canadian attitudes to the United States see S.F. Wise and R.C. Brown, *Canada Views the United States: Nineteenth-Century Political Attitudes* (Seattle, 1967); and W.M. Baker, 'The Anti-American Ingredient in Canadian History,' *Dalhousie Review*, LII (1973), 57–77.
28 *Freeman*, 30 Apr., 27 Oct. 1859; 20 Dec. 1860; 27 Apr. 1861; 20 May, 24 June 1875; 25 Apr. 1876; 20 May 1878
29 Ibid, 20 Dec. 1860; 12, 29 Jan., 23 Feb. 1861
30 The *Freeman*'s negative attitude towards the abolitionists paralleled Irish American views (see *Freeman*, 21 May 1861; and C. Wittke, *The Irish in America* [Baton Rouge, Louisiana, 1956], pp 125–34).
31 *Freeman*, 16 Apr. 1861. On New Brunswick attitudes to the war see G.E.

Gunn, 'New Brunswick Opinion on the American Civil War,' unpublished Master's dissertation, University of New Brunswick, 1956. Information is also to be found in J.K. Chapman, 'Relations of Maine and New Brunswick in the Era of Reciprocity, 1849–1867,' unpublished Master's dissertation, University of New Brunswick, 1951. The best source for material indicated by its title is R.W. Winks, *Canada and the United States: The Civil War Years* (Baltimore, 1960).

32 *Freeman*, 25 Jan 1862
33 Ibid, 25 Apr. 1861. See also ibid, 9, 18 Apr., 10 Sept. 1861.
34 Ibid, 25 Jan 1862; 31 Aug. 1861. See also ibid, 20 July 1861.
35 Ibid, 27 Apr. 1861. The *Freeman* still maintained, however, that the union could not be preserved by conquest.
36 A very full report of this lecture was given in the *Freeman*, 30 July 1863.
37 *Freeman*, 3 Aug. 1863. Anglin had previously drawn attention to the deleterious results of the 'puritan spirit' in the United States (see ibid., 9 Aug. 1862).
38 Ibid., 3 Aug. 1863
39 Ibid., 1 Aug. 1863
40 Wise and Brown, *Canada Views the United States*, pp 82–97
41 *Freeman*, 8 Aug. 1863; 15 Apr. 1865
42 Ibid, 8 Aug. 1863
43 Ibid, 1 Oct. 1861
44 M.B. Buckley, *Diary of a Tour in America*, ed K. Buckley (Dublin, 1886), p 96
45 *Freeman*, 22 March 1860
46 Ibid, 12 June 1860
47 Ibid, 7 Dec. 1861. See also ibid, 30 Nov. 1861.
48 Ibid, 17 Dec. 1861
49 Ibid, 31 Dec. 1861. See also ibid, 22 Jan. 1861.
50 See especially ibid, 24 June, 5, 7, 12 Aug. 1862.
51 Ibid, 12 June 1860
52 Ibid, 21 Sept. 1861
53 Ibid, 7 Aug. 1862
54 Ibid
55 Ibid, 30 July 1863
56 Ibid, 22 Nov. 1860
57 Ibid, 15 Aug. 1863. See also ibid, 31 Dec. 1861; 20 Sept. 1864. Goldwin Smith, interestingly enough, came to the conclusion that the Antis' argument on the question of military security was a good one (see A Bystander, 'Colonel Gray on Confederation,' *The Canadian Monthly and National Review*, II [1872], 175).
58 W.M. Whitelaw, *The Maritimes and Canada Before Confederation* (Toronto, 1966), pp 154–6; G.R. Stevens, *Canadian National Railways*, vol. I: *Sixty*

Years of Trial and Error (1836–1896) (Toronto, 1960), pp 170–4; and S. Fleming, *The Intercolonial: A Historical Sketch* ... (Montreal, 1876), pp 58–63. The agreement was never formally adopted by the Canadian government.

59 *Freeman*, 6, 13 Jan. 1863. That Anglin's analysis was correct is shown in Lord Stanmore (Arthur Gordon) Papers, Newcastle to Gordon, 31 May 1862, in UNBA; and Duke of Newcastle (Henry Pelham-Clinton) Papers, Gordon to Newcastle, 23 June 1862.

60 *Freeman*, 17, 20, 22 Jan. 1863

61 New Brunswick, Lieutenant Governor's Letter Books, vol LXII, Gordon to Newcastle, 6 May 1862; and Smith to Gordon, 10 Oct. 1862, enclosed in Gordon to Newcastle, 13 Oct. 1862

62 *Freeman*, 25 Aug. 1864; 11 Apr. 1863 (a report of Anglin's speech in the Assembly)

63 *Head Quarters* (Fredericton), n.d., quoted in *Freeman*, 11 Apr. 1863

64 Lieutenant Governor's Letter Books, vol LXII, Gordon to Newcastle, 16 Feb. 1863

65 See ibid, vol LXII, Gordon to Newcastle, 29 Aug., 28 Sept. 1863; and Canada, Governor General's Office, Telegrams, vol I, Lord Monck to Gordon, 1 Oct. 1863.

66 *Freeman*, 24 Nov. 1863; 14 Jan. 1864

67 Uncatalogued Tilley Papers, Boyd to Tilley, 10 March 1864

68 New Brunswick, Lieutenant Governor, Despatches Received, vol XLIV, Newcastle to Gordon, 5 March 1864; Uncatalogued Tilley Papers, C.J. Brydges to Tilley, 22 Jan., 13 Feb. 1864; ibid, H.J. Hubertas to Tilley, telegram, 17 Feb. 1864; and Sir Samuel Leonard Tilley Papers, McGee to Tilley, 1 Apr. 1864, in UNBA

69 *Freeman*, 12 Apr. 1864

70 Ibid, 26 Apr. 1864

71 Ibid, 4, 21 June 1864

72 On the history of Maritime union during this period see J.M. Beck, *The History of Maritime Union: A Study in Frustration* (Fredericton, 1969), pp 9–19; and P.B. Waite, *The Life and Times of Confederation, 1864–1867* (Toronto, 1962), pp 56–9.

NOTES TO CHAPTER FIVE

1 A concise account of the formation of the Great Coalition is P.G. Cornell, *The Great Coalition* (Ottawa, 1966).

2 New Brunswick, Lieutenant Governor, Despatches Received, vol XLIV, Lord Monck to Col. Cole, 30 June 1864. The Canadian government had apparently

planned to send a delegation under the leadership of McGee to the Maritime Union Conference even before the amazing coalition was founded (see Sir Samuel Leonard Tilley Papers, T.D. McGee to Tilley, 9 May 1864, in UNBA; and McGee to E. Watkin, 8 June 1864, quoted in R.B. Burns, 'D'Arcy McGee and the New Nationality,' unpublished Master's dissertation, Carleton University, 1966, p 104). Nevertheless the *Freeman*'s report of 4 June is curious, for as far as is known the Canadian premier had made no such statement at this early date.

3 New Brunswick, Lieutenant Governor's Letter Books, vol LXII, Cole to George Dundas, 25 July 1864; and Cole to Monck, 12 July 1864

4 *Freeman*, 9, 28 Oct., 18 Nov. 1858; 1 Sept. 1859; 22 Nov. 1860. The last-mentioned was occasioned by Charles Tupper's speech in Saint John (see his *Recollections of Sixty Years* (New York, n.d.), pp 14–38).

5 *Freeman*, 28 Oct. 1858

6 *Head Quarters* (Fredericton), n.d., quoted in *Freeman*, 11 Apr. 1863

7 The *Freeman* had argued the other side of the question in its discussion of Maritime union on 10 May 1862.

8 *Freeman*, 13 Aug. 1863

9 Ibid, 15 Aug. 1863

10 Ibid, 4 June 1864

11 Ibid, 25 Aug. 1864

12 Ibid, 5 July 1864

13 Ibid, 19 Nov. 1864

14 Ibid, 13 Aug., 3 Sept. 1864

15 Ibid, 3 Sept. 1864

16 Ibid, 20 Sept. 1864

17 Ibid, 24 Sept. 1864

18 Ibid, 15 Jan. 1863

19 Ibid, 22 Oct. 1864

20 Quoted in ibid, 1 Oct. 1864

21 Ibid, 8 May 1862

22 Ibid, 14 Oct. 1865. George Brown himself believed that Upper Canadians had 'all the advantages' in the Quebec Resolutions, but that it was 'a very serious matter for the Maritime provinces ...' (see George Brown Papers, Brown to Anne Brown, 4 March 1865).

23 *Freeman*, 15 Oct. 1864

24 Ibid, 22 Oct. 1864

25 Ibid, 3 Nov. 1864

26 This was assuming that Newfoundland and Prince Edward Island would join the union.

27 *Freeman*, 1 Nov. 1864

28 Ibid, 3 Nov. 1864
29 Sir Alexander Tilloch Galt Papers, Tilley to Gault [sic], 20 Nov. 1864
30 *Freeman*, 15 Nov. 1864
31 Ibid, 17 Nov. 1864
32 Ibid, 19 Nov. 1864
33 Reprinted in ibid, 22 Nov. 1864
34 Ibid
35 *The Colonial Presbyterian and Protestant Journal* (Saint John), 24 Nov. 1864
36 *Freeman*, 22 Nov 1864
37 Quoted in ibid, 3 Dec. 1864
38 Ibid, 6 Dec. 1864
39 Ibid, 15 Dec. 1864
40 Sir Samuel Leonard Tilley Papers, Wilmot to Tilley, 9 Dec. 1864, in UNBA
41 Sir John Alexander Macdonald Papers, vol LI, Tilley to Macdonald, 23 Nov. 1864
42 *Freeman*, 19 Nov. 1864
43 *Morning Telegraph* (Saint John), 25 Nov. 1864
44 The reasons for following this course of action are very complex and have been briefly dealt with in J.K. Chapman, *The Career of Arthur Hamilton Gordon: First Lord Stanmore 1829–1912* (Toronto, 1964), pp 30–2, and J.K. Chapman, 'Arthur Gordon and Confederation,' CHR, XXXVII (1956), 148–50; D.G. Creighton, *The Road to Confederation: The Emergence of Canada, 1863–1867* (Toronto, 1964), pp 230–2; W.S. MacNutt, *New Brunswick: A History, 1784–1867* (Toronto, 1963), pp 425–7; W.L. Morton, *The Critical Years: The Union of British North America 1857–1873* (Toronto, 1964), pp 173–4; and P.B. Waite, *The Life and Times of Confederation, 1864–1867* (Toronto, 1962), pp 241–2.
45 *Freeman*, 24 Jan. 1865
46 Tilley did, in fact, stress the power of the local government. See a speech by Tilley enclosed in Gordon to Cardwell, 2 Jan. 1865, quoted in G.P. Browne, ed, *Documents on the Confederation of British North America* (Toronto, 1969), pp 172–3.
47 Sir Samuel Leonard Tilley Papers (uncatalogued collection), Boyd to Tilley, 28 Sept. 1864
48 *New Brunswick Government Gazette*, XXIII, 25 Jan., 7 June 1865
49 *Freeman*, 9 Feb., 18 March, 6 Apr. 1865
50 Ibid, 13 Apr. 1865
51 Ibid, 5, 28 Jan. 1865. See also W.M. Whitelaw, *The Maritimes and Canada Before Confederation* (Toronto, 1966), pp 164–6.
52 *Freeman*, 9 Feb. 1865

53 Ibid, 14, 28 Jan. 1865
54 Galt Papers, Tilley to Gault, 26 Dec. 1864
55 Sir Samuel Leonard Tilley Papers, Macdonald to Tilley, 14 Nov. 1864; Tilley Papers, Galt to Tilley, 21 Dec. 1864, in NBMA; and Galt Papers, Tilley to Gault, 26 Dec. 1864
56 *Freeman*, 10 Dec. 1864
57 Galt Papers, Tilley to Gault, 26 Dec. 1864
58 *Freeman*, 24 Nov., 13 Dec. 1864; 12, 21 Jan. 1865
59 Ibid, 28 Jan. 1865
60 *Morning News* (Saint John), 8 May 1865
61 See A.G. Bailey, 'Railways and the Confederation Issue in New Brunswick, 1863–1865,' CHR, XXI (1940), 367–83.
62 Quoted in MacNutt, *New Brunswick*, p 428
63 D.G. Creighton, *John A. Macdonald*, vol I: *The Young Politician* (Toronto, 1952), p 404
64 Macdonald Papers, vol LI, Tilley to Macdonald, 13 Feb. 1865
65 *Freeman*, 16 Feb. 1865
66 Ibid
67 Uncatalogued Tilley Papers, S.T. Gore to Tilley, 17 Jan. 1865
68 *Freeman*, 21 Jan. 1865
69 Ibid, 21 Jan., 11 Feb. 1865
70 Ibid, 12 Jan. 1865
71 Uncatalogued Tilley Papers, Boyd to Tilley, ? Feb. 1865; and Watters to Tilley, telegram, 16 Feb. 1865
72 Macdonald Papers, vol LI, Tilley to Galt, undated
73 Sir Samuel Leonard Tilley Papers, McGee to Chief Clerk of the Provincial Secretary's Office, 28 Feb. 1865, in UNBA. One package was to be sent to Tilley, the second to Peter Mitchell, and the last to Charles Watters.
74 For Connolly's views on and role in Confederation see D.B. Flemming, 'Archbishop Thomas L. Connolly, Godfather of Confederation,' *Canadian Catholic Historical Association Study Sessions 1970*, pp 67–84.
75 Reprinted in *Freeman*, 17 Jan. 1865
76 Tilley Papers, Thomas Connolly, Jr, to Tilley, 23 Jan. 1865, in NBMA (this Connolly was a Catholic priest, but not the archbishop). See also Tilley Papers, David Wark to Tilley, 19 Jan. 1865, in UNBA.
77 *Freeman*, 17 Jan. 1865
78 Ibid, 9 Feb. 1865
79 See ibid, 4 Oct. 1864
80 The estimates vary, but twelve seems to be the most accurate figure (see J. Hannay, *History of New Brunswick* (Saint John, 1909), II, 235; *Freeman*, 30

March 1865; Lieutenant Governor's Letter Books, vol LXIII, Gordon to Cardwell, 27 March 1865; and *New Brunswick Reporter* (Fredericton), 31 March 1865).

81 The *Telegraph*, a Confederate newspaper, and the *Freeman* both played games with the statistics (see *Telegraph*, n.d., quoted in *News*, 29 March 1865; and *Freeman*, 30 March 1865).

82 Lieutenant Governor's Letter Books, vol XLIII, Gordon to Cardwell, 6 March 1865

83 Macdonald Papers, vol LI, Fisher to Macdonald, 5 Apr. 1865; and Gray to Macdonald, 13 March 1865. Tilley eventually acknowledged that Gordon was 'certainly not the *cause* of the failure' (see Galt Papers, Tilley to Galt, 13 May 1865). The *Freeman* scoffed at the belief that Gordon had played an important role (see *Freeman*, 18 March 1865). By pointing out that the Antis had carried every city and large town almost without exception, Anglin also rejected the argument than an ignorant, parochial vote had killed the Confederates (see *Freeman*, 23 May 1865).

84 Galt Papers, Gray to Gault, 9 Apr. 1865

85 Macdonald Papers, vol LI, Tilley to Galt, undated

86 Ibid, Gray to Macdonald, 13 March 1865

87 Brown Papers, Gray to Brown, 27 March 1865

88 *Freeman*, 21 March 1865

89 Ibid, 25 March 1865

90 Uncatalogued Tilley Papers, Mitchell to Tilley, 30 Jan. 1865

91 Macdonald Papers, vol LI, Tilley to Galt, undated

92 Uncatalogued Tilley Papers, Mitchell to Tilley, 30 Jan. 1865

93 See Bishop John Sweeny Papers, Connolly to Sweeny, 15 March 1865, in UNBA.

94 See W.M. Baker, 'No Shillelagh: The Life, Journalism and Politics of Timothy Warren Anglin,' unpublished Doctoral dissertation, University of Western Ontario, 1971, pp 548–9.

95 The attitude of the Acadians towards Confederation may provide an index of the views of French Canadians towards it. It is, at any rate, a factor that is usually ignored in attempting to assess the latter.

96 Macdonald Papers, vol LI, Tilley to Galt, undated

97 Galt Papers, Tilley to Gault, 22 Apr. 1865

98 Lieutenant Governor's Letter Books, vol LXIII, Tilley to Gordon, enclosed in Gordon to Cardwell, 30 Jan. 1865; and Uncatalogued Tilley Papers, Tilley to Gordon, 17 May 1865

99 Galt Papers, Gray to Gault, 9 Apr. 1865

100 *Freeman*, 18 March 1865

NOTES TO CHAPTER SIX

1 *Freeman*, 4 Apr. 1865
2 New Brunswick, Lieutenant Governor's Letter Books, vol LXIII, Gordon to Cardwell, 8 Apr. 1865
3 *New Brunswick: House of Assembly Debates, 1866*, p 95 (5 Apr.). See also Sir Samuel Leonard Tilley Papers (uncatalogued collection), Gordon to Tilley, 30 March 1865; and Mitchell to Tilley, 31 March 1865.
4 Lieutenant Governor's Letter Books, vol LXIII, Gordon to Cardwell, 8 May 1865
5 Ibid, vol LXIII, Gordon to Cardwell, 10 Apr. 1865. Wilmot did not become Auditor General, a fact which may have aided his disillusionment with the government by the fall of 1865.
6 Quoted in *Freeman*, 8 Apr. 1865
7 Arthur Hill Gillmor Papers, James Brown to Gillmor, 23 Apr. 1865, in PANB
8 Sir John Alexander Macdonald Papers, vol LI, Tilley to Galt, undated. See also Uncatalogued Tilley Papers, T.W. Bliss (?) to Tilley, 8 March 1865.
9 Uncatalogued Tilley Papers, Gordon to Tilley, 30 March 1865
10 *Assembly Debates, 1866*, p 95 (5 Apr.). The *New Brunswick Reporter* (Fredericton) was of the opinion that Anglin and Wilmot had vied so furiously for the office of Provincial Secretary that a substitute had to be selected. The *Freeman* denied the veracity of this assertion (see *Freeman*, 11 Apr. 1865).
11 See *Freeman*, 6 June 1876.
12 It seems likely that there would have been no contest as Tilley and Gordon had agreed that there was to be no immediate reagitation of the question of union and in the other by-elections no opposition was offered the government. Had there been a contest, it seems doubtful that the electors of Saint John would have defeated an Executive Councillor.
13 Gillmor Papers, Anglin to Gillmour [sic], 9 Oct. 1865; and *Assembly Debates, 1866*, p 98 (6 Apr.)
14 Gillmor Papers, Gillmor to Anglin, 10 Oct. 1865
15 Ibid; and ibid, Anglin to Gillmour, 12 Oct. 1865
16 Ibid, Gillmor to Anglin, 10 Oct. 1865
17 *Freeman*, 18 Apr. 1865. See also *Assembly Debates, 1866*, p 99 (6 Apr.).
18 *Freeman*, 1 June 1865. For Anglin's speeches on the subject in the Assembly see *Assembly Debates, 1865*, pp 85–6 (22 May).
19 *New Brunswick: House of Assembly Journal, 1865*, p 187
20 *Freeman*, 3 June 1865
21 Ibid, 6, 8 June 1865
22 Ibid, 6 June 1865

23 See Russell to Cardwell, 4 Sept. 1865, quoted in D.G. Creighton, *John A. Macdonald*, vol. I: *The Young Politician* (Toronto, 1956), p 423.

24 Edward Cardwell Papers, Cardwell to Gordon, 1 Apr. 1865

25 Ibid, Cardwell to Gordon, 13 May 1865. See also New Brunswick, Lieutenant Governor's Despatches Received, vol XLV, Cardwell to Gordon, 12 Apr. 1865.

26 Lieutenant Governor's Letter Books, vol LXIII, Gordon to Cardwell, 3 July 1865; and J.L. Muir, 'The New Brunswick Militia, 1787–1867,' *Dalhousie Review*, XLIV (1964), 337. During Gordon's governorship military expenditure had risen from $2,000 to $10,000 per year even prior to 1865 (see Lieutenant Governor's Despatches Received, vol XLVI, Hastings Doyle to Gordon, 30 Aug. 1865).

27 Lieutenant Governor Despatches Received, vol XLVI, Doyle to Gordon, 30 Aug. 1865; and *Freeman*, 15 July 1865

28 *Assembly Debates, 1865*, p 66 (17 May)

29 *Assembly Journal, 1865*, p 152

30 Lieutenant Governor's Letter Books, vol LXIII, Gordon to Cardwell, 22 May 1865

31 Ibid, vol LXIII, Gordon to Cardwell, 8 Apr. 1865. See also Uncatalogued Tilley Papers, Gillmor to Tilley, 30 May 1865.

32 Uncatalogued Tilley Papers, Gordon to Tilley, 30 March 1865

33 Lieutenant Governor's Letter Books, vol LXIII, Gordon to Cardwell, 22 May 1865. Gordon reported that Tilley had suggested that Confederation could be carried by money – £10,000 or £15,000 more than the $40,000 the Confederates had spent in the recent elections (see Cardwell Papers, Gordon to Cardwell, 5 June 1865).

34 Cardwell Papers, Cardwell to Gordon, 24 June 1865

35 Lieutenant Governor's Letter Books, vol LXIII, Executive Council to Gordon, enclosed in Gordon to Cardwell, 22 May 1865

36 *Freeman*, 20 May 1865

37 On the mission of Smith and Allen, see Lord Stanmore (Arthur Gordon) Papers, Smith to Gordon, 7 July 1865, in UNBA; Cardwell to Lord John Russell, 15 Aug. 1865, quoted in Creighton, *Macdonald*, I, 423; Gillmor Papers, Smith to Gillmour, 7 July, 5 Aug. 1865; and ibid, Allen to Gillmor, 22 July 1865.

38 Lieutenant Governor's Letter Books, vol LXIII, enclosed in Gordon to Cardwell, 15 July 1865

39 *Freeman*, 2 Sept. 1865

40 Ibid, 17 Apr. 1866. Professor Creighton recognizes that there are certain statements in the Minute that echoed Gordon's words of earlier letters to Cardwell. But Creighton also suggests that the external proof for the assertion that Gordon was one of the principal authors – the statement of Anglin – is not

good enough, for Anglin was 'not a very credible witness' (see D.G. Creighton, *The Road to Confederation: The Emergence of Canada, 1863–1867* (Toronto, 1964), p 294). This aspersion on Anglin's character is unfounded. Anglin made his statement in the House of Assembly and neither Wilmot nor anyone else present at the Council meeting nor a Gordon-directed member disputed Anglin's veracity (see *Freeman*, 19 Apr. 1866). The internal evidence of the Minute, verifying the delineation Anglin made between the passages he wrote and the rest, is conclusive. One segment of the memorandum talked about the Quebec scheme as separation rather than fusion as Gordon had done so often in the past. Anglin once again spoke of New Brunswick's loyalty, and of his belief that British North American union would bring about the disruption of the Empire. He again mentioned the fact that New Brunswick wanted no closer connection with Canada than that provided by the imperial tie. The *Freeman* of 23 April 1867 reprinted the Minute, showing the passages which Anglin had written.

41 See also *Freeman*, 15 June, 11 July 1865.
42 C. Martin, *Foundations of Canadian Nationhood* (Toronto, 1955), p 64.
43 Lieutenant Governor's Despatches Received, vol XLV, Cardwell to Gordon, 4 Aug. 1865
44 Galt Papers, Fisher to Gault, 17 Aug. 1865. Fisher called Anglin a 'thorough Jesuit' and accused him of disloyalty to the Empire.
45 See Montreal *Herald*, quoted in *Freeman*, 5 Sept. 1865; Uncatalogued Tilley Papers, Boyd to Tilley, 28 Aug. 1865; *Assembly Debates, 1866*, p 101 (6 Apr.); and Cardwell Papers, Cardwell to Gordon, 15 Sept., 12 Oct. 1865. Monck informed them that no substantial changes could be made to the Quebec Resolutions.
46 *Herald*, quoted in *Freeman*, 5 Sept. 1865
47 On the Quebec meeting see N.M. Rogers, 'The Confederate Council of Trade,' CHR, VII (1926), 277–86.
48 *Freeman*, 5 Oct. 1865
49 Ibid, 7 Oct. 1865
50 Ibid, 3, 7 Oct. 1865
51 Gillmor Papers, Anglin to Gillmour, 9 Oct. 1865
52 There are a number of works on the Fenians. Perhaps the best book on the subject is W. D'Arcy, *The Fenian Movement in the United States: 1858–1886* (Washington, 1947). P.S. O'Hegarty, *A History of Ireland Under The Union 1801 to 1922* (London, 1952), pp 411–54, has a good deal on Fenianism in Ireland. An interesting exception to the tendency to study Fenianism solely within national bounds is B. Jenkins, *Fenians and Anglo-American Relations during Reconstruction* (Ithaca, NY, 1969). An article well worth reading is C.P.

Stacey, 'Fenianism and the Rise of National Feeling in Canada at the Time of Confederation,' CHR, XII (1931), 238–61.

53 D'Arcy, *Fenian Movement*, p 15

54 C.L. King, 'The Fenian Movement,' *The University of Colorado Studies*, VI (1909), 195

55 Ibid, p 189

56 L. Winkler, 'The Fenian Movement and Anglo-American Diplomacy in the Reconstruction Period,' unpublished Master's dissertation, New York University, 1936, p 11. See also C. Wittke, *The Irish in America* (Baton Rouge, 1956), p 96; and E.R. Norman, *The Catholic Church and Ireland in the Age of Rebellion, 1859–1873* (London, 1965), pp 124–5. On 12 Jan. 1870 the Fenian Brotherhood was condemned by name by the Vatican.

57 There was little support in British North America for Fenianism (see D.C. Lyne, 'The Irish in the Province of Canada in the Decade Leading up to Confederation,' unpublished Master's dissertation, McGill University, 1960, p 264; and H. Senior, 'Quebec and the Fenians,' CHR, XLVIII [1967], 28). In Saint John it would appear unlikely that actual Fenianism held a position of any significant strength among the Irish community at this time (see W.M. Baker, 'No Shillelagh: The Life, Journalism and Politics of Timothy Warren Anglin,' unpublished Doctoral dissertation, University of Western Ontario, 1971, pp 266–7). Even the few colonial Irish who actively backed the Fenians supported the branch of that organization which apparently wished to restrict its armed movements to Ireland and leave British North America alone (see C.P. Stacey, 'A Fenian Interlude: The Story of Michael Murphey,' CHR, XV [1934], 140).

58 See, for example, *Freeman*, 7, 12 Jan. 1865.

59 Ibid, 21 Nov. 1863

60 See, for example, *Morning Journal* (Saint John), 25 Sept. 1865; and *Morning Telegraph* (Saint John), 30 Sept., 12 Oct. 1865.

61 Lieutenant Governor's Letter Books, vol LXIII, Cole to Cardwell, 21 Sept. 1865

62 Ibid, Cole to Cardwell, 21 Oct. 1865

63 Cardwell Papers, Gordon to Cardwell, 20 Nov. 1865

64 *Freeman*, 21 Oct. 1865

65 Macdonald Papers, Fisher to Macdonald, 11 Nov. 1865

66 *Daily Evening Globe* (Saint John), 7 Nov. 1865; *Head Quarters* (Fredericton), 15 Nov. 1865; *Reporter*, 3, 10 Nov. 1865; and *Freeman*, 31 Oct. 1865, 3 Apr. 1866

67 *Reporter*, 3 Nov. 1865

68 Quoted in *Head Quarters*, 15 Nov. 1865. See also *News*, 3 Nov. 1865; and *Telegraph*, 24, 26 Oct. 1865.

69 *Freeman*, 31 Oct. 1865. Anglin used the rather tenuous argument that Fisher's pledge made him an opponent of Confederation and meant that his election did not indicate a shift in public opinion towards Confederation (see ibid, 23 Nov. 1865).
70 Lieutenant Governor's Letter Books, vol LXIII, Gordon to Cardwell, 6 Nov. 1865; and 'Anti' to the Editor, undated, in the *Reporter*, 27 Oct. 1865
71 Creighton, *Road to Confederation*, p 320. See the reports of Fisher's nomination and declaration day speeches in the *Reporter*, 3, 10 Nov. 1865. See also *Head Quarters*, 8, 15 Nov. 1865; and Gillmor Papers, Gillmor to Anglin, 11 Nov. 1865.
72 Quoted in *Head Quarters*, 15 Nov. 1865
73 *Globe*, 7 Nov. 1865
74 *Telegraph*, 11 Nov. 1865
75 *Reporter*, 17 Nov. 1865
76 Sir Samuel Leonard Tilley Papers, Watkin to Tilley, 30 March 1865
77 Uncatalogued Tilley Papers, Parks to Tilley, 1 Apr. 1865
78 *Freeman*, 11 May 1865
79 Ibid, 5 May 1865
80 *Assembly Debates, 1865*, p 145 (6 June)
81 See *Freeman*, 15 June 1865
82 Ibid, 22, 24 June 1865
83 Ibid, 17 June 1865. It is possible that the government never asked the company to relinquish its charter.
84 See, for example, Gillmor Papers, Allen to Gillmor, 22 July 1865.
85 Quoted in *Freeman*, 12 Sept. 1865
86 Quoted in *Freeman*, 14 Sept. 1865
87 *Freeman*, 12 Oct. 1865
88 The information in this paragraph comes from Executive Council Papers, Anglin to Gordon, 10 Nov. 1865, in PANB; Gillmor Papers, Anglin to Gillmour, 9, 12 Oct., 14 Nov. 1865; and ibid, Gillmor to Anglin, 10 Oct., 11 Nov. 1865. The outlines of these developments can also be surmised from the comments of the *Freeman*.
89 *Assembly Debates, 1866*, p 103 (7 Apr.)
90 Executive Council Papers, Anglin to Gordon, 10, 21 Nov. 1865
91 Lieutenant Governor's Letter Books, vol LXIII, Gordon to Cardwell, 20 Nov. 1865; and *Freeman*, 23 Nov. 1865
92 Gillmor Papers, Anglin to Gillmour, 12 Oct., 14 Nov. 1865
93 *Freeman*, 4 Jan. 1866
94 *Globe*, 26 July 1867

NOTES TO CHAPTER SEVEN

1 *New Brunswick Reporter* (Fredericton), 17 Nov. 1865
2 George Brown Papers, Gordon to Brown, 21 Dec. 1865. Undoubtedly Anglin was one of those 'friends' (see Arthur Hill Gillmor Papers, Anglin to Gillmour, 14 Nov. 1865, in PANB).
3 *Freeman*, 17 Jan., 2 Dec. 1865
4 See W.M. Baker, 'No Shillelagh: The Life, Journalism and Politics of Timothy Warren Anglin,' unpublished Doctoral dissertation, University of Western Ontario, 1971, pp 87–9.
5 New Brunswick, Lieutenant Governor's Correspondence, Duplicate Despatches, Gordon to Cardwell, 4 Dec. 1865; and *Freeman*, 2, 5 Dec. 1865
6 Quoted in *Freeman*, 2 Dec. 1865. For more of the same see Sir Samuel Leonard Tilley Papers (uncatalogued collection), R.B. Cutler to T. Hanford, 2 Dec. 1865, enclosed in Hanford to Tilley, ? Dec. 1865; Charles Connell to Tilley, 5 Dec. 1865; S.J. Gore to Tilley, 5 Dec. 1865; and A.R. McClelan to Tilley, 15 Dec. 1865.
7 *Freeman*, 2 Dec. 1865
8 Ibid, 5 Dec. 1865
9 Gillmor Papers, Anglin to Gillmour, 14 Nov. 1865
10 Brown Papers, Brown to Anne Brown, 13, 18 Nov. 1865. See also J.M.S. Careless, *Brown of the Globe*, vol. II: *Stateman of Confederation 1860–1880* (Toronto, 1963), pp 208–10.
11 Gillmor Papers, Anglin to Gillmour, 14 Nov. 1865.
12 New Brunswick, Lieutenant Governor's Letter Books, vol LXIII, Gordon to Cardwell, 4 Dec. 1865. One reason Gordon suggested for the unpopularity of the government was its refusal 'to act with the injustice and partiality required by their supporters.'
13 Ibid. Gordon stated that some of the opposition wanted power even more than union and were clamouring for an immediate dissolution.
14 Edward Cardwell Papers, Gordon to Cardwell, 4 Dec. 1865; Sir Samuel Leonard Tilley Papers, Monck to Tilley, 23 Dec. 1865; and Sir John Alexander Macdonald Papers, vol LI, Monck to Macdonald, 28 Dec. 1865
15 Uncatalogued Tilley Papers, E. Willis to Tilley, 4 Dec. 1865; *News*, quoted in *Freeman*, 21 Dec. 1865; and Gillmor Papers, Anglin to Gillmour, 14 Nov. 1865. Anglin strenuously opposed Wetmore's becoming Attorney General because of his lack of experience (see *New Brunswick: House of Assembly Debates, 1866*, p 95 [5 Apr.]).
16 *Freeman*, 11 Jan. 1866. See also Cardwell Papers, Gordon to Cardwell, 14 Jan. 1866

17 Gillmor Papers, Anglin to Gillmour, 6 Nov. 1865. See also *Freeman*, 11, 20 Jan. 1866

18 Gillmor Papers, Anglin to Gillmour, 15 Jan. 1866

19 Lord Stanmore (Arthur Hamilton Gordon) Papers, F.W.A. Bruce to Gordon, 25 Aug. 1865, in UNBA. See also the printed *Report of the Conferences between the Colonial Delegation and the Committee of Ways and Means of the House of Representatives*, found in Macdonald Papers, vol CXLV.

20 Gillmor Papers, Anglin to Gillmour, undated [? Jan. 1866]

21 Ibid, Anglin to Gillmour, 9 Feb. 1866

22 Ibid, Anglin to Gillmour, 10 Feb. 1866. Unfortunately Gillmor's exact scheme is not known and can be surmised only in part from Anglin's letter to him.

23 Ibid

24 Ibid, Anglin to Gillmour, 9 Feb. 1866

25 Ibid, Anglin to Gillmour, 13 Feb. 1866; and John W. Cudlip to Gillmor, 13 Feb. 1866. Anglin divulged the contents of this note to both Gillmor and Cudlip (who had replaced Anglin on the Executive Council) in spite of it being a private letter, a fact which showed that Anglin was no more trustworthy than anyone else in keeping private information to himself if it would be useful to his party.

26 Cardwell Papers, Anglin to Gordon, 15 Feb. 1866, enclosed in Gordon to Cardwell, 20 Feb. 1866

27 Gillmor Papers, Anglin to Gillmour, 9 Feb. 1866

28 Lieutenant Governor's Letter Books, vol LXIII, Gordon to Cardwell, 12 Feb. 1866. The opposition was fully conversant with developments (see Sir Samuel Leonard Tilley Papers, Fisher to Tilley, 10 Feb. 1866, in NBMA; Sir Samuel Leonard Tilley Papers, Tilley to Rev. E. McLeod, 14 Feb. 1866, in UNBA; and Correspondence of the Military Secretary of the Commander of the Forces: Fenian Correspondence, vol CLXXXVIA, Mitchell to Gordon, 1 Feb. 1866). Gordon reported his movements to Lord Monck (see Canada, Governor General's Office, Telegrams, vol II, Gordon to Monck, two telegrams, 16 Feb. 1866). The big four of Gordon, Wilmot, Tilley, and Mitchell agreed that it would be best to meet the existing legislature even if a dissolution followed.

29 Lieutenant Governor's Letter Books, vol LXIII, Gordon to Cardwell, 21 Feb. 1866

30 *Freeman*, 22 Feb. 1866

31 Lieutenant Governor's Letter Books, vol LXIII, Gordon to Cardwell, 21 Feb. 1866

32 Gillmor Papers, Anglin to Gillmour, 10 Feb. 1866. See also ibid, Anglin to Gillmour, 19 Feb. 1866.

33 Lieutenant Governor's Letter Books, vol LXIII, Gordon to Cardwell, 5 March 1866

34 Ibid, vol LXIII, Gordon to Cardwell, 12, 21 Feb. 1866

35 *Assembly Debates, 1866*, p 104 (7 Apr.)

36 *New Brunswick: House of Assembly Journal, 1866*, pp 10–14

37 Ibid, p 21

38 W.S. MacNutt, *New Brunswick: A History 1784–1867* (Toronto, 1963), p 444

39 *Assembly Journal, 1866*, p 31. See also Lieutenant Governor's Letter Books, vol LXIII, Gordon to Monck and Sir F. Williams, 17 March 1866.

40 Quoted in *Freeman*, 13 March 1866

41 *Freeman*, 13 March 1866. As there was a problem involving the official reporters, it is necessary to consult the Saint John *Daily Evening Globe*'s account which was copied by the *Freeman*, 10, 12 Apr. 1866, as well as *Assembly Debates, 1866*, pp 94–105 (5–7 Apr.).

42 *Freeman*, 12 Apr. 1866

43 *Assembly Debates, 1866*, p 103 (7 Apr.).

44 Ibid, p 105 (7 Apr.).

45 See A.G. Bailey, 'Keystone of the Arch,' *Atlantic Advocate*, LIV (1964), 40–6; J.K. Chapman, 'Arthur Gordon and Confederation,' CHR, XXXVII (1956), 156–7; D.G. Creighton, *The Road to Confederation: The Emergence of Canada, 1863–1867* (Toronto, 1964), pp 362–6; MacNutt, *New Brunswick*, pp 446–7; and P.B. Waite, *The Life and Times of Confederation 1864–1867* (Toronto, 1962), pp 260–2.

46 *Freeman*, 17, 19, 24 Apr. 1866

47 Ibid, 24 Apr. 1866

48 Ibid, 2 Jan. 1866

49 Ibid, 25 Jan., 13 Feb. 1866

50 Ibid, 23 Nov. 1865

51 Lieutenant Governor's Letter Books, vol LXIII, Gordon to Bruce, 2 Dec. 1865. This was in response to Bruce's warning (see Stanmore Papers, Bruce to Gordon, 2 Dec. 1865).

52 *Freeman*, 9 Dec. 1865

53 *Reporter*, 29 Dec. 1865

54 *Freeman*, 20 Jan. 1866

55 See, for example, *Morning Telegraph* (Saint John), 10 Feb. 1866.

56 *Freeman*, 30 Jan. 1866. See also ibid, 20 Feb. 1866.

57 Ibid, 30 Jan. 1866

58 Ibid

59 Ibid, 20 Jan. 1866

60 Ibid, 15 Feb. 1866

61 Ibid, 3, 6 Feb. 1866

62 *Globe*, quoted in *Freeman*, 12 Apr. 1866

63 *Freeman*, 26 Sept. 1865
64 Fisher had been anxious that this be the case (see Macdonald Papers, Fisher to Macdonald, vol LI, 21 Feb. 1866).
65 Ibid, vol LI, Tilley to Macdonald, 20 Apr. 1866
66 D.G. Creighton, *John A. Macdonald*, vol. I: *The Young Politician* (Toronto, 1956), p 435. The *Freeman* claimed that the Confederates spent $50,000 in Saint John alone (see *Freeman*, 14 July 1866).
67 *Citizen* (Halifax), 2 June 1866; and Judge Patterson, 'Joseph Howe and the Anti-Confederation League,' *Dalhousie Review*, X (1930–1), 400–1
68 *Freeman*, 26 Apr. 1866; and Macdonald Papers, vol DXI, Macdonald to Mitchell, 10 Apr. 1866
69 *Freeman*, 26 Apr. 1866
70 Ibid
71 See ibid, 5, 19 May 1866
72 Ibid, 1 March 1866. Anglin was confident that Canada had no intention whatever of lowering the tariff.
73 Ibid, 23 Nov., 5, 16 Dec. 1865; 10 May 1866
74 There was some concern among Confederates that Gordon had given the Antis an exploitable issue. See Brown Papers, Monck to Brown, 17 May 1866; and Tilley Papers, D.L. Hannington to Tilley, 19 Apr. 1866, in NBMA.
75 *Freeman*, 12 Apr. 1866
76 Stanmore Papers, Bruce to Gordon, 2 Dec. 1865; and Governor General's Office: Drafts of Secret and Confidential Despatches to the Colonial Office, vol I, E.M. Archibald to Sir John Michel, 22 Dec. 1865
77 A good account of this episode is H.A. Davis, 'The Fenian Raid on New Brunswick,' CHR, XXXVI (1955), 316–34.
78 Quoted in ibid, p 322
79 *Freeman*, 5 May 1866
80 Ibid, 21 Apr. 1866
81 Ibid, 21 Apr., 3 May 1866
82 Ibid, 21 Apr. 1866
83 Ibid. The *Freeman* did not change its view about this in later years (see ibid, 23 Nov. 1869).
84 Ibid, 3 May 1866
85 In 1854 Killian had been a writer for the *American Celt*, a New York paper of which McGee was the editor and proprietor (see T.P. Slattery, *The Assassination of D'Arcy McGee* [Toronto, 1968], p 34).
86 *Telegraph*, 10 May, 5 June 1866
87 *Freeman*, 28 Apr. 1866
88 Tilley Papers, H.A. Vandenburg to Tilley, 25 Apr. 1866, in NBMA

89 Slattery, *Assassination*, pp 314–15; and Uncatalogued Tilley Papers, Jonathan McCully to Tilley, 27 Apr. 1866

90 Uncatalogued Tilley Papers, John McMillan to Tilley, 4 Oct. 1865; and T.W. Bliss to Tilley, 14 May 1866

91 Quoted in *Freeman*, 26 May 1866

92 *Freeman*, 26, 29, 31 May, 9 June 1866

93 Archbishop Connolly strongly approved of Rogers's controversy with Anglin (see Bishop James Rogers Papers, Connolly to Rogers, 16 Oct. 1866, in UNBA).

94 *Freeman*, 1 May 1866

95 Ibid, 20 Jan. 1866. See also ibid, 6, 23, 30 Jan., 3, 27 Feb., 1, 10 March, 24 Apr. 1866.

96 Ibid, 10 March 1866

97 Quoted in ibid, 20 Jan. 1866. According to Provincial Secretary Gillmor's son, the people of St George thought all Catholics were Fenians (see Gillmor Papers, D. Gillmor to Gillmor, 15 March 1866).

98 Quoted in *Freeman*, 22 May 1866

99 Lieutenant Governor's Letter Books, vol LXIII, Gordon to Cardwell, 13 June 1866. The results published in the *Freeman* and the *News* agree with Gordon's total.

100 The Confederates blamed clerical influence for their failure (see Uncatalogued Tilley Papers, J. Steadman to Tilley, 12 May 1866; and W. Gilbert to Tilley, 13 June 1866).

101 Quoted in *Freeman*, 16 June 1866

102 *Telegraph*, 7 June 1866

103 Sir Alexander Tilloch Galt Papers, Galt to Amy Galt, 14 Jan. 1867

104 Gillmor Papers, A.J. Smith to Gillmor, 31 June 1866

105 *Freeman*, 17 Nov. 1866. See also ibid, 26 July 1866; 9 Feb. 1867.

106 Ibid, 5 March 1867

107 Ibid, 15 June 1867

NOTES TO CHAPTER EIGHT

1 C. Murphy, ed, *D'Arcy McGee: A Collection of Speeches and Addresses* (Toronto, 1937), pp 18–19

2 *Freeman*, 12 June, 24 Nov. 1866; 12 March 1867

3 *Gleaner* (Miramichi/Chatham), 29 June 1867

4 Roman Catholic Diocese of Saint John Archives, Bishop John Sweeny Papers, James Rogers to Sweeny, 30 Oct. 1860

5 *Freeman*, 24 Apr. 1862; 2 Oct. 1860

6 *Canada: Census, 1870–71*, 1, 320
7 The man was hanged after confessing his crime (see *Freeman*, 31 Oct. 1874), but the woman, who protested her innocence, had her sentence commuted by the Governor General in Council to imprisonment for life (see *Freeman*, 29 Dec. 1874).
8 *Canada: Sessional Papers, 1867–68*, no. 41, p 74
9 *Freeman*, 20 March 1869
10 Ibid, 1 May 1860. This particular comment was made in relation to the failure of the government to provide support for French-language schools in New Brunswick.
11 Ibid, 7 March 1874
12 Ibid, 9 Feb. 1861
13 *New Brunswick: House of Assembly Debates, 1862*, p 36 (19 Feb.)
14 Sir John Thompson Papers, vol XXVIII, Anglin to Thompson, 5 July 1882. There is some possibility that Anglin may have been able to understand spoken French to some extent and it seems likely that he was able to read the language. When it was announced that classes of instruction in French were beginning in Saint John in 1868, the *Freeman* commented that 'a knowledge of French is always a great advantage, whatever may be a man's profession or occupation, and now that we are all Canadians by act of Parliament it has become almost a necessity' (see *Freeman*, 6 Oct. 1868).
15 *Freeman*, 3, 22 Aug., 3 Sept. 1867
16 Ibid, 29 June 1867. See also ibid, 13 Apr., 13 July 1867.
17 Ibid, 11 Apr. 1867
18 *Morning News* (Saint John), 31 July 1867, quoted in *Freeman*, 1 Aug. 1867; and *Religious Intelligencer*, n.d., quoted in *Freeman*, 3 Aug. 1867
19 *Freeman*, 3 Aug. 1867
20 *News*, 5, 8 July 1867; *New Brunswick Reporter* (Fredericton), 12 July 1867; and *Freeman*, 4, 9 July 1867
21 *Freeman*, 27, 29 Aug., 12, 26 Sept. 1867; and *Daily Evening Globe* (Saint John), 12 Aug. 1867. It was fortunate for Anglin that Bishop Rogers was absent from the province during the election for he would have opposed the newspaperman (see T.P. Slattery, *The Assassination of D'Arcy McGee* (Toronto, 1968), p 371; *Union Advocate* (Newcastle), n.d., quoted in *Freeman*, 8 Aug. 1868; and Bishop James Rogers Papers, Rogers to K.F. Burns, 9 May 1872, in UNBA).
22 *Freeman*, 21 Sept. 1867
23 Ibid, 26 Sept. 1867
24 Ibid
25 For an analysis of Anglin's volatile relationship with McGee see W.M. Baker,

'Turning the Spit: Timothy Anglin and the Roasting of D'Arcy McGee,' *Canadian Historical Association Historical Papers, 1974*, pp 135–55.
26 *Freeman*, 25 Nov. 1865. For the Wexford speech see Slattery, *Assassination*, pp 285–92. A typescript copy of the speech taken from a report in the *Dublin Evening Mail* is to be found in James Moylan Papers, pp 14341–7. McGee himself, in an afterthought, recognized that he might have been excessively severe 'on the Irish demagogues in the Atlantic cities' (see Slattery, *Assassination*, p 291).
27 McGee to Anglin, 1 June 1866, in *News*, 8 June 1866, quoted in *Freeman*, 12 June 1866
28 *Freeman*, 12 June 1866
29 Ibid, 26 June 1866
30 See ibid, 4, 9, 16 Oct., 6 Dec. 1866
31 See R.B. Burns, 'D'Arcy McGee and the Fenians: A Study of the Interaction between Irish Nationalism and the American Environment,' *University Review* (Dublin), 1967, pp 260–73, for an interesting fresh look at this question.
32 *Freeman*, 6 Aug. 1867
33 Ibid, 6 Aug. 1867. This was in response to a eulogistic letter written on McGee's behalf by Archbishop Connolly.
34 Ibid, 23 March 1867
35 Ibid. See also ibid, 12 March, 11 June 1867. There was, apparently, a growing accommodation between the Irish Fenians and the Catholic clergy in Ireland about this time (see E.R. Norman, *The Catholic Church and Ireland in the Age of Rebellion 1859–1873* [London, 1965], pp 124–5).
36 *Freeman*, 15 June 1867
37 On Irish Canadian attitudes towards Fenianism and McGee see H. Senior, 'Quebec and the Fenians,' CHR, XLVIII (1967), 26–44; R.B. Burns, 'D'Arcy McGee and the New Nationality,' unpublished Master's dissertation, Carleton University, 1966, pp 56–7; and Slattery, *Assassination*, pp 401–16.
38 *News*, 11 March 1867, quoted in *Freeman*, 12 March 1867
39 See Slattery, *Assassination*, p 424
40 Joseph Howe Papers, Wm.B. Lenihan to Howe, 10 Oct. 1867
41 The account of the speech which follows is taken from the *Freeman*, 12 Nov. 1867
42 *Globe*, n.d., quoted in *Freeman*, 4 Jan. 1868
43 'T.W.A.', 15 Nov. 1867, in *Freeman*, 21 Nov. 1867
44 Slattery, *Assassination*, p 429; and D.C. Lyne, 'The Irish in the Province of Canada in the Decade Leading up to Confederation,' unpublished Master's dissertation, McGill University, 1960, pp 260–1. On 11 Feb. 1868 the *Freeman* claimed that the names of many prominent Irishmen were painted on plaques

attached to the wall and had been hanging there for years before McGee decided to point out a couple to support his charge of Fenianism. McGee had, of course, been a prominent member of the society for all those years.

45 The speech is reported in 'T.W.A.', 15 Nov. 1867, in *Freeman*, 21 Nov. 1867. See also Slattery, *Assassination*, p 429; J. Young, *Public Men and Public Life in Canada* (Toronto, 1912), II, 44; and *Canada: House of Commons Debates, 1867–8*, ed P.B. Waite (Ottawa, 1967), pp 76–7 (14 Nov.).

46 *Globe*, 15 Nov. 1867, quoted in *Freeman*, 16 Nov. 1867

47 'T.W.A.', 15 Nov. 1867, in *Freeman*, 21 Nov. 1867

48 Slattery, *Assassination*, p 429

49 *Freeman*, 6 Feb. 1868. On the expulsion of McGee from the St Patrick's Society see Slattery, *Assassination*, pp 434–6.

50 *Gazette* (Montreal), 18 March 1868

51 *Canadian Freeman* (Toronto), 2 Jan. 1868

52 *True Witness and Catholic Chronicle* (Montreal), 13 March 1868; and *Irish Canadian* (Toronto), 1 Jan., 25 March 1868

53 'T.W.A.', 4 Apr. 1868, in *Freeman*, 11 Apr. 1868

54 'T.W.A.', 7 Apr. 1868, in *Freeman*, 14 Apr. 1868

55 *Canada: House of Commons Debates, 1867–8*, pp 479–80

56 *Freeman*, 7 Jan. 1868. Anglin's views on Fenianism during the first three months of 1868 remained about the same as they had been previously (see ibid, 8, 18 Feb. 1868; and 'T.W.A.', 30 March 1868, in *Freeman*, 7 Apr. 1868).

57 *Canadian Freeman*, 30 Apr. 1868; and *Evening Express and Commercial Record* (Halifax), 1 May 1868

58 'T.W.A.', 15 Apr. 1868, in *Freeman*, 21 Apr. 1868; and 'T.W.A.', 16 Apr. 1868, in *Freeman*, 23 Apr. 1868

59 *Freeman*, 13 Aug. 1868

60 Ibid, 5 Dec. 1867; 5 Nov. 1868

61 Ibid, 15, 18 July 1871

62 'T.W.A.', 15 Dec. 1867, in *Freeman*, 24 Dec. 1867

63 *Freeman*, 5 May 1868

64 House of Commons Sessional Records, 1.

65 *Freeman*, 19 May 1868. See also 'T.W.A.', 21 June 1869, in *Freeman*, 1 July 1869; and 'T.W.A.', 29 Apr. 1873, in *Freeman*, 8 May 1873.

66 *Freeman*, 28 Oct. 1869. As the representative of Gloucester Anglin was not perturbed about the selection of the North Shore route (see 'T.W.A.', 26 March 1868, in *Freeman*, 4 Apr. 1868; and *Freeman*, 20 Oct. 1868).

67 See *Freeman*, 25 Jan., 4, 22 Feb., 12 March, 12 May 1868; and *Morning Telegraph* (Saint John), 11 Feb. 1868. Saint John financial institutions fared badly in their competition with Montreal-based establishments (see J.R.

Petrie, *The Regional Economy of New Brunswick* [A Study Prepared for the Committee on Reconstruction, 1944], p 107). The Commercial Bank, for example, was forced to close its doors in 1868 (see *Freeman*, 12 Nov. 1868).

68 See *Freeman*, 4, 14 Jan. 1868; Rogers Papers, Sweeny to Rogers, 27 Jan 1868; and *Telegraph*, 29 Feb. 1868, quoted in *Freeman*, 3 March 1868. In 1869 John Cudlip moved a resolution in the legislature urging the House to consider whether the province should seek entry into the American Union (see *Freeman*, 20 March 1869).

69 See, for example, *Reporter*, 15 Apr. 1870; and the *Daily Telegraph and Morning Journal* (Saint John), 22 June 1870. The latter paper was a combination of the two formerly separate papers indicated in the title.

70 *Freeman*, 7 Jan. 1868

71 Ibid, 16 July 1868

72 Ibid, 18 Jan. 1868. See also ibid, 11 Jan. 1868; 20 March 1869

73 Ibid, 6 July 1869

74 Ibid, 18 Jan. 1868

75 See ibid, 31 Jan., 6, 8 July, 7 Oct., 7 Nov. 1871

76 Ibid, 11 Jan. 1868. See also ibid, 3 July 1869.

77 Ibid, 2 Nov. 1867

78 Anglin opposed the appointment very strenuously (ibid, 29 Oct. 1867; 4 Feb., 25 July 1868). Wilmot returned the antagonism in full measure (ibid, 24 Oct. 1871).

79 Ibid, 4 Feb. 1868. See also ibid, 5 March, 20 June, 8 Aug. 1868.

80 'T.W.A.', 15 Nov. 1867, in *Freeman*, 21 Nov. 1867; and *Freeman*, 5 March, 20 June 1868

81 Ibid, 4 Feb. 1868. See also ibid, 8 Aug. 1868

82 Ibid, 20 June 1868. The *Freeman* felt that Howe acted the traitor in accepting Confederation and a seat in the government. What else he could have done it did not say (see *Freeman*, 8, 11 Aug. 1868).

83 Ibid, 17 Dec. 1868. Anglin was absent from Ottawa when the votes on the Nova Scotian question were taken. He had, however, spoken in support of the government's position on the second reading of the bill (ibid, 29 June 1869).

84 Ibid, 5 Dec. 1867

85 'T.W.A.', 12 Dec. 1867, in *Freeman*, 21 Dec. 1867

86 'T.W.A.', 28 May 1869, in *Freeman*, 3 June 1869

87 *Freeman*, 15 June 1869

88 *Freeman*, 16 Sept., 16, 25 Nov., 2, 21 Dec. 1869; 6, 8 Jan. (incorrectly dated 11 Jan. on editorial page), 23 Apr. 1870. See also 'T.W.A.', 3 March 1870, in *Freeman*, 15 March 1870.

89 *Freeman*, 7 May 1870

90 'T.W.A.', 29 May 1869, in *Freeman*, 5 June 1869; and *Freeman*, 12 Aug. 1869

91 *Freeman*, 26 Jan. 1871; 4, 7 May 1872; and 'T.W.A.', 31 March 1871, in *Freeman*, 11 Apr. 1871

92 *Freeman*, 6 Feb., 16 July, 22 Oct., 10 Nov. 1868; 3 June 1869. Anglin felt sure that the Dominion could not and ought not to support a vast military force to replace the vacuum left by Britain (ibid, 6 Feb. 1868; 'T.W.A.', 8 May 1868, in *Freeman*, 16 May 1868; and Arthur Hill Gillmor Papers, Anglin to Gillmour, 24 Oct. 1867, in PANB).

93 Ibid, 12, 22 June, 31 July 1869. In Anglin's eyes British failure to protect Canadian fisheries against American encroachments was the most flagrant and most concrete example of Britain's unwillingness to meet her responsibilities (ibid, 25 Aug. 1868; 25 Feb., 26 Oct. 1869).

94 Ibid, 31 July 1869

95 See, for example, ibid, 24 Nov. 1870

96 Ibid, 18 Nov. 1869. See also ibid, 10 Aug., 14 Sept. 1869

97 Ibid, 26 Feb. 1870

98 Ibid, 12 July 1870. See also ibid, 23 June 1870

99 'T.W.A.', 13 Feb. 1871, in *Freeman*, 18 Feb. 1871

100 *Freeman*, 11 May 1871

101 Ibid, 18 May 1871

102 Ibid, 13 June, 11 July, 18 Nov. 1871

103 Ibid, 18 Nov. 1871

104 'T.W.A.', 8 May 1872, in *Freeman*, 23 May 1872; and 'T.W.A.', 17 May 1872, in *Freeman*, 4 June 1872. See also *Canada: Parliamentary Debates, 1872*, pp 606–20 (16 May).

105 *Freeman*, 23 May 1872

106 Gillmor Papers, Anglin to Gillmour, 24 Oct. 1867

107 'T.W.A.', 6 Nov. 1867, in *Freeman*, 14 Nov. 1867

108 *Globe*, n.d., quoted in *Freeman*, 4 Jan. 1868

109 *Freeman*, 15 Oct. 1867; and *Globe* (Toronto), n.d., quoted in *Freeman*, 16 Nov. 1867

110 Some of the more important writings concerning the development of political parties after Confederation are: F.H. Underhill, 'The Development of National Political Parties in Canada,' CHR, XVI (1935), 367–87; E.M. Reid, 'The Rise of National Parties in Canada,' *Papers and Proceedings of the Fourth Annual Meeting of the Canadian Political Science Association, 1932*, pp 187–200; and E.V. Jackson, 'The Organization of the Canadian Liberal Party, 1867–1896: With Particular Reference to Ontario,' unpublished Master's dissertation, University of Toronto, 1962.

111 Two interesting letters dealing with the organization of the Reformers in these

early years are Alexander Mackenzie Papers, Mackenzie to Brown, 8 Nov. 1867; and Brown to Mackenzie, 20 Aug. 1869.

112 *Freeman*, 25 July 1868

113 See, for example, ibid, 31 Oct., 7 Nov. 1868; 15 Apr. 1869.

114 The statistics to verify this assertion have been compiled by the author from *Canada: House of Commons Journals, 1867–8* through to *Commons Journals, 1870*.

115 This is surmised from the fact that Prince Arthur danced with Mrs Anglin, among others, at a levee on the night of 25 Feb. (see *Freeman*, 1 March 1870).

116 'Letters of Hon. Alexander Mackenzie to Hon. A.G. Jones, 1869–1885,' *Report of the Board of Trustees of the Public Archives of Nova Scotia, 1952*, Mackenzie to Jones, 12 Apr. 1870

117 *Globe* (Toronto), 29 Nov. 1870. See also *News*, 5 Dec. 1870; and *Freeman*, 6 Dec. 1870. Only one year earlier the *Globe* had labelled the *Freeman* a ministerial paper (see *Freeman*, 4 Nov. 1869).

118 Sir John Alexander Macdonald Papers, vol CCCXLII, Anglin to Macdonald, 3 Dec. 1870. See also 'T.W.A.', 4 Apr. 1871, in *Freeman*, 13 Apr. 1871.

119 John O'Connor Papers, Macdonald to O'Connor, 26 Dec. 1870

120 Macdonald Letterbooks, vol XV, Macdonald to Anglin, 10 Jan. 1871

121 Mackenzie Papers, Anglin to Mackenzie, 6 Sept. 1872. Anglin mentioned at the end of the letter that he had received a note from Edward Blake.

122 At least he spoke at a meeting of stockholders (see *Freeman*, 4 Nov. 1869).

123 See ibid, 2, 4 Dec. 1869; 2 Dec. 1871; 27 Jan. 1872.

124 A brief report of one sumptuous affair given by Anglin is presented in M.B. Buckley, *Diary of a Tour in America*, ed K. Buckley (Dublin, 1886), pp 132–3.

125 *Freeman*, 28 Aug. 1873

126 Two figures on newspaper values in the nineteenth century are mentioned in W.H. Kesterton, *A History of Journalism in Canada* (Toronto, 1967), pp 24, 55. Total stock for the newspaper Anglin later edited, the Toronto *Tribune*, was $25,000 in 1883 (see Edward Blake Papers, draft of a circular, ? Feb. 1883, in PAO).

127 *Freeman*, 6 July 1872; and *Daily Evening Globe* (Saint John), 6 July 1872. The taxes were based on assessments of both real estate and personal estate including all goods, chattels, moneys, and capital effects (see *Statutes of New Brunswick*, 22 Vict. Cap. XXXVII and the 1868 revisions to that Statute). As the *Globe* gave the total assessments as well as the total taxes levied for Saint John, it is possible to calculate Anglin's assessed value on the basis of the taxes he was expected to pay. Assessments were normally lower than actual value (see *Freeman*, 15 Nov. 1860). The purchasing power of money in the last third of

the nineteenth century was approximately eight times greater than it is today. Thus Anglin's assessed value was equivalent to a current assessment of over $100,000.

128 *Freeman*, 12 May 1870; 9 Apr. 1872
129 Ibid, 18 Feb. 1871
130 Ibid, 1 Feb. 1872
131 Ibid, 20 Apr. 1872
132 Ibid, 18, 22 Jan., 22 Feb. 1872

NOTES TO CHAPTER NINE

1 There are several useful studies of the New Brunswick schools question which treat the subject from a wider perspective than can the present account, which must concentrate on Anglin's role. The predetermined outlook and heavy reliance on secondary sources makes the account in C.B. Sissons, *Church and State in Canadian Education: An Historical Study* (Toronto, 1959), pp 227–43, barely adequate. J. Hannay, *History of New Brunswick* (Saint John, 1909), II, 295–317, has some merit despite its age but has been superceded by K.F.C. MacNaughton, *The Development of the Theory and Practice of Education in New Brunswick 1784–1900* (Fredericton, 1947), pp 187–222. The account in D. Argue, 'The Separate School Question in New Brunswick,' unpublished Master's dissertation, Carleton University, 1967, is well done but contains little new material. M.F. Hatfield, ' "La Guerre Scolaire": The Conflict Over the New Brunswick Common Schools Act 1871–1876,' unpublished Master's dissertation, Queen's University, 1972, is a helpful synthesis. The most interesting work on the topic and one which has shed much new light on the question by making use of material in the Catholic Archives of Saint John and Chatham (now Bathurst) is P.M. Toner, 'The New Brunswick Separate Schools Issue 1864–1876,' unpublished Master's dissertation, University of New Brunswick, 1967. See also P.M. Toner, 'The New Brunswick Schools Question,' *Canadian Catholic Historical Association Study Sessions 1970*, pp 85–96. Despite the impression given in many accounts, the use of the French language was a minor issue at the time. In fact the regulations of the Board of Education showed that there was no intention of eliminating the use of French in public schools in New Brunswick (see M.H. Hody, 'The Development of the Bilingual Schools of New Brunswick,' unpublished Doctor of Education dissertation, University of Toronto, 1964, p 54; and M. Hody, 'The Anglicizing Common Schools Act of 1871: A Study in Folklore,' *La Société Historique*

294 Notes to Pages 145–7

Acadienne, XI [1968], 347–9). The question was one of religion, not one of language, and it was Irish Catholics – Anglin, Costigan, Rogers, and Sweeny – who led the agitation.

2 'Syllabus of Errors,' no. 48, in *Introduction to Contemporary Civilization in the West*, 3rd ed (New York, 1961), p 644

3 Toner, 'New Brunswick Separate Schools Issue,' p 1

4 W.L. Morton, *The Critical Years: The Union of British North America 1857–1873* (Toronto, 1964), p 205

5 J.B. Bury, *History of the Papacy in the 19th Century: Liberty and Authority in the Roman Catholic Church*, rev ed (New York, 1964), p 16

6 *Freeman*, 28 Jan. 1860

7 See, for example, ibid, 1 Nov. 1860

8 P.S. O'Hegarty, *A History of Ireland Under the Union 1801 to 1922* (London, 1952), pp 390–1; D. Gwynn, *Young Ireland and 1848* (Cork, 1949), pp 26, 36–7, 40; R.A. Billington, *The Protestant Crusade 1800–1860: A Study of the Origins of American Nativism* (Chicago, 1964), p 143. In Upper Canada the common school system was directed at or against Irish Catholics (see S. Houston, 'Politics, Schools, and Social Change in Upper Canada,' CHR, LIII [1972], 264–5).

9 See W.S. MacNutt, *New Brunswick: A History, 1784–1867* (Toronto, 1963), pp 365–6; Sir Samuel Leonard Tilley Papers (uncatalogued collection), C.N. Skinner to Tilley, 9 Jan. 1858; and ibid, G.E. Fenety to Tilley, 12 Jan. 1858.

10 *The Law Relating to Parish Schools in New Brunswick, 1858*, p 7

11 Uncatalogued Tilley Papers, Sweeny to Tilley, 7 Feb. 1862; and *New Brunswick: House of Assembly Debates, 1862*, p 114

12 Onésiphore Turgeon, the Gloucester MP from 1900 to 1922 and long-time senator, mentions this fact and somewhat unfairly places blame on Anglin for failing to bring up the subject in the New Brunswick Assembly (see O. Turgeon, *Un Tribut à la Race Acadienne: Mémoires, 1871–1927* [Montreal, 1928], p 23). As has been seen, Anglin had brought up the issue in 1862. Moreover, he was not a member of the Assembly which met when the 1866 election had shown that Confederation was a 'fixed fact,' and it was only the BNA Act, drafted late in 1866, which made the legal situation of Catholic education of significance.

13 See Toner, 'New Brunswick Separate Schools Issue,' pp 22–8, for the story of Archbishop Connolly's efforts in this regard. Connolly was so anxious to win for the Catholics of Nova Scotia educational rights akin to those of the Protestant and Catholic minorities of Canada East and Canada West respectively that he was willing virtually to guarantee 'nearly every Catholic vote in the Province' if Tupper arranged for such educational changes (see Sir Charles Tup-

per Papers, vol III, Connolly to Tupper, Wednesday [10 Apr. 1867]). The wording of Section 93 of the BNA Act, the section relating to minority education rights, was one of the few important issues at the London Conference (see D.G. Creighton, *The Road to Confederation: The Emergence of Canada 1863–1867* (Toronto, 1964), pp 410–12; and Morton, *Critical Years*, p 208).

14 Sir Samuel Leonard Tilley Papers, Tilley to E. McLeod, 4 Jan. 1867, in UNBA
15 *Freeman*, 20, 22, 25 Jan. 1870
16 Ibid, 16 July 1870
17 *Morning News* (Saint John), n.d., quoted in *Freeman*, 16 July 1870
18 *Freeman*, 16 July 1870
19 Ibid, 16 Aug. 1866
20 Ibid, 16 July 1870
21 MacNaughton, *Education in New Brunswick*, p 188
22 Ibid, p 191. Counter petitions, numerously signed, were also in evidence.
23 *Freeman*, 20, 22 Apr. 1871
24 Ibid, 22 Apr. 1871
25 Ibid, 4 May 1871
26 Ibid, 6 May 1871
27 Ibid, 9, 16, 30 Jan., 20 Feb. 1872. See Toner, 'New Brunswick Separate Schools Issue,' pp 39–40.
28 *Freeman*, 3 Feb., 21 March 1872
29 Ibid, 6 Jan. 1872
30 Ibid, 20 Feb. 1872
31 Ibid, 6 Apr. 1872
32 *Canada: Sessional Papers, 1872*, no. 36, pp 1–2, 6–7
33 Sir John Alexander Macdonald Papers, vol CCCXLIII, Anglin to Macdonald, 5 Oct. 1871
34 *Sessional Papers, 1872*, no. 36, pp 2–4. See also *Freeman*, 1 Feb. 1872; and Toner, 'New Brunswick Separate Schools Issue,' pp 41–4.
35 'T.W.A.', 30 Apr. 1872, in *Freeman*, 11 May 1872; *Canada: Parliamentary Debates, 1872*, pp 197–206 (29 Apr.); and *Canada: House of Commons Journals, 1872*, p 60 (29 Apr.).
36 'T.W.A.', 21 May 1872, in *Freeman*, 6 June 1872; *Parliamentary Debates, 1872*, pp 705–11 (20 May); and *Commons Journals, 1872*, p 134 (20 May).
37 Bishop James Rogers Papers, Anglin to Rogers, 20 May 1872, in UNBA
38 *Commons Journals, 1872*, p 156 (22 May)
39 Rogers Papers, Anglin to Rogers, 22 May 1872 (with a postscript on 23 May). The letter requested that the bishop telegraph his views in order that they might be acted upon.

40 *Freeman*, 25 May 1872; *Parliamentary Debates, 1872*, pp 758–66 (22 May); and *Commons Journals, 1872*, pp 155–6 (22 May).
41 Macdonald Papers, vol CCLXXVI, Tilley to Macdonald, 25 May 1872
42 *Freeman*, 25, 28, 30 May 1872
43 The information in this paragraph has been gleaned from 'T.W.A.', 28 May 1872, in *Freeman*, 13 June 1872; 'T.W.A.', 30 May 1872, in *Freeman*, 15 June 1872; and Rogers Papers, Anglin to Rogers, 30 May 1872.
44 Rogers Papers, Anglin to Rogers, 1 July 1872
45 'T.W.A.', 28 May 1872, in *Freeman*, 13 June 1872; 'T.W.A.', 30 May 1872, in *Freeman*, 13 June 1872; *Parliamentary Debates, 1872*, pp 898–909 (29 May); and *Commons Journals, 1872*, pp 175–9 (29 May). Anglin voted against the Colby amendment.
46 Rogers Papers, Anglin to Rogers, 30 May 1872; and *Freeman*, 1 June 1872. See also Rogers Papers, Anglin to Rogers, 1 July 1872; and *Freeman*, 2 July 1872.
47 *Freeman*, 25 June 1872. Of course, the bill could still be declared unconstitutional and therefore illegal by judicial decision.
48 Rogers Papers, Rogers to Burns, 9 May 1872
49 Ibid, Rogers to Rev. T.F. Barry, 15 May 1872
50 Ibid, Anglin to Rogers, 13 Sept. 1872
51 Anglin's reports to Rogers on political developments in the constituency are found in Rogers Papers, Anglin to Rogers, 20 May, 12 July 1872.
52 Ibid, Anglin to Rogers, 13 Sept. 1872
53 *American Newspaper Directory* (New York, 1873), p 226. These figures are certainly open to a good deal of scepticism.
54 *Freeman*, 4 July 1872
55 Ibid, 22 Oct. 1872
56 Rogers Papers, Anglin to Rogers, 21 Oct. 1872
57 Ibid, Anglin to Rogers, 19 Nov. 1872
58 *Freeman*, 8 Feb. 1873
59 W. Pugsley, ed, *Reports of Cases Determined by the Supreme Court of New Brunswick ...*, vol. I: *1872–1873* (Saint John, 1876), pp 273–300. The judgment was reprinted in *Sessional Papers, 1873*, no. 44, pp 66–84. Judges Allen and Weldon had stated that the question was a legitimate subject for remedial legislation by the Canadian parliament (see *Freeman*, 22 Feb. 1873).
60 *Freeman*, 20 Feb. 1873.
61 Ibid, 25 Feb. 1873; and *News*, 24 Feb. 1873.
62 Rogers Papers, Anglin to Rogers, 13 March 1873
63 It seems likely that the child was either stillborn or survived for only a very short time.
64 'T.W.A.', 14 March 1873, in *Freeman*, 20 March 1873

65 'T.W.A.', 4 March 1873, in *Freeman*, 8 March 1873
66 'T.W.A.', 25 March 1873, in *Freeman*, 1 Apr. 1873
67 Rogers Papers, Anglin to Rogers, 13 March 1873
68 The question of the New Brunswick schools had been more significant in Quebec than in New Brunswick itself in the 1872 elections (see Rogers Papers, Anglin to Rogers, 13 Sept. 1872).
69 Rogers Papers, Anglin to Rogers, 13 March 1873
70 *Globe* (Toronto), n.d., quoted in *Freeman*, 10 Apr. 1873; *Canada: Scrapbook Hansard, 1873*, p 61 (3 Apr.); and *Commons Journals, 1873*, p 120 (3 Apr.)
71 *Sessional Papers, 1873*, no. 44, p 63
72 *Freeman*, 17 Apr. 1873; and 'T.W.A.', 17 Apr. 1873, in *Freeman*, 22 Apr. 1873. The Law Officers did not change their views.
73 'T.W.A.', 18 Apr. 1873, in *Freeman*, 25 Apr. 1873
74 Rogers Papers, Anglin to Rogers, 5 May 1873; and John Costigan Papers, Costigan to Sweeny, 28 Apr. 1873
75 Rogers Papers, Sweeny to Rogers, 12 May 1873
76 Ibid, Anglin to Rogers, 16 May 1873; *Freeman*, 15, 17 May 1873; 'T.W.A.', 15 May 1873, in *Freeman*, 24 May 1873; *Scrapbook Hansard, 1873*, pp 176–9 (14 May); and *Commons Journals, 1873*, pp 345, 347 (14 May).
77 Rogers Papers, Anglin to Rogers, telegram, 15 May 1873
78 'T.W.A.', 15 May 1873, in *Freeman*, 24 May 1873
79 Lord Kimberley Papers, Dufferin to Kimberley, 16 May 1873. See also ibid, Dufferin to Kimberley, 29 May 1873; and Canada: Governor General's Office, Telegrams, 1862–1883, vol v, Dufferin to Kimberley, 17 May 1873.
80 *Freeman*, 24 May 1873. There was great pressure on Macdonald from Maritime Protestants on this question. Their reaction to the resolution of 14 May had been swift and furious (see *News*, 16 May 1873; and Rogers Papers, Anglin to Rogers, 20 May 1873).
81 *Freeman*, 24 May 1873. See also ibid, 20 May, 14 June 1873. Kimberley agreed with Dufferin's right to take this course. Edward Blake took up the constitutional question and in 1875 gave notice of a resolution to clarify ministerial responsibility in cases of disallowance (see W.R. Graham, 'Liberal Nationalism in the Eighteen Seventies,' *Canadian Historical Association Report, 1946*, pp 116–17).
82 Rogers Papers, Anglin to Rogers, 20 May 1873. Two decades later Bishop Rogers placed full blame on the decision of the Quebec bishops (see Toner, 'New Brunswick Separate Schools Issue,' pp 83–4).
83 There are many accounts of this famous debate in Canadian history. Two which tell the story in detail, but from very different perspectives, are D.C. Thomson, *Alexander Mackenzie: Clear Grit* (Toronto, 1960), pp 146–68; and

D.G. Creighton, *John A. Macdonald*, vol. II: *The Old Chieftain* (Toronto, 1955), pp 129–79.

84 'T.W.A.', 3 Apr. 1873, in *Freeman*, 12 Apr. 1873

85 'T.W.A.', 18 Apr. 1873, in *Freeman*, 25 Apr. 1873; *Freeman*, 19 Apr. 1873; 'T.W.A.', 22 Apr. 1873, in *Freeman*, 29 Apr. 1873; *Scrapbook Hansard, 1873*, pp 80–4 (17 Apr.); and *Commons Journals, 1873*, pp 167–72 (17 Apr.). The *Times* (Ottawa), 27 March 1874, recalled that when Anglin had risen to reply to the charges, there had been a discourteous rush of a number of MPs from the House. An article in the *Canadian Monthly* agreed that the *Freeman*'s article was worthy of contempt but considered that it was little worse than publications in other journals and that the censure motion presented to the House was ill-advised and useless, passed, as it was, by the party strength of the government (see Anon., 'Notes on the Session,' *Canadian Monthly and National Review* [Toronto], III [1873], 534).

86 Alexander Mackenzie Letterbooks, vol I, Mackenzie to Anglin, 29 July 1873

87 See ibid, Mackenzie to Pickard, 25 July 1873; ibid, Mackenzie to Anglin, 1 Aug. 1873; and Mackenzie Papers, Anglin to Mackenzie, 1 Aug. 1873.

88 'T.W.A.', 5 Nov. 1873, in *Freeman*, 11 Nov. 1873. The same was true for the selection of the Nova Scotian cabinet ministers (see K.G. Pryke, 'The Making of a Province: Nova Scotia and Confederation,' *Canadian Historical Association Historical Papers, 1968*, p 42).

89 *Freeman*, 13 Nov. 1873

90 Rogers Papers, Anglin to Rogers, 21 Nov. 1873

91 *News*, 12 Nov. 1873. See also ibid, 6 Nov., 1 Dec. 1873; *Le Moniteur Acadien* (Shediac), 6, 13 Nov. 1873; *New Brunswick Reporter* (Fredericton), 19 Nov. 1873; *Mail* (Toronto), 11, 12 Nov. 1873; and *True Witness and Catholic Chronicle* (Montreal), 16 Jan. 1874. A contrary view was expressed by *New Dominion and True Humorist* (Saint John), 15 Nov. 1873. See also ibid, 29 Nov. 1873; 10 Jan. 1874.

92 Mackenzie Letterbooks, vol III, Mackenzie to Anglin, 12 Nov. 1873

93 *News*, 17 Nov. 1873

94 *Freeman*, 18 Nov. 1873

95 Rogers Papers, Anglin to Rogers, 21 Nov. 1873

96 Ibid, Anglin to Rogers, 2 Jan 1874

97 Bishop Rogers had given his support to Anglin (and to Peter Mitchell) once again (see Rogers Papers, J. Sivewright to Rogers, 24 Jan. 1874; and Rogers to Sivewright, 27 Jan 1874). John Costigan had solicited and received support from both bishops (see *Costigan Papers*, vol I, Sweeny to Costigan, 18 Jan. 1874; and Rogers to Costigan, 20 Jan. 1874).

98 *Freeman*, 28 March 1874; and *Scrapbook Hansard, 1874*, p 1 (26 March)

99 Mackenzie Letterbooks, vol III, Mackenzie to Father Quin, 3 Jan. 1874
100 Rogers Papers, Anglin to Rogers, 6 March 1874. Not all New Brunswick priests agreed with their bishops in thinking that Anglin ought to become Speaker (see Costigan Papers, Rev. James Quin to Costigan, 2 Apr. 1874).
101 W.F. Dawson, *Procedure in the Canadian House of Commons* (Toronto, 1962), p 63

NOTES TO CHAPTER TEN

1 The Marchioness of (Lady) Dufferin and Ava, *My Canadian Journal 1872–8: Extracts from My Letters Home Written while Lord Dufferin was Governor-General* (London, 1891), p 213
2 See *Freeman*, 14 July 1874; 8 July 1875
3 *Canada: Scrapbook Hansard, 1874*, p 1 (26 March). Holton denied that he had turned down the office of Speaker but thanked Macdonald for his expression of confidence. He then assured the House that Anglin would be a capable person. There was a feeling in many circles that Holton would be a better candidate for the office than Anglin (see Anon., 'Current Events,' *Canadian Monthly and National Review*, V (1874), 424; *Nation* (Toronto), 2 Apr. 1874; and *Mail* (Toronto), 26 March 1874).
4 *Scrapbook Hansard, 1874*, p 1 (26 March)
5 This is seen very clearly in part of a letter from Macdonald to Geroge Kirkpatrick reprinted in P.B. Waite, 'The Political Ideas of John A. Macdonald,' *Les idées politiques des premiers ministres du Canada | The Political Ideas of the Prime Ministers of Canada*, ed M. Hamelin (Ottawa, 1969), p 58.
6 *New Brunswick Reporter* (Fredericton), 25 Feb. 1874. See also *Mail*, 26 March 1874.
7 *Daily Citizen* (Ottawa), 26 March 1874. See also ibid, 20, 24 March 1874
8 'Current Events,' *Canadian Monthly*, V (1874), 424; *Citizen*, 20 March 1874; and *Nation*, 2 Apr. 1874
9 *Citizen*, 24 March 1874
10 *Globe* (Toronto), 27 March 1874; *Times* (Ottawa), 27 March 1874; and *Free Press* (Ottawa), 27 March 1874
11 *Globe*, 27 March 1874
12 W. Leggo, *The History of the Administration of the Right Honorable Frederick Temple, Earl of Dufferin, Late Governor General of Canada* (Montreal, 1878), p 206
13 *Scrapbook Hansard, 1874*, pp 7–8, 15–16 (31 March, 9 Apr.).
14 See, for example, *Citizen*, 2 May 1874; *Free Press*, 13 May 1874; and P.B.

Waite, 'Sir Oliver Mowat's Canada: Reflections on an Un-Victorian Society,' *Sir Oliver Mowat's Ontario*, ed D. Swainson (Toronto, 1972), pp 21–3.

15 Roman Catholic Archdiocese of Toronto Archives, Archbishop John Joseph Lynch Papers, Anglin to Lynch, 25 March 1875

16 *Globe*, 26 May 1874; and *Free Press*, 27 May 1874

17 See, for example, *Commons Debates, 1876*, pp 601–2 (13 March).

18 However, see ibid, pp 288–90 (28 Feb.).

19 'Chaudiere,' 18 Apr. 1874, in *Canadian Illustrated News* (Montreal), 18 Apr. 1874. 'Chaudiere' noted that Holton seemed to take 'a little malicious delight' in rescuing the Speaker at the beginning of the 1874 session. Holton's one-upmanship continued in subsequent sessions but Anglin soon became as expert as Holton (see, for example, *Commons Debates, 1877*, pp 875–6 [21 March]).

20 J.H. Aitchison, 'The Speakership of the Canadian House of Commons,' *Canadian Issues: Essays in Honour of Henry F. Angus*, ed R.M. Clark (Toronto, 1961), pp 31–2

21 However see *Commons Debates, 1874*, p 56 (27 Apr.); and *Commons Debates, 1877*, pp 1171–4, 1178 (5 Apr.).

22 *Freeman*, 29 March 1877; and Bishop James Rogers Papers, Anglin to Rogers, 4 Apr. 1878, in UNBA

23 Quoted in W.F. Dawson, *Procedure in the Canadian House of Commons* (Toronto, 1962), p 80. This was part of Anglin's testimony before the Committee on Privileges and Elections in 1877.

24 Anglin later acknowledged that he followed the apparently traditional practice of appointing those nominated by members of his party (see *Commons Debates, 1880*, pp 1030–2 [2 Apr.]).

25 Ibid

26 House of Commons Sessional Records, Anglin to Hartney, 10 Aug. 1876

27 *Citizen*, 28 March, 1874, 9 Feb. 1877; and *Free Press*, 5 March 1877, 11 Feb. 1878.

28 *Saint John Watchman*, n.d., quoted in *Citizen*, 12 Apr. 1877

29 *Citizen*, 18 Apr. 1874. See also ibid, 28 March 1874

30 See, for example, ibid, 26 Feb., 13 March 1877; and *Free Press*, 7 Apr. 1877.

31 *Globe*, 9 Feb. 1877

32 *Free Press*, 25 Apr. 1877

33 See Alexander Mackenzie Letterbooks, vol I, Mackenzie to Anglin, 28 Sept. 1875; vol IV, Mackenzie to Anglin, 26 May, 14 June, 7, 14 Oct. 1875; vol V, Mackenzie to Anglin, 6 Dec. 1875; vol V, W. Buckingham to Anglin, 16 Feb., 29 March 1876; vol VIII, Buckingham to Anglin, 22, 31 Oct. 1877; and Alexander Mackenzie Papers, Anglin to Mackenzie, 25 July 1877. See also Arthur Hill Gillmor Papers, Anglin to Gillmour, 23 June 1874, 16 July 1875, in PANB;

Rogers Papers, Anglin to Rogers, 6 March 1874, 6 Dec. 1875; and *Freeman*, 23, 30 May 1876.

34 See Mackenzie Papers, Isaac Burpee to Mackenzie, 14 Oct. 1876; and A.J. Smith to Mackenzie, 23 Sept. 1877.

35 Charles Marcil who was Speaker from 1909 to 1911, had been a journalist but does not appear to have been actively involved in newspaper work while he was Speaker (see J.K. Johnson, ed, *The Canadian Directory of Parliament 1867–1967* [Ottawa, 1968], pp 350–1).

36 See, for example, *Freeman*, 4 Apr., 6 June 1874; 11 March 1875; 27 May 1876.

37 *Commons Debates, 1877*, pp 1267–74 (9 Apr.).

38 Edward Blake Letterbooks, vol IX, Blake to Anglin, 23 Sept., 26 Dec. 1876; 9 Jan. 1877, in PAO. The issue of whether W.B. O'Donoghue, the Irishman involved in the Riel uprising of 1869–70 and later with the Fenian invasion of Manitoba, should receive amnesty aroused some interest among Irish Canadians (see *Freeman*, 1 Apr. 1876; 29 Nov. 1877).

39 *Freeman*, second and third week of November 1872; Rogers Papers, Anglin to Rogers, 15 Dec. 1872. Froude's views were, of course, also challenged in the United States (see J. Bland, *Hibernian Crusade: The Story of the Catholic Total Abstinence Union of America* (Washington, 1951), p 73). On 7 Jan. 1873 the *Freeman* refuted Goldwin Smith's arguments concerning Ireland and its history.

40 *Freeman*, 27 March 1877

41 Ibid, 5 June 1877

42 Ibid, 27 March 1877

43 Ibid, 5 June 1877

44 Ibid, 19 June 1877

45 Ibid, 5 June 1877

46 P.M. Toner, 'The New Brunswick Separate Schools Issue 1864–1876,' unpublished Master's dissertation, University of New Brunswick, 1967, pp 86–8.

47 *Freeman*, 20 Sept. 1873

48 Ibid, 31 July, 2 Aug. 1873; and *Morning News* (Saint John), 1 Aug. 1873

49 *Freeman*, 5 July 1873

50 Ibid, 30 Sept., 11 Oct. 1873; ibid, 6 Jan. 1874; and *News*, 17, 18 Dec. 1873. The meeting may have been the result of the mission of Macdonald's henchman, L.-F.-R. Masson, to patch up the schools difficulty, win Bishop Sweeny's approval, and alleviate the position of the federal government in a very difficult situation (see Toner, 'New Brunswick Separate Schools Issue,' p 91).

51 *Freeman*, 15 Jan. 1874. See also ibid, 26 Feb. 1874.

52 Ibid, 24 March 1874

53 John Costigan Papers, Costigan to Sweeny, 3 May 1874

54 *Freeman*, 23 May 1874

55 Ibid, 9 Apr. 1874

56 Costigan Papers, Sweeny to Costigan, 7 May 1874; and Sweeny to Costigan, telegram, 20 May 1874

57 J. Pope, ed, *Correspondence of Sir John Macdonald* (Toronto, 1921), pp 213–14 (Macdonald to Father Quin, 29 May 1873); and Mackenzie Letter-books, vol iii, Mackenzie to Quin, 3 Jan. 1874

58 *Freeman*, 25 June 1874. The election results are compiled in C.H. Mackintosh, ed, *The Canadian Parliamentary Companion, and Annual Register, 1878* (Ottawa, 1878), pp 307–8.

59 *Freeman*, 4 July 1874

60 *New Brunswick School Act: The Argument before the Privy Council of Great Britain in the Judicial Committee of the Privy Council, July 17, 1874: Maher Vs. the Town Council of the Town of Portland.* See also *Freeman*, 18 July 1874.

61 A detailed account of these events is in G.F.G. Stanley, 'The Caraquet Riots of 1875,' *Acadiensis*, ii:2 (Autumn 1972), 21–38. The issues of the *Freeman* relating to the disturbances and eventual court cases are 19, 30 Jan., 2 Feb., 9, 11 Sept., 7 Oct., 9 Nov., 9 Dec. 1875; 29 June, 1 July 1876. See also Rogers Papers, Anglin to Rogers, 6, 10, 27 Dec. 1875.

62 *Freeman*, 11 Feb. 1875

63 *Daily Evening Globe* (Saint John), 1 Feb. 1875, quoted in *Freeman*, 2 Feb. 1875. The *Globe*, along with the *Freeman*, felt that the government was using the religious – educational issue to obscure its incompetence and keep itself in power.

64 Rogers Papers, Anglin to Rogers, 28 March 1875

65 Costigan Papers, Sweeny to Costigan, 25 Jan. 1875

66 Ibid, Sweeny to Costigan, 12 Feb. 1875

67 *Canada: House of Commons Journals, 1875*, p 179. An indication of Protestant reaction in New Brunswick to Costigan's resolution is found in Gillmor Papers, John Boyd to Gillmor, 6 March 1875.

68 The consensus seemed to be that Costigan's motion would have passed had it come to a vote that evening (see Rogers Papers, Anglin to Rogers, 28 March 1875; George Brown Papers, Brown to Anne Brown, 9 March 1875; and *Freeman*, 16 March 1875).

69 *Commons Journals, 1875*, p 197; Rogers Papers, Anglin to Rogers, 28 March 1875; and *Freeman*, 16, 18 March 1875

70 Rogers Papers, Anglin to Rogers, 28 March 1875. If he had done this, Mackenzie certainly was not guaranteeing his support should it become a matter of changing the constitution. In a letter to the persistent Father Quin he had given no encouragement to that idea; claimed that such a change could not be made

'without the consent of every party to the compact'; and doubted that Quebec or even Ontario would accept such a modification (see Mackenzie Letterbooks, vol IV, Mackenzie to Quin, 18 Jan. 1875).
71 Rogers Papers, Anglin to Rogers, 28 March 1875. When back in Saint John, Sweeny reported to his parishioners that, if the appeal to the Queen did not succeed, the case could be carried to the Commons once again (see *Freeman*, 4 May 1875).
72 *Freeman*, 18 March 1875
73 Rogers Papers, Anglin to Rogers, 28 March 1875. It is apparent that Catholic Conservatives, such as Costigan, felt that the bishop was not in favour of the Liberal amendments (see Costigan Papers, Masson to Costigan, 16 July 1877). Anglin's own position is well outlined in the *Freeman*'s defence of Bernard Devlin (see *Freeman*, 29 March 1875).
74 *Commons Journals, 1875*, pp 202–3
75 Rogers Papers, Anglin to Rogers, 28 March 1875. Anglin was disappointed that both New Brunswick cabinet ministers, especially Smith, had been in opposition to the Catholic requests for 'justice.'
76 Lynch Papers, Anglin to Lynch, 25 March 1875
77 *Freeman*, 17 Apr. 1875
78 Quoted in ibid, 14 Aug. 1875
79 Blake Papers, Anglin to Blake, 25 June 1875
80 Mackenzie Letterbooks, vol V, Mackenzie to Anglin, 6 Dec. 1875. The letter contained a copy of Carnarvon's despatch of 18 Oct. 1875. The letter was printed in *Commons Journals, 1876*, p 55; and in *Freeman*, 15 Feb. 1876.
81 Mackenzie Letterbooks, vol V, Mackenzie to Anglin, 6 Dec. 1875
82 Rogers Papers, Anglin to Rogers, 10 Dec. 1875. Anglin tried to make use of it nevertheless (see *Freeman*, 17 Feb. 1876).
83 Rogers Papers, Anglin to Rogers, 10, 27 Dec. 1875; and Anglin to Rogers, 18 Jan. 1876
84 Ibid, circular letter from Rogers to the priests in his diocese, 7 Jan. 1876
85 *Freeman*, 24, 27, 29 March, 3 May 1877
86 Ibid, 3 Apr, 12 May 1877. Negotiations in Fredericton, however, failed in August (see *Freeman*, 30 Aug. 1877).
87 Rogers Papers, Rogers to Anglin, 8 May 1877
88 *Freeman*, 26 Apr. 1877. A copy of the evidence given before the Committee on Privileges and Elections was reprinted in the 24 and 26 Apr. 1877 issues of the *Freeman* (it may also be found in *Commons Journals, 1877*, appendix no. 8., *First Report of the Select Standing Commitee on Privileges and Elections*). Footnote references to these two issues of the *Freeman* relate to this evidence.
89 *Canada: Sessional Papers, 1877*, no. 59, pp 5–6

90 *Freeman*, 14 Apr. 1877. A lengthy report of the debate in the House of Commons of 7 and 9 Apr. 1877 was given in the *Freeman*, 12, 14 Apr. 1877 (see also *Commons Debates, 1877*, pp 1222–1316). Footnote references to these two issues of the *Freeman* relate to this debate. It is interesting to note that at the same time that Huntington was taking away Post Office printing from the *Freeman*, Anglin was publicly objecting to Huntington's stand against the Catholic Church.

91 *Freeman*, 12 Oct. 1876. See also *News*, 3, 8 July 1874; ibid, 11 Sept. 1876; *Freeman*, 4, 7, 9, 25, 28 July 1874; and ibid, 12, 14, 19, 21 Sept. 1876.

92 *Freeman*, 6 June 1868

93 Bowell had brought up the question in the House the year before but had not made much use of it (see *Commons Debates, 1876*, pp 837–8 [24 March]). See also Anon., 'Current Events,' *Canadian Monthly*, x (1876), 445.

94 *Commons Debates, 1877*, p 1830 (25 Apr.).

95 Ibid, p 1171 (5 Apr.). See also ibid, pp 470, 485 (5 March).

96 *Freeman*, 10 Apr. 1877. On the question as a whole see Young, *Public Men*, II, 270–2; W. Buckingham and G.W. Ross, *The Hon. Alexander Mackenzie: His Life and Times* (Toronto, 1892), pp 451–2; D.C. Thomson, *Alexander Mackenzie: Clear Grit* (Toronto, 1960), pp 301–3; N. Ward, *The Canadian House of Commons: Representation* (Toronto, 1950), pp 86–7; and C.W. de Kiewiet and F.H. Underhill, *Dufferin-Carnarvon Correspondence 1874–1878* (Toronto, 1955), p 345 (Dufferin to Carnarvon, 19 Apr. 1877).

97 *Mail*, 10, 15 Feb., 6, 9, 16, 19, 23 Apr. 1877; and *Citizen*, 13 Feb., 9, 10, 13, 30 Apr. 1877

98 *Globe* (Toronto), 4, 10, 12, 16 Apr., 2, 4 May 1877; and *Free Press*, 9, 10, 21 Apr. 1877

99 *Collingwood Bulletin*, 3 Feb. 1887

100 *Freeman*, 24 Apr. 1877

101 Ibid, 1 and 3 May 1877. Blake's view of the matter irked Anglin (see Gillmor Papers, Anglin to Gillmour, 7 May 1877). There were a number of others who were affected by the decision of the committee (see *Freeman*, 17 Apr. 1877; Young, *Public Men*, II, 271–2; Ward, *Commons: Representation*, pp 86–7; and de Kiewiet and Underhill, *Dufferin-Carnarvon Correspondence*, p 345 [Dufferin to Carnarvon, 19 Apr. 1877]).

102 Gillmor Papers, Anglin to Gillmour, 11 July 1877

103 Ibid; Rogers Papers, Anglin to Rogers, 21 June, 9 July 1877; Mackenzie Papers, Anglin to Mackenzie, 25 July 1877; and O. Turgeon, *Un Tribut à la Race Acadienne: Mémoires, 1871–1927* (Montreal, 1928), pp 38–45. Because the 1877 Great Fire of Saint John destroyed the *Freeman* office and because Anglin was tied up in Gloucester, no issues of the *Freeman* were published between 19 June and 29 Aug. 1877. Thus what one might expect to be the best

source of information on the election is non-existent. One interesting aspect of the election is that the government took no part in the contest and did not even communicate with Anglin (see Gillmor Papers, Anglin to Gillmour, 11 July 1877). After the election Anglin took steps to have dismissed those office-holders who had been conspicuous opponents (see Mackenzie Papers, Anglin to Mackenzie, 25 July 1877).

104 *News*, 27 Aug. 1877; Rogers Papers, Anglin to Rogers, 2 Sept. 1877; and Mackenzie Papers, Anglin to Mackenzie, 9 Jan. 1878

105 Mackenzie Letterbooks, vol vi, Mackenzie to Anglin, 3 Jan. 1878. General accounts of the issue are contained in Buckingham and Ross, *Mackenzie*, pp 459–61; Thomson, *Mackenzie*, pp 321–2; and Dawson, *Procedure in Commons*, p 59.

106 Mackenzie Papers, Anglin to Mackenzie, 9 Jan. 1878

107 Ibid, Holton to Mackenzie, 19 Jan. 1878; and Brown to Mackenzie, 2 Feb. 1878

108 *Herald* (Montreal) n.d., quoted in *Freeman*, 12 Feb. 1878. See also *Freeman*, 13 Feb. 1878. Papers such as the *Mail* and *Citizen* argued the Conservative case while the *Free Press* answered for the Reformers (see *Mail*, 8, 9 Feb. 1878; *Citizen*, 5, 8 Feb. 1878; and *Free Press*, 6, 8 Feb. 1878). A fairly complete and relatively judicious contemporary assessment of the matter is Anon., 'Current Events,' *Canadian Monthly*, xiii (1878), 317–20.

109 *Freeman*, 24 Apr. 1877

110 See Dawson, *Procedure in Commons*, p 66; Thomson, *Mackenzie*, pp 326–7; and Buckingham and Ross, *Mackenzie*, pp 468–9.

111 *Freeman*, 21 Jan. 1878

112 Ibid, 30 Apr. 1878. See also ibid, 21 March 1878.

113 *Daily Sun* (Saint John), 5 Sept. 1878. See also *Commons Debates, 1878*, pp 2402–4 (3 May).

114 *Sun*, 5 Sept. 1878

115 Anon., 'Current Events,' *Canadian Monthly*, xiii (1878), 671

116 *Freeman*, 6 May 1878; and *Commons Debates, 1878*, p 2499 (4 May). The bill was geared to overcome a deplorable situation which had developed in Montreal.

117 Rogers Papers, Anglin to Rogers, 4 Apr. 1878

118 *Freeman*, 11 May 1878

NOTES TO CHAPTER ELEVEN

1 *Freeman*, 20 Nov. 1877

2 Ibid, 25 Apr. 1876

3 Ibid, 20 May 1875

4 Ibid, 4 Dec. 1877
5 Ibid, 19 Nov. 1872. A good example of this is Benjamin Disraeli's Crystal Palace speech of June 1872 (see W.F. Monypenny and G.E. Buckle, *The Life of Benjamin Disraeli, Earl of Beaconsfield*, rev ed [New York, 1968], III, 533–6).
6 *Freeman*, 3 Nov. 1874; 27 June 1876
7 Ibid, 3 Nov. 1874. The *Freeman* was, however, critical of British imperialism in Asia (see ibid, 24 June 1875).
8 Ibid, 25 Nov. 1875
9 See, for example, ibid, 19 March 1881.
10 Ibid, 27 June 1872; 24 Feb. 1874; 5 Feb., 22, 25 July 1878
11 It has been suggested that the latter third of the nineteenth century was a period in which the level of violence in the United States was particularly high (see H.D. Graham and T.R. Gurr, eds, *Violence in America: Historical and Comparative Perspectives* [New York, 1969], p 3).
12 See H. Senior, *Orangeism: The Canadian Phase* (Toronto, 1972) for a brief history of Canadian Orangeism.
13 *Freeman*, 30 May 1876
14 *Morning News* (Saint John), 31 May 1876, quoted in *Freeman*, 1 June 1876
15 *Freeman*, 1 June 1876
16 Ibid, 22 June 1876. The *Freeman* all along felt that Willis was trying to gain political strength from the agitation.
17 Ibid
18 Ibid, 24 June 1876
19 Ibid, 11 July 1876
20 Ibid, 13, 15 July 1876
21 *News*, 14 July 1876, quoted in *Freeman*, 15 July 1876
22 *Freeman*, 15 July 1876
23 A valuable survey of the development of social welfare and the role of the state is E. Wallace, 'The Origin of the Social Welfare State in Canada, 1867–1900,' *Canadian Journal of Economics and Political Science*, XVI (1950), 283–93.
24 A.I. Abell, *American Catholicism and Social Action: A Search for Social Justice 1865 to 1950* (Notre Dame, Indiana, 1963), pp 7–8. See also ibid, pp 26, 47.
25 *Freeman*, 2 Sept. 1875; 25 Oct. 1878
26 Ibid, 28 Oct. 1875; 12 Nov. 1874
27 Ibid, 7 June 1870
28 In fact he considered that private charity was about all that was required in this area of social welfare (see ibid, 17 July 1869; 21 Dec. 1875).
29 *New Brunswick: House of Assembly Debates, 1862*, p 38 (8 March)

30 *Freeman*, 18 July 1872
31 For an analysis of early labour organization in Canada see S. Langdon, 'The emergence of the Canadian working class movement, 1845–75,' *Journal of Canadian Studies*, VIII:2 (May 1973), 3–13, and VIII:3 (Aug. 1973), 8–26. Goldwin Smith was one contemporary who demonstrated some objectivity on the labour question (see G. Smith, 'The Labour Movement,' *The Canadian Monthly and National Review* [Toronto], II [1872], 513–32).
32 J.R. Rice, 'A History of Organized Labour in Saint John, New Brunswick 1813–1890,' unpublished Master's dissertation, University of New Brunswick, 1968, p 33
33 Sir Samuel Leonard Tilley Papers (uncatalogued collection), 'One of Them' to Tilley, 26 Dec. 1859
34 *Freeman*, 10 Aug. 1867. See also ibid, 23 Oct. 1862; 27 Nov. 1866.
35 Ibid, 22 Feb. 1870. This was also true of the Shipwrights' Union (ibid, 9 Jan. 1875).
36 This judgment is confirmed in Rice, 'History of Labour,' pp 63–4.
37 *Freeman*, 17 Apr. 1869. See also ibid, 14 June 1870.
38 Ibid, 14 March 1874
39 Ibid, 9 Apr. 1874
40 Ibid, 25 Apr. 1874
41 Ibid, 30 Apr., 14 May 1874
42 Ibid, 7, 14 May 1874
43 Ibid, 2 May 1874. Even the Toronto *Nation* noted the incident and commented unfavourably on the activities of the workers while praising the 'firmness and judgment' of the mill owners (see *Nation*, 7 May 1874, p 63).
44 *Freeman*, 5 Nov. 1874
45 Ibid, 31 Oct. 1874
46 Ibid, 11 March 1875. The Society decided, within a few weeks, that it would reduce its wage-rate demands to $2 a day (ibid, 6, 8 Apr. 1875).
47 Ibid, 1 May 1875
48 Ibid, 29 May, 17 June 1875
49 Ibid, 6 May 1875
50 Ibid, 4 May 1875
51 Further indications of Anglin's position on this question are given in ibid, 10, 24, 26 Aug., 21 Dec. 1875; 18 Apr. 1876; 6 Feb. 1877.
52 Ibid, 17 Apr. 1869
53 Ibid, 21 Dec. 1877
54 It appears that the hostility of other English Canadian Catholic papers towards labour unions moderated as time went along (see *True Witness and Catholic Chronicle* [Montreal], 20 Sept. 1867, 1, 15 May 1874; and *Evening Express and*

Commercial Record [Halifax], 25 Nov. 1867, 9 Apr. 1869), but that the *Freeman* was more favourably disposed to unions than most.
55 *Freeman*, 1 June 1871
56 Ibid, 12 Nov. 1870
57 Ibid, 22 Aug. 1878. See also ibid, 13 Oct. 1877.
58 Ibid, 30 Apr. 1878
59 Ibid, 8 June 1878
60 Ibid, 16 Dec. 1875. See also ibid, 7 Oct 1876; 11 Dec. 1877. For a brief analysis of the antagonism between scientific rationalism and Catholicism in the nineteenth century see H. Daniel-Rops, *The Church in an Age of Revolution 1789–1870*, trans J. Warrington (London, 1965), pp 313–14. See also C.J.H. Hayes, *A Generation of Materialism 1871–1900* (New York, 1941), pp 143–8.
61 *Freeman*, 1 Aug. 1872
62 Ibid, 25 Jan. 1877. The *Freeman* had become involved in the question of divorce when the Toronto *Globe* argued in favour of a liberalization of the divorce laws. Anglin claimed that this would lead to many social evils (see *Freeman*, 13 Jan. 1877) – to which the *Globe* replied on 22 Jan. 1877. See also 'T.W.A.', 7 May 1868, in *Freeman*, 16 May 1868; and *Freeman*, 3 Nov. 1868.
63 *Freeman*, 23 Jan. 1877. Anglin viewed Jews as one of the most formidable agents of infidelity (ibid, 25 Feb. 1873; 28 July 1874; 1 July 1875).
64 The conflict was centred in Quebec. Useful sources in English are: M. Wade, *The French Canadians 1760–1967*, rev ed (Toronto, 1968), I, 341–70; O.D. Skelton, *Life and Times of Sir Wilfrid Laurier* (Toronto, 1965), I, 21–48; J. Willison, *Sir Wilfrid Laurier* (Toronto, 1926), I, 253–313; P.B. Waite, *Canada 1874–1896: Arduous Destiny* (Toronto, 1971), pp 45–52; and L.C. Clark, *The Guibord Affair* (Toronto, 1971), pp 1–21.
65 *Freeman*, 19 June 1860. Anglin often pointed out the Protestants double standard on the issue of clerical influence. See, for example, ibid, 21 March 1865. Interference of Protestant clergymen in political affairs was not unusual. A particularly blatant example occurred during a Toronto mayoralty contest in the 1880s (see D. Morton, *Mayor Howland: The Citizens' Candidate* [Toronto, 1973], p 99).
66 *Freeman*, 9 Feb. 1865; 19 June 1866
67 Ibid, 15 Nov. 1866
68 Ibid, 25 March 1865
69 Ibid, 30 July 1868
70 Ibid, 27 July 1875. The *Witness* (Montreal) was a rabidly Protestant newspaper with readers throughout the country. Its anti-Catholicism stemmed from the belief that priests controlled the politics of the Dominion.

71 *Freeman*, 18 Jan. 1876. For other criticisms of the *Globe*, see *Freeman*, 27 Jan. 1876; 25 Sept., 15 Nov. 1877.
72 D.C. Thomson, *Alexander Mackenzie: Clear Grit* (Toronto, 1960), pp 255–6; and Willison, *Laurier*, 1, 264–8. Patrick Power wrote to Huntington and the latter replied that he had not directed his remarks against the Catholic Church as a whole (see ibid, 1, 268–9). The *Freeman* was willing to accept Huntington's explanation although it felt his original words were all too clear (see *Freeman*, 15 Feb. 1876).
73 *Freeman*, 15 Feb. 1876. Mackenzie's speech in the House of Commons had been guarded (see Willison, *Laurier*, 1, 269–77). There is evidence, however, of Mackenzie's real feelings in a letter to Blake in which he said: 'If the liberal R Catholics are trampled down by the Clerical despotism the protestant wire fence will not long defend liberty of thought and action or protestant rights in Quebec (see Edward Blake Papers, Mackenzie to Blake, 28 Sept. 1875, in PAO). On the same day he wrote to Anglin in a tone which implied a quite different attitude to the question of ultramontanism (see Alexander Mackenzie Letterbooks, vol 1, Mackenzie to Anglin, 28 Sept. 1875). Further evidence of Mackenzie's views may be found in Thomson, *Alexander Mackenzie*, pp 256–7. The *Freeman* claimed that the Conservatives labelled the Liberals anti-Catholic in order to gain political advantage (see *Freeman*, 20 Jan. 1876; 24 Jan. 1878).
74 *Freeman*, 15 Nov. 1877. See also ibid, 23 July 1867; 29 Jan., 23 Dec. 1876; 14 June, 27 Sept. 1877.
75 Roman Catholic Archdiocese of Toronto Archives, Archbishop John Joseph Lynch Papers, Anglin to Lynch, 6 May 1878
76 *Freeman*, 28 March 1876. See also ibid, 15 Nov. 1877.
77 The entire issue of clerical influence and the meaning of Liberalism was debated again in the winter of 1876–7 (ibid, 2, 19, 23 Dec. 1876; 2, 20 Jan., 10 Feb., 6, 8 March, 10 Apr. 1877).
78 Ibid, 17 March 1877. See also ibid, 30 Nov 1876.
79 Ibid, 4 Sept. 1877. This issue of the *Freeman* applauded Laurier's famous defence of Liberalism (see Wade, *French Canadians*, 1, 362–7; Willison, *Laurier*, 1, 315–47; and J. Schull, *Laurier: The First Canadian* (Toronto, 1965), pp 113–22) in fitting Canadian Liberalism into the British rather than the European tradition, but it proclaimed that the speech was weak in its defence of the right and duty of clerics to speak out on moral and ethical matters.
80 *Freeman*, 6 March 1877. See also ibid, 10 Feb., 8 March 1877.
81 Bishop James Rogers Papers, Rogers to Anglin, 8 May 1877, in UNBA
82 Ibid, Anglin to Rogers, 10 May 1877

83 Pastoral Letter of Bishop Rogers, 24 June 1877, reprinted in *Freeman*, 5 Sept. (incorrectly dated 7 Sept. on p 1 and 4 Sept. on p 2) 1877.
84 See O. Turgeon, *Un Tribute à la Race Acadienne: Mémoires, 1871–1927* (Montreal, 1928), pp 39–45; Rogers Papers, R. Young to Rev. T. Allard, 26 July 1877, enclosed in Young to Rogers, 26 July 1877; ibid, Conroy to Rogers, 27 July, 2 Aug. 1877; ibid. Anglin to Rogers, 2 Sept. 1877; and *Freeman*, 5 Sept. (incorrectly dated 7 Sept. on p 1 and 4 Sept. on p 2) 1877, which printed letters of Turgeon to Rogers, 27 July 1877, and Rogers to Turgeon, 30 July 1877, along with the pastoral letter of 24 June 1877.

NOTES TO CHAPTER TWELVE

1 Alexander Mackenzie Papers, Burpee to Mackenzie, 20 June 1879. Burpee had asked A.J. Smith to split the cost but the latter had claimed he could not afford it. Smith, however, was far from poor. The value of his estate at the time of his death in 1883 was sworn to be $175,000 (see *Freeman*, 4 Aug. 1883).
2 Bishop James Rogers Papers, Anglin to Rogers, 25 Sept. 1878, in UNBA
3 Mackenzie Papers, Anglin to Mackenzie, 25 July 1877
4 Ibid; and Roman Catholic Archdiocese of Toronto Archives, Archbishop John Joseph Lynch Papers, Anglin to Lynch, 6 May 1878
5 *Freeman*, 18, 19 Sept., 1878; *New Brunswick Reporter* (Fredericton), 18, Sept. 1878; *Le Moniteur Acadien* (Shediac), 19 Sept. 1878; and *Daily Sun* (Saint John), 23 Sept. 1878
6 Mackenzie to James Young, n.d., quoted in J. Young, *Public Men and Public Life in Canada* (Toronto, 1912), II, 317–18
7 Mackenzie Papers, Anglin to Mackenzie, 21 Sept. 1878
8 Rogers Papers, Rogers to Anglin, 27 Sept. 1878
9 Mackenzie Papers, Anglin to Mackenzie, 27 Sept. 1878
10 P.B. Waite, *Canada 1874–1896: Arduous Destiny* (Toronto, 1971), p 92; and D.C. Thomson, *Alexander Mackenzie: Clear Grit* (Toronto, 1960), p 341
11 The procedure today is that Speakers 'are removed automatically by the dissolution of the House over which they have presided' (see W.F. Dawson, *Procedure in the Canadian House of Commons* [Toronto, 1962], p 67).
12 Alexander Mackenzie Letterbooks, vol II, W. Buckingham to Anglin, 3 Oct. 1878. See also ibid, vol. II, Buckingham to Anglin, 8 Oct. 1878.
13 'Dominion Parliament,' 18 Feb. 1879, in *Freeman*, 22 Feb. 1879
14 The account which follows is based on the Toronto *Globe*'s summary of the correspondence on the question of Anglin's appointments laid before the House of Commons and quoted in *Freeman*, 1 March 1879. See also *Freeman*,

14 Dec. 1878, 22 Feb. 1879; J.E. Collins, *Canada Under the Administration of Lord Lorne* (Toronto, 1884), pp 109–11; and Sir John Alexander Macdonald Papers, vol CCCLIV, A. Patrick to Macdonald, 22 Jan. 1879.

15 'Dominion Parliament,' 18 Feb. 1879, in *Freeman*, 22 Feb. 1879, 1 March 1879

16 Collins, *Canada Under Lorne*, pp 109–11; H.J. Morgan, ed, *The Dominion Annual Register and Review, 1879* (Ottawa, 1880), pp 22–5; and 'Dominion Parliament,' 18 Feb. 1879, in *Freeman*, 22 Feb. 1879. It appears that the Speaker's powers during an interregnum have never been clarified. In the last two decades, however, it has become usual to make at least the more important appointments of parliamentary employees on the basis of competitive examinations. Thus the problem of the patronage power of a 'lame-duck' Speaker is not likely to become an issue in the future. Professor W.F. Dawson of the University of Western Ontario had been kind enough to supply information on this constitutional question.

17 *Freeman*, 1 March 1879

18 H.J. Morgan, ed, *The Dominion Annual Register and Review, 1878* (Montreal, 1879), pp 255–6

19 'Parliamentary Summary,' 25 Apr. 1879, in *Freeman*, 3 May 1879

20 For Anglin's speeches on the tariff see 'Dominion Parliament,' 9 Apr. 1879, in *Freeman*, 12 Apr. 1879; and *Hansard* report of Anglin's speech, quoted in *Freeman*, 17 May 1879; 'Dominion Parliament,' 9 Apr. 1880, in *Freeman*, 17 Apr. 1880; and *Hansard* report of Anglin's speech quoted in *Freeman*, 12, 19 June 1880. For his speeches on the CPR see *Hansard* report of Anglin's speech quoted in *Freeman*, 24, 31 July 1880; 'Dominion Parliament,' 21 Dec. 1880, in *Freeman*, 25 Dec. 1880; and *Canada: House of Commons Debates, 1880–81*, pp 196–204 (1 Dec.).

21 J.E. Collins, *Life and Times of the Right Honourable Sir John A. Macdonald* (Toronto, 1883), p 342

22 *Freeman*, 22 Feb. 1879

23 'Letters of Hon. Alexander Mackenzie to Hon. A.G. Jones, 1869–1885,' *Report of the Board of Trustees of the Public Archives of Nova Scotia, 1952*, Mackenzie to Jones, 14 May 1879

24 Quoted in *Freeman*, 3 May 1879

25 *Freeman*, 19 July 1879

26 Ibid, 26 July 1879

27 For confirmation of these attitudes see ibid, 8 Sept. 1877, 11, 18 Oct., 15, 22 Nov., 13, 27 Dec. 1879, 5 June, 10 July, 14 Aug., 6, 13 Nov. 1880; and Rogers Papers, Anglin to Rogers, 26 Nov. 1880.

28 *Freeman*, 27 Dec. 1879

29 On Anglin's views on the Irish situation see especially *Freeman*, 24 Feb., 14

Apr., 28 July 1874; 8 Sept. 1877; 17 Jan., 25 Sept., 16 Nov., 14, 21 Dec. 1878; 11, 18 Oct., 22 Nov., 13 Dec., 1879; 31 Jan., 2 Oct., 27 Nov. 1880; 1, 15, 29 Jan., 5, 12 Feb., 5 March, 2, 23, 30 Apr., 4, 11 June, 2 July, 15, 29 Oct., 19 Nov. 1881; and 11, 25 Feb. 1882.

30 See ibid, 2, 7 Oct., 16 Nov. 1878; 17 Jan. 1880; 15 July, 7 Oct. 1882.

31 Ibid, 10 Jan. 1880; 6, 13 Jan., 17 Feb. 1883

32 Ibid, 8 Feb. 1879. See also ibid, 24 May 1879.

33 Ibid, 14 June 1879; 2 Apr. 1881; 18 Nov. 1882

34 Ibid, 17 Jan., 14 Feb., 24 Apr. 1880

35 Costigan to Macdonald, 7 Feb. 1880, cited in S.W. Horrall, 'Canada and the Irish Question: A Study of the Canadian Response to Irish Home Rule, 1882–1893,' unpublished Master's dissertation, Carleton University, 1966, p 11

36 'Dominion Parliament,' 13 Feb. 1880, in *Freeman*, 21 Feb. 1880

37 *Commons Debates, 1880*, pp 126–7 (20 Feb.); and *Freeman*, 28 Feb. 1880

38 See Horrall, 'Canada and the Irish Question,' pp 12–37; D.L. Poynter, 'The Economics and Politics of New Brunswick, 1878–1883,' unpublished Master's dissertation, University of New Brunswick, 1961, pp 139–45; J. Pope, *Memoirs of Sir John Alexander Macdonald* (Ottawa, n.d.), II, 228–9; and W.S. MacNutt, *Days of Lorne* (Fredericton, 1955), pp 162–6.

39 Macdonald Papers, vol CCVI, Costigan to Macdonald, 6 March 1882

40 *Sun*, 30 May 1882; *Fredericton Evening Capital*, 10 June 1882; and *Commons Debates, 1882*, p 1066 (20 Apr.). Senator Power had been the only Reformer to attend the meetings throughout, and on one occasion Costigan had requested Anglin's assistance by way of the senator.

41 *Freeman*, 29 Apr. 1882

42 Ibid

43 The *Freeman* of 1 Apr. 1882 had criticized the original resolutions of the committee for detailing only 'selfish' reasons for Home Rule.

44 *Commons Debates, 1882*, pp 1060–5 (20 Apr.); and *Freeman*, 29 Apr. 1882. See also ibid, 1 Apr. 1882.

45 The *Freeman*, along with nearly all Irish newspapers, deplored the murders (see *Freeman*, 27 May 1882; 3, 31 March 1883).

46 Pope, *Memoirs of Macdonald*, p 229

47 Lord Kimberley Papers, Kimberley to Lorne, 11 May 1882. See also ibid, Lorne to Kimberley, 22 Apr. 1882; Kimberley to Lorne, 25 May 1882; and Kimberley to Queen Victoria, 8 June 1882. Kimberley's attitude was the sort which doomed any hopes of imperial federation.

48 *Freeman*, 6 May, 15 July, 5 Aug. 1882

49 *Commons Debates, 1877*, pp 1267–74 (9 Apr.); Mackenzie Papers, Anglin to Mackenzie, 25 July 1877; and O. Turgeon, *Un Tribut à la Race Acadienne: Mémoires, 1871–1927* (Montreal, 1928), p 40. See also *Freeman*, 23 July 1878.

50 *Commons Debates, 1880–81*, pp 483–5 (14 Jan.); and *Freeman*, 22 Jan. 1881. In 1877, of course, Anglin had been Speaker and therefore was unable to reply to Costigan.

51 Sir Samuel Leonard Tilley Papers, G.A. Girouard, J. Costigan, P.A. Landry, and O. Turgeon to Tilley, 18 Apr. 1882. The letter claimed that, if a Catholic were appointed, Anglin could be defeated in Gloucester.

52 *Capital*, 25 May 1882

53 Rogers to Costigan, 23 May 1882, quoted in *Sun*, 7 June 1882

54 C. Cormier, 'The Acadian Outlook (II),' *French Canada Today*, ed C.F. MacRae (Sackville, NB, 1961), pp 28–9; M.-A. Savoie, 'Varieties of Nationalism. (I) The Acadians: A Dynamic Minority,' *French Canada Today*, p 81; and Poynter, 'Economics and Politics,' pp 109–12

55 *Freeman*, 7 March 1874; 14 Oct. 1878

56 Ibid, 19 June 1880

57 Ibid, 23 July 1881

58 Ibid, 15 July 1882

59 See, for example, *Moniteur Acadien*, 8 juin 1876.

60 H. Thorburn, *Politics in New Brunswick* (Toronto, 1961), p 26. The college was forced to close its doors. Evidence of hostility between Acadian leaders and the Irish clergy as far back as 1867 is presented in N. Griffiths, 'The founding of *Le Moniteur Acadien*,' *Acadiensis*, II:2 (Spring 1973), 80–90.

61 *Freeman*, 1, 15 Feb. 1879

62 Rogers Papers, Anglin to Rogers, 28 Aug. 1879

63 Quoted in Poynter, 'Economics and Politics,' p 139. See also *Freeman*, 29 Jan. 1881.

64 Rogers Papers, Anglin to Rogers, 9 July 1877

65 *Sun*, 27 May 1882

66 Edward Blake Papers, Anglin to Blake, 4 July 1882, in PAO

67 Rogers Papers, Anglin to Rogers, 28 June 1882

68 Lucian [S.D. Scott], 'Politics in this Province in the Old Days,' Willet Scrapbooks, vol VII, n.p., in SJRL. See also *Chatham Advance*, n.d., quoted in *Freeman*, 22 Apr. 1882. Both Burns and Turgeon made trips to Ottawa just before the campaign got underway in earnest (see *Advance*, n.d., quoted in *Freeman*, 22 Apr. 1882; *Advance*, n.d., quoted in *Freeman*, 6 May 1882; and *Freeman*, 20 May 1882). Turgeon was not consciously a party to the plan, but he did not drop out of the race in spite of his knowledge that a three-cornered

contest would be of great aid to Burns (see Turgeon, *Un Tribut*, p 49). Verification of the Conservative plan to defeat Anglin can be found in Tilley Papers, T. Des Brisay to Tilley, 5 Nov. 1888.

69 *Sun*, 23, 26 May 1882. See also Blake Papers, Anglin to Blake, 4 July 1882. Burns's personal interest in the Caraquet Railway is indicated in G. Myers, *A History of Canadian Wealth* (Toronto, 1972), pp 320–3.

70 *Capital*, 11 May 1882; and Blake Papers, Anglin to Blake, 27 June, 4 July 1882. Both Turgeon and Anglin claimed Burns used money freely during the campaign and both were convinced that the election could have been voided on grounds of bribery and corruption (see Turgeon, *Un Tribut*, pp 52, 54–6; *Freeman*, 24 June 1882; Rogers Papers, Anglin to Rogers, 24, 28 June 1882; and Blake Papers, Anglin to Blake, 27 June, 4 July 1882). Turgeon pressed charges but these were not upheld (see Toronto *Globe*, 25 Oct. 1883).

71 F.J. Robidoux, *Conventions Nationales des Acadiens* (Shediac, 1907), p 15

72 See, for example, *Moniteur Acadien*, 16 sept. 1880.

73 Turgeon, *Un Tribut*, p 51; *Freeman*, 24 June 1882; Rogers Papers, Anglin to Rogers, 12 June 1882; and Blake Papers, Anglin to Blake, 27 June, 4 July 1882. Anglin was convinced that Langevin had been largely responsible for developing the feeling that Acadians should have a French-speaking representative.

74 *Freeman*, 3 June 1882; *Sun*, 16 June 1882; and *Advance*, n.d., quoted in *Freeman*, 17 June 1882

75 Rogers to Barry, 26 May 1882, quoted in *Freeman*, 10 June 1882. The *Freeman* also published a French translation.

76 Macdonald Papers, vol CCLXXVII, Tilley to Macdonald, 25 June 1882. He also claimed that the opposition Anglin was facing in Gloucester had brought out Bishop Sweeny and nearly all Irish Catholics against him (Tilley) in Saint John.

77 Blake Papers, Jones to Blake, 23 June 1882. Cartwright, Mills, Huntington, Smith, Jones, Laird, and Laflamme, as well as Anglin, had been defeated (see O.D. Skelton, *Life and Letters of Sir Wilfrid Laurier* [Toronto, 1965], 1, 74). Of these the *Dominion Annual Register* rated only Cartwright, Huntington, Mills, and Anglin as men who were 'not easily replaced' (see H.J. Morgan, ed, *The Dominion Annual Register and Review, 1882* [Toronto, 1883], p 121).

78 *Sun*, 21 June 1882

79 Sir John Thompson Papers, vol XXVIII, Anglin to Thompson, 5 July 1882. See also ibid, vol XXVIII, Anglin to Thompson, 31 July 1882. It is worthwhile noting that at the time of this exchange of correspondence Thompson was temporarily removing himself from the arena of partisan politics for he resigned as premier of Nova Scotia and was appointed to the Supreme Court of Nova Scotia during the month of July.

80 Macdonald Papers, vol CCCLXXXV, part 2, anonymous to Macdonald, 28 June

1882. The letter had a Saint John postmark and stated that 'Though young the writer will soon prove a useful friend.'

81 Blake Papers, Anglin to Blake, 27 June 1882; ibid, I. Burpee to Blake, 18 July 1882; and Rogers Papers, Anglin to Rogers, 24 June 1882

82 Rogers Papers, Anglin to Rogers, 24 June 1882. There was no possibility of opening a seat for him (see Blake Papers, I. Burpee to Blake, 25 June, 18 July 1882). Anglin doubted that he could take Gloucester even if Burns's election was voided (see Blake Papers, Anglin to Blake, 4 July 1882).

83 See T.W. Acheson, 'The National Policy and the Industrialization of the Maritimes, 1880–1910,' *Acadiensis*, I; 2 (Spring 1972), 3–28, for a most useful analysis of the attempts of Maritime businessmen to shift their energies from failing shipbuilding and lumbering enterprises to industrial undertakings. The tonnage of ships built in New Brunswick declined from the Civil War high of 92,605 in 1864, to 33,353 in 1870, to 14,528 in 1880, and to 6,501 in 1890 (see S.A. Saunders, *The Economic History of the Maritime Provinces* [Ottawa, 1939], pp 110–11).

84 See, for example, *Freeman*, 6 March 1875; 30 March 1876; 27, 30 Jan. 1877; 24 Sept. 1878; 22 March, 31 May, 7 June, 15 Nov. 1879; 3 Jan. 1880; 30 Apr., 7 May 1881. Other more objective writers accepted the view that Confederation and the National Policy probably had a detrimental effect upon the development of the Saint John valley (see W.A.Mackintosh, *The Economic Background of Dominion-Provincial Relations* (Toronto, 1964), pp 34–5; Thorburn, *Politics in New Brunswick*, pp 15, 20; and J.R. Petrie, *The Regional Economy of New Brunswick* (n.p., 1944), p 398).

85 The fire was a terrible conflagration which destroyed almost all of the business section of the city. See G. Stewart, *The Story of the Great Fire in St. John, N.B. June 20th, 1877* (Toronto, 1877); and R.H. Conwell, *History of the Great Fire in St. John* (Boston, 1877). See also Rogers Papers, Anglin to Rogers, 21 June 1877.

86 Mackenzie Papers, Anglin to Mackenzie, 23 July 1877

87 Rogers Papers, Anglin to Rogers, 9 July 1877

88 *Freeman*, 20 Oct. 1877. Undoubtedly this resulted from the decision of the Committee on Privileges and Elections (see Arthur Hill Gillmor Papers, Anglin to Gillmour, 11 July 1877, in PANB). The *Freeman* of 29 Aug. explained the new arrangements and why its publication had been delayed so long.

89 The *News* of 27 June 1877 indicated that Anglin claimed $800 from the Liverpool, London and Globe Co. He must also have had other insurance coverage.

90 The exact figure is not known. What is known is that Anglin received about $800 annual interest from his investment (see Roman Catholic Diocese of Saint John Archives, Bishop John Sweeny Papers, Anglin to Sweeny, 10 May 1887).

Interest rates of 6 per cent on investments were not uncommon, as seen in the returns on the 1872 bonds of the city of Saint John (see *Statutes of New Brunswick*, 35 Vict. Cap. xxxviii [passed 11 Apr. 1872]). Canadian railway bonds in the 1880s were also in the 5 to 6 per cent interest range, as shown in the annual publications of *Poor's Manual of Railroads*. Anglin's bond investment was equivalent to a current investment of approximately $96,000.

91 *Freeman*, 29 Aug. 1877

92 *New Dominion and True Humorist* (Saint John), 1 Sept. 1877

93 *Acadian Recorder* (Halifax), n.d., quoted in *Freeman*, 9 Nov. 1877

94 *Freeman*, 7 Dec. 1878

95 *Sun*, 29 Jan. 1879; and *Freeman*, 8 Feb. 1879. Plans to have Anglin publish a strictly Catholic paper had just fallen through (see Rogers Papers, Sweeny to Rogers, 11 Jan. 1879). It is probable, however, that the church provided some financial assistance to the *Freeman* (see Griffiths, 'The founding of *Le Moniteur Acadien*,' p 89).

96 See, for example, *Freeman*, 21 June 1879.

97 Ibid, 6 Dec. 1879; 4 Dec. 1880; 31 Dec. 1881; 16 Dec. 1882

98 *American Newspaper Annual, 1881* (Philadelphia, 1881), p 315. One would be justified in being sceptical of these figures.

99 Blake Papers, I. Burpee to Blake, 25 June, 18 July 1882. It was expected that Anglin would revive the *Freeman* and turn it from a weekly publication into the tri-weekly it had been from 1850 to 1877 (see ibid, Burpee to Blake, 25 June 1882).

100 Rogers Papers, Anglin to Rogers, 26 Feb. 1883

101 Without Anglin the *Freeman* was very flat and its ultimate demise came on 2 Aug. 1884. On 6 Jan. 1900 the *New Freeman*, a Catholic paper, was begun in Saint John. Its name was chosen in commemoration of Anglin's paper and it is published to this day.

102 *Freeman*, 3 Dec. 1881, 25 Nov. 1882; Sun, 8 Dec. 1881, 11 Dec. 1882; and *News*, 9 Dec. 1881

103 *Freeman*, 19 May 1883

104 Anglin left on 11 May 1883. Exactly one week later celebrations were held in honour of the one hundredth birthday of the founding of the city.

105 *Freeman*, 12 May 1883

106 *Evening Globe* (Saint John), 11 May 1883, quoted in *Freeman*, 19 May 1883. At first it had been intended to hold a non-partisan affair but then the organizers thought that it would be wiser to give Anglin the opportunity to speak freely. Still, the list of guests was fairly extensive, including Bishop Sweeny, General Warner (the American Consul), Sheriff Harding, Mayor Jones, Wm. Elder, J.V. Ellis, and G. McLeod. Isaac Burpee sent his regrets.

107 *News*, 11 May 1883. Other New Brunswick papers paid tribute to Anglin as he departed (see *Capital*, 10 May 1883; and *Sun*, 12 May 1883). Interestingly enough, the *Moniteur Acadien* merely stated that Anglin was leaving the province.

NOTES TO CHAPTER THIRTEEN

1 Compare *Canada: Census of 1880–81* with *Canada: Census of 1890–91* for an indication of the different rates of expansion of Saint John and Toronto. On Toronto's growth see also C.S. Clark, *Of Toronto the Good. A Social Study. The Queen City of Canada as it is* (Montreal, 1898), pp 1–2; D.C. Masters, *The Rise of Toronto 1850–1890* (Toronto, 1947), pp 165–207; and the relevant sections in P.G. Goheen, *Victorian Toronto, 1850 to 1900* (Chicago, 1970).
2 Roman Catholic Diocese of Saint John Archives, Bishop John Sweeny Papers, Anglin to Sweeny, 4 Nov. 1884
3 *The Toronto Daily Mail*, an anti-Reform paper, recognized the Liberal strategy (see *Mail*, 1 June 1886).
4 Edward Blake Papers, draft of a circular, ? Feb. 1883, in PAO. See also Sir James David Edgar Papers, Blake to Edgar, 17 Feb. 1883 in PAO. The *Tribune* had been founded in 1874 and had come to support the Liberals by 1876 (see *Freeman*, 3 Sept. 1874; 28 Sept., 5 Dec. 1876).
5 Roman Catholic Archdiocese of Toronto Archives, Archbishop John Walsh Papers, Walsh to Anglin, 30 March 1883
6 Blake Papers, Anglin to Blake, 16 May 1883
7 Ibid. Smith's visit was surprising, for the *Freeman* had once called him 'a glum, gruesome, gloomy man, who hates any one who ever slights or displeases him …' (see *Freeman*, 7 June 1879).
8 *Globe* (Toronto), 6, 8 June 1883
9 See also *Mail*, 2, 5, 6, 7 June 1883; *Globe*, 7 June 1883; and *Freeman*, 16 June 1883. The factual inaccuracies in the poem are legion. For example, a toast to the Queen was given at the beginning of festivities; Cook did not even attend the banquet; and Irish affairs were hardly mentioned (see *Globe*, 6, 8 June 1883). For another critical assessment of the Anglin banquet see Sir John Alexander Macdonald Papers, vol CCIL, D.L. Macpherson to Macdonald, 6 June 1883.
10 On the initial phase of the 'exposure' see *Globe*, 1, 2, 4, 5, 7 June 1883; *Mail*, 2 June 1883; and *Freeman*, 9 June 1883.

11 *Globe*, 16 June, 28 Nov. 1883. Anglin's authorship of the article is assumed in Shield's letter to the *Mail* which appeared in the issue of 2 June 1883.

12 *Globe*, 9 Jan. 1884. See also ibid, 28 Nov. 1883.

13 John O'Donohoe Papers, Macdonald to O'Donohoe, 30 June 1883

14 K.W.K. McNaught, 'The *Globe* and Canadian Liberalism,' unpublished Master's dissertation, University of Toronto, 1946, pp 122–64

15 *Globe*, 10 Apr. 1884; 20 Oct. 1885

16 *Tribune*, 7, 14 Oct. 1885; *Globe*, 8 Dec. 1885, 17, 20 March, 28 Apr. 1886; and Lord Lorne Papers, Lorne to Anglin, 8 June 1883. Lorne also asked Costigan to make a submission (ibid, Lorne to Costigan, 8 June 1883). On the subject of Canadian activity in regard to Irish Home Rule see S.W. Horrall, 'Canada and the Irish Question: A Study of the Canadian Response to Irish Home Rule, 1882–1893,' unpublished Master's dissertation, Carleton University, 1966.

17 At least this is what the *Mail*, 5 Nov. 1884, quoted the *Globe* as having said a year and a half previously.

18 The more important issues of the *Globe* dealing with the Irish situation between 1883 and 1887 are 3, 31 March, 29 June, 10 July, 2 Aug.,14, 20 Sept., 10 Oct. 1883; 28 March 1884; 4 July, 28 Aug.,3 Sept., 23 Nov., 2, 15 Dec. 1885; 8 Jan.,9, 11 March, 10, 12 Apr., 6, 7, 8, 12 May, 9 June, 10 July, 10, 21 Sept., 1, 2 Oct. 1886; 9, 30 March, 4, 5, 8, 15, 18, 22, 25, 27 Apr. 1887.

19 See, for example, *Globe*, 17 Oct. 1885.

20 *Tribune*, 28 Oct. 1885. See also ibid, 11, 29 July, 12 Aug., 12 Oct., and 21 Nov. 1885.

21 Sweeny Papers, Anglin to Sweeny, 22 Nov. 1883

22 *Globe*, 14 March 1884

23 Blake papers, draft of a circular, 6 Jan. 1885

24 Ibid, Blake to Mowat, 23 Jan. 1886

25 Sweeny Papers, Anglin to Sweeny, 15 Nov. 1886. When the *Tribune* again became a weekly is not known; it was still a twice-weekly at the beginning of 1886.

26 Blake Papers, draft of a circular, ? Feb. 1883, draft of a circular, 6 Jan. 1885, and Blake to Mowat, 23 Jan. 1886; and Sweeny Papers, Anglin to Sweeny, 15 Nov. 1886, 11 Apr. 1887

27 Sweeny Papers, Anglin to Sweeny, 4 Nov. 1884. Saint John street directories show Anglin's house vacant until 1888–9.

28 Sweeny Papers, Anglin to Sweeny, 22 Nov. 1883

29 Ibid, Anglin to Sweeny, 16 Apr. 1885. Fortunately for Anglin the bishop took a friendly and lenient attitude about the debt Anglin owed him.

30 Ibid, Anglin to Sweeny, 22 Nov. 1883. Whether Anglin was able to find cheaper and yet suitable accommodation in later years is not known.

31 Ibid, Anglin to Sweeny, 10 May 1887. This amount was an interest rate of 6 per cent on the loans Sweeny had made to Anglin. The story of Anglin's finances in these years can be traced in more detail in ibid, Anglin to Sweeny, 22 Nov. 1883; 24 Apr., 3 May, 4 Nov. 1884; 16 Apr. 1885; 28 May, 7 June, 15 Nov. 1886; 10 May 1887.

32 Ibid, Anglin to Sweeny, 24 Apr., 8 Nov. 1884

33 Ibid, Anglin to Sweeny, 7 June 1886; 12 Dec. 1887; 6 June 1892

34 Ibid, Anglin to Sweeny, 22 Nov. 1883; 24 Apr. 1884

35 Ibid, Anglin to Sweeny, 4 Nov. 1884; 16 Apr. 1885. Frank received his degree from the University of Ottawa.

36 'Letters of Hon. Alexander Mackenzie to Hon. A.G. Jones, 1869–1885,' *Report of the Board of Trustees of the Public Archives of Nova Scotia, 1952*, Mackenzie to Jones, 2 Apr. 1883; A.E. Byerly Papers, Mackenzie to William Buckingham, 1 May 1883, in PAO; *Freeman*, 24 May 1884; and Macdonald Papers, vol CDVI, J.B. Plumb to Macdonald, 29 July 1884.

37 *Globe*, 12, 13 Dec. 1883; 10 May, 12, 13, 18, 21, 26, 30 June, 5, 30, 31 July, 3, 20, 22 Sept. 1884

38 J.K. Foran, *Irish-Canadian Representatives: Their Past Acts, Present Stand, Future Prospects. A Review of the Question* (Ottawa, 1886), p 20

39 *Globe*, 17 Apr. 1886

40 Sweeny Papers, Anglin to Sweeny, 11 Apr. 1887. In Dec. 1886 Anglin had made a speech in Halifax and at the time it was rumoured that he might become a candidate in that constituency (see *Daily Evening Globe* [Saint John], 15 Dec. 1886).

41 Sweeny Papers, Anglin to Sweeny, 11 Apr. 1887

42 Ibid

43 W.T.R. Preston, *My Generation of Politics and Politicians* (Toronto, 1927), p 171; and J. Willison, *Sir Wilfrid Laurier* (Toronto, 1926), p 471

44 Blake Papers, Blake to James Somerville, 24 Feb. 1887

45 Blake had encountered this for some time (see Edgar Papers, Blake to Edgar, 15 May 1882).

46 Sweeny Papers, Anglin to Sweeny, 11 Apr. 1887

47 Ibid

48 M.A. Banks, 'The Change in the Liberal Party Leadership, 1887,' CHR, XXXVIII (1957), 109–28; and W.R. Graham, 'Sir Richard Cartwright, Wilfrid Laurier, and Liberal Party Trade Policy, 1887,' CHR, XXXIII (1952), 1–18

49 Edgar Papers, Cartwright to Edgar, 9 Aug. 1886. Cartwright was undoubtedly referring to E.E. Sheppard, the editor of the *News* (Toronto) from 1883 to 1887.

50 Sweeny Papers, Anglin to Sweeny, 12 Dec. 1887

51 T.W. Anglin, 'What Does Home Rule for Ireland Mean?' *The Lake Magazine*, I (Nov. 1892), 200–9.

52 *Daily Sun* (Saint John), 7 Apr. 1893; and *Globe* (Saint John), 7 Apr. 1893. In the course of his speech he indicated that he had spoken on the same topic in Saint John four years earlier.

53 See also Sweeny Papers, Anglin to Sweeny, 6 Dec. 1890; *Toronto World*, 20 Aug. 1892, in Blake Papers, scrapbook 36, p I; and *Catholic Weekly Review* (Toronto), 24 Sept. 1892.

54 *Globe* (Toronto), 11, 15 Oct. 1887; and *Catholic Weekly Review*, 4 Jan. 1890; 18 Apr. 1891; 27 Feb., 5 March, 2, 30 July 1892

55 T.W. Anglin, 'The Life and Times of the Most Rev. John Joseph Lynch, Archbishop of Toronto,' *Jubilee Volume: The Archdiocese of Toronto and Archbishop Walsh, 1842–1892*, ed Rev. J.R. Teefy (Toronto, 1892), pp 169–96. Lynch died in 1888. He was succeeded as Archbishop of Toronto by John Walsh (1889–1898).

56 The general reason for the conflict and the actual campaign are dealt with in F.A. Walker, *Catholic Education and Politics in Ontario: A Documentary Study* (Toronto, 1964), pp 60–81. See also *Catholic Weekly Review*, 17 Sept. 1887, 18 Feb. 1888; and Roman Catholic Archdiocese of Toronto Archives, Archbishop John Joseph Lynch Papers, Lynch to Anglin, 1888, and *Mail*, 20 Apr. 1888. Reports in the *Catholic Weekly Review* indicate that he was a trustee in July 1892, but not in January 1893.

57 Anglin to the editor, 22 Aug. 1892, in *Empire* (Toronto), 25 Aug. 1892. See also *Empire*, 20, 25 Aug. 1892; and Sweeny Papers, Anglin to Sweeny, 5 Sept. 1892.

58 T.W. Anglin, 'The School Question in Manitoba,' *The Lake Magazine*, I (Sept. 1892), 73–80. See also Sweeny Papers, Anglin to Sweeny, 5 Sept. 1892. The *Globe*, 29 Aug. 1892, criticized Anglin's analysis and Anglin replied in a letter to the editor, 29 Aug. 1892, in *Globe*, 30 Aug. 1892, and reprinted in *Catholic Weekly Review*, 10 Sept. 1892. The Feb. 1894 edition of the *Catholic World*, an American periodical, carried an article in which Anglin boosted the Ontario school system as a good example of his contention that national harmony did not require or benefit from a single school system (see T.W. Anglin, 'How Canada Solves the Problem We Shirk,' *Catholic World*, LVIII (Feb. 1894), 609–27).

59 Sweeny Papers, Anglin to Sweeny, 10 May 1887

60 Ibid. See also ibid, Anglin to Sweeny, 12 Dec. 1887.

61 Ibid, Anglin to Sweeny, 12 Dec. 1887

62 *Globe*, 16 Oct. 1885

63 *First Report of the Commission on Municipal Institutions*, Ontario, *Sessional*

Papers, 1888, no. 42. The report was supposed to have been given by the beginning of February (see Sweeny Papers, Anglin to Sweeny, 12 Dec. 1887).

64 *Second Report of the Municipal Commission, Ontario, Sessional Papers, 1889*, no. 13. The *First Report* was 96 pages long; the *Second Report* 233 pages.

65 Information on Anglin's experience as Ontario Commissioner at the Cincinnati Exposition is contained in *Ontario's Exhibit at the Centennial Exposition of the Ohio Valley and Central States: Report of Hon. Timothy W. Anglin, Ontario, Sessional Papers, 1889*, no. 30; and in Sweeny Papers, Anglin to Sweeny, 7 Dec. 1888.

66 *Ontario's Exhibit ...*, p 6

67 Sweeny Papers, Anglin to Sweeny, 7 Dec. 1888

68 D.G. Creighton, *John A. Macdonald*, vol. II: *The Old Chieftain* (Toronto, 1956), p 484

69 Sweeny Papers, Anglin to Sweeny, 21 May 1888

70 *Globe*, 1 Oct. 1889

71 Sir Samuel Leonard Tilley Papers, F.C. Law to Tilley, 28 Jan. 1890, in NBMA, Tilley replied that according to New Brunswick custom Anglin had the right, although he thought the custom inadvisable (see Miscellaneous Collections 1865–1969, Tilley to Law, 31 Jan. 1890, in PAO). Law's notation on this letter was that neither pre-Confederation ministers nor an ex-Speaker of the House of Commons had any right to be styled 'Honourable.' Law was correct, as apparently Lord Monck's 1868 suggestion that the Speakers of the two Houses should be sworn in as privy councillors and thus retain the title of 'Honourable' for life, had never been acted upon (see Monck to Macdonald, 2 Sept. 1868, quoted in J. Pope, *Correspondence of Sir John Macdonald* [Toronto, 1921], p 73).

72 Sir John Alexander Macdonald Papers, vol CDLXXIII, Mrs E. Anglin to Macdonald, 6 May 1889. In a postscript she enjoined Macdonald to strict secrecy 'as not even my husband is aware of my effort to render his life a less anxious one.' No reply from Macdonald could be found.

73 Macdonald Letterbooks, vol XV, Macdonald to Anglin, 10 Jan. 1871

74 Macdonald Papers, vol XXI, Mrs E. Anglin to Macdonald, 9, 14 Dec. 1889; and vol DXXIX, Macdonald to Mrs E. Anglin, 13 Dec. 1889.

75 The information given regarding the Prison Commission and Anglin's role on it has been gleaned from the 799-page *Report of the Commissioners Appointed to Enquire into the Prison and Reformatory System of Ontario, 1891, Ontario, Sessional Papers, 1891*, no. 18; and Sir John Thompson Papers, Anglin to Thompson, 16 July, 4, 20 Aug. 1894. While Anglin was secretary, the commission also had a stenographer who recorded the evidence presented.

76 R.B. Splane, *Social Welfare in Ontario 1791–1893: A Study of Public Welfare Administration* (Toronto, 1965), p 56. See also ibid, pp 54–6, 103, 106–9, 188–93, 213, 268–71 for an admirable discussion of some aspects of the commission's study.

77 Thompson Papers, vol CXXXI, Frank Anglin to Thompson, 26 June 1891; and vol CXXXII, Frank Anglin to Thompson, 6 July 1891. As to the assertions of Frank and Mrs Anglin that Timothy knew nothing of their appeals, is it possible that Timothy was a Henry II?

78 *Report of the Commissioners Appointed to Enquire Into the Claims Made by the Township of Proton to certain sums of money payable as alleged to that municipality under the Act 16 Vict. Cap. 159, Sec. 14, Ontario: Sessional Papers, 1892*, no. 89

79 Anglin's letters to Bishop Sweeny indicate that by 1888 Anglin was receiving only $698.76 in interest per annum and by 1890 only $519.20. As there is no further mention of the debentures in Anglin's correspondence with Sweeny after June 1892, it is reasonable to assume that the term of the bonds had expired. If the bonds were held at a 6 per cent interest rate, then the debentures when cashed in 1892 would have provided Anglin with a sum of $8,653.33.

80 Register of Deeds Office Provincial Building, Saint John, Saint John Country Registry of Deeds, Vol. Lib 42, pp 75–7 (no. 63386). Frank Anglin had drawn up the bill of sale. Timothy's occupation was listed as 'Gentleman.'

81 W. Buckingham and G.W. Ross, *The Hon. Alexander Mackenzie: His Life and Times* (Toronto, 1892), p 641

82 Thompson Papers, vol CLVIII, E. Anglin to Thomson [sic], 9 July 1892. Thompson wrote back to say that the government did not intend to appoint a commission on prisons (see ibid, vol CCLVI, Thompson to Mrs T.W. Anglin, 12 July 1892).

83 Sweeny Papers, Anglin to Sweeny, 8 Aug. 1892

84 Ibid, Anglin to Sweeny, 14 Feb. 1891. See also ibid, Anglin to Sweeny, 9 June 1890; 4 June, 4 Dec. 1891.

85 Bishop James Rogers Papers, Anglin to Rogers, 8 Aug. 1892, in UNBA. See also Sweeny Papers, Anglin to Sweeny, 8 Aug., 5 Sept. 1892.

86 To Sweeny Anglin stated that quick action along these lines would prevent the government from putting their machine into gear (see Sweeny Papers, Anglin to Sweeny, 8 Aug. 1892).

87 Sweeny Papers, Anglin to Sweeny, 5 Sept. 1892

88 The rumour that Anglin might be a candidate in Kent brought out a vicious 'communiqué,' published in *Le Moniteur Acadien* (Shediac), 27 Sept. 1892, against Anglin.

89 *Report of the Commission on Municipal Taxation, 1893 (with a Supplement by Hon. T.W. Anglin), Ontario, Sessional Papers, 1893*, no. 73
90 Anglin's rejection of George's theories was in line with contemporary Catholic thinking (see *Catholic Weekly Review*, 16 July 1887; and A.I. Abell, *American Catholicism and Social Action: A Search for Social Justice* [Notre Dame, Indiana, 1963], pp 61–89).
91 *Official Report of the Liberal Convention Held in Response to the Call of Hon. Wilfrid Laurier, Leader of the Liberal Party of the Dominion of Canada. Ottawa, Tuesday, June 20th, and Wednesday, June 21st, 1893* (Toronto, 1893), pp 134–40. Anglin had written Laurier suggesting that, if he did not wish to chair the convention, 'perhaps as the only ex-speaker of the House of Commons in the party I would be next best' (see Sir Wilfrid Laurier Papers, vol VII, Anglin to Laurier, 5 June 1893). The post went to Oliver Mowat.
92 Thompson Papers, vol CCXV, Anglin to Thompson, 16 July 1894; vol CCXVII, Anglin to Thompson, 4 Aug. 1894; and vol CCXVIII, Anglin to Thompson, 20 Aug. 1894
93 Ibid, vol CCLXX, Thompson to Anglin, 30 July, 21 Aug. 1894
94 Laurier Papers, vol IX, Anglin to Laurier, 16, 21, 26 Feb. 1895
95 Ibid, F.A. Anglin to Laurier, 16 Feb. 1895. See also ibid, F.A. Anglin to Laurier, 23 Feb. 1895.
96 *Toronto City Directory for 1892* (Toronto, [1891?]), p 505; and *Toronto City Directory, 1896* (Toronto, 1896), p 419
97 M. Englin, 'My Margaret Anglin Story,' *Atlantic Advocate*, LIII (March 1963), 47. One might surmise that the trip Anglin and his wife took to New York in 1892 was to make arrangements for Margaret and to see her safely established (see Sweeny Papers, Anglin to Sweeny, 6 June 1892).
98 *Toronto City Directory*, 1896, p 419. The assessment rolls show that the value of the lot and house which Anglin rented was $6,160, the house itself being valued at $4,000 (see Toronto City Archives, Assessment Roll for the Ward of St. Patrick, City of Toronto, 1892). It is possible that Eileen was already attending school in Montreal or Paris by 1896 (see appendix).
99 Sweeny Papers, Anglin to Sweeny, 12 Dec. 1887
100 This is apparent by the names given on the firm's letterhead (see, for example, Blake Papers, Blake to J.S. Willison, 23 Feb. 1892).
101 *Catholic Weekly Review*, 16 March 1889; 17 Sept., 26 Nov. 1892. Timothy Anglin was a pall-bearer at O'Sullivan's funeral (see ibid. 17 Sept. 1892).
102 Sweeny Papers, Anglin to Sweeny, 6 June 1892
103 *Catholic Weekly Review*, 13 June 1891
104 Thompson Papers, vol LXXXIII, Frank Anglin to Thompson, 28 March 1889;

and vol CCXXXVIII, Thompson to Frank Anglin, 2 Apr. 1889. Thompson's letter indicated that Frank had written a letter to the *Empire*.

105 *Catholic Weekly Review*, 28 March 1891

106 Laurier Papers, Frank Anglin to Laurier, undated (but must have been at the beginning of March 1895), 26 March, 5 Apr. 1895. While the emphasis in these letters was on the political expediency of supporting remedial legislation if necessary, Frank was convinced of the benefits of Catholic education (see Hon. Mr. Justice Anglin, *Catholic Education in Canada in its Relation to the Civil Authority* [Toronto, 1910], p 3). See also F. Anglin to editor, 23 March 1895, in *Globe*, 26 March 1895.

107 Laurier Papers, Frank Anglin to Laurier, 27 Feb. 1895. Apparently Frank did not get the Liberal nomination in any case, for he did not run against the Conservative candidate in 1896.

108 When Timothy died, Mrs Anglin was only fifty-three years old. She lived until 1923, not quite long enough to see her eldest son become chief justice of the Supreme Court of Canada, but certainly long enough to see Margaret establish herself as an internationally known actress.

109 On the Citizen's Committee and municipal reform in Toronto in 1895 see J.C. Weaver, 'The Meaning of Municipal Reform: Toronto, 1895,' *Ontario History*, LXVI (1974), 89–100.

110 *Globe*, 4 May 1896

111 Raymond Scrapbooks, XIV, 28, in SJRL. One must assume that a typographical error had been made in giving the name of one of the pall-bearers as 'Goodwin Smith.' Smith had been a member of the 1895 Citizens' Committee along with Anglin.

112 *Globe*, 5 May 1896

113 *Freeman*, 15 May 1880

Appendix

Francis Alexander (1865–1933), chief justice of Canada (1924–33), was born at Saint John on 2 April 1865. He was educated at St. Mary's College, Montreal, and at Ottawa University (BA, 1885), and was called to the bar of Ontario in 1888 (KC, 1902). He was appointed a judge of the High Court of Ontario in 1904, and of the Supreme Court of Canada in 1909. He became chief justice of Canada in 1924 and in the same year became an imperial privy councillor and a Knight Commander and Knight of the Grand Cross of the order of St Gregory the Great. He retired as chief justice in 1933 because of illness and died shortly thereafter at Ottawa. In 1892 he married Harriet Isabel, daughter of Archibald Fraser, of Fraserfield, Glengarry. The couple had one son and three daughters.

Arthur Whyte (1867–1955), lawyer, was born at Saint John on 10 January 1867. He attended St Mary's College, Montreal, and Ottawa University. He became a partner in Blake, Lash, Anglin and Cassels, Barristers, in Toronto. In 1894 he married Madeline St George, daughter of the Honourable Sir William Glenholme Falconbridge, chief justice of the King's Bench for Ontario. Arthur sired eleven children.

Mary Ellen (1869–1873), was born at Saint John in April 1869 and died from whooping cough on 22 February 1873.

Margaret (1871–1873), was born at Saint John, 7 November 1871 and died of whooping cough on 22 February 1873.

Infant son, born and died sometime late in 1872 or early in 1873 at Saint John.

Timothy Warren Jr (1873–1933), was born at Saint John on 9 October 1873. Little is known about Timothy Jr except that he was working as a clerk for Sloan and Crowther, Toronto, in 1891, and in 1896 was a teller in the Canadian Bank of Commerce. Timothy Jr remained a bachelor and died in New York on 11 September 1933.

Mary Margaret (1876–1958), actress, was born in the parliament buildings in Ottawa on 3 April 1876. She was educated at Loretto Abbey, Toronto, and at the Convent of the Sacred Heart, Montreal; and she studied at the Empire (Wheatcroft) School of Dramatic Acting in New York. Although she has never received the recognition she deserves, she was the first internationally renowned Canadian actress, residing in New York but making appearances as far away as Australia. For a time she managed her own touring company. She married Howard Hull in 1911; the couple had no children. She died in a nursing home outside Toronto on 7 January 1958.

Eileen Mary Warren (1879–1952), was born at Saint John on 16 January 1879. She was educated at Loretto Abbey, Toronto, the Convent of the Sacred Heart, Montreal, and the Convent of Assumption, Paris. For a time before her marriage she was an actress in the professional theatre in the United States. On 11 July 1910, at St Patrick's Cathedral, New York, she married Lieutenant (afterwards Captain) Charles Thomas Hutchins, usn, son of Rear Admiral Charles Thomas Hutchins, usn. Captain Hutchins was afterwards for some years the naval attaché of the us Legation at Peking. In 1946 Captain Hutchins was residing in Shanghai; presumably Eileen was there also.

Basil Haliburton (1881–1957), business executive, was born at Saint John, 20 March 1881. Nothing is known of Basil's education. He was engaged in the brewing business in Portsmouth, New Hampshire, and Albany, New York. Subsequently he became involved in the oil industry with Indiana Refinery Company, of which he became vice-president, until it merged with the Texas Oil Company. With Texas Oil he worked first in Chicago and by 1946 his place of residence was Bronxville, New York. His first marriage took place in 1903 at Roanoke, Virginia, to Clyde Elsbeth Helms; they had two children, one of whom received educational training at Columbia University and Oxford University, and the other at the Sorbonne in

Paris. Basil's second marriage was to Marie Therèse Tracey at Albany in 1916; they had no children.

Alexander Edward (1883–1899), was born at Saint John on 29 April 1883 and died in San Antonio, Texas, on 3 May 1899.

Index